Praise for *Care*

“Extraordinary, profound, enlightening, and entertaining. Tenenbom’s best book to date.” – ***Der Spiegel*** (Germany)

“With a lot of humor, and in countless anecdotes, Tuvia Tenenbom opens the doors to a world that doesn’t reveal much about itself at first.” – **Bayerischer Rundfunk** (Germany)

“Tuvia Tenenbom has written a fascinating book, shedding light on the world of ultra-Orthodox Jews. The intensity of Jerusalem, evident to the casual visitor of the city, builds up in the reader the more he reads this book. The tourist, who will hopefully come to Jerusalem again soon, will now see the people of Mea Shearim with totally different eyes.” – ***Süddeutsche Zeitung*** (Germany)

“Tenenbom writes down the facts as they are – and, as it is usually with him, they are often bizarre and hilarious.... Tenenbom succeeds here in painting an exhilarating description of a largely unknown group of people who, out of ignorance, are often depicted as a negative caricature of ‘the Jew.’” – ***Hamburger Abendblatt*** (Germany)

“A book full of warmth and benevolence.” – ***tz München*** (Germany)

“Gripping, extremely funny, mercilessly direct, this first-person report – subjective, pointed and biting as one could expect from the suspenders-wearing chubby man – is rousing and very human.” – **NDR** (Germany)

“He provokes, but he also has a lot of humor.” – **Deutschlandfunk Kultur** (Germany)

“You read this smart, funny book with curiosity. Tenenbom’s delicate and biting, ever humane gaze into the sometimes irrational is a blessing – especially since the 7th of October.” – ***Kurier*** (Austria)

MW00465745

"Along with his sharp sense of humor, which runs through almost every line he writes, Tenenbom's ability to assimilate into ultra-Orthodox society turns his book into a fascinating in-depth journey of ultra-Orthodox existence."
– **Walla!** (Israel)

"A mind-changing book, an extraordinary, brilliant, fascinating, and entertaining anthropological journey into the world of the ultra-Orthodox."
– **Kikar Hashabat** (Israel)

"Superb, superb, superb book. Tenenbom is the funniest, most entertaining writer in Israel."
– **Channel 13 TV** (Israel)

"Tenenbom is the smartest, most entertaining researcher in town."
– **Attila Somfalvi's Barricade Podcast** (Israel)

"Those who loved his previous books will undoubtedly return and find here the good old Tenenbom again. As for those who have not yet been exposed to his writing, they will do well to be exposed to it now, for they will gain not only a new and refreshing insight into the Ḥaredi world, its parodies and humanity, but also an insight into Tuvia, a unique and colorful figure in the gallery of present-day Judaism."
– ***Makor Rishon*** (Israel)

Praise for Tuvia Tenenbom's Previous Work

"Tenenbom's laughter touches our soul in places where mere intellect could never reach."
– ***Die Zeit*** (Germany)

"A mystical provocateur, unstoppable director and iconoclastic playwright."
– ***Le Monde*** (France)

"*Catch the Jew!* offers one of the more interesting portraits of Palestinian politics to have appeared in English. Illuminating and alarming."
– ***Wall Street Journal***

"Irresistibly fascinating, emotionally explosive, seductive and engaging. Bluntly satirical."
– ***New York Times***

"Hugely entertaining, terribly funny, sarcastic, engaging, powerful, accusatory, judgmental, good!"
– ***National Review*** (USA)

"Here is a man, a writer, who does not follow patterns of thought dictated by others, nor does he abide by a code of language that the others have imposed. And yet, he keeps his sense of humor throughout the pages."
– ***Der Spiegel*** (Germany)

"Highly engaging and emotional, eminently readable, brutally honest."
– ***Publishers Weekly*** (USA)

"One of the most iconoclastic and innovative of contemporary dramatists."
– ***Corriere Della Sera*** (Italy)

"Read what Tenenbom has to tell us, without bias. We don't have the privilege not to know."
– ***Haaretz*** (Israel)

"Tuvia Tenenbom is Michael Moore and Borat in one."
– ***Die Welt*** (Germany)

"Every word that comes out of Tenenbom's pen can set the world on fire." – ***Forward*** (USA)

"Dazzling. A free artist who fights for truth and tolerance." – ***Le Vif/L'Express*** (Belgium)

"*The Lies They Tell* ranks Tenenbom among the best social anthropologists, like Comte Alexis de Tocqueville and Mark Twain." – ***American Thinker*** (USA)

"If J.D. Salinger and John Steinbeck collaborated on antisemitism in the UK, they might have written *The Taming of the Jew*." – ***Jewish Press*** (USA)

"Quizzical and tragic at the same time, the sort of comedy sketches that Samuel Beckett might have written if he were Jewish rather than Irish." – ***Algemeiner*** (USA)

"Tenenbom is the Egon Erwin Kirsch of our time." – ***Achgut*** (Germany)

"If Kafka had written non-fiction, he could not have bested Tenenbom's latest book." – ***Asia Times***

"A brilliant journalist, Tenenbom is straightforward, fearless, politically incorrect, courageous – and very funny." – ***Jerusalem Post*** (Israel)

"Tenenbom goes where it hurts...he wants to know what the reality is, not what we would like the reality to be." – ***Mitteldeutsche Zeitung*** (Germany)

"Tenenbom's hodgepodge of politics, zealotry and literary genres is fresh and audacious." – ***Village Voice*** (USA)

"The most important play of the year." – ***StadtRevue*** (Germany)

"Full of investigative chutzpah and laughter...mixing British wit and Talmudic subtleties." – ***Die Weltwoche*** (Switzerland)

"Tenenbom dares." – ***La Razon*** (Spain)

"Amazingly original." – ***Jewish Currents*** (USA)

"Tuvia is curious as a cat, sly as a fox, friendly as a Labrador, and is also a man with seismographic sensitivities." – ***Mida*** (Israel)

"A daring and hilariously written account." – ***Commentary*** (USA)

"A piercing storyteller whose writing is full of humor and irony." – ***Frankfurter Allgemeine Zeitung*** (Germany)

"Brilliant." – **Deutschlandradio** (Germany)

"Tenenbom rides the razor's edge...and goes all the way off." – ***Amsterdam News***

"A force of nature...provocative, satirical, intellectual."

– ***La Repubblica*** (Italy)

"He sees and he hears. Exactly as it is." – ***Frankfurter Rundschau*** (Germany)

"A New Jew." – ***Maariv*** (Israel)

Tuvia Tenenbom

Careful, Beauties Ahead!

MY YEAR WITH THE ULTRA-ORTHODOX

gefen גפן
publishing house בית הוצאה לאור
JERUSALEM • NEW YORK Est. 1981

Copyright © Tuvia Tenenbom
Jerusalem 2024/5784

All rights reserved. No part of this publication may be translated, reproduced, stored in a retrieval system or transmitted, in any form or by any means, electronic, mechanical, photocopying, recording or otherwise, without express written permission from the publishers.

Scripture quotations are modified from *The Holy Scriptures According to the Masoretic Text*, published by the Jewish Publication Society in 1917.

Editor: Kezia Raffel Pride
Photos and eytses: Isi Tenenbom
Cover illustration: Shay Charka
Photos on pages 13, 95, 260: Florian Krauss
Photo on page 493: Avi Gadlovich, Behadrei Haredim
Cover design: Optume Technologies
Typesetting: Optume Technologies

ISBN: 978-965-7801-55-0

1 3 5 7 9 8 6 4 2

Gefen Publishing House Ltd.
6 Hatzvi Street
Jerusalem 9438614,
Israel
972-2-538-0247
orders@gefenpublishing.com

Gefen Books
c/o Baker & Taylor Publisher Services
30 Amberwood Parkway
Ashland, Ohio 44805
516-593-1234
orders@gefenpublishing.com

www.gefenpublishing.com

Printed in Israel
Library of Congress Control Number: 2024933162

My deepest gratitude to Isi, the charm of my life, who worked day and night to immortalize every person and each event with her ever-present lenses, entertained everyone who came to our abode with food and drinks in abundance, and was ever by my side with words of comfort and wisdom.

This book is dedicated to you.

Contents

Are They Announcing My Funeral?
Infidel, get out! ... 1

What's a Better Way to Fly, on a Plane or an Eagle?
White donkeys, mules, a prophet, and a messiah in search of a wall ... 18

Passage for Dogs and Zionists Is Totally Forbidden
Also forbidden: Looking at beautiful queens, birds, and sweeties ... 24

Mourning a Destroyed Temple
The Law of Moses: A man cannot look at a beautiful woman, but he can look at an ugly woman ... 37

Looking for a Mate? Go to a Grave
Taliban ladies marry seed-spilling men ... 41

Shaved Heads Covered by $24,000 Hats
"Is she skinny, or is she fat? What color is her skin? What color is her hair?" ... 44

One Hour + One Prayer = One Billion Shekels
"When you give a Jewish beggar a shekel, he is upset. When you give a goy twenty cents, he's happy." ... 52

A Litvak Rabbi Looks at His Wife and Runs to Tell
What exactly does resurrection of the dead mean? ... 57

Jewish Men Must Wear Tails of Cats on Their Heads
It's time to pray to God at a grave while holding two Palestinian flags 63

Welcoming the Nazis with Bread and Salt
"I would rather be with the Nazis than with the Zionists." 74

Oh, God, Give Me a Mate
Or a pinky, a little sweet pinky 76

The Quickest Way to Get Healthy: *Na, Naḥ, Naḥma, Naḥman*
If this fails, try: Pa, Pat, Patri, Patricia 79

The Prince of Torah Will Find You a Girl
God accepts prayers today until 13:30 only 82

Fashion Parade on Mea Shearim
Where are the nicest-looking Jews in the world? In Mea Shearim, of course 85

As the Ladies Are Gone, Crowds of Angels Arrive
Visions of Sabbath: a beard of a Rebbe and birds around a child's neck 89

The Real Name of God Is Revealed to Me in a Dream
A man unites with the Logic of God, and a woman "forgets" to go to the mikveh 97

Would You Desecrate the Sabbath to Save a Dying Zionist?
Women: You can sleep with them, but you can't look at them 102

Would You Risk Your Life to Save a Dying Ḥasid?
"For five years, my rebbe raped me four times a week." 108

Did King David Sleep with a Married Woman? No, He Just Put on the Tallit over His Body
Good Jews don't ask questions – period 117

You Never Met a Woman in Your Life, and Then One Night, There Is a Woman in Your Bed. What Do You Do?
"When we united, the Holy Presence came to be with us." 127

Beware Women's Fingers When They Pick Up Chicken
She is Ḥaredi. Her father is a convert. Who will marry her? 131

Does the Modesty Guard Exist?
Be careful: Satan is hiding under her clothes 141

The Woman Who Can't Wait to Shave Her Head
And the Ḥasidim who wear Hamas yarmulkes 147

The International Jewish Parliament Convenes at the Pickle Shop
Are you an Ashkenazi or a Jew? 151

The Language of God: Ta, Ta, Ta, Oy, Oy, Oy, Pam, Pam, Pam
"We prefer that people like you, an outsider, don't show up at our tish." 155

We Want You Dead. Would You Like Another Portion of Egg Salad?
If you know how to sing Sabbath songs, my dear man, Ḥaredi ladies request your company 159

Sephardi Jews Would Like to Have Free Coffee, Please
"No studying in the impure Hebrew language" 164

It Takes 3,500 Years for a Soul to Descend from Heaven to the Womb
The story of a rabbi who calls himself a liar, and he is 168

In the Devil's House
How to get ten little Ḥaredim free of charge 171

When You Walk on the Street, Take Off Your Glasses; When You Bike, Close Your Eyes
Do rich Ḥasidic men look at rich Ḥasidic women? 175

Dressed in Arab Garb, Stoned by Palestinians, Protected by Nazis
From the depth of his grave, the Rebbe will give you a gift 179

When God Loves a Jew, He Finds Him a Parking Spot
"My Soul Thirsts for God, for the Living God." 186

Watching a Rebbe Lick a Gefilte Fish Is Extremely Sexy
Should I hide under the Rebbe's bed on Friday night? 197

You Can Create Black Angels or White Angels; It All Depends on You
The cheapest health insurance in the world: Rebbes 201

A Litvak Explains the Unexplainable
But who has more spirituality, a kishke or a Litvak? 207

The Stunning Beauty Who Won't Talk
And the mother who burned her daughter 213

Fact: Moses the Lawgiver Was Wearing a Shtreimel
Theatrical fireworks at the Lord's Holy Seat in Heaven performed by fiery angels 217

The Belzer Rebbe Is in My Belly
When angels and dead Rebbes unite for the last meal of the Sabbath 224

God Is Alive and Well inside a Ukrainian Grave
White angels roaming the streets of Jerusalem 230

Open Your Faucet and All Your Sins Will Be Washed Away
What happens if you spilled your seed in the previous incarnation? 236

God Speaks Yiddish
A Rebbe agrees to sit down for an interview 244

What's Mightier, a Mea Shearim Rooster or an Iranian Atomic Bomb?
Nothing beats drinking wine while staring at a photo of an old Litvak 249

Beware: Don't Snap a Photo of the Taliban Ladies
Got coronavirus? Come to shul! 254

When Lilith Meets Palestine
Will I have a Mea Shearim baby of my own? 261

The Palace of Ger at the Bottom of Hell
Turn off the lights, put on your clothes, and have fun in your bed .. 265

The Fake, True Story of the Brothel on Tsfanya Street
In Yiddish, yes can mean no 270

The Rebbe Carries a Pistol to Protect Himself from the Ger Ḥasidim
Have you heard of the Real Estate Rebbe? 275

Could You Donate a Burial Plot, Please?
How to sell a five-shekel fruit for two thousand 281

The Rebbe Owns My Testicles, and Sometimes He Squeezes Them
All married women have the same name: "Pss, pss, pss" 284

The Messiah Will Arrive on a Saudi Arabian Airliner
A match made in Heaven: Ḥaim Kanievsky and Greta Thunberg 291

Got a Problem? The Ḥasidim Got a Crane!
It doesn't matter if God exists or not. Just believe! 299

Can You Give Me Your Smartphone and I'll Break It for You?
Welcome the Łódźer Rebbe, Me 303

These Jews Think They Are Jordanians
Death to the Zionists! 309

Why Can't Reform Jews Have Good Food?
To avoid getting sick, take off your clothes and stand naked facing the moon 313

How to Purify the Bodies of Dead Jews
Do Rebbes give interviews? 318

God's Name Revealed: Yaakov Aryeh Alter
Give me money and I will resurrect your dead relatives 323

Come to Vizhnitz, Stand with the Boys and Experience It
How to make sure that your soul does not burn for eternity in boiling excrement 327

Your Daughter Is Pregnant!
A gefilte fish can bring you closer to God 332

Excuse Me, Are You in Touch with the Holy Spirit?
Make sure that your children aren't anywhere near this Torah scroll 342

When in the Toilet, Don't Think of Women
An Arab cabbie dreams of Ḥasidic women begging him for sex 345

Future Husbands of Taliban Ladies Try to Set People on Fire
A hot coffee mixed with a hot kiss in the most extreme of synagogues 353

Who Is a Bigger Idiot, the Litvak or the Ḥasid? Both, Says the Litvak
Two young Litvaks spend their nights dreaming of blonde Germans 360

A Conversation with the Rebbe of Toldos Aharon
The Rebbe speaks, uncensored, and drops a bombshell 367

The Rebbe Is in Your Bed
The Ḥasid who did not spill his seed for a decade 376

Honoring Sabbath with Cannabis
Why are Sephardi rabbis honoring a pedophile? 382

This Sephardi Rabbi Is So Holy, His Eyes Have Never Seen a Woman
An Ashkenazi rabbi arrested as a suspect in a murder case 387

The Price of a Blessing: From 20 Shekels to 50,000 Shekels
A man gets rewarded in the World to Come, a woman gets rewarded in This World 391

A Rabbi Hiding behind the Foreskin of a Baby
The Prophet Elijah appears, but the rabbis are afraid to talk to him 396

The Best Way to Find a Mate: Hang a Scarf on a Tree Next to a Grave
American Jews who care about transgender and proper Halloween dress: read Psalm 15 402

Fact: A Sheep Says "Amen" to a Rabbi
Fact: A dead man will resurrect the other dead 411

A Conversation with the Rebbe of Shoimrei Emunim
Who is God? What is God? What is a kvittel? 415

A Miracle: A Rebbe Comes to Visit, but He Didn't
What's the difference between Ḥaredim and Catholics? 427

She Died, but Her Rabbi Resurrected Her
The Romanian nun feeds me Palestinian cookies 432

A Conversation with the Karliner Rebbe
Why the Boyaner Rebbe is a smart man 439

God Wants Ḥaredi Litvaks to Be Poor
A Yiddish-speaking camel enters a yeshiva 442

They Are Ready to Die for Their Faith, but What Is It?
A dead man, covered with a tallit, at the entrance to Jerusalem 449

Emergency! This Is Your Last Chance to Find a Mate!
If you can't find a girl in a grave, come here! 459

The Haters and the Terrorists Join in Prayer
The dissonance between students and rabbis, at the time when the Ḥaredi world opens a little and the Free World closes a lot 465

If the Wind Blows on Your Hair, You Will Be Thrown Out of School
Why are the streets of Bnei Brak so dirty? Because Bnei Brak is a liberal city 476

Did My Father Rise from the Dead?
An old Jew rents a room next to the grave of his late wife 481

If You Want to Get Married, Wear a Tallit That Was in a Grave
The exciting Bnei Brak show: an old lady feeding a street cat 484

The Power of the Pinky of the Ḥasidic Lady
The luckiest of men get a bite of Holy Gefilte 486

God Is a Word. Period.
Beautifully clad Ḥaredi women kill righteous Ḥaredi men 489

A Ḥasid with a Beard Declares War on God
When Ḥasidim try to blow up the head of a fellow Ḥasid 493

What Is God? A Battery
Swallow this pill, and you will never spill your seed again 503

An Invite for a Sabbath Meal Is Withdrawn
"What's your name and the name of your mother?" 506

A Bored Litvak Is Looking for Something Exciting to Do
Do angels interfere with cellular connections? 509

What's Better, Cutting Off the Attorney's Sidelocks or His Beard?
Ḥaredi journalists afraid to report the news 512

Hand in Hand, God and I Go for a Walk with a Quail in Kiryat Vizhnitz
A Gypsy with a shtreimel 518

Der Heilige and die Schwänze
Have you got one million for me? 524

Ḥaredim in Appearance, Atheists at Heart: These Are the Anusim
Am I a Ḥaredi or an infidel? 532

The Light Train Carries Your Bulls to the Holy Temple

Murderers, get out! 539

Thanks and Acknowledgments 553

About the Author 555

Are They Announcing My Funeral?

Infidel, get out!

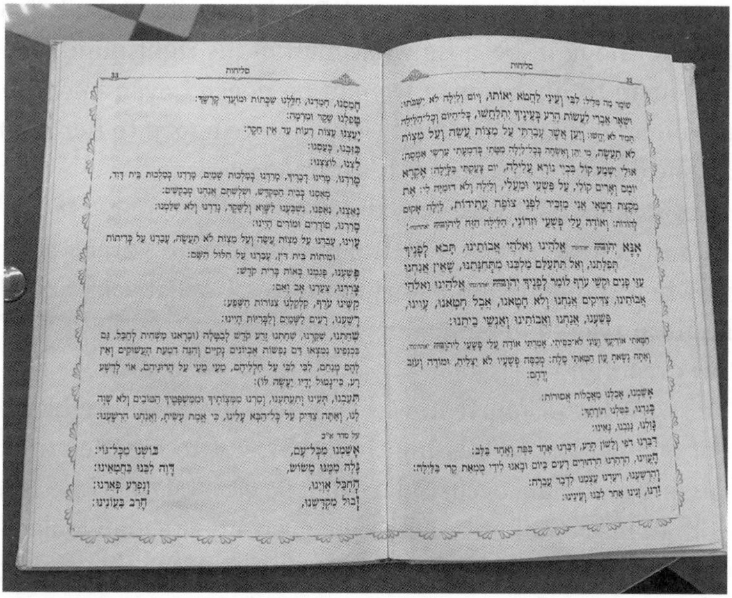

Lately I see him, dancing before my eyes, a sweet kid of twelve, then thirteen, and finally fourteen years of age. He wears a white shirt, black pants, black shoes, a black skullcap, and he has two beautiful sidelocks. His teachers admire him and have him skip a grade or two here and there. And when he reaches fourteen, while his classmates are eighteen and nineteen, he tries to fit in socially by starting to smoke.

One day, at fourteen, he got pneumonia or some similar illness, and he was stuck in bed in the dormitory of his yeshiva (rabbinical seminary), unable to study, his favorite activity. A classmate, nineteen years of age, gave him a book to read, a novel, about John and Patricia, names unfamiliar to him. *Which Jew in his right mind would call himself John when he could be called Moishe?* he asked himself. *Which Jewess in her right mind would walk on the street with the name Patricia when she could be called Zisale?* And even more interesting, and enormously strange, was what this John and this Patricia did. They were acquainted with each other, so he read, at a romantic candlelight dinner, one which John invited Patricia to – or was it the other way around, Patricia invited John? That's absurd, he thought, because what man in his right mind would ask a woman to his home, a woman he doesn't even know, and what woman in her right mind would invite a man to her home, a man she doesn't even know? It's immodest.

But as strange as it was, they did it.

They ate a little, drank a little, ate a little more, drank a little more, when suddenly John started undressing Patricia, and she smilingly answered in kind.

How dreadful!

The sweet kid of fourteen was shocked. Never before had the idea of one person undressing the other, not to mention a man undressing a woman, occurred to him. *Do people do that?* he asked himself. In his community, where he grew up, if a man looked at a woman, it was considered a major sin; why was this strange-sounding-name of a man undressing this strange-sounding-name of a woman?

When he thought about it a little more and tried to analyze it, the idea came to his mind that undressing a woman, or being undressed by a woman, was an interesting concept after all, and one that had to be explored.

How to explore it? This he didn't know.

Not yet.

He got up from bed, as sick as he was, and went to the window to look out at the street outside. He saw men and women walking, and for the first time in his life, he didn't avert his eyes at the sight of women. Yes, this is what he always did. When a woman passed by him, he always lowered his head and looked the other way, so his eyes wouldn't catch sight of a woman, because, his rabbis always told him, Satan hides under the clothes of women. Yeah. And if, Heaven forbid, a wind would blow, let's say, the dress of a woman, and his eyes met Satan, he would be snapped up by Satan for life and be his eternal slave.

But now, he looked at the women. They looked nice, he said to himself, and nothing Satanic did he find in them. Women, the thought came to him, were much more beautiful than men. What were their names, he wondered? Were they all Patricias? Could he, too, invite them for a candlelight dinner and undress them?

No, he said to himself, I could not. I'm no John.

But could he become John?

He stood at the window, looked up to Heaven, and thanked God, whom he called The Name, for creating such beautiful creatures.

He got dressed, a renewed energy filling his body, and walked out to the street to see women up close.

He liked what he saw so much that he didn't know what to do anymore, and he ran to his rabbis.

He approached them, one by one, and demanded to know why he was not allowed to look at women. Was he not allowed to look at women because they were beautiful and he was supposed to deny himself all pleasures, he asked his rabbis, or because the rabbis considered them ugly and wanted to protect him from the ugliness of life? And, by the way, he asked them: Where was it written that men cannot look at women? Was it The Name, at Mount Sinai, who said to Moses, *Thou shalt not look at females*? If He did, where exactly does it say that He did? And furthermore, who came up with the idea that Satan was hiding under women's clothes, and where was that written?

These questions, the rabbis answered, were *kfireh*, heresy, and one should never entertain such questions. Only infidels, they said, looked at women, and only infidels would ask questions on issues of faith and belief. Was he, they asked, an infidel? Had Satan, The Name forbid, entered his body?

He heard them, listened to them, and asked: Why not ask questions? When, exactly, did The Name decree that only infidels may ask questions? Why did it require a Satan inside of him to ask a question? And, as long as they were talking about it, who and what was Satan? And, by the way, in what woman did Satan reside before entering his body? Could he look at that woman, now that Satan had left her? Did Satan, he kept at it, plan to enter the bodies of his rabbis as well? And one more question: Why is it that looking at women is an act of heresy? Did he deny the existence of The Name at the very moment that he looked at a woman?

There were many more questions that came out of his mouth, day after day and month after month, until one shiny day he left the Ḥaredi (ultra-Orthodox) community, the world of his birth. Outside the Ḥaredi world, he hoped, he would be able to look at anyone he wanted – male or female, a cat or a monkey – and ask any question he would feel like asking, and say anything that came to his mind.

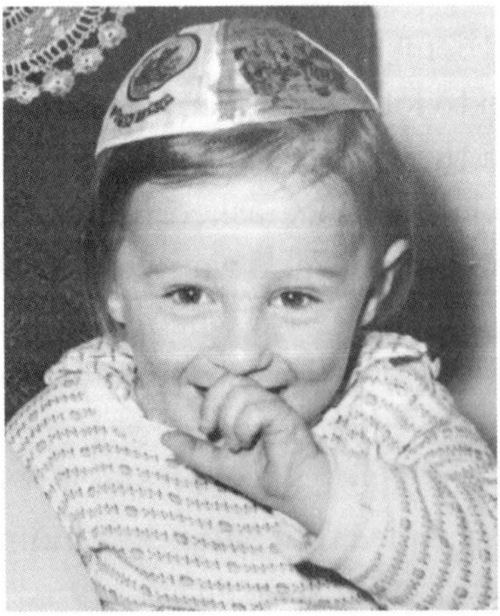

This story of the sweet, inquiring, tough boy – but mostly sweet – took place many years ago.

Who is that sweet boy? That boy, that sweet boy, is me.

And when I left, I didn't leave only my community. I also left Jerusalem, left Israel, and the sweet boy in me went into hiding.

I moved to the United States, where I spent many years in New York studying in various universities, collecting degrees and half degrees in several disciplines. As the years passed, I founded a Jewish theater company in New York City, became a journalist on top of that, made Germany my second home, and authored a few bestsellers.

Yet, parallel to my personal achievements, there was something else taking shape in my two adoptive countries, a slow process aimed at eventual mind control.

Wow. Strong words, I know. But true.

When I made America my home, I thought that in the Land of the Free and the Home of the Brave, I would be able to say whatever I wanted to say and do whatever I wanted to do. But with time, it slowly dawned on me that, perhaps, I was deluding myself for the second time in a row.

As the years passed by, one after another, I gradually had to be more and more watchful of what I looked at, more and more careful of what I said, and more and more mindful of what I did. When I first came to New York, I could, if I wanted, read conservative and liberal views on the opinion pages of leading mainstream newspapers, but then the conservatives left, and slowly the liberals disappeared as well, and both were replaced by Puritan extremists. In the old days of New York, I could, if I wanted, put up shows that included nudity, combined with unfettered social criticism. But no more. Such theatrical shows, hatched in the astoundingly brilliant Theater of the Absurd, became things of the past. Slowly, step by step, a new religion was born, championing ideas and ideals that once belonged, if anywhere, to the fringes of society: Sexual Puritanism, Gender Sensitivity, Climate Change Activism,

Veganism, Cancel Culture, Non-Binary Language, Open Borders, Palestine, and Marijuana.

And then COVID came. The coronavirus, a plague of enormous proportions, took millions of lives, and with it, the Western world as I knew it. The process of change that I had witnessed gradually taking hold in society, small step by small step, year by year, suddenly took a giant leap forward. For the first time in their lives, people across national borders realized the limits of their powers and with dread watched death approaching their homes, crossing every border and barrier, and they couldn't stop it. If once they thought that they had conquered the world, proud to be part of a generation that invented the smartphone, a solid proof of their genius and intelligence, they now looked in horror at the endless parades of coffins on the shiny screens of their newest smartphones.

And through it all, as the Angel of Death was dancing inside their bedrooms, the people who cherished liberal ideas and always believed in free speech hid in their beds, shaking under their blankets, while the Puritans marched on the streets, shouting as loud as they could, and the process of change intensified a hundredfold. What once was right became wrong, and behavior once considered normal became criminal.

The issue most impacted by the harsh change, at least for the people around me, was the most intimate, the sexual: who may sleep with whom and who may not, who can touch whom and who cannot, what may one do with the other, if anything, and what exactly are humans supposed to do with their sexual organs, if anything.

That's on the left side of politics, where the Puritans are more commonly known as Progressives.

On the right side of politics, an equally senseless phenomenon soon came into view. Many of the anti-vaxxers, for example, were to be found on the right side of American politics, and they claimed that more people were dying from taking COVID vaccines than from the coronavirus itself. If people who followed them ended up in the cemetery, so be it; they didn't care. It was bizarre, totally ridiculous, dangerous, and poisonous. They had not one iota of sense or science to prove what they were saying, but they were viewed as righteous, truth tellers, and world savers. They lived in a bubble of lies, and no force in the world could stop them.

This schism between left and right became highly pronounced as the plague savagely claimed more and more of us, but people like me who live in New York City, a bastion of the left, were affected primarily by the left side of politics. Our old world, the one we knew, collapsed in front of our eyes. And on this day in New York City, if you are a man and you want to keep your good name, your best bet is to avoid contact with the city's ladies. If my Ḥaredi rabbis of old came to New York today, they would feel at home with the most ardent of its atheists.

Funny world.

A year follows a year, the number of the dead and dying increasing, though at a slower pace, and the boy, the sweet me that once was, is lately starting to stare at me frequently. What would have happened, I keep asking myself, if I had stayed the course, remained in the Ḥaredi world, and a new Patricia, or maybe Madonna, came my way today – would I now leave the Ḥaredi world and join, let's say, the anti-vaxxers?

The sweet boy, now out of his hiding place, stares at me ever more profoundly and asks: *Shouldn't you, with the world in such a mess, make a U-turn and rejoin the world you left behind?*

The truth is, I don't know much about the world I left behind. I left it too young to understand it fully. And now that I'm an adult, that world might also be different, just like the world surrounding it.

Is it?

I loved the years of my childhood and my youth, and if not for the rabbis and the ever-increasing prohibitions, I would have stayed there to this day. I loved Jerusalem, a city of ancient history and present intrigue, and I never stopped loving it.

And now, disappointed as I am in the world around me, I sometimes dream of taking a journey back to my past, a trip back to the spiritual world that I ran away from, a world that I loved, and a world that I betrayed.

If I am to take that journey and go to Jerusalem, where in Jerusalem would I go to?

Mea Shearim, my dear.

Mea Shearim is one of the most authentic Ḥaredi neighborhoods in Israel and the most colorful of them all, and even though I lived there for a while, I left it at an early age and didn't really know it. Though there's one thing I know for certain: if God occasionally takes walks on Planet Earth, you can be assured that He does it in Mea Shearim.

Myself, I come from a highly religious family, Godlier than the Lord, with deep roots in Eastern Europe. On my father's side, I am a descendant of the Radzyner Rebbe, the leader of the Ḥasidic dynasty of Radzyn, Poland, a dynasty that was practically eradicated from the face of the earth by Nazi Germany. Very few Ḥasidim survived, including my grandfather, but the dynasty's glory is buried in ashes. On my mother's side, I am the grandson of a Romanian rabbi whose life, like those of most of his family, was cut short by a bullet because he was a Jew.

Death, sadly, did not end there.

As I am writing these words, this very week, it is the anniversary of my father's death well over a decade ago, when he returned his soul to Heaven, and his bodily remains were buried in the Holy City of Jerusalem.

"Returned his soul" – that's the way we described those who passed away in our community.

Sitting in a café, staring at the void, I see the image of my father staring back at me. He was a man of sharp intelligence and immense knowledge who would look at people he had never met and analyze them correctly to the last detail. He was a rabbinic scholar, a Talmudic genius, and a loving father who showered me with money for as long as he lived. And I see my mother, a great hostess, a good storyteller, a woman who paid me cash every time I ate chicken (which I hated), and a lady with an excellent eye for art, who miraculously survived the Nazis. She, too, returned her soul to Heaven some years back, and her bodily remains were also buried in the Holy City of Jerusalem.

Where am I now? I'm in Prenzlauer Berg, Berlin, a neighborhood I have come to like over the years, sipping a hot Italian coffee.

Often in the summer, if I don't have anything better to do, I stay in Prenzlauer Berg. Every morning, I choose a different sidewalk café, order coffee and cake, often an omelet, light up a cigarette, and watch the people passing by. Yes, I'm a dedicated people watcher. I am a son of dead Jews, grandson of burned Jews, and I like to see living people. Go blame me.

I will never admit it in public, but it is true that the people I like to watch the most are the ladies, the young German ladies passing by me.

At times, the images mix in my mind: my dead Jewish parents on one side and the living German ladies on the other side. Sometimes the images mix even more: the faces of my parents above and the legs of the ladies below.

I light up a cigarette, look at the smoke rings carried by the soft winds up to the sky, and imagine them flying all the way to Israel, where both my parents joined the earth.

Should I follow the winds and the smoke?

Well, why not?

Having finished my cigarette, I reserve a room in a Jerusalem hotel, take a taxi to the airport, board the British EasyJet plane, and fly to the Holy Land.

Yes, you've got to move fast in life: think it, do it. Done.

Funny, I say to myself when sitting on the plane: the same fire I had in me when leaving the Ḥaredi world of my past, I now have when leaving the Western world of my present.

I think – don't tell anybody I said it – that I'll stay in Israel for a while, at least for a few months.

Hell, why not?

Upon landing, just a few short hours later, I take a taxi to Jerusalem, a city whose dead rise from graves, like Jesus Christ; where prophets conduct direct flights to Heaven, like the Prophet Mohammed; and whose kings have 999 wives and concubines waiting to entertain their master, King Solomon. In short, the City of God.

The cabbie drops me at my future abode, Tzefania Hotel, a boutique hotel on Tsfanya Street in the Mea Shearim area. Inside, the place looks more like an Austrian home from a century past than an Israeli hotel of the present day, and for a moment, I wonder where exactly I am.

Well, in Mea Shearim.

To be Germanically exact, my hotel, down the block from the famous Sabbath Square (Kikar Hashabbat), is in Kerem Avraham. But in real life, and if you're not German, the areas immediately surrounding Mea Shearim – Geula, Kerem Avraham, Batei Ungarin, Beth Israel, and such – are viewed as greater Mea Shearim.

Mea Shearim. Have you heard of it before?

Mea Shearim, which literally means One Hundred Gates, has many connotations depending on who you are. To some, it's the holiest place on earth; to others, it's the dirtiest. There are still others, the independent thinkers, and they say that it's a combination of the two.

I remember Tsfanya Street, which I have not been on for decades. On both sides of the street, I remember, at its beginning and at its end, there used to be frequent clashes between the police and Ḥaredi demonstrators who demanded that the area be closed for traffic on the Sabbath.

Are the demonstrations still going on?

Just before boarding the plane to Israel, I told a few Jews that I planned to stay in Mea Shearim, and they strongly advised me against it. "You will not last there more than one night," one religious man told me. "Twenty Ḥaredim will gather next to your hotel, immediately after you get there, throw stones at your room, and yell, 'Infidel, get out!'"

Well, being that some years, many years, have passed since the first "Infidel," I hope I'll know how to handle it better this time around.

Be that as it may, let me first acquaint myself with my new surroundings.

After parking my suitcases at the hotel, I go out and start walking the narrow streets of Mea Shearim.

If I'm lucky, and if God indeed takes walks in the neighborhood on occasion, I'll get to meet Him face to face. You never know, but maybe we will even walk hand in hand one day. That would be something, wouldn't it?

Unlike Prenzlauer Berg, adorned with cafés and restaurants, the streets of Mea Shearim are adorned with signs that request women who pass by to dress modestly. What is modest? "Modest clothes include: Closed blouse, with long sleeves. Long skirt. No tight-fitting clothes," per one of the signs. I'm not sure why they have these signs. If a man is not allowed to look at a woman, what difference does it make how she is dressed?

In addition to the signs, there are countless paper posters covering the neighborhood walls. Above them are strange-looking balconies, structures that seem to have been designed not by engineers but by dumpster manufacturers.

The posters, glued on boards that cover rows of houses, contain obituaries of people who have "returned their souls," as well as various announcements, known as *pashkevils*.

If I remember correctly, the balconies were built for the yearly celebration of the Sukkot holiday, when Ḥaredi Jews live in a sukkah, a temporary hut, for seven days, celebrating the freedom of their ancestors from slavery in Egypt that, they believe, took place thousands of years ago.

The grandparents of the Ḥaredi Jews living here, if one is to judge by their family names, were Europeans, Belarussians, Ukrainians, and Russians who spoke in Yiddish, a language derived from the German, without a trace of any Egyptian accent. At what point they stopped speaking Egyptian and started speaking Yiddish is a secret known only to the Jewish God, The Name.

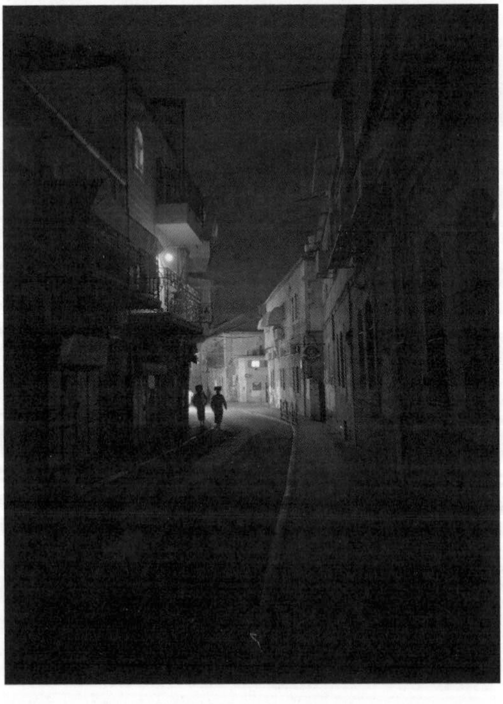

What I know is this: I would like to go to a café.

Old habits die hard, and I toy with the idea of sipping Italian coffee in an outside café and watching nice-looking Germans. But this is not to happen: I can neither spot a single German around me nor a single outdoor café.

This is not Prenzlauer Berg, this is Mea Shearim.

There are a few restaurants here, I see, mostly hidden either behind closed doors or downstairs in basements, but no place to look at German legs.

Instead of an array of cafés, what my eyes see is an array of stores, where I could buy, if I wanted, kosher herrings and mezuzahs (sacred scrolls to mount on doorposts), silver cups and pickles, plastic plates and expensive jewelry, wigs and *tiḥel*s (headcovers) for married women, "Ḥasidigel" and "Ḥasidishkids" for maintaining perfect rounded sidelocks for men, fashion shops and groceries, bakeries and bookstores.

What a different world.

The narrow streets, some of which are not fit for cars, are not very clean. Hopefully, the homes where people live are not as dirty. I have never been inside a private residence in Mea Shearim, not even when I lived here while I was a yeshiva student, back when, but I'd love to.

I stop next to a synagogue, called a shul in Yiddish, and am told by an old, *tiḥel*-wearing Ḥaredi lady standing near it that the members of this shul are the biggest troublemakers in all of Mea Shearim. "But they are nice people," she adds.

This is Jerusalem, I say to myself, a city that for thousands of years has known more troublemakers than any other city I know of, and one little shul with troublemakers won't make one bit of difference.

I ask the lady if she lives in the area, and she says that she does. Where do you live? I ask her.

She points at a little abode across the narrow pathway from the shul. When she sees me looking at it absorbedly, she asks if I would like to go in.

Yes, I say, and she invites me to come in.

And in we walk.

In this very house, she tells me, she grew up as a child.

It's a small unit, with two tiny rooms, each of them the size of about two twin beds, plus a small kitchen and a small bathroom.

"When we were children, nine of us slept here, and the rest of my siblings slept at grandfather's."

I have no idea how nine souls could fit in such a room.

"Those days," she tells me, "were my happiest days."

Inside the house, it is immaculate, spotless.

I leave her abode and go to the troublemakers' shul, just out of curiosity, but it's empty. The roaring lions, if that's what they are, must be sleeping.

I keep on walking.

On Mea Shearim Street, a car with a loudspeaker mounted on top passes by, announcing: "The funeral of the righteous rabbi, Reb Dovid Shloime Birnhak, of the important Toldos Aharon Ḥasidim, son-in-law of the pious rabbi Reb Eliyohu Steinberger of blessed memory, will leave at six o'clock [p.m.] from Toldos Aharon to the Mount of Olives." This is a call to the neighborhood people to pay their last respects by attending a funeral that will take place later in the day. The car drives slowly, making sure everybody is aware of the impending funeral and stops everything they are doing in order to attend the funeral.

What exactly are they doing? Of this I'm not sure. But they better stop whatever they are doing, because, so says tradition, attending a funeral is one of the most critical mitzvahs (God's commandments) a man can do, and he who does it will be handsomely rewarded from Heaven.

What will the reward be? Of this I'm also not sure.

If I had stayed in the Ḥaredi world and died here, they would have announced my funeral for all to hear. "The funeral of the pious rabbi, Reb Tuvia Tenenbom of blessed memory, will leave at six o'clock from Toldos Aharon to the Mount of Olives."

For a moment there, in my mind's ear, I hear them announcing my funeral.

It gives me chills.

I look at the passing car, and for a fraction of a second, it seems as if there is something in the back of it, something that I can't identify. Is that God?

What's a Better Way to Fly, on a Plane or an Eagle?

White donkeys, mules, a prophet, and a messiah in search of a wall

I know some of the rules and traditions of the Ḥaredi people, but many years have passed since I was Ḥaredi, and I'm not sure if the rules of today are the same as the rules of yesterday. The world outside Mea Shearim has changed, and perhaps Mea Shearim has changed as well.

The funeral announcer repeats his call several times, again and again urging people to give their last respects. A man is about to be buried, and this is the last chance to honor him.

Do I know this man? Did I see him in my youth?

It doesn't matter. All that matters now is that he's going to be interred on the Mount of Olives, God's favorite cemetery.

The Mount of Olives, as far as I know, is a burial place for the righteous and the rich; a burial plot in it costs more than an average café in Prenzlauer Berg.

Why is it so expensive? If memory serves me right, when the Jewish Messiah, known as Messiah ben David, arrives in Jerusalem at the End of Days, mounted on the white donkey of the Patriarch Abraham, he will first appear at the Mount of Olives, where he will bring back to life all the dead interred in the belly of the mountain. He will walk through the graves, one grave after the other, calling the names of those buried deep in the soil, and they will come out of the graves alive, breathing beautifully, with sparkling eyes. One after the other, their bodies will rise, as if they were never dead.

How do we know, you may ask, that Messiah ben David will come riding on Abraham's white donkey?

The answer is not short, but I'll give it to you.

In the biblical book of Zechariah, as you surely know, it is written:

> Rejoice greatly, O daughter of Zion; shout, O daughter of Jerusalem: behold, your king comes unto you: He is triumphant, and victorious; lowly, and riding upon a donkey, and upon a colt the foal of a donkey.

Who is the king? The Messiah.

How do we know, you may ask, that this is the donkey of the Patriarch Abraham?

It says in Exodus, as is known to all:

> Moses took his wife and his sons, and set them upon a donkey, and he returned to the land of Egypt.

And the Sages (Talmudic rabbis) say, as written by the most important Bible commentator, Rashi, that Moses the Lawgiver used the same donkey that the Patriarch Abraham used.

And since this donkey is the Patriarch Abraham's donkey, we know that whenever the Bible says "donkey," it refers to the Patriarch Abraham's donkey, the white donkey.

Where exactly is this donkey coming from? According to some kabbalists, this donkey was created at the end of the Six Days of Creation, right before the Sabbath entered. Full stop.

How do we know, you may be inclined to ask, that Zechariah's "king" refers to Messiah ben David? There are many answers to this question, and the best of them is this: asking too many questions is not suitable for the tongue.

Still, you can ask this question: What will the donkey do when the Messiah wakes up the dead?

Case in point: the Western Wall. The Jews say that the Western Wall is part of their ancient Holy Temple complex, but the Muslims of Israel say, no way! What's the name of the wall, you ask the Muslims? Al-Buraq Wall, they answer. No Temple, Holy or not. And no Western. Al-Buraq! Why al-Buraq?

Well, there's a story here; be patient and listen.

When the Prophet Mohammed, peace be upon him, came to Jerusalem from what is now Saudi Arabia, Allah provided for him a heavenly animal, al-Buraq, for the ride. What is the Buraq? According to the Hadith, it is "a white animal smaller than a mule and bigger than a donkey." Yes, kind of a White Donkey Plus. In any case, just before the prophet, peace be upon him, flew to Heaven, together with the Angel Jibril, Allah built a special wall for the purpose of tying al-Buraq to it while the prophet, peace be upon him, was up in the sky. Now, since there is a similarity between the white donkey and al-Buraq, the question arises: Will God build a wall for the Messiah's white donkey while he's busy raising the dead?

The answer is this: we will have to wait and see.

What we do know already is this: just before the Messiah arrives, perhaps three days prior, the biblical prophet Elijah will ride into town. What will he ride on? It could be – and of this I'm not sure – that he'll ride on some other ancient animal, maybe a cow or a camel, preferably white.

When all this takes place, I was told years and years ago, many eagles will fly in, carrying Diaspora Jews from places like New York and London and dropping them off in the Holy Land.

I should have flown here on an eagle; it beats EasyJet any day of the year.

In any case, once all the dead on the Mount of Olives have been resurrected, the Messiah will go to other cemeteries in the Holy Land, Israel, and resurrect the dead buried in the other cemeteries as well. That's why, it's important to remember, burial plots on the Mount of Olives are so expensive. Wouldn't you, if you had the money, want to be the first of the resurrected? I would. No waiting in line: Messiah arrives, and I'm alive.

As is written in the Bible, the Patriarch Abraham died long, long ago, but his donkey survived him. Why so? Nobody knows. In fact, nobody knows anything. Some people, known as scientists, think they know everything. They don't. When I was a little kid, studying in *ḥeider* (elementary school), my rebbe told us a story. A few so-called scientists made a highly acclaimed scientific experiment not long ago. They caught a fly with their hands, cut off its wings, and said to it: Fly, fly! But the fly wouldn't fly. Why? Because, the so-called scientists concluded, if the wings of a fly are cut, it becomes deaf.

Nice, isn't it?

That's how I, a little Ḥaredi Jew, started my life as a Ḥaredi – with sayings like that.

Do you know what "Ḥaredi" is?

The word *ḥared* in Hebrew has more than one meaning. It could be, for example, afraid, in awe, or fearful. A man is Ḥaredi, a woman is Ḥaredit (or Ḥaredis, in Ashkenazi pronunciation), and the plural, in masculine form, is Ḥaredim. (The spelling of the eighth letter of the Hebrew alphabet differs from place to place, language to language. Some spell it *h* or *ḥ*, others *ch* or *kh*. On these pages, it's spelled *ḥ*. Easy does it.) In America, where many people find it hard to pronounce the *Ḥ* of Ḥaredi, they prefer to say "ultra-Orthodox" instead of "Ḥaredi."

Now, there's more than one kind of Ḥaredim, meaning those who fear God. The most common, at least visually speaking, is the Ḥasidim.

To become a Ḥasid, genuine and pure, one had better have a Rebbe to follow.

Ḥasid, by the way, literally means "pious person," but in vernacular use, it means "follower."

The word *rebbe*, Yiddish for "rabbi," has more than one meaning. It can refer to a Grand Rabbi, a leader of a Ḥasidic sect (or court, or dynasty), and it can refer to an elementary school teacher. (On these pages, a Grand Rabbi is spelled with capital *R*, Rebbe.) "Rabbi," on the other hand, can refer to a non-Ḥasidic rabbi, at times also to Ḥasidic Rebbes, and on occasion to any fat man with a beard and a yarmulke (skullcap). "Reb," another derivative of *rabbi*, is a title bestowed on any man with a beard, if he is Ḥaredi and older than, say, thirty-one.

A rebbe for the little ones teaches in a *ḥeider*. In a *ḥeider*, you study everything you will need to know in life, from the Hebrew alphabet to the Talmud. In other words: alphabet and Talmud. In my *ḥeider*, where I studied when I was a sweet boy, we studied the Five Books of Moses as well as the Talmud, a series of tractates composed by the Jewish Sages following the Destruction of the Second Temple. Those Sages established Rabbinical Judaism, which is Judaism as we know it to this day.

If, God forbid, you have already forgotten some of the definitions hereabove explained, you will still be able to maintain a healthy and happy life, God willing.

As for me, I walk a bit more until I see some stone steps, where I sit down.

The sound of the funeral announcer is playing in my mind, an echo of what I heard. It's quieter, but the words are the same: "The funeral of the righteous rabbi, Reb Dovid Shloime Birnhak, of the important Toldos Aharon Ḥasidim, son-in-law of the pious rabbi Reb Eliyohu Steinberger of blessed memory, will leave at six o'clock from Toldos Aharon to the Mount of Olives."

I light up a cigarette, and I think. I think of my immediate area, of the areas surrounding it, and of the history surrounding all of us here.

The Second Temple and its Destruction, which Ḥaredi Jews mourn to this day, was located where al-Aqsa Mosque now stands in the Old City of Jerusalem. Today, all that's left of the prominent Jewish compound of old is the Western Wall, or Wailing Wall, the holiest place of the Jews, where they go to wail, pray, and dance. The Palestinians, who call that same wall al-Buraq, claim that no Jewish Temple ever existed in the area. Full stop. Many Palestinians – and countless Muslims worldwide – likewise claim that no Jew exists anywhere in the world. Full stop.

Are they right? According to some left-wing scientists, the Jews, also known as Hebrews and Israelites, are the forefathers of the present-day Palestinians. In other words, the Palestinians are the real Jews. And flies with no wings are deaf.

Yeah, really.

The Christians, followers of a faith derived from Judaism, believe that Jews exist but claim that the Jews got it wrong with their Messiah, since the real Messiah is Jesus Christ. The Christians also believe that Jesus is the Son of God, born of a virgin mother, while Jews believe that each one of them is a son of God, and some of them also think that their mother is a virgin, not Jesus's mother.

Islam, which is also derived from Judaism, rejects the Virgin Birth. Islam believes in other virgins, the Virgin Brides of Paradise, but that's a different story altogether.

The burning question that I have now, just popping in my head, is this: What happens to the dead people before any Messiah resurrects them? Do they exist anywhere? If so, do they do anything? If they do, what is it they are doing?

Unlike the Muslims, who believe that the dead get Virgin Brides to enjoy in perpetuity up there in Heaven, Jews and Christians are not very much into sex in Heaven. How sad.

Passage for Dogs and Zionists Is Totally Forbidden

Also forbidden: Looking at beautiful queens, birds, and sweeties

I get up to shake away the sad thoughts and resume walking the streets of Mea Shearim when another car passes by, also with a loudspeaker. Another man, clearly as rich or righteous as the other, has died. And he, too, is going to his resting place on the Mount of Olives.

All the dead and dying, let's hope, will soon be resurrected.

It will be nice to see my father again, with his long beard and sidelocks, his penetrating eyes, and his cigars. Yeah, my father loved cigars and pipes. He was a chain smoker, never inhaling but always on fire. I wonder, though, how he will look once resurrected. Will he be as old as he was when I last saw him? And what will be with me – if I stay alive for many years, will I be older than my father when he gets out of the grave?

Good question.

The walls on my right, where I now walk, are covered with obituaries of men and women who have just passed away. No German dies in Prenzlauer Berg, but here every Jew is dying. How come?

A group of girls, chatting in Yiddish and dressed like princesses, pass by me, one more beautiful than the other. I look at them intently; each of them is much more attractive than Patricia.

How could that be?

I never thought that Jews could look more beautiful than Germans. Had I known, I guess, I would have invited them all for a candlelight dinner. How could I have missed them?

It would be nice to see what happens once the Messiah resurrects all the Jewish ladies of the past. Will this Holy City suddenly explode with Jewish beauties, all the millions of them that I missed all these years?

The Messiah, unfortunately, is not coming today. Yes, every good Ḥaredi declares daily that *I shall wait for him every day*, but it's not going to happen today. Why? Because today is Thursday, a day before Friday, when Jewish women, the most famous cooks on earth, have no time to greet Abraham's donkey. Sorry. It is on Thursday evening, as is known, that Jewish wives and mothers start preparing the cholent, a food that cannot be described by words, only tasted by tongues, and no Messiah is going to intervene with this process.

The Messiah, a thought suddenly pops into my mind, shares one vital attribute with The Name: he has no name. He is known as Messiah ben David, meaning Messiah Descendant of King David, but what does this mean? Messiah is not a real name; it just means "Anointed One." That could be me, maybe?

The Name.

In this Ḥaredi neighborhood, as in any other Ḥaredi environment, God is not called God, but "The Name." At times, Ḥaredim also refer to Him as der Bashefer, meaning "the Creator," while more imaginative folks refer to Him as Master of the Universe, the Holy One Blessed Be He, and The Space. But no specific name.

In short: the Anointed will be sent by The Name to save the Jews.

At least the Jews have a name.

Messiah ben David might indeed be the Messiah, whatever his real name is. Still, there's a little problem here: there's another messiah in Judaism, and he is known as Messiah ben Yosef,

Messiah the Descendant of Josef. So, the question arises, who is the real Messiah, or do we have two messiahs?

Good question.

Messiah ben Yosef has no specific name either.

Why? Good question.

In any case, name or not, The Space will make sure that the Messiah is not coming today.

And neither is he going to come on Saturday. Why not? Because on the Sabbath – please don't advertise it – Ḥaredi men are supposed to "serve the bed," meaning have sex with their spouses, and no Messiah is big enough and strong enough to stop a Jew in bed. How would anyone expect to have Jewish children if a messiah and a donkey ride into the bedrooms of Jewish couples in the middle of "serving"? No way!

It is on Sabbath, the Jewish rest day, that serving is best. It took The Name six days to create the world, as is recorded in the Book of Genesis, and on the seventh day, the Sabbath, He rested. And that is why we, the people here, otherwise known as the Chosen People, were told by The Name, also known as The Space, to rest on the Sabbath and "serve" while resting. We are already in bed, so why not serve? That's how we kill two birds with one stone.

How was the world, all its planets and galaxies, stars, and the living beings, created in just six days? I don't know; I don't know everything. And if anyone told me that it took a gazillion years to get the world to be what it is, I wouldn't see how that could happen either.

The time passes, and I keep on walking. Back and forth, forth and back, over and over and over. I occasionally stop at the hotel, look at the interesting collection they have there of menorahs and other Judaica, and catch a nap. Then I go out again, again and again, breathing the air of my youth.

As I walk, I notice one thing missing here: dogs. In my New York abode, on the Upper East Side of Manhattan, almost everybody has a dog. Back there, where people are afraid to say anything about anything for fear that they will be ostracized by those surrounding them, dogs are the perfect tool to avoid loneliness. Dogs, who are not Progressive, perform all kinds of pleasurable acts that their owners don't dare do, but love to watch, because it reminds them how life used to be in the past, before the Progressives came into being.

What's "Progressive"? It's something you must be, clothes you must wear, words you must use, and a mindset you must adhere to if you want to be counted. Progressives teach, among other things, that you shouldn't say *he* or *she*, only *they*. Why? I'm not sure. I know that Progressives, judging by what they say, are not very much into sex. For Puritans like them, so it seems, sex is the domain of the Backwards and the Populists. They get their pleasures from other things, such as worshiping the environment, healthy food, marijuana, and dog walking.

There are no dogs in Mea Shearim. And no Progressives.

And now it's Friday, late afternoon.

On Friday, the eve of the Sabbath, men and women shower, or immerse their naked bodies in a ritual bath, known as a mikveh, cut their nails, and dress in holiday clothing. When the Sabbath enters, about half an hour before sunset on Friday, the women light the Sabbath candles and ask The Name to protect their mates and children.

In honor of the coming Sabbath, the streets of Mea Shearim change 180 degrees. All stores close their doors, traffic lights go off, "No buses coming soon" signs light up at bus stops, and sirens sound to announce the arrival of the Bride. Who is the Bride? The Sabbath, not Patricia.

Emptied of cars, the streets fast turn into sidewalks, and the people stroll in the middle of the streets. Women are dressed in fabulous dresses, looking like queens, and often push baby carriages. Men and their children – the fathers being the kings and the children the princes – walk, dressed in their finest, to the synagogue, where they will sing: "Go, my beloved, and welcome the Bride."

I could have been one of them. Walking the streets with Patricia and our little children, enjoying the quiet of the Sabbath and the kids' laughter.

No, no, no. Patricia would never be here. What would a Patricia do in Mea Shearim – undress in the middle of the street?

No, no Patricia. It would be, if it were to be, Rachel (the biblical Jewish foremother), Feigale (meaning bird), Malke Sheine (beautiful queen), or Zisale (sweetie). When I was a young boy, I dreamt of marrying a Rachel, because in the Bible, Rachel is described as a gorgeous girl, or a Zisale.

The temperature today is over 90 degrees, it's steaming hot, but the men are dressed in fur hats and long coats, some of them in double coats. These clothes, they say, are Jewish clothes, and they are the clothes, so they told me back then, that saved the Jews from certain death for the past thousands of years, especially since the Destruction of the Second Temple in Jerusalem and the loss of the Holy Land. Another reason Jews have been saved from total annihilation, they taught me, is because the Jews did not change their tongue, meaning their language.

What are the exact clothes that have never changed? Most visible of them on these streets is the *shtreimel*, a fur hat. But not all people agree on the fine details of how a *shtreimel* looks precisely and how thick it should be. A similar disagreement goes for the other never-changed Jewish clothing. Some believe that the pants, for instance, must be only three-quarters the length of the legs and are to be tied under the socks, long socks that cover the calves, while others argue that ankle length is the authentic Jewish clothing. Some believe that the socks must be white, and others believe that they must be black. There are white-sockers, if I remember, who will not intermarry with the black-sockers. Though in some Ḥasidic courts, the two socks are used, one kind for the married men and the other for the single ones. And in yet some other courts, so they tell me, the men who are part of the Rebbe's family dress in one kind of socks, while all others in another kind.

Go figure.

Truth be told, the likelihood that the Patriarch Abraham, or Moses the Lawgiver, wore a *shtreimel* thousands of years ago in Egypt is less than zero, and no *shtreimel*s are ever mentioned in the Bible or the Talmud. Yet in true Ḥasidic thought, Mea Shearim-style, this does not mean that the Patriarch Abraham did not wear a *shtreimel* while riding his white donkey.

What language, you may ask, did Abraham the Patriarch speak with his white donkey? Yiddish, of course. In what other language, let's be honest, could a *shtreimel*-wearing Jew living in Egypt communicate with his white donkey? Only Yiddish.

Factually speaking, Yiddish is mostly a dialect of German, and no Jewish donkey has been proven to speak German at any point in history, but we are not deaf flies, and we stick by our story.

"Passage for dogs and Zionists is totally forbidden," I read on a wall ahead of me, spray-painted in black over white paint. There must have been another graffiti underneath the white paint, but I can't decipher it. "Zionists are not Jews," proclaims another sign. "Do not read *Hamevaser* [a Ḥaredi newspaper]," I read in one of the *pashkevil*s near me, written by people associated with competing Ḥaredi newspapers.

How many people live in Mea Shearim? Rumor has it that even God doesn't know. How many Ḥaredi groups live in this neighborhood? Legend has it that there are more opposing groups in Mea Shearim than people. Is that true? Of course not, but the legend is lovely, nevertheless.

Once upon a time, Jews were led by one leader, such as Moses the Lawgiver or King David, but since the Destruction of the Second Temple, there have been more Jewish leaders in the Land of Israel than cats, and there are more cats in the Land than humans. How could these two statements coexist? Good question, but the fact is that they exist side by side in peace and harmony.

The Destruction of the Second Temple, which once stood proudly a mere twenty-minute walk from here, hastened the creation of Jewish settlements in many parts of the world, a period known as the Galut (Diaspora). All that, according to the Sages, will change when the Third Temple is built. Miraculously, no architect will be needed to design the Third Temple, since it will descend upon the earth from Heaven when the right time comes, meaning upon the arrival of Messiah ben David.

When will he come? That's anybody's guess, but if all the Jews alive observe even just one Sabbath, he will show up at once. If this theory is correct, others say, he'll never show up.

Here in Mea Shearim, though, the Sabbath is fully observed.

Once the father and the children are back from shul, the family sits together at the Sabbath table and sing. They welcome the Sabbath Angels to their homes, and the husband sings, "A woman of valor, who can find?" from the Bible (Proverbs 31), praising his wife as the best of the best there is, then the husband blesses his children that they may live forever, and then he makes a Kiddush, in which he sanctifies the Sabbath wine. They all proceed to eat a three-course meal, or a four-course meal, and some families prefer even more, plus sweets and drinks, all the while singing and celebrating the day of rest. If a non-Jew walked in and watched this, he would think that these people were celebrating Christmas. He doesn't know it, but these Jews celebrate "Christmas" every seventh day.

Observing the Sabbath requires more than just eating, drinking, resting, and serving, by the way. Driving, working, using an elevator, buying, selling, writing, watching TV, using electronic devices, smoking, cooking, boiling, and a series of other things are forbidden.

Ḥasidic Jews, if you are curious to know, also use the Sabbath to feast on different alcoholic drinks: brandy, whisky, wine, vodka, and a host of other delicacies, and if they have any energy left, they get up and dance.

Why not?

It is on this Sabbath day, on Saturday, that I go to attend a Sabbath morning meal with a religious family at their home in the Jewish Quarter of the Old City, by the Western Wall, al-Buraq Wall.

Surrounded by Arabs, Armenians, Greeks, and all kinds of other goyim (gentiles), the Jewish Quarter is a unique place in Israel. It is in the middle of one of the most contested real estate properties of the world, a place that has seen much blood spilled on its grounds for thousands of years, and is currently guarded around the clock by the Israel Police and Border Police.

Homes in the Jewish Quarter are very expensive, and only a select few can afford to live in them. Yet the home I'm visiting is decorated so simply that it hurts. A few photos, a big table, and the food is served on plastic plates. If John invited Patricia to this home, nothing would have happened, for there's not one romantic thread in this place.

Sitting down at the table, I try to understand the depth of this family's faith. And instead of dwelling on the high theological issues of the day, such as the religious origin of *shtreimels*, I go for the simplest: a man looking at a woman.

When you walk on the street, do you look at women? I ask a sixteen-year-old boy sitting next to me.

"No, of course not."

Why not?

"It's forbidden."

Says who?

"It's written."

Written where?

"In the Talmud."

Where in the Talmud?

"In tractate *Avodah Zarah*."

Where in tractate *Avodah Zarah*? What page? Can you show it to me?

"Yes, I can."

Will you do that?

"Let me bring the book."

While he's out looking for the book, I ask his fourteen-year-old sister to share her thoughts with me.

May a man look at a woman who's not his wife, mother, or daughter?

"No, he may not."

May a woman look at a man, any man?

"Yes."

Do you look at men while walking on the street?

"Yes."

Is it permitted?

"Yes."

A woman can look at a man, but a man cannot look at a woman. Is that so?

"Yes."

Why cannot a man look at a woman, but a woman can look at a man?

"Because –"

Because of what?

"Because, a man, a man, because."

What?

"A woman is, she is, she."

Excuse me?

"It's because, because, because."

Because of what?

"It's because, how should I say it? I don't know if you want me to say it, all of it –"

Yes, please, all of it.

"You mean that I should, eh, eh?"

Yes.

"The reason is, well, it's because, I don't know how to say it."

Say whatever comes to your mind.

"Do you want me to tell you what I was taught or what I think?"

You can tell me both, but what I'm most interested in is what you think.

"What do I think?"

Yes.

"What I think is that, yes, that, yes."

She smiles. Meanwhile, her brother returns to the table, the Talmud volume in his hands.

"I'll now show you," he says.

Well, I am ready.

"You will see it, right on these pages."

Great.

He opens the book and looks for the quote. He turns a page, then another page, and then one more page. And then he turns back the pages. One page, two pages, five pages. He goes on and on, page here and page there, but no quote is to be found.

So, it's not there? I ask him.

"No, it *is* here."

Where?

"In the book."

Where in the book?

"In one of these pages."

Which one of them?

"I read it once. I know it's here!"

Though he can't find anything of the kind in the book, he's right – to an extent. The Talmud in tractate *Avodah Zarah* does mention an opinion that a man better not look at a "beautiful woman," but it does not say that such an act is forbidden.

In general, the Talmud contains a collection of opinions, often contradictory opinions, and such is the case on the issue of a man looking at a woman. The Talmud, this young man was obviously never taught, also tells of prominent rabbis who couldn't stop looking at women.

I stick around a little longer, observing the people around me.

This family is Ḥaredi but not Ḥasidic. The Ḥaredim are divided into groups, subgroups, and sub-subgroups. The three main groups, from which many other subgroups have been born along the ages, are the Ḥasidim, followers of a religious movement that originated in the eighteenth century in the Kingdom of Poland; the Litvaks, opposers of the Ḥasidic movement, created in the Grand Duchy of Lithuania; and the Sephardim, a term that most often refers to Jews who come from families that immigrated to Israel from Muslim-majority countries. (Sephardim means "Spanish," because they were Spanish residents earlier on.)

Ḥasidim love to sing – sometimes for hours – dance, eat, pray, and spend precious time with their Rebbes. Litvaks, also known as "Misnagdim" ("Opposers," meaning of the Ḥasidic movement), love to study, dress simpler than the Ḥasidim, sing for up to four minutes, and collect prohibitions of all kinds because the more that is forbidden, the better it is for their psyche. Sephardim love everything mystical, whatever mysticism means, and dream of catching a Litvak for a spouse, even if that Litvak is sick, ugly, fat, old, or has slight brain damage.

I come from a Ḥasidic background, but I was educated in Litvishe yeshivas. This means that I grew up half and half, half a Ḥasid and half a Litvak.

Had the Temple not been destroyed and had the Jews of thousands of years ago not been expelled from the Holy Land or fled from it on their own, there would be no Ḥasidim, no Litvaks, and no Sephardim. But the Temple was destroyed, and it was destroyed on the ninth day of the Hebrew month of Av, meaning on this very evening on the Jewish calendar, close to two millennia ago.

Mourning a Destroyed Temple

The Law of Moses: A man cannot look at a beautiful woman, but he can look at an ugly woman

When the Sabbath ends, on Saturday evening, I get ready to go to the Old City again, this time not for the purpose of eating. The Ninth of Av is a fast day, when Jews mourn the destruction of the House of God in Jerusalem, the Holy Temple.

The ride to the Western Wall is almost impossible in private cars, but public buses go there, and buses leave my neighborhood every few minutes.

I mount one of them.

The bus, in this case a double-length bus, is packed to capacity. All riders in it are religious Jews who want to mourn the Destruction of the Temple near its only surviving part. The holiest site of the Jews, how depressing, is one remaining wall of a magnificent Temple compound that no longer exists, and these Jews are flocking to be next to it, to unite with it. No Patricia and no John would understand this logic, but Rachel, Zisale, and Feigale would.

The ride to the Western Wall is slow – there is traffic bumper-to-bumper – and at some point, I give up on the bus, get off, and proceed on foot.

After a while, I arrive. And here it is, facing me: the very place of the destroyed Temple.

I used to come here as a young boy, stare at the old stones of the Wailing Wall, and ask The Name to give me Patricia, and if that was impossible to give me Rachel, Zisale, and Feigale.

The Sages say that from the Day of Destruction, the Shḥinah (often spelled Shechinah) has never left the Western Wall, and that's one of the reasons people come to pray here. What's the Shḥinah? Nobody can tell, even though many try. Shḥinah can be translated as a feminine entity that dwells within. Within what? What entity? Nobody knows exactly. There are those who say that the Shḥinah is the feminine side of The Name, whatever that means, while some so-called kabbalists, relying on the mystical book the *Zohar*, say that the Shḥinah is The Name's wife or something like that. In short: nobody knows anything, and that's why everybody thinks that she's so great.

Whatever she is, or isn't, she is here, and she's watching the Children of Israel, the Jews, reciting in the tens of thousands the biblical Book of Lamentations, which mourns the fall of Jerusalem:

> How does the city sit solitary, that was full of people!
> How is she become as a widow, she that was great

> among the nations, and princess among the provinces, how is she become a tributary!
>
> She weeps sore in the night, and her tears are on her cheeks: she has none to comfort her among all her lovers; all her friends have dealt treacherously with her, they have become her enemies....
>
> The hands of the pitiful women have sodden their own children: they were their meat in the destruction of the daughter of my people.
>
> The Lord has accomplished his fury; He has poured out His fierce anger, and has kindled a fire in Zion, and it has devoured the foundations thereof.

I approach two yeshiva students, who usually spend their time studying Talmud, asking: Are you allowed to look at women?

Their response? Yes and no, it all depends on the circumstances, they say.

When are you not allowed? I ask.

"If the woman is beautiful, you are not allowed to look at her," comes the learned reply. "One is permitted to look only at an ugly woman, not at a pretty one."

Why that?

"Because it's written."

Where is it written?

"In the Talmud."

Which tractate of the Talmud?

"In tractate *Niddah*."

Not in *Avodah Zarah* but in *Niddah*. What page in tractate *Niddah*? Neither of them knows. What's the exact phrasing of this prohibition? Neither of them remembers. But it's undoubtedly written, something, somewhere, to such an effect. Does it say specifically that one is not allowed to look at a pretty woman?

"For sure."

Does it say, let me try to refresh your memory, Thou shalt not look at a pretty lady?

Well, "not exactly in these words, but something similar."

The question, of course, is how do you know if a woman is beautiful or ugly? You must look at her first, but then you might be committing a sin at the very moment you're looking at her, if she happens to be beautiful. If you are lucky, and she's ugly, then you have committed no sin.

How does Heaven determine if a woman is beautiful or ugly?

That's a good question, and neither of these yeshiva guys can supply the answer.

On the Ninth of Av, a day that recalls the time when Jewish mothers were so starving that they ate the flesh of their children, I talk to these two Jews about looking at beautiful ladies. And they are answering. It's a bit bizarre, I must admit.

In due course, as the descriptions of destruction go on and on in the Book of Lamentations, I mount a bus to take me back to Mea Shearim.

The streets of my new abode are almost empty of people when I arrive, and only a few cars are moving around. It is at this time that the most visible elements one can see on the streets are the *pushkes*, charity boxes, all around, attached to many a pole, gate, fence, and wall.

The people here, it seems, are taking good care of their poor.

Looking for a Mate? Go to a Grave

Taliban ladies marry seed-spilling men

When morning arrives, the temperature reaches 99 degrees, and the bright sun shines magically on the furnace down under, illuminating a big announcement on the main street of Mea Shearim. What is it about? Finding a mate. He who is lonely and looking for a mate, the announcement shares with us, can take a ride to a place called Amuka, in the far away Upper Galilee, and visit the grave of the Talmudic Sage Jonathan son of Uzziel. Special transportation will take place on Tu b'Av, the Fifteenth of Av, in just a few days, and famous, righteous rabbis will be in attendance.

How could a Sage, a Talmudic rabbi, soundly dead for hundreds and hundreds of years, make matches between lonely Jews? The answer is – brace yourself here – it's scientific. There are thousands and thousands of witnesses, the announcement authors say, who can verify the power of the grave and testify that they have found their mates within less than one year after visiting it.

When I was a sweet lad, back then, I went to Amuka, joining a few classmates who didn't have anything better to do other than rent a car and drive up north. We were the only ones anywhere near that grave – nobody else anywhere close. Today, it seems, the place is a popular tourist attraction.

Times are a-changing, I guess.

A woman walks in front of me now, but I can't tell if she's beautiful or ugly. She is covered from the top of her head to the tip of her shoe soles in black textile, a curtain perhaps, and people tell me that in Jerusalem, women like her, extra-modest Jewish women, are called "Taliban." Who are these Taliban?

I ask Yossi, a Sephardi Jew from the neighborhood who knows everything and anything, and he says: "For the most part, the Taliban are newly religious women who, in their past, slept with everybody and walked in bikinis on the streets. Now that they are religious, they cover their bodies as much as possible, believing that this new dress code will purify their sinful bodies. Their men, also newly religious, like their spouses' new look, because the longer it takes them to undress their wives, the more pleasure they extract, imagining that they are going to find diamonds under the black sheets."

And he goes on, after a short pause: "These newly religious men join the Ḥasidic court of Breslev, at the end of Mea Shearim Street. They have a unique problem: they used to have sex with all kinds of characters, and now they fear that they have accumulated so much spilled semen in their lives that The Name will never forgive them because spillage of men's seed is a great, great sin – the biggest sin ever. That's why they go to Breslev. The Rebbe of Breslev, who's been dead for over two centuries but is still very active in Heaven, promised that he would collect all the spilled seed of such men and turn their mountains of semen into mountains of diamonds."

The Breslever Rebbe also promised his followers, according to a Breslev Ḥasid I meet on the street, that if they grow long sidelocks, he will, in the World to Come, snatch them by those sidelocks from the gates of Hell, in case the Heavenly Court decides to send them there, and schlep them with him to Paradise.

That's what happens to the people who die here, I finally understand: their bodies go to the Mount of Olives, or another cemetery, and their souls fly to Rabbi Naḥman, the Breslever Rebbe.

Good for men, but what about women? Mea Shearim's women, after all, don't grow sidelocks, which means that Rabbi Naḥman won't schlep them with him to Paradise. Is that indeed so? Well, don't worry. Women are guaranteed to go to Heaven, meaning Paradise, I read in signs posted around the neighborhood, if they follow the rules of modesty while in This World, namely: arms must not be exposed from the elbows up, legs must be covered by black or by non-transparent brown stockings, skirts must reach well below the knees. All other parts of the body, excluding the face, the neck above the collar bone, and the lower part of the arms, must be covered. Fitted clothes, those that show the body's figure, are frowned upon; but many wear pretty tight sleeves, showing the exact shape of the arms, under the elbows.

Oh, God, I remember these rules so clearly! It's as if somebody took me out of here as a young teenager, flew me somewhere far on al-Buraq, and then dropped me back here on a white donkey.

How old is Patricia now? Is John still alive?

Shaved Heads Covered by $24,000 Hats

"Is she skinny, or is she fat? What color is her skin? What color is her hair?"

Walking the streets of the righteous, I pass various Ḥasidic courts and sects on my way. Karlin-Stolin, Satmar, Lelev (or Lelov), Dushinsky, Breslev, Toireh v'Yireh, Toldos Aharon, Toldos Avrom Yitzḥok, Shoimrei Emunim, and many others that only the Lord can read and pronounce.

I remember some of the courts, but the one that sticks with me the most is Toldos Aharon, whose members are known as Reb Ahrelaḥ, meaning the followers of Rabbi Aharon Rote, who was known as Reb Ahrele. I don't know much about them, except what I heard when I lived here. They were, so I was told back then, a Yiddish-speaking fanatic group dressed in golden caftans, whose members were ardent anti-Zionists. Is it true? I don't know. All I know is that I avoided them at the time, but now I would like to find out who they really are one of these days.

Yes, I know precious little about them. But if I remember correctly, they are a Ḥasidic court initially called Shoimrei Emunim, which Reb Aharon Rote established in the 1920s. That court was eventually split into three courts: Toldos Aharon, Toldos Avrom Yitzḥok, and Shoimrei Emunim, all of which are presently flourishing in Mea Shearim and other places. The married women of these three Ḥasidic courts, as I have been told, shave their heads after marriage. Their men, on the other hand, shave their heads from the age of three. Will anyone from these three courts talk to me if I, a man with round red eyeglasses and an impressive belly, approach them?

I get the answer to my question quicker than I could have dreamed.

A young lady, a *rebbetsen* (wife of a rabbi), is the one supplying the answer. Her name is Rebbetsen Leah Miriam Kohn, and she has, if I may say so, a face that shines in beauty and a smile that could melt the most hardened mafia boss in Sicily. She is, if I understand correctly, married to a son of the Toldos Aharon Rebbe, and he calls himself, if I'm not mistaken, the Rabbi of London. Funnily, she looks a bit like the "Rachel" I imagined years and years ago, the Rachel I would marry if Patricia didn't materialize.

We have a little chat.

Some people claim, I say to her, that the women of her community are degraded, abused, and spend their lives in depression and sorrow. Is that true?

I have no idea what made my tongue and lips utter such words, but they did.

The Rebbetsen gives me a smile, that greatest of smiles, and asks: "Do I look depressed to you? Abused? Degraded?"

Not exactly, but what do I know?

"I will tell you: I am happy to be who I am, I am proud to be part of my community, and I feel lucky that I belong to this community."

I would love to meet your husband. Can this be arranged?

"I will ask him if he wants to meet with you, and I will let you know. Call me."

She gives me her cell number.

Would you, my dear, give your cell number to a stranger who had just told you to your face that your community practically stinks all the way up to the sky? I wouldn't, but she did.

An older woman, whose children, grandchildren, and great-grandchildren combined surpass one hundred, walks by, and she stops to say hello to the Rebbetsen. The Rebbetsen, smilingly, says to me that perhaps I should talk a bit to this woman to find out how depressed she is. The ladies laugh, and the older lady invites me to her home.

We walk together, and once we are inside her home, a place that's a bit messy but very clean, she offers me a liter of cold soda and shows me photos of her family in a photo album – not on a smartphone, a device she doesn't own.

As I look at the photos, happy faces all, the woman's son enters. He is here to check if everything is okay, his mom tells me; he comes every day, she says. Understandably, he didn't expect to see a man, me, in the house, and he is more than surprised. He examines me, a stranger, a total stranger, perhaps even an infidel.

His mom, looking at her son, tells him that Rebbetsen Leah introduced the stranger to her. Hearing this, he promptly relaxes and welcomes me kindly.

The lady of the house has more children, she tells me. In fact, her young son is getting married next month, and she's busy these days raising funds for the occasion.

How much money is she trying to raise? The wedding will cost, she says, NIS 200,000, an amount equal to the average annual salary in the USA, and there are people and institutions in the community that will help her raise every penny of it.

She teaches me a few things, which I find interesting.

The rich of the community, she says, invest part of their earnings in the community, sharing what they have with those who don't. There's also the possibility of borrowing money without interest from a *gmaḥ*, a free-loan fund.

Why is the wedding so expensive? I ask.

It's not just the wedding itself that's so expensive, but other related expenses, comes the answer.

What are they?

A bridegroom, for instance, must wear a *shtreimel* on the Sabbath, and "the cheapest *shtreimel* costs NIS 6,000," the son says. There are *shtreimels*, for those who can afford quality, that go for up to $10,000. And there are other *shtreimels*, for those who lead a very comfortable life, that cost $24,000.

I would like to have the $24,000 one.

Do you know what the *shtreimel* is made of? I ask the son, who now sits down on a sofa in the room, ready to chat more comfortably.

"The tail of the sable, many sables for each hat," he says.

How many sables?

The Name knows, but not he.

That's for the hat, but the soon-to-be-married man will need more than just a hat. He will need, for instance, a couple of caftans, a golden one for the Sabbath and a bluish one for regular days, and each caftan costs NIS 1,000. Then there's the *gartel*, the unique belt that goes with the caftan, which also costs a pretty penny. And then there is a coat over the caftan, known as a jubbah, which he will also need. Not to mention that he will need nice shoes and nice socks for the Sabbath, black or white, and we didn't even talk yet about new shirts, new pants, new underwear, and of course a nice watch, preferably gold.

There's one more expense that one should never forget, because, without it, there's no wedding and no marriage: the matchmaker's fee. Since men cannot even look at women, and young men and women are not allowed to be together, how would a young boy and a young girl find each other? Enter the matchmaker. The matchmaker, man or woman, professional or not, knows the two families, or pretends to know them, and is well versed, hope be to the Lord, in the personal traits and history of the young man and the young woman, to make sure the two really fit.

That's how it works in the Ḥaredi world.

When I was part of it, I remember the story of a nineteen-year-old yeshiva student who was sitting in front of an open book, but his eyes were staring in a different direction, somewhere very far away. The rabbi, walking by, stopped, and sat next to him. "How does she look?" the rabbi whispered in the student's ears. "Is she tall? Is she short? Is she skinny, or is she fat? What color is her skin? What color is her hair? How does she sound?"

It didn't take the rabbi long to get the boy under the canopy.

And now I have a question: Is it true that a person from a family whose men wear white socks on the Sabbath won't marry a person from a family whose men wear black socks?

True, says the mother.

I thought so.

There are more costs one must think of, by the way, before getting married: women's clothes.

Being dressed modestly, covering as much flesh as possible, is much more expensive than going naked.

Ḥaredi women, like any other human, want to look attractive. You can be modest, cover most of your body, and yet look sexier than any woman in a bikini. That's the biggest secret of fashion: you can take anybody, beauties or uglies, and make them look stunning via the cover of cloth. Some Ḥaredi women – you should not be shocked by this little fact – are more gorgeous than Ms. Universe. But, yes, there are some rules beyond just fashion dictates. For example: married Reb Ahrele women, at least from what I can tell, wear a white cover on their heads on Friday night, when the Sabbath starts. During Sabbath day, if I'm not mistaken, they can wear their hat in any color they want as long as it's not too showy (for example, fire engine red).

In any case, I bid my hosts goodbye and make my way to a wig shop.

Yeah.

I love fashion, and I find Ḥaredi fashion quite intriguing. And so, I go to the wig shop near Sabbath Square to examine what a newlywed woman would need to have before a ring finds its way onto her finger. Some Ḥaredi communities, such as the Reb Ahrelaḥ, dictate that a married woman wears a headscarf, a *tiḥel*, not a wig, but other Ḥaredi women wear wigs and love it.

A married Ḥaredi woman, let me break the news to you, is not allowed to show her hair to anyone but her husband, and some say not even to him. Hair, an old rabbi whose name nobody knows determined long ago, is hugely tempting, and if married women were to walk with their heads uncovered, God save us, men would get extremely tempted, their membrane would go nuclear, and they would lose their minds for good. To save men from such a disaster, God in His mercy created wigs, and that's why this wig shop exists.

If you wonder how, in real life, the wigs look on these women, here goes: it depends on which wig they have. Some of the wigs are so gorgeous that they could make every woman a porno star.

Yes, the very idea of covering the head is to make sure that the men are not tempted, and yet some wigs are potential membrane blowers, which logically would mean that wigs should be the Most Forbidden. But no, because not everything in the world makes sense. Is there any sense in having snakes in the world? They are there, and we have to live with them, and with the tempting women too.

The wig store, in the basement level of a building, sells wigs natural and artificial, those made from human hair and others that are synthetic. A natural wig on a shelf near me costs NIS 5,800, and a synthetic one next to it goes for NIS 1,700. Cheaper than a *shtreimel*.

That's all I wanted to know. Why? I have no clue.

I go out of the wig shop to the street.

What do I see? A big announcement: Public Prayer at the Western Wall for Matches. The Ḥaredi community is invited to gather at the Western Wall and pray to The Name for help in finding a mate.

This makes me think: assuming, let's just say, that the prayers for matches are answered, and all singles find their mates, what will happen next? If a wedding costs NIS 200,000, not to mention the cost of buying or renting a living space, how many will be able to afford it? Judging by the inner streets of Mea Shearim, where I now stand looking around and noticing yet again all the garbage strewn around, it doesn't strike me that many of these people can afford NIS 200,000 just to stand under the canopy. Could it be that the community helps each newlywed with NIS 200,000 just to get married?

By the way, in case you wondered: the streets might be dirty, but the people walking by are super clean.

And here's a Ḥasidic couple walking by me, a man and a woman. The man seems to be mentally retarded, and so is the woman. Together, they look very happy. A perfect match! Lucky them, there's a matchmaker in town. Otherwise, most likely, they would have lived alone and had miserable lives.

One Hour + One Prayer = One Billion Shekels

"When you give a Jewish beggar a shekel, he is upset. When you give a goy twenty cents, he's happy."

I keep on walking and pass by a money-changing shop. I stop for a little chat with the owner. In our day and time, I ask him, who needs money changers? I stopped using money changers ages ago; why would anyone use them in our tech-advanced age?

"You'd be surprised," he replies. "The transactions that I make, just me, are in the hundreds of thousands every day."

Who has this kind of money, my dear money changer?

"I don't know. Maybe they are donations from abroad, to keep the community going."

This is the strangest exchange I've ever had with a money changer.

I walk toward the area where my old yeshiva, Beis Hatalmud, once was until I reach a restaurant called, wild guess, The Restaurant (Hamisadah). The Restaurant, near one of the buildings of the Mir Yeshiva, is run by Motti and his wife, Tehilah. Here one can get, among other things, *yaptchik* (a mixture of potato kugel and meat) for 28 NIS; cholent, for as little as NIS 17 and as high as NIS 60 (depending on the size); a meat patty for NIS 10; and a single cigarette for NIS 2.50. Yes, they sell single cigarettes here, and you can smoke anywhere in the restaurant. Motti used to be an attorney, and now he sells a single Marlboro for 2.5 shekels and feels he's in Heaven.

Are the people around here poor or rich? I ask Motti, a maven in the community.

"Nobody knows," he answers.

A family can have millions, living next to a family that has nothing, and no outsider would be able to tell the difference, Motti says.

What is it with the streets – why are they so dirty?

A way of life, Motti answers. One day, he tells me, a very famous philanthropist came to the neighborhood to visit. When the people heard that he was coming, they each took a big plastic bag, went outside, and picked all the garbage on the streets. The philanthropist came, was impressed, and left in good spirits, very good spirits. Once he left, the residents went out of their homes, with the plastic bags in their hands, and emptied the garbage back on the streets. Why are you throwing garbage on the streets, a passerby asked them? They looked at him in surprise and said: "Where else should we throw our garbage? That's where we found it!"

Is this story true? I don't know. It might be an allegory, a tale, or just an excuse by the teller to entertain himself.

Truth be told, if you compare the streets here to New York subway stations, for example, you will say that the streets here are spotless.

Well, whatever.

Steps away from Motti's restaurant is Kuperman's Free-Loan Fund – *gmaḥ*, in Hebrew – reportedly Israel's largest *gmaḥ*, with transactions of up to one billion NIS. The Fund is not easy to spot, as its offices are on the lower level of an unassuming building, where you might expect to find a toilet, not a multi-million-shekel financial office. But that's the way they like it, and that's where I go.

"Thousands of *gmaḥ*s are believed to be operating in Israel's Ḥaredi society," Israeli media write. And Kuperman, if I get it right, is the king of *gmaḥ*s.

The office is small. Five clerks are sitting in the back, behind see-through windows, with a similar number of seats opposite them for the loan seekers. Opening hours, I read: five days a week, one hour per day. How do you turn over a billion shekels from an office that looks like a small barbershop, and while operating five hours a week? I don't know. What I do know is this: if you plan to get married and wonder where you'll find NIS 200,000 to pay for your change in status, try your luck here.

There are a few plastic chairs in the room, and I sit on one of them, next to Shimon. Shimon is here to ask for a $20,000 interest-free loan, payable in fifty installments. He has some financial difficulties due to an apartment he just bought – long story, he says. He works for a living in the food industry, but the bills due each month are overwhelming. Enter Kuperman's *gmaḥ*. He has taken a loan before, and he expects no difficulties this time either. For new borrowers, he tells me, it takes six months to two years to get an appointment at Kuperman's, and guarantors are required before a loan is given.

How many guarantors?

"It depends on how good your guarantors are," a man standing near us says, with a smile on his face. "I'm not here to take a loan," the man adds. "I am here to deposit money. Banks today give very nominal interest rates, and I prefer to deposit my money in a *gmaḥ*. When I deposit my money here, I know that my money helps people in need. If I need the money back, the *gmaḥ* will give it back to me immediately. Have a good day."

Is he really a depositor and not a borrower? Only The Name, Kuperman, and he know.

Shimon speaks unto me. "When you give a Jewish beggar a shekel, he is upset. When you give a goy twenty cents, he's happy. Why? Because a Jewish beggar thinks what he would be giving a poor man if he were rich – at least NIS 10, and that's why he's not happy with the one shekel. A goy also thinks what he would be giving if he were a rich man approached by a beggar: zilch, and that's why he's thrilled with the twenty cents."

Suddenly all transactions stop. What happened? Did the New York Stock Exchange collapse? No. Something much more important is happening: it's prayer time!

What do the Jews pray about while moving millions? Well, first and foremost, about the resurrection of the dead. Yeah. All the billions in the world are not worth a single penny if you can't use them once you get up from your grave. It makes perfect sense to me.

With the prayer over, I leave the place, and I see an ocean of yeshiva students on the street outside. One of them tells me that there are about eight thousand students in the Mir Yeshiva.

The numbers in this area – of shekels and students – are astronomical.

When I lived here, in the Beis Hatalmud Yeshiva, the yeshiva was under the leadership of its founder, Rabbi Berel Schwartzman, who was a close friend of my father. Rabbi Berel, who passed away about a decade ago and is buried on the Mount of Olives, was a genius, versed in the Talmud and many other Jewish books. On occasion, he visited my parents at their home in Bnei Brak, visits that I still remember as if they were yesterday. He was an interesting man, with a unique personality. One day, when he gave a lecture, a fly flew next to his face. He stopped the lecture and followed the fly's movements. He wanted to know why the fly was flying the way it did and what made it fly round and round, seemingly in the pointless pursuit of something. Reb Berel was curious: What was it that the fly was looking for?

Beis Hatalmud moved to another location a few years after I left it. According to his biography, at some point in his rich career, Rabbi Berel joined a rabbi named Nota Schiller and others to establish the famous Jerusalem yeshiva for penitent Jews (*baalei tshuvah* in Hebrew, meaning "returnees to Judaism" or newly observant Jews), Ohr Somayach.

It would be nice to meet Rabbi Nota Schiller one of these days.

Which reminds me: I have not been inside a yeshiva for a long, long, long time.

A Litvak Rabbi Looks at His Wife and Runs to Tell

What exactly does resurrection of the dead mean?

On the following day, I go to one of the biggest yeshivas in Jerusalem to participate in a Talmud lecture. The students sit on countless benches in a big hall, Talmud books open before them, and they listen to the learned rabbi explaining a complex Talmudic concept to them. Some of the students write down every word he says, others just stare at him, and still others look away, traveling in their inner thoughts and dreams.

Once the rabbi is done with the lecture and starts walking out of the hall, many of his students follow him, refusing to say goodbye to their beloved teacher. As far as I can tell – don't laugh – he has more admirers than the king of Saudi Arabia. And the king has many, many admirers, according to the Saudi press.

Outside, another car with a loudspeaker drives by, announcing yet another funeral.

Nobody around me seems to be saddened by this announcement. To these people, I guess, a funeral is not the end of the world, since the dead will be resurrected anyway.

I approach one of the rabbi's followers and ask him to ask the rabbi if he wouldn't mind, please, meeting me in person. The rabbi tells him that he would gladly do so, and I go to the rabbi's home to meet him in private.

He lives modestly, quite unlike the Saudi king, and we sit down in his living room, a place surrounded by books. I can tell there's somebody else in the house, as I hear footsteps, but I see no face. Perhaps it's his wife and maybe an angel. Rabbis and angels go hand in hand, I was once taught.

The rabbi gives me a shy smile, then a look, just so, and then he shows me a telephone directory. I have not seen a telephone directory in ages, but the people of his community, where smartphones are frowned upon, are still using it. He opens the directory to the "charity" category, the *gmaḥs*. The charity-listing pages consume many, many pages of this directory. "This is our world," he says to me, meaning the Ḥaredi world. "We help each other, and we won't let anyone fall. Where else do you have this?"

Some of the *gmaḥs* give out loans that are to be repaid but with no interest; others are *gmaḥs* for various needs, such as medicines, that don't have to be repaid. There are *gmaḥs* that offer baby carriages, there are *gmaḥs* that provide use of computers for just a few shekels, and there are *gmaḥs* that provide air conditioners for reduced prices. In short: help for the needy however it is needed.

This done, he takes one long look at me and says: "I have one condition. Don't mention my name or my yeshiva."

I didn't expect this, but I guess I don't have any other choice, and I accept his condition.

What is he afraid of? That's for him to know, but it's interesting to notice that even in communities like his, where leaders are worshipped, there are leaders who are fearful of their followers.

He speaks in a soft but determined voice. There is a softness to his voice, mixed with stubbornness and a self-recognition of authority. And though he doesn't want his name to be made public, he wants his words to be heard. And I notice another thing about him: he is not a Ḥasid but a Litvak (referring to the Misnagdim's origin in Lithuania), part of a people who pride themselves on knowledge and not on emotions, on study and not stories, and it shows. There's no warmth projected from him, and a smile seems to be a language he doesn't speak in. He would do well in Hamburg, I think.

Do you believe that the Messiah will come and resurrect the dead? I ask the learned man.

"The Name will."

Let me rephrase my question: Do you believe that the Messiah will come, call on the dead to rise from their graves, and with The Name's help, all of them will be resurrected?

"Not all of them, but certainly those who have studied the Torah."

Can you paint for me the picture: How will the resurrected dead look? Let's say one of them died at the age of eight and another at eighty. Will they come back eight- and eighty-year-olds? Also: Will the resurrected stay forever at the same age as when they are resurrected, or will they grow year by year?

"I have been thinking about this, but I have no answer. Not everything has an answer."

Let me ask you another question: Why would The Name kill people and then resurrect them? Can't He just let them stay alive?

"When people depart from this world, they will either be rewarded for what they did while alive or punished if they deserve to be punished."

Can't The Name punish them without burying them first?

"It says that the suffering in Hell is so severe that no pain that exists in This World is comparable to it."

The Name, if I get this correctly, wants to inflict upon the sinners the harshest, cruelest punishment that exists, and this can be achieved only in Hell, once they are dead.

But those who spent their lives studying the Torah will be rewarded, correct?

"Of course."

What is the Torah? The Torah is a set of rules and regulations. Let's take an example, from tractate *Baba Kama* (as translated by

Sefaria online): "If an ox gored a cow, causing it to die, and its newly born young was found dead at its side, and it is not known if the cow gave birth before the ox gored, or if after the ox gored the cow gave birth, the owner of the ox pays half damages for the cow and one-quarter damages for the newborn." Very interesting. But why is studying these laws so crucial to The Name? It's not much different than students studying law in university, and they are not rewarded with a good place in Heaven, as far as I know. Why do those who study laws about bulls and cows get rewarded so handsomely?

"The Torah are laws of The Name. And why does He want us to study them? Because The Name is the Utmost Good, and He wants to do us good. After all, that's why The Name created the world, because He wants to do good."

It takes a rabbi to tell you how cruel God is and how good He is in a stretch of just minutes.

I move on. Why, I ask the esteemed and secretive rabbi, can't a man look at a woman?

"Because it says so in the Bible."

Where?

"In the Book of Numbers. 'Do not allow your heart and eyes to direct you to what you lust after.'"

Does that mean women?

"Certainly."

There's no arguing this, because he is "certain."

Can a woman look at a man? I ask him.

"Yes."

Why is it that she can and he can't?

"When a man looks at a woman, it arouses desires in him, and this can lead to forbidden acts."

But women also have desires, and they too might end up doing forbidden acts – isn't it so?

"Men's desires and women's desires are different."

Perhaps you are not aware of it, but a man's desires and a woman's desires are pretty similar.

"Not the same."

As far as I have seen, it's pretty much the same!

"Not that I know. In any case, after marriage, a man can look at his wife often, and I do it too. It's a good deed to look at one's wife and please her with such looks. This is also the will of The Name."

That would be funny to watch: a rabbi taking a chair to the kitchen, where his wife prepares chicken for the Sabbath meal, and he sits there looking at her, admiring her beauty compared to the chicken.

Tell me something, I say, moving on to a different subject matter altogether – his Ḥaredi clothes. Why are you wearing black clothes? Is that, too, the will of God? Did the Patriarch Abraham wear them? Did Moses the Lawgiver?

"Rabbis of past generations instituted that we wear these clothes, and whatever they told us to do, we do. Rabbi Israel of Salant said that a man could shave his beard, and that's why some of us do. He also said that a man should wear a tie, so his followers wear ties. On the other hand, some rabbis say that men shouldn't shave their beards, which is why many don't. We follow our rabbis!"

Do they really follow their rabbis of old? Well, not exactly. Being that he is a Litvak, part of a people who in my day didn't go to rabbis asking that they pray for them, I tell him that some time ago I happened to see people standing in line in front of a Litvishe rabbi's home to have him bless them, a custom that Litvishe rabbis of the past condemned. When I was a kid, I also share with him, this rabbi lived across from my family's home in Bnei Brak, and I remember that I wasn't that much impressed with him. But things obviously changed, and many Ḥaredi Jews now believe this rabbi to be a miracle maker and a future teller. They go to him to cure them when they are sick, enrich them if they are poor, and solve their various personal problems, whatever those may be. When I saw this, I said to myself: these people say that they believe in The Name, but they believe in a rabbi, as far as I can tell. Am I wrong?

"Not totally wrong. During and after the Holocaust, the faith weakened. And even though many years have passed since the Holocaust, the faith that the people of our generation have is much less than in the generations before the Holocaust."

In other words, the people who go to that rabbi (Rabbi Ḥaim Kanievsky) are rabbi believers and not God believers, praying to a rabbi instead of praying to God.

It is on this note that we depart, he to his world and I to mine, and the secret meeting comes to an end.

I go back to my hotel, where the thought comes to me that I should talk with the husband of Rebbetsen Leah, a holy rabbi, who is a Ḥasid. Maybe he will explain to me the idea of praying to a rabbi instead of praying to God.

I call the Rebbetsen, that gorgeous Rebbetsen, and her husband picks up the phone.

He speaks: "It will be nice to meet you, but I don't see how this could take place. I spend every available moment studying the Torah, as I should, so how could we find the time to meet? Right now, I'm playing with my kids, because I love them very much, but when I'm not with them, I study all the time. There is no time to meet."

I wonder if this London rabbi talks like this to British people. They would most likely show him the way to the airport, out of the UK, if he did.

It is time, now that I'm done with these two spiritual men, to take care of my belly. Yes.

Jewish Men Must Wear Tails of Cats on Their Heads

It's time to pray to God at a grave while holding two Palestinian flags

Hadar Geula, just a few minutes' walk from my hotel, is mainly a food shop, but there is a room with a few tables and chairs in the back of the shop.

There I go, and you're welcome to join me.

On me. It's my treat!

What am I having? Well, two slices of gefilte fish, a potato kugel, and a Jerusalem kugel, which is a lokshen kugel, meaning noodle kugel. And then I order eggplant salad mixed with sweet and spicy chili. Delicious! My belly, sensing a food it recognizes from years past, is jumping for joy. My tongue and palate, feeling like those of a sweet boy again, sing twenty-six Hallelujahs.

If I had married a Rachel back then, or a Zisale, I would get this food at least seven times a week. Oh, Rachel, oh, Zisale, where are you?

Do you accept credit cards? I ask the Ḥasidic man behind the counter, remembering that in Prenzlauer Berg, some establishments accept cash only.

"Well, that depends," the man answers.

Depends on what? I ask.

"If it's valid, we accept. Otherwise, no."

The man makes me laugh.

Funny people, these Jews.

With my belly happy, my feet ask if I wouldn't mind taking a little walk.

Well, of course. I'll never say no to my feet, entities that have served me faithfully since my birth, more or less.

And walk I do.

Ahead of me, I see two young men. One is dressed in a blue caftan, with white stripes all over, and one in a black coat. What does the blue caftan indicate, and what's the difference between those who wear blue and those who wear black? And what about those who wear golden caftans? I ask them.

The blue, explains the blue man, is for every day, while the gold is for the Sabbath, and both indicate followers of Toldos Aharon, and other "Chalmers," meaning Ḥaredim who are Jerusalemites. The black ones with no stripes, they tell me, are for single men.

Good to know. I move on.

Two young men well dressed in Ḥasidic attire, black with no stripes, now approach me. They ask for tzedakah, alms for the poor, and say that it would be great if I could help. I don't have cash on me, I tell them. No problem, they answer, and one of them promptly produces a wireless credit card machine and tells me that he'll be happy to charge my credit card in any amount I wish. I can pay in installments, any amount I wish, and it will be charged to my card once a month or once a week, whatever I wish.

I burst out in laugher, unable to believe my eyes. Nobody, be it in New York or Berlin, ever tried to charge my credit card just like that, on the street, but this is Mea Shearim. The young men see me laugh, and they join in the laughter. They laugh so hard that they forget about the alms they requested moments before.

I keep on walking until my eyes catch sight of a Palestinian flag flying high above a shul, in addition to several Palestinian flags painted on houses and walls near it. "Zionists are not Jews," I read on a couple of walls. In addition, I see advertisements for trips to the graves of rabbis where prayers are answered, and where miracles happen. If I've got this right, anti-Zionists love to spend their lives in tombs while holding Palestinian flags. That would fit with some currents in the Palestinian culture of our day. When sick, those Palestinians go to the graves of suicide bombers, believing that they will get healed as a result.

Who put up these flags, and who are the ones who do the graffiti? I ask an older Ḥasid with a welcoming smile on his face.

"You have to stay here for some time, understand how the community here works, to know who does what."

You won't hear this kind of an answer in Bnei Brak, the Ḥaredi city near Tel Aviv, where I spent my first years in this world. In Bnei Brak, if I remember correctly, they would rather you don't stay amongst them if you don't understand such simple things. You've got to be a Ḥasidic Jew in Mea Shearim to give the answer that I was just given.

No wonder, I now think, that at a very early age, I decided to move to Jerusalem, a holy city of prophets, donkeys, and stunning ladies.

Did I just say, "stunning ladies"? Yes, I guess I did. Well, what can I say? Since I started walking the streets of Mea Shearim, I look at Ḥaredi women more than I ever looked at any woman in any unholy city. Yes, when sitting at Prenzlauer Berg cafés, I did look here and there, like any healthy Jew whose brain is not on weed, but not constantly. Here, so strange, I can't stop looking at the Mea Shearim beauties.

There's something about this Mea Shearim that draws me in, and I wonder what makes Mea Shearim what it is.

Go to Yoilish Krois, a journalist tells me, and he'll explain to you everything you need to know about Mea Shearim.

I don't have much faith in journalists these days, but I go to Yoilish anyway.

Yoilish lives on Honi Hameagel Street, inside the "real" Mea Shearim neighborhood. Everybody knows where Yoilish lives because Yoilish, I'm told, likes to talk to journalists, and the more people who know his address, the better. Everybody knows the address of the Israeli prime minister, on Balfour Street in Jerusalem; why wouldn't everybody know where Yoilish lives? Isn't Yoilish, after all, more important than a prime minister?

Yoilish Krois is a big troublemaker, I am also told, and he is known as the *kambats* (operations officer) of the Ḥaredi Council, whatever that means, if it indeed means anything.

And here I am now, in front of his house, and Rachel, his wife, greets me.

Rachel, a princess in the closed world of Mea Shearim, comes from the highly respected families of Rabbi Aharon Katsnelenboigen and Rabbi Amrom Bloi, founders of the extremely anti-Zionist Toireh v'Yireh Yeshiva and the Neturei Karte movement. Yoilish and Rachel are, so I hear, the most extreme of the extreme of Israel's Judaism, and both would be honored, I think, to have such a title.

Of course, it all depends on what "extreme" is.

Late in his life, Rabbi Amrom Bloi, founder of the "most extreme" Ḥaredi movements of his time, married a beautiful former Catholic, Ruth, about twenty years his junior, when he was in his mid-sixties. It didn't matter that almost everyone around, rabbis and what have you, threatened to boycott him. They reminded him, as if he needed any reminder, that she's a former Catholic, much younger than him, and they tried to convince him that what he was doing shamed his honor. He didn't care a bit; love won over, of a man for a woman and a woman for a man. Extreme maybe, but in love.

Just as the street leading up to Yoilish and Rachel's place is dirty and messy, so is the front of their house. Their abode, sad to say, is one big mess.

Here is an empty plastic bag, here is a broken plastic chair, here is a plastic plate, a plastic bottle, a few mattresses one on top of the other, and no order anywhere. This would be a total disaster for the average German, but for the eighteen children plus the two parents, twenty in all, everything here is in perfect order.

Yes, Rachel and Yoilish have eighteen children.

Not all the children, I assume, live in the house. Some must be married, but there's quite a bunch of them around, and I'm impressed how well educated they are. When visiting a "normal" family of one or two children, be it in the USA or Germany, I'm used to encountering screaming or spoiled-rotten kids bossing their parents around. Not here. The children of Yoilish and Rachel behave like flowers in the desert, beautiful and welcoming, offering me warm smiles as if I were the long-lost, beloved uncle they have all dreamt of meeting one day.

And they chat with me.

One of the youngest children, a charming boy, teaches me the Book of Genesis in Yiddish. He sings the verses in juicy Yiddish as his dedicated mama cheers him on. One of their daughters, as charming as the boy, serves me a cup of cold water by placing it next to me on a chair, to avoid giving it to me straight, for fear, of course, of accidentally touching me, which is a major sin, since it might make me desire her, The Name save us.

Rachel, a friendly woman, strikes me as a happy person, ever a smile on her face, despite some of her teeth being missing.

She kindly shows me to my seat in the living room.

We sit down, Reb Yoilish and I, at a big table in front of a bookcase, to have a little chat in Yiddish, his Mamme Lushn, mother tongue. We would have spoken in Hebrew, the language of the land, but he doesn't speak Hebrew, he says.

Good, let it be Yiddish.

For years and years, he tells me, he organized demonstrations against the desecration of ancient Jewish graves by the Zionist government.

Yeah, he thinks that I am like some other Western journalists who come to hear him speak against the horrible people of the State of Israel, the cursed Zionists, and how murderous is the country called Israel, a country in which he resides. For those Western journalists who come to interview him, or his upstairs neighbor Rabbi Hirsh, he offers a great visual: he looks like a "Jew," the most authentic Jew possible, one with extra-long sidelocks, long beard, a huge white yarmulke, and he fights the Jewish state, and he supports the Palestinians. They love it, since it offers them a visual that they crave: an "authentic" Jew who is against the Jewish state, a state that they don't like much. But I don't want to talk politics, and I'm not impressed by the "Jewish" visuals. I want to know other things. Faith, for example.

I tell him as much.

I have noticed, I say to him, a popular trend in the Ḥaredi world: prayer travel to graves of dead Jews. Isn't that a form of idol worship? Why would anyone who believes in The Name go to pray at a grave?

"In this generation, people are weak, people are broken, they don't know where to go and what to do, and that's why they go to the graves."

I have heard this excuse before from the rabbi who spends his time at home looking at his wife.

How about the generations before that? I ask him.

"They studied the Torah, and they didn't need to go to graves. They had more faith."

Why is it that in this generation, Ḥaredi people have less faith?

"Because of the Zionists."

He tries, desperately, to direct the conversation to his anti-Zionist propaganda. But I am not willing to go there.

Why, I ask the man, do Ḥaredim wear *shtreimels* and black clothes?

Reb Yoilish, a product of Toldos Aharon's institutions, is surprised by the question, but he accepts the challenge. The reason Ḥaredim wear black clothes and *shtreimels*, he tells me, is that 350 years ago, more or less, there was a *gzeireh*, a decree by a non-Jewish authority, forcing Jews to wear a tail of a cat on their heads and to dress up in black, to denigrate them.

It is over 90 degrees out, steaming hot, but Reb Yoilish wears the *shtreimel*, a fur hat suitable for the freezing winters in Siberia, because some *shmeckale beckale* king at some point in time had this bizarre idea that Jews should have tails of cats on their heads.

And what is the reason for having a caftan? What's the story behind that?

"I don't know," says Reb Yoilish, and adds: "I never asked questions like these." What he does know is this: "The caftan is made out of twenty-six pieces of textile, since twenty-six is the numerical value of The Name." What he also knows is that a man is not allowed to wear a wristwatch, because a wristwatch is an item of female clothing, and a man is forbidden from wearing female attire. "It's written in the Torah."

He has a pocket watch, and he's proud to show it to me.

I'm happy for him.

But enough talking about men and watches, I say to myself; let's talk about women and *tiḥels* or wigs.

I want to know, I share with him, at what point in history were married women prohibited from exposing their hair, and where in the Bible does The Name command women to cover their hair?

"This started during the time of Moses, when a woman was ordered to wear a covering on her head."

The time of Moses the Lawgiver?

"Yes. It's written in the chapter of Koraḥ."

You have the Bible, let's see it, I tell him while pointing to his bookcase, where he has at least one Bible.

He takes the Holy Book from the bookcase, opens it to the Koraḥ chapter (in Numbers), and I read aloud:

> Now Korah, the son of Izhar, the son of Kohath, the son of Levi, with Dathan and Abiram, the sons of Eliab, and On, the son of Peleth, sons of Reuben, took men; and they rose up before Moses, with certain of the children of Israel, two hundred and fifty princes of the congregation, the elect of the assembly, men of renown; and they assembled themselves together against Moses and against Aharon, and said unto them: "You take too much upon you, seeing all the congregation are holy, every one of them, and the Lord is among them; wherefore then lift you up yourselves above the assembly of the Lord?"

What does this have to do with a woman covering her head? I ask.

In response, Reb Yoilish, the famed Operation Officer, reads the Holy Book and spends a considerable amount of time trying to find the head covering commandment inside the Koraḥ story. He turns the pages here and there, there and here, but he comes up empty at the end. "My head doesn't work anymore," he says. His head, he explains to me, is full of idiotic elements, and because he's too busy eating and drinking instead of studying, he can't find the verse.

Good. Let's, then, try something easier to deal with: Why can't men look at women?

"Because men don't have 'brakes,' they have no stop signs."

But women have stop signs?

"Yes. Women, unlike men, possess wisdom, as is written."

Are women better than men, then?

"Certainly."

When you say that men are not allowed to look at women, does it mean long looks or any looks?

"Any looks."

Where does it say that a man is not allowed to look at a woman?

It's written somewhere, he says, but he doesn't know where. "This is a tradition, and one shouldn't ask questions; one shouldn't ask why."

Why shouldn't one ask why?

"Because it says that one shouldn't ask."

Where does it say so?

Well, this Reb Yoilish doesn't know. The gefilte fish and the lokshen kugel consumed via the mouth in his head distract quite a bit.

The Bible says, I tell him, that Moses looked at women. I might not be able to prove it, since I don't know where the Bible says such a thing, but who cares?

Such an idea, or an argument, is too much for his head now, and we leave it as is.

Is it true, I change the topic, that "Zionists are not Jews"?

I don't want to talk about Zionism with him, but I'm trying to figure out if the kugels and the gefilte fish will distract him on this issue as well.

That graffiti, says Reb Yoilish, was "written by *baalei tshuvah*."

And the Palestinian flags, what are they about?

"They are against the *baalei tshuvah*."

Why that?

"The *baalei tshuvah* have a lot of money, and they force us out of our apartments because they can pay top prices, but when they see the Palestinian flags, they don't like being here, and they walk away" from the neighborhood.

Who are these *baalei tshuvah*? Well, Zionists who became Ḥaredi, and nobody needs them here, because "they are not Jews." Yeah, he suddenly, without warning, changes his mind and says that the Zionists are indeed not Jewish, and the *baalei tshuvah* don't understand it. The Zionists are the source of the Satanic forces, pure goyim. They are part of the "Erev Rav," the non-Jewish Egyptians who joined the Israelites out of Egypt in biblical times and sneaked into Mount Sinai, like thieves in the night, where the early Jews, the Israelites, were given the Torah from God Himself on the Mount, as recounted in the Bible. But they are not Jews, and after their deaths, they are not to be buried in a Jewish cemetery. They are, in short, Egyptians. Or Kurdish, he says. And then he tops this statement: everyone who serves in the Israeli army is not a Jew.

The gefilte fish and the kugels don't blur his vision once the topic of "Zionists" is brought up.

Interesting.

Reb Yoilish lives well with contradictions. When he gets up from the table at the end of our talk, his cellphone rings, and he goes to chat with the caller at a safe distance from me. But I can still hear him, hear him talking, and he's talking in Hebrew. The man knows Hebrew, I see, contrary to what he told me. I guess he didn't want me to know that he speaks in a "Zionist" language.

Welcoming the Nazis with Bread and Salt

"I would rather be with the Nazis than with the Zionists."

Zionists and Ḥaredim have been clashing for decades, though as far as I can tell, both are getting a bit tired of it.

The conflict between the Ḥaredi Jews and the Zionist Jews dates back to the beginning of modern Zionism, starting with Dr. Theodore Herzl, the Zionist visionary who turned Zionism from a concept in the head to a plan on a page. Zionism, as a concept of Jews living in the biblical Land of Israel, is as old as the Bible, the original Zionistic text known to man. But *Der Judenstaat*, Dr. Herzl's 1896 book, helped Jews realize that a Jewish state could be a reality in their day and time and that the Diaspora was not necessarily the perpetual fate of the Jew. Ḥaredi Jews, people who are willing to risk their lives for the Bible, should have been the first converts to such an idea, a biblical idea, but they were not. In fact, they were – and some still are – the biggest opposers of Zionism.

Why?

When Zionism, modern Zionism, started in earnest, Ḥaredi leaders feared that Ḥaredi life would be over if a Jewish state were created and governed by Jews. Why did they think so? Well, many of the early modern Zionists were not religious, and the Ḥaredim were afraid that Yiddish would stop being the mother tongue of Jews, and their cherished Ḥasidic courts and Lithuanian (Litvak) yeshivas would perish. In essence, and this might be hard for some to digest, Ḥaredi leaders were afraid that if Jews were to free themselves from their anti-Semitic enemies in various European countries, the rank and file of European Jewry would turn their backs on Jewish religion, and the Ḥaredi world would cease to exist. This did not happen. Ḥaredi Jews never had it so good as they now have it in Israel, where their numbers reach well above one million.

During World War II, my maternal grandfather was given the opportunity, by members of the Jewish Agency, to save himself and the community he led from the approaching Romanian Fascists, aided and guided by the Nazis, who were about to catch up with the Jews of his town. The Jewish Agency people offered to smuggle him and others of his community out of Romania and into the soon-to-be-formed State of Israel. He refused. "I would rather be with the Nazis," he said to them, "than with the Zionists." When the Fascists and the Nazis finally arrived at the gates of his town, he welcomed them with bread and salt, the way kings were once welcomed when entering a city. In response, they emptied their bullets on his head, took those of his children who were in town to the nearby Răut River, threw them into the water, making sure they drowned to death, then shot his wife, the mother of the drowned children. His daughter, my mother, never forgave the Zionists for the Nazis' crimes. Makes sense? No. Man's reality is rarely logic's best friend.

On the other side of my family, the story was different. The Radzyner Rebbe in the Holocaust years, the last of the Radzyner Rebbes, called upon his Ḥasidim to pick up arms, join the partisans, and fight the Nazis by all means possible. The Nazis caught up with him and murdered him, and the Dynasty of Radzyn is no more.

But now, enough about Nazis. It's time you get yourself a mate, if you haven't gotten one yet.

Oh, God, Give Me a Mate

Or a pinky, a little sweet pinky

The day of the Public Prayer at the Western Wall for Matches has arrived, and I go to see how this prayer takes shape.

The Western Wall, al-Buraq Wall, is packed with worshippers. Not all of them have come for the purpose of matching, but if my memory doesn't fail me, there was a note in the big advertisement: the prayer for matching, it said, will take place next to the partition between the men's section and the women's section. Yes, in this holy place, men pray on their own and women on their own, so the sexes don't mix, God forbid, and fall in love near the remains of His Home.

I look at the worshippers.

The women and the men next to the partition can't see each other, but they feel, perhaps, each other's presence while praying. It would be much simpler and easier to match the two by taking the partition down so that the two sides could see each other and perhaps even fall in love. But nothing is simple in Jerusalem, and logical arguments are doomed to fail.

I talk to the praying people near me, trying to find out why they came here instead of, let's say, going to a matchmaker.

Some of them tell me that, in their case, the usual matchmakers didn't come up with anything viable, and they need the Ultimate Matchmaker: The Name. Others tell me that they are here not for themselves but for members of their families. A yeshiva boy, seventeen and a half years old, tells me that he came here to pray for his two brothers, twenty-two and twenty-five years of age, who are single. His friend came to pray for his sister, twenty-one and a half years old; he's afraid she'll die a spinster.

What kind of prayer are they reciting? "I say the Psalms, chapter by chapter," one young man answers me.

Don't you ask The Name specifically for a match?

"No need. The Name knows what I want."

If He knows what they want, the question arises, why are they here to start with? Does He know what they wish for at the deepest corners of their hearts only when they are here?

Well, who am I to argue with lonely souls looking for company?

I eavesdrop on this guy's prayer. *Do not hide your face from me when I am in distress*, he prays, reciting Psalms.

Once the prayers are over, the match worshippers take a public bus. Men sit in the front half of the bus, while the women sit in the back half of the bus. Why? Because this way, the men won't look at the women, the famous tempters of mankind, while the bus drives on the holy streets of Jerusalem. Though from time to time, I notice when I look at them, they steal a tiny glance, no longer than a second and a half, at the ladies in the back. Oh, how much they want them! Oh, how much they desire them! The sexual tension on this bus, let me tell you, could power the heaviest spaceship to the moon in no time.

And this tension, between the intense desires and the total suppression, creates a constant obsession about all matters sexual.

When I was a sweet boy, I remember, I stealthily touched the pinky of a Georgian girl on the street not far from my yeshiva for, maybe, one second. I went nuts for days, if not for weeks. Oh, how much I wanted that pinky!

When night falls, I have a dream, a beautiful dream about a little pinky. The sweet little pinky, just one, flies above the Western Wall, then to a café on Jaffa Street in Jerusalem, and from there to the top of the highest mountains of Austria, until it finally lands in a café, where else, in Prenzlauer Berg.

Oh, Lord, am I losing my mind in this Holy City?

The Quickest Way to Get Healthy: *Na, Naḥ, Naḥma, Naḥman*

If this fails, try: Pa, Pat, Patri, Patricia

I'm going to Jaffa Street, on the opposite side from Ḥaredi Judaism, to take a little break from the holy. Jaffa Street, where Jerusalem's light rail passes, connecting East and West Jerusalem, also serves as an invisible border between the Ḥaredim and the secular. Jaffa Street is just a few minutes' walk from Mea Shearim, but it's another world, a world that is anything but Ḥaredi.

Sitting at a café, I order an omelet with all kinds of salads, cheeses, spreads, bread – what you call Israeli breakfast.

It's almost like being in Prenzlauer Berg, only there are no Germans around.

Oh, Lord of Lords, I can't believe what my eyes see! On the sidewalk only feet away from me, a group of Breslev Ḥasidim, five men in total, shows up, and they sing. I thought to take a break from the holy and the sacred, but holiness follows me wherever I go, Heaven save me.

The holy men of Breslev sing. Loud. They have their car parked next to them, with "*Na, naḥ, naḥma, Naḥman me'Uman*" signs all over it, and they dance in honor of their holy rabbi, Rabbi Naḥman, who is buried in Uman, Ukraine. Rabbi Naḥman passed away in 1810, but this means nada to them. They think Rabbi Naḥman can hear them from all the way up in Heaven or from his grave thousands of miles away in Ukraine, and they dance for him to cheer him up. They have a bottle of some drink with them – I'm not sure what exactly it is – and they all drink from the same bottle. Next month, if only The Name wills, they will fly to Ukraine to prostrate themselves over their Rebbe's grave. It is good to be with the holy dead, because the holy never really die, and their souls are hovering over their own graves.

Who is more bizarre, I ask myself: they with their grave or I with my pinky?

I don't know.

One day, so the story goes, a man went to visit his friend, a Breslev Ḥasid. The Breslever was lying in bed, sick to his bones, maybe pneumonia and maybe something else, and couldn't do anything, except for reading his favorite book, a book written two hundred years or so ago by the Breslever Rebbe, Rabbi Naḥman. But now the sick Ḥasid didn't do even that. His body was so weak that he fell asleep at midday. The visitor, a man with a funny bone and pretty bored, took a little piece of paper and wrote on it something that he thought was funny: "He who says, '*Na, naḥ, naḥma, Naḥman me'Uman*' three times will be cured of all diseases." He put the paper inside the Breslever's book and left.

Hours later, the Breslever woke up from his sleep, opened his favorite book and, what a miracle, a piece of handwritten paper dropped on his bed. He picked it up, read it, and he had no doubt that Rabbi Naḥman himself, or an angel from Heaven sent by him, had put that piece of paper in the book for him. He looked up to Heaven and said "*Na, naḥ, naḥma, Naḥman me'Uman*" three times, again, and again, and again. After a week or so, when he finally recovered, he had no doubt that he recovered because of the healing powers of the words "*Na, naḥ, naḥma, Naḥman me'Uman.*" He told the story to his friends, Breslever Ḥasidim, and they ran out to the streets and spray-painted "*Na, naḥ, naḥma, Naḥman me'Uman*" all over Israel, until thousands of thousands of religious Jews started believing in it. When his friend told him, after seeing the graffiti all over, that he was the one writing the *Na, naḥ* and that it was meant as a joke, it was too late to go back.

I should have done the same: "Pa, Pat, Patri, Patricia." Imagine, all over Israel you would see this sign: Pa, Pat, Patri, Patricia. Wouldn't that be fun? Imagine tens of thousands of Israelis spending their days and nights shouting, "Pa, Pat, Patri, Patricia."

And imagine, just imagine, that the visitor had given the sick Breslever the book about John and Patricia, instead of writing that little "*Na*" thing. Nobody in Israel would go "*Na, naḥ, naḥma, Naḥman me'Uman.*" Can you imagine that?

Wow.

I return to my hotel.

The Prince of Torah Will Find You a Girl

God accepts prayers today until 13:30 only

I sit in one of the hotel's terraces and notice on a chair next to me, probably left there by one of the guests, a Ḥaredi newspaper by the name of *Yated Ne'eman*, one of several Ḥaredi papers.

It reminds me what my rebbe in *ḥeider* used to say: "Everything written in the newspaper is a lie, except for the date; everything the radio says is a lie, except for the hour."

But let me see what's new today, at least according to this newspaper. Today, Friday, is the eve of Tu b'Av, the fifteenth of the month of Av, which is regarded as one of the best and most blessed days on the Jewish calendar. And today, so I read in *Yated Ne'eman*, "Their Redemption Has Come!" Who is being redeemed? Well, Tu b'Av, it turns out, is the day on which the Gates of Heaven open for prayer for those who have not found their *zivug*, their mate. And so today, a special prayer will take place in Bnei Brak at the home of Rabbi Ḥaim Kanievsky, who was born ninety-four years ago or so and is known in the Ḥaredi world, so I read, as the Rabbi of All the Children of Israel in the Diaspora, and also as the Prince of Torah. If you are looking for a *zivug*, I read on, send in your name until 13:30 p.m. today, and the Diaspora Prince will mention your name to The Name, and you will find your mate in no time. No need, by the way, to drive to Amuka, because Rabbi

Ḥaim will pray, and The Name will obey. As it says: the righteous decree, and The Name makes it happen.

When I was a kid, Ḥaim Kanievsky was called Ḥaim'ke, or the Weird Ḥaim'ke, as I called him, because he was quite strange, with a weird smile on his face. At the time, I thought that he was an idiot too. But these days, he is the holiest man in town, the smartest, and a prince no less.

Is he?

I'm not so sure. The Prince of Torah, and his followers, seem to have totally forgotten the Talmud, the very essence of what they call Torah.

Here's what the Talmud (tractate *Ta'anit*) says about Tu b'Av, and how the day was celebrated at the time when the Holy Temple was standing proud in Jerusalem and God Himself ruled over the Holy Land, not Ḥaim'ke and not any other.

> There were no joyous days for the Jews as Tu b'Av, the fifteenth of Av, and Yom Kippur, the Day of Atonement.

> On these two days, the daughters of Jerusalem, the single girls, dressed themselves in white garments and went to the vineyards to dance for the boys. The beautiful girls of them showed off their beauty while dancing, saying to the boys: "Look at our beauty! Why else would you want a woman?" The well-pedigreed girls danced and said: "Think of your children. Why else would you want a woman, if not for the children?" The ugly ones, having nothing to sell, danced as well and said: "Marry us for Heaven's sake, and once we are married, buy us nice clothes."

"He who didn't have a woman went there," the Talmud adds.

What a difference between then and now! When The Name was in control, Jewish boys and girls had lots of fun, with wild parties in the vineyards celebrating sexuality, and, oh boy, did the boys look at the girls.

In our day and time, when a Ḥaredi Jew can't find a girl, he visits a grave, weeps at the site of a destroyed temple, or connects with a man over ninety.

How did we get here? I don't know.

Yes, of course: the Talmud is a collection of endless opinions, by as many Sages, where one can also find the opinion, for example, that a man should not listen to a woman singing. Why would anyone rely on this opinion and not on the others, which was the norm before ultra-Orthodoxy took shape, is anyone's guess.

Be that as it may, as evening comes and the Sabbath is about to enter, I go for a *Spaziergang* on Mea Shearim streets. Yet again.

Fashion Parade on Mea Shearim

Where are the nicest-looking Jews in the world? In Mea Shearim, of course

Some people like to go to the zoo, where they get immense pleasure out of watching camels, baboons, giraffes, lions, birds, and snakes. That's nice, I admit, but I prefer people. I'm a people watcher.

If you like watching people, my dear, come here and wash your eyes in the beauty of humankind.

Take a look. What a sight!

Let's start, as already alluded to before on these pages, with the ladies.

They are out, dressed in their finest, and they look like princesses – Jerusalem princesses, that is, not British princesses. Remember Princess Diana, the dream of so many men? Forget her. Jerusalem princesses are something else, out of this world. You can't compare them at all to the ladies of Prenzlauer Berg, for example. Oh, no. There, those goy ladies show their legs, or parts of their legs, their breasts, or parts of their breasts, depending on what they assume will ignite the imagination of men, other women, women who used to be men, men who used to be women, and humans who used to be cats. Here, you better forget it. No breasts here. I mean, of course they are there somewhere, but you can't see them. You can imagine them, but you can't see them. Nope.

No legs, and thighs is a word no one mentions. No way. And as for genital organs, forget them. I mean, yes, you can imagine them, but they have no names, just like God. The words *penis* or *vagina* don't even exist in classical Hebrew, and you won't find them anywhere in the Bible. (In Yiddish, you say *Shmuck*, "jewelry" in German, for penis.) That's why Biblical Hebrew is called a pure language, a holy language. Imagine, my dear, but don't utter. Imagine. Just imagine. No objectifying here, it's only imagination. Mea Shearim, my dear, is the perfect place for Ḥaredim and Progressives. Yeah. What you see here are the dresses, gorgeous dresses, and no dress looks like the other, and no *tiḥel* looks like the other. But you can look at the arms, below the elbow, something that Progressives might object to. And you can look at the faces. What faces! Like angels from high above.

Oh, if only I were as holy, wise, and smart as King Solomon, a holy man surrounded by 999 ladies. Though I must admit that I am probably more fortunate than him. How many of his ladies, you tell me, spoke Yiddish, the sexiest of languages? How many of them were dressed like these Mea Shearim ladies?

These ladies, let me share with you, are much sexier than Mother Teresa, of blessed memory.

Mary, the Virgin Mother, the desired image of billions of Christians throughout the centuries, looked exactly like the Ḥasidic women of Mea Shearim. No wonder, you may say, since she was a Jewess just like the Feigales and Zisales walking these streets right now.

The Virgin Mother, I bet, spoke fluent Yiddish.

And in case you have never been here before, let me give you some details: the clothes the Ḥaredi women of Mea Shearim wear are made of classic, high-quality material (at least it looks like it) and are of clever design and cut, all of which accentuate the female body in delicate yet clear lines. Some of the clothes are similar in design to classic evening dresses, some are more in the haute couture direction; but most, yes, very similar to classic European paintings of Mary. Not to forget the makeup that women here use: ever delicate, never too showy, and well applied. For the most part, they present an attractive figure, and very few are overweight (this is true also for the men).

That said, the Sabbath is not just for *Spaziergang* but also a time for prayer. In the prayer, the Ḥaredi Jew asks God to return to Zion, build the Temple anew, and resurrect the dead. "And You are trusted to raise the dead. Blessed be You, He Who Resurrects the dead."

But of course, once the prayers are done, in yeshivas or shuls, the people return to the streets of the neighborhood, parading once more their beautiful selves for all to see. *A gitten Shabbes*, Have a good Sabbath, I say to them as I pass by them, and one after another answers *A gitten Shabbes* in return; some even sing it, and they give me a little smile for no additional charge.

The men, with their golden caftans and gorgeous *shtreimels*, are so handsome that they look much nicer than any British royalty, even nicer than Charles.

Yeah.

What would a transgender Ḥaredi choose to wear, I wonder, a gorgeous dress or a gorgeous *shtreimel*? Perhaps both.

Passing by me right now is a bunch of the Golden, the sexiest men of history.

Come here, O you, gays and queers of the world, come here to the holy city of Jerusalem, and wash your eyes with the rosiest fragrances of male sexuality. These Ḥasidic men will tempt you; they will challenge you, and though you'll never be allowed to touch them, look you will. Yes, you can look at them for as long as you want. Just like that Litvak rabbi, whose quality time at home is looking at his wife cutting chicken in the kitchen.

The only problem, sorry, is that the Golden Boys are not known to dirty their soft hands with dead chicken.

Oh, well.

Ḥasidic men, of any age, grow beards. Litvaks usually shave their beards until they are married, but when they start viewing themselves as more important than others, they grow those beards as well. Most of the men in Mea Shearim have beards, some long, some short, in this shape and that. I'm not a beard man, but I've seen some ladies in my life who would kill for a bearded man. Go figure. All Ḥasidic men, in case you are into men and want to know more details, shave their heads, save for their sexy sidelocks.

Back in my hotel room, a thought comes to me: If everything were permitted, and boys could go with the girls, would the girls of Mea Shearim be so beautiful? Would the boys of Mea Shearim be so handsome? Would I stay here, in this neighborhood, for more than one day? Would Mea Shearim even exist?

The Sabbath is not over yet, and I can't wait for Sabbath morning.

As the Ladies Are Gone, Crowds of Angels Arrive

Visions of Sabbath: a beard of a Rebbe and birds around a child's neck

It's Sabbath morning.

It's hot, as hot as can be, and the ladies of the night are not to be seen. Only some men are on the street here and there, and not that many of them, but I enjoy looking at these men, warmest of hats on their heads and golden caftans on their bodies, as they walk by me.

Right ahead of me is a Ḥasidic guy, a handsome young man with golden hair and golden caftan, standing next to a cute boy with a sweet face and golden sidelocks. They are at the entrance of the shul of Shoimrei Emunim, the original, I think, of the Toldos Aharon dynasty, of the Reb Ahrelaḥ.

Is morning prayer over? I ask the two beauties. No, no, they say. Yes, they started three hours before, at nine thirty, but they have a couple of hours left until the end of the service. Morning prayer on Sabbath takes about an hour and a half at most places, but not here. Here it takes five.

That's my place!

This place, someone once told me, is the place of the most extreme of the extreme, a usual reference to almost any community in Mea Shearim, where Ḥasidic Yiddish is spoken, a language that loves exaggerations.

Yes, there are many Yiddish dialects, but the Ḥasidic one is the most prone to exaggerations, and the most humorous.

It's more than just mere humor, mind you.

Yesterday, someone told me that when I speak in Ḥasidic Yiddish, "it's not you and me talking, but your grandfather and my grandfather talking; that's how we feel it." If I speak Ḥasidic Yiddish with the people here, he said, "we immediately connect with you, even though you are not a Ḥaredi. When you speak Ḥasidic Yiddish with us, you are one of us."

Yes, I speak Yiddish here, the Ḥasidic kind. I never, either in my childhood or during my studies in Mea Shearim (I studied in a Litvishe yeshiva), spoke more than two sentences in Yiddish, but now I speak it like a native. How did that happen? I don't know how the linguistic mind works, but I guess that since I understood some Ḥasidic Yiddish before, from my early days in the USA when I stayed for a few months in Williamsburg, Brooklyn, and since I understand German as well, the two tongues miraculously combined in my head on the day I arrived in Mea Shearim.

In any case, as I step into the shrine of the Most Extreme, I look at the worshippers. They have sidelocks longer than I ever imagined existed. Some of these sidelocks go down to the hips. How do they manage to keep them perfectly round, at such a length? Perhaps, you never know, the Angels of Sabbath are taking care of their sidelocks and constantly keeping them round and sexy.

It could be, of course, that they use Ḥasidigel. In any case, and as is always the case in Jewish prayer, prayer direction is of utmost importance. Prayer direction here, as anywhere in Jerusalem, is the Temple Mount, where the Jewish Temple once stood. Worshippers in Israel outside Jerusalem pray in the direction of Jerusalem, and Jews outside of Israel pray in the direction of Israel. All of them, in essence, are praying in the direction of the Temple Mount, the Western Wall.

Looking at the worshippers, it seems that the order of their seating is organized according to marital status. One side of the shul appears to be for married men, since they have the tallit (they say *tallis*) over their clothes; and on the other side, there are worshippers without the tallits, and I assume that these are the unmarried folks.

I sit in between the two.

The women are sitting upstairs or wherever, and I can't see any of them. It's essential not to see women while praying, because otherwise, you will be thinking of them instead of The Name.

The Rebbe, an older man with a tallit that covers most of his head, except for his beard, is mumbling verses from the Bible, it seems to me. One of the Ḥasidim opens the Holy Ark, revealing various Torah scrolls that contain the Five Books of Moses. A scroll or *sefer Torah* is taken out and carried in the direction of the bimah, an elevated platform on which the *sefer Torah*, written on parchment, will soon be laid and read from.

As the Torah scroll is carried around, people congregate next to it, bring their lips over it, and drop a hot kiss. They do this one by one, and then, when the Torah scroll is laid on the bimah, it is rolled open, and a member of the congregation picks it up and presents it to the congregants, who each point with the right pinky in its direction and say, "This is the Torah that Moses placed before the Children of Israel..."

The Torah scroll is then laid down on the bimah again, and the Rebbe, named Rabbi Shloime Rote, as I'm told, starts reading aloud.

The Five Books of Moses, also known as the Pentateuch, are divided into more or less equal parts so that every Sabbath morning, another portion, or *parshah*, is read from it in shul throughout the year. This Sabbath's weekly portion is Vo'esḥanan ("And I besought the Lord"), a portion of the Bible that is emotional at the same time that it contains some of the essential elements of Judaism. Here we read about Moses telling the Israelites he guided out of slavery in Egypt that he would love to join them on their journey to the Land of Israel as free people. But God, he tells them, refuses to allow him to enter the Land, a punishment for hitting a rock instead of speaking to it. As is told in the Bible early on, God had told Moses to speak to a rock, and water would come out of it, but Moses hit the rock instead, an act that angered The Name tremendously.

Moses tells the people that The Name had told him to stand over a hill, look north and south, east and west, and see with his own eyes the beautiful Land of Israel that he would never enter. You will die outside of the great Land of Israel, The Name tells him.

Moses reminds the people of their slavery in Egypt, of the miracle of their freedom, and of their journey, their long journey into Israel, and he tells them to obey The Name's commands. If they do not, he warns them, The Name will throw them out of the Holy Land and disperse them all over the world.

Moses also reminds the people of the Ten Commandments given to them at Mount Sinai: Observe the Sabbath, Honor your parents, Don't steal, Don't murder, Don't desire your friend's wife, among others.

And here it is that Moses utters the most famous of Jewish lines: "Hear, O Israel, the Lord our God is One." This is the verse that, reportedly, many religious Jews uttered just before their last breath in Nazi gas chambers.

As the Rebbe recites the Ten Commandments, worshippers stand up and gather around him. He reads the verses excruciatingly slowly, very, very, slowly, and his followers listen to every syllable as if they have never heard these commandments before.

Eventually, after a long while, the Torah reading is over, and the Torah scroll is escorted back to the Holy Ark.

The Sabbath prayer service continues.

In the part of prayer called Kedushah, the congregation, all up on their feet, sing and pray as loudly as humanly possible, as if God above were 100 percent deaf.

> Crowds of angels above,
> With Your nation, Israel, below,
> Will crown You, Lord our God,
> Thrice sanctify You together,
> As told by Your prophets:
> And they call one unto the other, saying: Holy, Holy, Holy...

Holy, Holy, Holy, the Ḥasidim shout, as if these were the finest words a human ear has ever heard.

This is a very different prayer service than the one I was used to while a sweet boy. When we prayed, we, like most other Ḥaredim, didn't dwell much on content. There was a text on the page, in the *siddur*, the book of prayers, and we said the words. Did we think about the meaning of the words? Rarely if ever. Not here. The people here think of every word and perhaps every letter.

God must love it slow. These worshippers, after all, have entered the Holy Land.

With the service done, the Ḥasidim form a line to say *A gitten Shabbes* to the Rebbe, and I join them. The Rebbe watches me as I pass by him and motions something to his followers, pointing one finger at me and three fingers at his lips. What does this mean? I don't know. But a Ḥasid immediately approaches me, asking if I would like to join the congregation for a Kiddush.

I say yes!

What a Kiddush!

I get to eat their version of the Jerusalem kugel, the most delicious of its kind ever to reach my tongue. It is dark, dark brown, sweet, and spicy, hot, and incredibly delicious, and it comes with an ice-cold Pepsi-Cola.

Hopefully, one day I'll get to meet this Rebbe in private and thank him for thinking of me. I have no clue how to get a private audience with a Rebbe, but maybe I'll find out one day. At the moment, I'm thankful for this Kiddush, a word that implies holiness.

Yes, this is a holy kugel. Really.

I love Kiddushes. A public Kiddush, food and drinks offered at the end of a Sabbath prayer service, is something only Ḥasidim do. Litvaks, who don't cherish the joys of life as much as Ḥasidim, don't have it. They pray and go home; what a pity.

Following the Kiddush, I open a book I see on a table, a book written by the founder, Rabbi Aharon Rote, and in it I read that when it comes to faith, no questions are to be asked. You just believe. Period.

Yoilish, I think, goes by it, especially after he fills his stomach with gefilte fish and kugels.

Sabbath.

On the Sabbath, as we all know, the Shḥinah, the Holy Presence, descends to the face of the earth to join with the people of Israel, the Jews, and unite with them. And if you ever come to Mea

Shearim on a Sabbath, you can feel it. There's something special in the air, something otherworldly. Call it Holy Presence, call it Sabbath, call it Christmas, call it Jerusalem Kugels, call it Beauty Pageants. Call it whatever you want; it's in the air, and in your belly.

And while walking back to my hotel, as the sun is slowly setting and darkness gradually descends on the earth, I see a family sitting around a table in their living room, singing goodbye to the Sabbath. The youngest member of the family, a kid of ten or so, sings so beautifully that I imagine birds sitting next to his throat, accompanying him, and I stop to watch.

His father, who notices me watching his son, comes out to chat with me. I tell him, in Yiddish of course, what an amazing son he has. *Seit ihr a igger?* are you a local? he asks me, wondering how come he has never seen me before.

He is connecting, I guess, with my grandfather.

What's next, you may ask, now that the Sabbath is over?

Stay tuned.

The Real Name of God Is Revealed to Me in a Dream

A man unites with the Logic of God, and a woman "forgets" to go to the mikveh

With the Sabbath now over, tradition calls for a little meal known as Melaveh Malkah, Accompanying the Queen, referring to the Holy Presence, as was taught to me by my rabbis when I was that sweet boy.

And now, I sit down with a few Ḥaredi people, mostly men and one married couple, to accompany the Queen together on one of the terraces of my hotel.

All present at the table are Litvaks, not Ḥasidic, which means they are supposedly moved by logic, not emotions, by analyzing, not singing.

How is it to be a Ḥaredi woman? I ask the woman.

"Great!"

Why so?

"The most important thing for me," she answers, "is that my husband will not look at other women." He is a faithful man, she shares with me, and "he looks only at me."

Wow!

What does it mean to be Ḥaredi? I ask the people.

"A life devoted to getting closer to The Name," one says, and all agree.

How does one achieve such a goal?

"By studying the Torah."

How does that go?

"The logic of the Torah is the logic of The Name, and when you study the Torah, you connect with The Name through His logic. This is the closest you can get to The Name."

Is it also important to God that you study the Torah?

"Yes!"

Why?

"Because this is what The Name wants, and that's why He created the world."

Why does He want this?

Well, I better ask Him, one of the men tells me, and all agree. They have faith, they say, and faith doesn't share a space with logic. Period.

The married couple, a nice-looking pair, knew that they belonged with each other very early in their relationship, they say. When? The second time they met. Their second date, they tell me, took six hours. No, they both say, they did not touch each other before they got married, much less have sex or even exchange a kiss. They just talked to each other.

Did you, I ask the man, look at your future wife when talking to her?

"Yes, at her face."

Only at her face?

"Mostly. But from time to time, I did steal a few glances below the face as well."

And?

"I liked what I saw."

His wife is delighted to hear him say that.

The husband studies in a *koilel*, a yeshiva for married men, and the wife works in real estate to support the family. She is very happy, she shares with me, to be the provider of the family, because this will enable her husband to devote his life to the study of the Torah.

"I have a weakness," she adds, elaborating on what she said before, "I'm a jealous person, and I want my husband never to look at other women." There are no women in the *koilel*, thanks be to the Creator, and life's good.

There are some beautiful ladies walking outside on the street right now. Should I warn the husband by saying, "Careful, beauties ahead!"? I probably better not.

Yet, since the lady is so much into her man, I feel it's time I touch on an intimate issue or two. I heard a rumor, I tell them, that Ḥaredi couples have sex while they are fully clothed. Is that true?

Oh, no. According to some rabbis, the husband informs me, a woman can ask for a divorce if her man refuses to be naked during sex. But there is a trick here: the sex must take place in the dark and under the blanket. Yes, the bodies join, skin to skin, but you don't see the naked body of the other. Not knowing how the naked body of your spouse looks, I am informed, has many advantages, because in your mind, your partner is the sexiest, handsomest creature ever created by The Name.

There are times, they tell me, when husband and wife cannot unite. For example, during the woman's period. During that time, I'm told, the woman is "impure" and cannot even touch her man.

Shortly after her period is over, the woman must go to a mikveh to become pure again, and then she can rush to her bed (yes, they sleep in separate beds), and her husband will run after her, and together they will have tons of fun in the dark, under the blanket.

Oy to the man, let it be known to all, who does not treat his wife well, for she might "forget" to go to the mikveh, and he will not be permitted to have any fun under any blanket anytime, day or night. In such a case, of a wife who forgets to become pure again, it is forbidden for the husband even to touch her pinky. Yeah, not even the tip of her pinky!

And he who thinks that he could masturbate for a while is in for the biggest shock of his life: masturbation is one of the most significant offenses against The Name.

Yes.

The male genital organ is known in the Ḥaredi world not as a penis, or even a genital organ, but as the *bris*, meaning covenant. It's in that place of the body that every Jewish baby boy eight days of age is circumcised, a process known as *milah*, and this is regarded as a covenant that The Name has with every Jew. The covenant was first introduced in the Bible, in Genesis:

> This is my covenant, which you shall keep, between Me and you and your seed after you: every male among you shall be circumcised.
>
> And you shall be circumcised in the flesh of your foreskin; and it shall be a token of a covenant between Me and you.

The circumcision is, therefore, a stamp, a mark of God on the man's genital organ. If a man masturbates, our rabbis taught us – and I remember it well – he is betraying the covenant with The Name, no less, and is worse than the average goy.

As for our dear husband: if he improves his ways and, let's say, buys his wife something nice like a new pair of shoes, or a fresh apple strudel with vanilla sauce just for her, the dear wife will suddenly recall that she had forgotten to go to the mikveh and will run to a mikveh faster than al-Buraq, jump on her bed, cover herself with the blanket, and the starving husband will appear from under the sheets, screaming for joy.

Yeah, yeah, yeah.

By the way, in my youth, just like many others in my community, I never understood why baby girls don't get their *bris* circumcised. It did not occur to me, back then, that women don't have a *bris*. What else could they have if not a *bris*?

In any case, and coming back to reality, Queen Sabbath departs, and at the end of our wonderful conversation, the Ḥaredim around me bid me goodbye, and I'm left alone.

I fall asleep.

In my dream, I see myself in a mirror, a sweet boy walking the streets of Mea Shearim, searching for The Name. Where is He? Is He hiding in an apartment somewhere? Which apartment? I walk, walk, and walk until my eyes fall on a Ḥasidic woman's pinky. I look at the pinky and follow it, street after street. Such a sweet pinky! Just a pinky and yet so powerful! Is this pinky God? Maybe. Who else, truth be told, could that pinky belong to? I stop walking, the pinky slowly disappears, and I know: I have seen The Name, and He is the best entity there ever was, and He has a name, a real name: Pinky.

I wake up from this, my second pinky dream, and make myself a cup of Turkish coffee, a bitter and sweet coffee. If I were a full-fledged resident of Mea Shearim, I would now spray-paint the word Pinky all over the neighborhood: Pi, Pin, Pink, Pinky.

I dress up and go out.

Would You Desecrate the Sabbath to Save a Dying Zionist?

Women: You can sleep with them, but you can't look at them

I walk the streets of my pinky dream and find myself twenty minutes later in Shoimrei Haḥoimois, a Jerusalemite Ḥaredi community in Mea Shearim. Two teenagers, sixteen years of age, walk by. Each of them sports two sidelocks but no beard yet. They are dressed to perfection with not a spot on any of their clothes, and they behave like the most respected of adults. Normal sixteen-year-olds outside this area are one big pain in the neck, shouting and yelling. Not these.

Are they deaf-mutes? Maybe, who knows, they are two angels from the crowds of angels at the Shoimrei Emunim. Could be, no? Well, not really. They can hear, and they can speak, and they have flesh. Yes, they do; they shake my hand.

Surprisingly, one of the two invites me to a special celebration that will take place later in the week. It's the *siyum*, completion, of Tractates *Sukkah* and *Makkes* (*Makkot*), and he will deliver a speech at two o'clock in the afternoon. He would love for me to attend. Could I make it, he asks?

I'll try, I say. With my busy schedule, a full-time street walker, I never know. Maybe, who knows, I will meet a *rebbetsen* at that very moment, two o'clock sharp, and she will show me her pinky.

I will never, ever say no to a Ḥasidic pinky. It's as if somebody offered you a gefilte fish; would you say no? Of course not.

I keep on walking, letting my feet lead me wherever they like in Mea Shearim, as my eyes wander over the many institutions on my path. At almost every corner and every couple of buildings, an institution stands proud. Be it a yeshiva, a school for boys, a school for girls, a *koilel* for married men, a shul – anything goes. The elders of the people living here, it strikes me, invest enormous resources, time, and money, on raising the next generation.

And it shows.

Let me meet one of the elders, I say to myself.

Of the Mea Shearim public personalities, one of the most interviewed by foreign media, other than Reb Yoilish, is Rabbi Hirsh, or Reb Israel Meir Hirsh, the son of the late Rabbi Moishe Hirsh, who was known as the "foreign minister" of Neturei Karte, the group of people whose profession is anti-Zionism. Yeah, yeah, some Jews work in high tech, others in anti-Zionism.

Reb Israel Meir lives one floor above Reb Yoilish, but what a difference! His place is spotlessly clean, featuring a brownish bookcase and cabinet, a long table with comfortable chairs, white tablecloth on the table, shiny glasses, and different kinds of unopened soft drinks for the guest.

On his business card, which features the Palestinian flag, his title appears as "Leader of Neturei Karte, Palestine." Palestine, not Israel. We, he and I, are in Palestine, not Israel. That's his shtick. He doesn't believe in the State of Israel, and for him, the Zionists are an expression of evil, which makes him a darling for those foreign journalists looking to smear Israel.

I, for I one, prefer not to get involved with his thoughts about others, be they Zionists or Yazidis. I ask him, instead, to tell me what it means to be Ḥaredi, but he immediately gravitates to his chief enemies, the Zionists. The word *Ḥaredi*, he says to me, was invented by the Zionists. Where he got this idea from, I don't know and, frankly, don't care. I'm not interested in who he is against, only in what he is for. Yet he goes on. The Zionist obsession is too hard to get out of. Zionists are not Jews, he informs me. "Anyone who does not believe in the Thirteen Principles of Faith, as Maimonides dictated them, is not a Jew."

Hearing him talk, I give in, but just a bit. According to Jewish law, a man is allowed to desecrate the Sabbath – for example, to drive a car (otherwise forbidden to Ḥaredim on the Sabbath) – to save a life. Would he, Reb Israel Meir, drive a vehicle on the Sabbath to save the life of a Zionist, let's say a victim of an accident?

No, he says. "He may be sick, he may face death, we are still not permitted to save his life. That's the Law."

Would you, Reb Israel Meir, let that Jew die?

Well, this he doesn't know. It's hypothetical, not real, he says, well aware of the explosive nature of his assertion. "I just gave you the Law. According to the Law, we are not allowed to save him."

Well, since he relies so much on Maimonides, I say to him: according to Maimonides (as cited by Nachmanides), a man can have sexual relations with a woman who is not his wife, if the woman is neither married nor menstruating. Is that okay with you?

"This is the Law, and so yes."

Does this mean that you agree with the rule that men can have sex with women outside of marriage?

"It's against the Torah."

What? Haven't we just agreed that it's permitted?

Well, yes and no. Yes, there's a Law, and by the Law of the Torah a man can sleep with as many women as he wishes, but no, because according to the Torah, a man is not allowed to look at women.

How could these two rules coexist? That's a stupid question, mind you, because everything is possible in Mea Shearim, especially if you say it in Yiddish, the language he and I communicate with.

But to be fair, these two rules can coexist very well in any language. Don't married couples, after all, "serve" in dark rooms?

Bottom line: if you are a male, make sure you don't shine a light on the lady while you are having sex with her. If you do, my dear, you might desire her, and then you will have sex with her, The Name save us. Yes, I know that this makes no sense to you, but that's because – guess what? – you don't understand Yiddish.

Why can't a man look at a woman? I ask Reb Israel Meir.

"It's written."

Where?

Oops, this he is not sure; he'll check it out and get back to me, hopefully before the Messiah arrives. He also tells me that Jewish law dictates that a married woman must cover her head. Where is this written? Well, he'll check this out as well and let me know, hopefully before we meet again after the resurrection.

That all said, the foundation of the Jewish home, he teaches me, is modesty. In simpler words: that a woman must cover her flesh and that a man must not look at her is the basis of Judaism. I wonder aloud why, then, didn't Maimonides include modesty as one of the Thirteen Principles of Faith? The Thirteen Principles of Faith, for example, include the belief in the coming of the Messiah and the resurrection of the dead. Why not modesty?

Regretfully, this is a question he cannot answer.

A man, by the way, is also not allowed to chat with a woman who is not his wife, he tells me. It's written.

Where?

Somewhere.

To Reb Israel Meir – I see a pattern – everything is somewhere high up beyond the clouds, in the ether, except for the Zionists, who are always here.

But he knows a great deal about *shtreimels*, thank God. The *shtreimel*, he teaches me, became a Jewish hat after the rulers of

Russia ordered the Jews to wear the tail of an animal on their heads two hundred years ago, a date different from the one Reb Yoilish told me. But who cares? One hundred years here, one hundred years there; it's all the same.

I wonder what would have happened if the rulers of Russia two hundred years ago had ordered Jewish females to walk around in red bikinis. Would Ḥasidic women, following the same logic of men wearing *shtreimels*, parade with red bikinis on Friday nights on the streets of Mea Shearim?

I don't ask him this question because I'm afraid this would be one more question that he can't answer, and I didn't come here to embarrass the man.

For his part, he keeps talking. The golden caftan of Sabbath, he informs me, is an Arab coat, and it comes from Syria.

Good to know. But I have another question for him. There is a famous Jewish saying, "It's hard to be a Jew." What's the hardest mitzvah for you to observe? I ask the Syrian Arab.

Reb Israel Meir thinks about it and comes up empty. "There's nothing hard," he finally says. The simple fact is, he tells me, that it's pretty easy to be a Jew. Observing the Sabbath, one of the essential basics of Jewish law, is not hard. What's so hard in eating cholent, gefilte fish, and kugels?

Dead Rebbes, sadly, don't eat cholent and kugels, not even gefilte fish, and many Ḥaredim go to visit their graves and pray there. What do you think of that?

"Praying by the dead is idol worshipping," he answers.

I'm taken by surprise here; I didn't expect this answer.

Why is it, then, that the rabbis don't stop it? I ask the Palestinian Syrian Arab.

"Because the whole Ḥaredi world is one big idol worshipping. All those rabbis, what are they? Pure idol worshippers. All the rabbis, all those Rebbes, let me tell you again, are idol worshippers."

Including those in Mea Shearim?

Yes, and Toldos Aharon as well.

The interview soon ends, and I leave the Palestinian, the most dedicated Palestinian there is, in his Palestine, and move back to Israel, to Mea Shearim.

I might disagree with this Hirsh, but I can't avoid one little fact: this man is a likable person.

I have been prewarned about the people of Mea Shearim, but so far, I like them. Is something the matter with me?

Would You Risk Your Life to Save a Dying Ḥasid?

"For five years, my rebbe raped me four times a week."

I start doubting myself. From my first day in journalism, I don't remember ever being so positive about the people I cover, thinking they are all beautiful and handsome. Yes, I have to report what I see, whatever that is, and if it's positive, let it be positive; but could it be that I've simply become blind to all that's negative and am seeing only the positive?

I ask people I know to introduce me to thinkers who are strong opposers of the Ḥaredi world. Such a person, my hope is, will be able to point me in the right direction.

There is a professor, I'm told, living in the city of Givatayim, who is a top thinker, and he knows about the Ḥaredi world from A to Z.

I board the train to Tel Aviv, from which I'll take a taxi to the professor's home in Givatayim.

Just minutes after I board the train, a religious Jew comes to sit next to me. He has a skullcap on his head, and he loves schmoozing. His name, he tells me, is Yossi. Yossi is a bit overweight, dresses schlumpy, and he seems to be a man who doesn't have many pleasures in life.

He tells me he is thirty-two years old, was married for three months, and divorced. Once, he says, he was Ḥaredi, but today he is no more. He's still wearing a skullcap, true, but he does it for the sake of his parents. He tells me that his father was a *rosh yeshivah* (head of a yeshiva), but now the father is retired. From the age of eight, when Yossi was still studying in *ḥeider*, and for five years, Yossi's rebbe raped him four times a week, he tells me. This rebbe was a resident of Mea Shearim, a Satmar Hassid, but today he lives in Bnei Brak. "He has all kinds of organizations, connections with everyone, including the police."

Why did you divorce?

"Because I could not have a relationship with my wife."

Did you love her? Did she love you?

"Yes."

Why couldn't you have a relationship with your ex-wife?

"Whenever we got intimate, I started thinking of the rebbe."

And that's it.

Today, he tells me, he has no sexual attraction to any woman in the world.

When you see a beautiful woman or porn movies, are you attracted?

"No."

Let's say that a naked woman and a dog pass by you. Would you feel the same for both, sexually speaking?

"Yes."

Perhaps you are attracted to men?

"No."

Have you ever seen your wife naked?

"I saw her silhouette, but not her skin. Not the flesh. When we tried to have intimate contact, there was no light in the room. That's the law."

If I was looking for something negative about the Ḥaredi world, well, I just found it, and from a person I didn't plan to meet. The question is, is Yossi's story indicative of a wider trend, or just an isolated case?

The issue of pedophilia in the Ḥaredi world pops up in the secular media often, giving the impression that there's much more pedophilia in the closed communities of the Ḥaredi world than anywhere else in the land. "There is not one child here," the internationally acclaimed newspaper *Haaretz* quotes an unnamed source from Mea Shearim, in an article extremely critical of Ḥaredi society, "who was not [sexually] abused." As if this was not enough, the article further states that what's happening in Mea Shearim is "a silent plague of murdering young souls." Is this true? Generally speaking, it's hard for me to believe that there are more pedophiles and rapists in any one community of people than in the others. If I'm wrong, and if the trend of abuse has been going on for ages in the Ḥaredi world, as many seculars believe, I ask myself: How come I never experienced it when I was at the tender age of childhood and early adulthood? Was I so ugly that nobody had any interest in me? I don't think so.

In New York, a city where I spent most of my life, if any journalist wrote an article in which he or she accused a whole society, be it Blacks, Hispanics, or Asians, of being a bunch of pedophiles, that journalist would immediately be fired. In this land, on the other hand, stories about sexual abuse and outright rape in the Ḥaredi world are a favorite topic in the secular media, and nobody is planning to fire anybody.

Are there rapists in the Ḥaredi world? I'm sure there are, just as in any other community of people. How many? This I don't know.

Hopefully, the professor I'm about to see will enlighten me.

The professor's home in Givatayim is a short taxi ride from the Tel Aviv train station, and I am physically, psychologically, and mentally ready to meet him. His name is Dan Shiftan, a nice name.

It's not easy to find the abode of this man, as his apartment is part of a complex created by, I think, a Talmudic scholar, but he comes out of his apartment, and I now spot him: a man with a pink shirt and dark blue jeans, and no *shtreimel* in sight. He leads me to his abode, and once there, he points me to a room with tons of drawers, a couple of office chairs, a desk, and a bookcase, all very clean and in meticulous order.

I'm impressed.

I go to the toilet before starting the interview and steal a glance at the rest of the place. What do I see? In the adjacent room, perhaps it's the kitchen, my eyes see an enormous number of plastic bags, some with stuff in them, others not, and it looks as if somebody had built a public garbage container inside the apartment. I've never seen anything like this in any house I've ever visited.

Dr. Sigmund Freud, maybe, could explain this dichotomy between the two rooms; I can't.

I can't tell what's in the plastic bags, if they are stuffed with garbage or, perhaps, the man is hoarding all kinds of stuff in case all stores are shut down and he can't buy anything for the next ten years. I don't know. It looks like trash, yeah, even if the bags are stuffed with goodies.

This trash display reminds me of the garbage depository rooms along the sidewalks near my hotel. They are pretty, made of Jerusalem stone, but the garbage dumpsters that are supposed to be inside them are nowhere to be seen. The Jerusalem Municipality, I was told, took the dumpsters away and replaced them with huge, ugly containers (known as "frogs") that it placed on the streets, taking up parking places. Reason? In the past, so I was told, young men used to set the dumpsters on fire and then pushed them into main intersections during violent demonstrations in order to block traffic. The municipality had enough of that and figured that frogs wouldn't be pushed due to their weight.

Is this story true? I don't know. Being that this is a Ḥaredi neighborhood, not everybody agrees on anything, and many tell me that the municipality garbage containers story has no basis in reality. Whatever. What were the demonstrations about? That's hard to know. When asked, one person told me: "The Ḥaredim are not allowed to go to gyms or do any kind of sport; they are not allowed to watch TV, go to a theater or cinema, and they are supposed to study Torah all day long. But there are those who can't study because they don't have the brains for it, so they demonstrate. What else do you expect them to do?"

If those good-for-nothings need trash or some other kind of material in plastic bags, there's enough of it in this house to light up a fire, in any violent demonstration.

I wonder if my professor knows if the container story is indeed true.

But perhaps I better not raise the issue of garbage with him; it might be too sensitive of an issue.

When I return from the toilet, we sit down to chat.

"In my view," the bags professor tells me, "the Ḥaredim are the number one threat to the Jewish people."

And who is he?

"I'm a Zionist, a fundamentalist Zionist," he says.

Why are the Ḥaredim such a threat to the rest of the Jews?

"We have one group of Jews at the moment who are growing in numbers in a way that is dramatic, and frightening and damaging, and this is the ultra-Orthodox community."

He clarifies that his comments about the Ḥaredim refer only to those who don't serve in the Israeli army and don't contribute financially to society. In other words, the majority of Ḥaredi men, if I'm to trust what I've heard a thousand times from non-Ḥaredim: Ḥaredim don't work.

"The way of life of the ultra-Orthodox in Israel is a danger to the future of the Jewish people," he goes on to say, "because they have 7.2 children per family, 7.2 primitive children per family." They are "parasites," he says, quite passionately and angrily. "They live on the sweat of my brow and my blood," he rages on, adding: "A person who doesn't work doesn't deserve to live."

Strong words.

Given that the Ḥaredi worldview is that men should dedicate their lives to the Torah, don't they have a democratic right to practice their faith? I ask my new intellectual acquaintance.

No, he says. No man in a democracy has a right to rape, and democracy can impose its wishes on its citizens and demand that they dedicate part of their time to work for a living. He raises his voice, exploding in anger, and he repeats his assertion over and over that the Ḥaredim are "parasites."

If a non-Jew said this, I pause to think, he would be classified as an anti-Semite. How else would you classify someone who says to you that a particular group of people have too many children, all parasites?

You served in the Israeli army, I ask him, willing to risk your life in defense of your fellow Jews; would you be as willing to risk your life in defending ultra-Orthodox Jews, in defending Mea Shearim, for example?

He tries as hard as possible not to answer this question, arguing that this is not a fair question. Still, in the end, after I repeat my question numerous times, he says that, yes, he would risk his life defending Mea Shearim, not because of the people living there, but because Mea Shearim is part of Israel.

"The people of Mea Shearim are not even proper Jews, based on Maimonides, because they don't work for a living."

Can he show me where Maimonides writes what he claims he does? Like Reb Yoilish and Reb Israel Meir, he cannot.

I look at him and I see, at least partially, a mirror image of Reb Yoilish and Reb Israel Meir; each side of the equation is claiming that his community, and only his, is Jewish, and no other. And as far as each is concerned, let the other drop dead, preferably today or better yet yesterday. Both these sides quote sources, but none can give me an exact reference where I could verify their sources, and each is as passionate as passionate can be about why the other side is so bad, neglecting to tell me why their side is so great.

From the data that I remember reading a while ago, 80 percent of Ḥaredi women participate in the workforce, and the difference between the work habits of the religious and the secular is not that big to start with. But there's no point arguing this, for his heart is full of hate.

His cellphone rings, and he takes the call. After hanging up, he tells me that the caller is a very important person, in a very high position, and that very important people are often reaching out to him for advice.

Good.

I leave the garbage bags professor, light up a cigarette on the street outside, and think: From where did the professor suck his intense hatred of the Ḥaredim? What have they done to him that hurt him so much to make him so angry? I expected strong arguments, factual data and accurate statistics, intense philosophical discussions, and great theological arguments, but I ended up with raging hate.

According to *Haaretz*, I see on my iPhone as I smoke my cigarette, the Ḥaredim are the happiest people in Israel.

I look at the smoke rings coming out of my mouth and think about The Name. Does The Name really have no name?

I don't know what you're thinking when you're having a cigarette, if you do, but this is what I'm thinking of: Does The Name, Lord of the Parasites, really have no name?

Well, He has a name, kind of. It's referred to as The Explicit Name, but nobody knows what it is. There are stories of some people who know The Explicit Name, and when they utter it, they can resurrect the dead, fly above countries faster than eagles, and destroy or save whole cities. When I was a kid – don't tell anybody what I'm telling you now – I really wanted to know the name of The Name. I checked many Kabbalah books in search of the name of The Name. No, I didn't want to destroy cities or resurrect the dead – that kind of stuff I leave for The Name to do on His own. I wanted to create a living creature for myself, a lovely girl, of course, since those who know The Explicit Name can also create other people. Yes. That's how, as everybody knows, the Maharal of Prague, a world-renowned rabbi, created the Golem, an all-powerful creature who saved the Czech Jews from their goy enemies who wanted to kill and rape them hundreds of years ago.

I probably won't find any answer to any question about The Name in Givatayim. The Name is in Jerusalem, right by His destroyed Temple, and I board the train to Jerusalem.

Did King David Sleep with a Married Woman? No, He Just Put on the Tallit over His Body

Good Jews don't ask questions – period

Back in Jerusalem, I learn a bit. What do I learn? "He who says chapter 27 of Psalms every day during the month of Elul [the month following the month of Av], in the morning and in the evening, is guaranteed a wonderful year ahead."

Who teaches me this lesson? A Sephardi Jew out of a job who spends his time collecting blessings and healings and miracles in his spare time, which is practically all the time.

As for me, I want to attend the *siyum* celebration of Tractates *Sukkah* and *Makkes* and listen to the speech of the teenager I met earlier in Shoimrei Haḥoimois. But this event could be off limits to a man like me, a man with no beard and no sidelocks, unless I find a Ḥaredi Jew who will facilitate my entrance.

To solve this little problem, I go to Reb Yeḥezkel David Lefkovits, who has been involved in rebuilding the Shoimrei Haḥoimois community for the past few decades; he can get me anywhere in this little part of the world. I don't really know Reb Yeḥezkel, but I know a guy in New York named Mordy, a fine man, and he knows a guy by the name of Itsik, a lovely man, and Itsik introduces me to Reb Yeḥezkel.

Wonderful, isn't it?

As I arrive in Reb Yeḥezkel's corner on Earth, the first thing I see are the kids of the neighborhood, who look very clean and very sweet, but seem to be tough creatures, if my impression of them is correct. The moment they spot me in their neck of the woods, they immediately approach me and examine me, just to make sure that I'm not an enemy, maybe a German Nazi or a Russian tsar. But then Reb Yeḥezkel comes to greet me, and the kids promptly assume that I am no danger to them and go on to play with each other.

Reb Yeḥezkel gives me a little tour of the area.

Forty years ago, he tells me, Shoimrei Haḥoimois was a "*ḥurveh*," a slum, but now it is a fascinating place, with hundreds of families. We are walking together on the streets of Shoimrei Haḥoimois, and I see older people whose years make it hard for them to walk, and next to them are little kids running and jumping all over. For a second there, it feels like watching a movie: here life starts, there it ends.

The houses we pass by are tiny, but most seem to be well maintained. All are stone houses, made of what is known as Jerusalem stone, resembling the walls around Jerusalem's Old City.

In front of us, I see a couple of men standing next to cartons of fruits and vegetables. What is that? These fruits and vegetables, Reb Yeḥezkel tells me, are given for free or sold at cost to the needy members of the community. Here one also can get a little card, the size of a credit card, to be redeemed before the Sabbath in a bakery for a couple of *ḥallah*s, free of charge.

These people take care of one another. It's touching.

After the tour, we go to sit for a chat at Reb Yeḥezkel's office on Spitzer Street. His office is simple: a couple of rooms, a calculator, a refrigerator, a table, some chairs, and an air conditioner. Would you like tea, coffee? he asks, as he offers sweet cookies to his guest.

Reb Yeḥezkel's cellphone rings, and he takes the call. It's a cellphone he's talking on, not a smartphone. Here, my dear, smartphones are forbidden.

Do Ḥaredim really, really have no smartphones?

They say that they don't have them. But they say it in Yiddish, and a no sometimes means yes in Yiddish. Yiddish is all about nuance, fine nuances, and if you don't understand nuances, don't speak this language.

Soon Reb Yeḥezkel hangs up, and he offers me more sweets.

He was born in Hungary, he tells me, where his father lost his wife and three children during the Holocaust. Reb Yeḥezkel's father married again, and he and his new wife, Reb Yeḥezkel's mother, were successful in business. But life under the new bosses, the Russians, was hard, and they immigrated to Israel. Young Yeḥezkel worked in the family's curtain business, but one day he had an accident, and he couldn't stand as a result. Looking for a job where he wouldn't have to stand, he found a finance-related job in the Shoimrei Haḥoimois foundation, which oversees Shoimrei Haḥoimois. To raise money and spend it, you need a tongue, not legs. All in all, Reb Yeḥezkel worked full-time for a couple of decades, and to a degree, he is still involved in the financial side of the community's management.

Reb Yeḥezkel is a man of discipline and patience, and he knows that to build anything requires time, discipline, and patience. It took time to turn Shoimrei Haḥoimois from the slum that it was to the nice place it is now. The Book of Esther, he says to me, tells a story that spanned twelve years. When reading the book, people tend to think that the events described in it lasted for just a few days or a few weeks, at the most, but no. Twelve years. Everything takes time.

Interesting that he mentions a biblical book, I say to myself. Ḥaredi Jews hardly read the Bible, except for a few books: the Five Books of Moses and a select list of other biblical books, one of which is Esther. The juicy books, the books that wash the dirty Jewish laundry in public – and there are several of them – are being skipped, and as a result, many of the biblical stories are not known to Ḥaredi people. The biblical story of King David, whose descendant is the Messiah, and how he tempted a married woman, slept with her, and then sent her husband to die in a battle, is off limits to the Ḥaredim. But if, on a rare occasion, it is mentioned, it comes wrapped with all kinds of excuses. Classic excuses can be hugely inventive. For example: yes, King David slept with a married woman, but what does "slept" mean? "Slept," in its mystical meaning, refers to the act of putting on the tallit.

Makes no sense to you? Of course not. But try this in Yiddish, and it will make *perfect* sense!

Why all this inventiveness, you may ask? Simple: it's too much for Ḥaredi people to digest the fact that a sexual story is written in the Holy of Holies, the Bible, because for them even the mere mention of the word *sexual* is forbidden. In addition, to read that the author of Psalms (religious Jews believe that King David is

Psalms' author), the most admired of kings, not only looked at a woman but slept with her as well is too much to swallow. Not to mention the story of Pilegesh ba'Givah (the Levite's Concubine), a biblical story about the Children of Israel from the tribe of Benjamin who went berserk one day and raped a woman, one after the other, until she dropped dead. How could the Jews of biblical times, regarded as the best of Jewry by the Ḥaredim, do such a thing? Well, the response is: Don't read it. Cover it up. Put on the tallit.

Reb Yeḥezkel, not aware of the thoughts running in my head, shares with me how a Jew like him starts the day.

"First, I wash my hands. I don't put my feet down on the floor before washing my hands. I have a *shissel* [bowl] of water and a cup under my bed. Always. Then I say the Moideh Ani: 'I thank You, living and eternal King, for mercifully returning my soul within me; Your faithfulness is abundant!' Next, I go to the toilet; and after that, I go to the mikveh. Having done these things, I pray the morning prayer, then I study the Talmud. After that I have breakfast, and once finished, I go to work. I start my day at about four thirty in the morning, and at ten o'clock I start to work."

What is a Jew? What does it mean to be a Jew? I ask the money man.

"You are born a Jew, and you are a Jew. A Jew has distinct rules, and he must observe them. The Torah has 613 different commandments that we must observe, and I thank The Name for being a Jew. A Jew has to go to shul, he has to go to a mikveh, his wife has to go to a mikveh, and she has to wear a *tiḥel*."

Wow, that's the million-dollar answer!

What about a Jewish person who doesn't observe the commandments – is he still a Jew?

"It depends. There are Jews who don't observe because they don't know any better; they are like little kids kidnapped by an enemy. But if a person knows and he doesn't observe, let's say, the Sabbath, or if he doesn't put on the tefillin [which religious Jews put on their head and arm every morning, except on the Sabbath and Jewish holidays], then he is the one who cut himself off from the Jewish people. As it says (in Exodus): 'Wherefore the children of Israel shall keep the Sabbath, to observe the Sabbath throughout their generations, for a perpetual covenant.' If a person doesn't observe this covenant, he cuts himself off, and in that case, I don't have to save him on Sabbath."

This means, of course, that one shall not desecrate the Sabbath to save the life of such a person.

Do you think, I ask him, that most secular Jews should be regarded as kidnapped kids, or are they the kind of Jews who know and still don't observe?

Most people in Israel, he answers, are the kid kind, and Ḥaredim must desecrate the Sabbath to save their lives.

Benjamin Netanyahu, a secular Jew, served as prime minister of Israel for many, many years. Should he be saved on the Sabbath if the only way to save him was by desecrating the Sabbath?

"I think not. It will not be allowed to desecrate the Sabbath to save him."

Before we finish our chat, Reb Yeḥezkel says to me: "I don't ask questions. I don't know. You asked me: What is a Jew? I'll tell you: We are Jews not because we understand, we are Jews because we were born Jews, and we have to be Jews."

Reb Yeḥezkel is ready to take me to the *siyum* celebration, he tells me, only not at this very moment. He has some affairs to attend to, but we will go there together if I come back in a couple of hours between four and five in the afternoon.

Yeah, this is Mea Shearim, not Germany. Two hours here or there won't make much difference in anyone's life, will it?

I take a walk in the neighborhood and notice a significant change from yesterday: the old obituaries are gone, replaced by new ones. More and more people die daily, and their names are posted for all to see, so that people can pay condolences at the homes of grieving families.

I drink a small bottle of Diet Coke, then another one, and by four thirty, Reb Yeḥezkel takes me to the Shoimrei Haḥoimois yeshiva for the *siyum* celebration.

We are late, but the celebration is still going on. Boys, thirteen to sixteen years of age, fill the hall where the celebration takes place, all dressed in the finest and cleanest of their Ḥasidic outfits. Parents and relatives sit in the back, and rabbis sit at a long table in the front of the hall, speaking into a microphone. To my right side, I see a bunch of musicians and a singer, whose job it is, I assume, to make us all as happy and merry as we can be. In the front, on the left side, I see many framed certificates, one for each student, listing their specific achievements. This boy is rewarded for knowing the tractate of *Sukkah* by heart, that one for knowing *Makkes* by heart, and here is one who gets the Golden Certificate for knowing *Sukkah* or *Makkes*, or both of them, in depth.

All the people – students, rabbis, and relatives – sit around tables, where various foods and drinks are served. Cold beverages with or without caffeine, cold orange juice, and lots of sweet cookies, sweet cakes, potato kugels, lokshen kugels, and anything in between that has sugar in it. The rabbis deliver speeches, the students deliver speeches as well, and I think to myself: they look so much like I did at their age.

Looking at them, I'm looking at me, am I not?

With one difference: they have no clue that there's a Patricia somewhere on this planet. There is no Patricia in their hearts. They have a sukkah in their heads.

Sukkah is a tractate in the Talmud dealing with the sukkah and the holiday of Sukkot. According to the Bible, on the holiday of Sukkot, Jews are expected to sit in a sukkah, to remind themselves of their miraculous voyage out of Egypt and the temporary shelters they lived in before reaching the Land of Israel. In any other culture, this would be quite an easy act to follow: put a chair and a table on your balcony or in some park, have a bite to eat, share a cup of coffee or a glass of wine with someone, and you're good to go. Done. Not so in Judaism, especially Rabbinical Judaism, the Judaism recognized as the "real" Judaism since after the Destruction of the Temple or somewhere near it. Yes, a sukkah is a temporary place, say the Sages, but what does "temporary" mean? Does it have a size? Does it have a width? Does it have a length? Does it have walls, and if so, how many? Does it have a ceiling, and if so, what's the ceiling made of? Can you build a sukkah inside your home? Do you have to eat there, and if so, how often? Do you have to sleep there, or is it enough to just look at it?

And these are just the first questions.

When I listen to these boys, young men who spend their time studying which sukkah is kosher and which is not, not to mention all the blessings that they are supposed to recite every time they put anything in their mouths, in addition to other blessings, totaling at least one hundred blessings a day, not to mention all other kinds of prayers, I suspect that most of them won't have much time for questions such as how the dead look will when resurrected and what's the actual name of The Name.

The music guys start playing.

The tables are pushed to the sides, and slowly but surely, the certificates are being given to the students, one by one. The rabbi in charge reads the name of each student, who then approaches the front table to get his certificate. When he does so, the rest of the students start dancing wildly in his honor.

This repeats itself each and every time one of the students gets rewarded with a certificate. At times, one of them picks a "certified" student high up, carrying him on the shoulders, and the rest of the students dance around the couple with more energy than you would find in a semitrailer full of Coca-Cola bottles.

The friendship between the students and the happiness they exhibit when any of them gets awarded is heartwarming, and it makes you want to hug each of them. The human love outpouring from this group of youngsters is contagious, hugely refreshing.

Be it in Germany or America, I'm often surrounded by people who declare to me and to everyone else in earshot their love for fellow humans and their devotion to the whole of humanity, climate, nature, and all other good causes. None of them – not even all of them combined – has exercised the love bursting out of each student here. Look how these students dance with each other, how they tap each other's shoulders in appreciation for their achievements, and how they hold each other's hands as if they were Siamese twins, connected by one soul.

Looking at them, I start doubting both Krois and Hirsh. Krois and Hirsh know a great deal about journalists, ever busy with their hatred for Zionism, but neither of them exhibited before me the warmth seen here, the love shining here, and the happiness sounded here. I doubt if they even know that such a feeling exists.

I spend an hour, two, three, The Name knows how many, with these students, not realizing the time's passing. When the student

I met a few days ago spots me in the crowd, he runs over to ask me why I didn't come earlier, when I could have heard him delivering his speech. I tell him that I wished I could, but Reb Yeḥezkel was not available at the time. He understands and is thankful that I wanted to come. Oh, God, how sweet these students are!

The question is, What happens to these sweet students when they grow up and get married?

Reb Yeḥezkel, who walks around talking with people while I'm sitting in the same spot throughout, comes over to me and asks me for my impression. I tell him that I'm very impressed and ask him to introduce me to some people in the area.

He agrees. He introduces me to Reb Dovid (David), a follower of the Toldos Avrom Yitzḥok court. Reb Dovid, I'm told, is a convert, a German convert to Judaism. He might embody, the thought comes to me, kind of a marriage between Prenzlauer Berg and Mea Shearim. How does such a combo work? I'm not sure, but hopefully I'll find out come Friday night. Yes, I'm going to spend Friday night with the Convert. Are you jealous?

You Never Met a Woman in Your Life, and Then One Night, There Is a Woman in Your Bed. What Do You Do?

"When we united, the Holy Presence came to be with us."

Friday night is two days away and, in the meantime, I'd like to meet a married man who grew up here, a man who used to be a sweet student like the ones I just met. There is this kosher restaurant a couple of kilometers from my hotel, and I heard that they offer *heimishe essen* (if you don't know what these words mean, I will pray for you next time I go to shul), and I think I should try it out and, hopefully, there I will find my young man.

I go to the restaurant, and I invite a young Ḥasidic man, who is married, to join me. We talk, and he tells me that he will gladly share with me a chapter from his life if I don't mention his name, and preferably not the name of the restaurant we are sitting in, a restaurant he often frequents. No problem with me. Order whatever you want, I tell him; it's all on me. I place the order, for him and for me, and we schmooze.

Young men of the community who are about to get married, he tells me, have a story to tell like no other. What is it? Well, on their wedding day, or maximum a day before, a guide comes, takes the bridegroom aside, and explains to him everything he will have to do with his bride on their first night together. She is a woman, a girl, a wife, a person he hardly knows, never touched, but suddenly he will have to unite with her in the most intimate way.

In this community, he explains to me, where unmarried men and unmarried women don't meet, the first time a couple meets, on a date arranged by the parents or a matchmaker, is the first time either of them has met the other sex. Most often, if they like each other, they will get to meet – never in private – two or three more times. If all goes well, they get engaged and marry. And then, hardly knowing each other, they find each other in the same bed.

Can you recall that day? I ask the Ḥasid.

Yes, he can.

It was tough, the toughest day of his life so far. For someone who grew up in Mea Shearim, he shares with me, the act of being with a woman alone in a room is tough. You don't know what to do, he says.

So, the guide came to you a day before your wedding, right? I got that. What did he say to you?

"He asked me if I've seen blue movies before. I said: 'Blue movies? What are they?'"

How did he react?

"He told me what to do with my new wife and how to do it."

What did he say, can you give me the details?

"This is very hard for me to talk about."

Why?

"He explained the 'details.'"

What are they?

"I can't repeat that."

Were you and your wife naked on the bed on your wedding night? I mean, is it allowed for a man and a woman to be naked when intimate?

"If you are in a closed room, I think it's allowed."

Do married couples see each other in the nude?

Well, he explains to me, the sexual act should take place in the dark. But they can still see each other's bodies. How can they, I ask, since they are in the dark? He looks me in the eye and says: "By 'darkness,' I didn't mean the darkness of Egypt" (referring to the Plague of Darkness, one of Ten Plagues that The Name inflicted on the Egyptians, according to the Bible, to force them to free the Jews).

Let me ask you something: Can a married man look at his wife in the nude in daylight?

"Oh, that's not modest."

Have you ever seen your wife in the nude in the daytime?

This, he tells me, is a secret he will never reveal.

Let's go back to the day before your wedding night. You were given instructions on what to do, step by step. How did you feel when you listened to those instructions?

"I was shocked. I was afraid. I was lost."

How about your wedding night – do you view it as a dark night, a bad night?

"No, I won't say that. It was a holy night because the Holy Presence came to be with us in that room when we united. It was a special night. I don't know how to describe it. A pure night. At the time, it was confusing, you know; it's something I'd never done before."

Lucky me, later on I get to meet a Ḥasidic woman in my hotel, and she explains to me what this guy wouldn't. The details.

"Before I got married, I met the marriage guide and she explained to me everything."

What did she say?

"When she talked about the *bris*, I didn't know what she was talking about, so she drew it for me. 'This is how a *bris* looks like,' she said, 'and your husband will put it inside you. Then he will make a certain sound, jump out of your bed, and it will be over. That's it. Easy.'"

Now I can imagine what the guide of my restaurant guest drew for him before the Big Night. And he is an example of what the young students I met at the *siyum* might experience once they get older.

Yeah. But Reb Dovid the Convert will have a different story to tell, I'm sure.

Beware Women's Fingers When They Pick Up Chicken

She is Ḥaredi. Her father is a convert. Who will marry her?

Reb Dovid lives in Shoimrei Haḥoimois, where most people are of Hungarian origin, and I go to his home on Friday night. Two of his children, Eliezer and Scheindel, are also at home. Eliezer, still a little kid, has a rocket toy he's playing with. Scheindel is into fashion, wearing flashy jewelry, and she dreams of being a dancer one day, a bird whispers in my ear. Could a Mea Shearim girl be a dancer? Of course not, but she can still dream.

Before sitting for the Sabbath meal, Reb Dovid takes me to shul, his shul, the shul of Toldos Avrom Yitzḥok, to participate in the Friday evening prayer. There are not many people in shul this evening, he tells me as we walk in. As far as I can tell, the place is packed, and as far as I can see, every seat is taken, but this is not how he sees it. The Rebbe, he says, is vacationing in Europe at the moment, and when he's not here, many of the Ḥasidim go to other shuls to pray. If Reb Dovid is right, I have no idea where the other Ḥasidim could fit when the Rebbe is present. Of course, The Name is a known miracle maker, and if He could create the whole world in six days, as is written in the Bible, there should be no doubt that He can fit six million people in this very building.

Squeezing onto a wooden bench, I sit down and look around me. There's a little poster on a pole next to me, and I read its content: If people do not talk during prayer, many miracles will happen. And it gives an example: "There was a couple who tried to have children for many years and finally had, all because you did not talk during prayer."

A good lesson to remember: if you don't talk while praying, somebody out there will become a papa.

At a table to my right is the candy man, a man who comes to shul on the Sabbath with bags of candies for the kids who are attending services. I watch how this works in practice. Here goes: the candy man sits at the table, with the bags next to him, and prays. So far, pretty simple, right? Well, this is not the end. Some kids come over and ask for a candy or two, others take without asking, some check what's available and others don't, some choose the flavor they prefer and others not; and for those who don't come, the candy man gets up at some point and distributes the rest of the candies amongst them.

It's interesting to watch the kids and how they go about their candies. You can tell who's a born leader and who's not, who will make a good living and who will end up a beggar.

At the table to my left sits a man who might be a member of the Modesty Guard, an organization rumored to operate in Mea Shearim. Members of this organization, so the rumors go, are men whose life mission is to make sure that modesty rules are observed. Usually, rumors have it, these men are people who can't study because their IQ or EQ is limited, but they have muscles, want to be counted as righteous, or whatever, and spend their time telling others that they must improve or else. Why do I think that he's a member of the Modesty Guard? Well, he gets up every few minutes, goes out and comes back, and he seems to have difficulty concentrating.

The congregation sings "Leḥa Dodi": "Go, my Beloved, to the Bride, let us welcome the Sabbath..."

They sing, sing, and sing, everyone as excited as if they had never prayed this prayer before in their lives.

Having done this, they recite from the *Zohar*.

> Just as they unite above in One, so too does She unite down in the Secret of One to be above with them One to One. The Holy One Blessed Be He will not sit on His Seat of Honor above until She joins in the Secret of One. Like Him, to become One in One. And here we have explained the Secret of "the Lord is One and His name is One." The Secret of the Sabbath: the Sabbath unites in the Secret of One, so that the Secret of One may dwell on her.

Does this make any sense? Not to me, and most likely not to 99.9 percent of the worshippers.

This classic kabbalistic text requires a very imaginative and creative brain to interpret. If you have that talent, the interpretation of such a text will depend on what kind of person you are and why exactly you are willing to spend your time interpreting such a text. If you are into porno, for instance, you can adapt this text into a steamy hot sexual encounter between God and His Partner. Suppose you are into Ḥasidic tales, on the other hand, you will interpret this text as an avowedly sacred text whose every word will spread sacred holiness across the universe at the very exact moment that the Sabbath enters and the Secret of the Unity of One fills the globe. As for me, years back, I might have interpreted it as the story of John and Patricia, but that couple is so old by now that such an interpretation doesn't ring reasonable anymore.

In any case, the prayer goes on.

The "Modesty Guard," who left some twenty minutes ago, suddenly returns with hundreds of copies of Sabbath bulletins to be distributed among the worshippers.

What are Sabbath bulletins? Sabbath bulletins are various weeklies, usually two to four pages long, distributed in synagogues on the Sabbath and containing commentaries for the weekly Torah reading and stories of a religious nature.

I pick up a few.

As part of what seems like a series titled "The Holy One Blessed Be He said, 'No one who listens to Me loses'" in one of the bulletins, I read about a person named Reb Berish Cornblit. Reb Berish had a butcher shop in the holy city of Jerusalem where the righteous in the Jewish community used to shop. As part of doing this kind of business, the story goes, he had to sell his goods to women as well, not just men, a fact that could lead, The Name forbid, to being tempted by the women. To make sure he was never tempted, he was very careful not to look at the women he served. Not even once, the story goes, did he see the face of his female clients. How did he achieve this admired goal? Well, simple: when serving female clients, he did it from a dedicated table in his shop, where he had a board with a hole at its bottom. He would hand over the meat through that hole, and they, the women, would leave the money on the table instead of giving it to him. This way, clearly, there was never the possibility that he would see, God forbid, the face of any woman or her fingers, The Lord save us.

One day, oy vey, a chicken that he sold to a woman whose face, fingers, belly, or toes he did not see was later revealed to be non-kosher. This means that if he did not go to the woman to tell her not to eat the chicken, she and her family would eat it and fill their bellies with, Heaven protect us, all kinds of horrible spirits that reside in non-kosher foods.

Normally, in cases like this, he would run to the buyer to warn him that the chicken should not be eaten. But since this particular chicken was sold to a woman, a creature he didn't see, he could not run to her to warn her that the food she bought from him was not to be consumed.

Brokenhearted and saddened beyond sadness, Reb Berish immediately closed his shop and ran to the shul to pray to The Name, beseeching Him to solve this dangerous situation. After a long prayer, weeping and crying, Reb Berish returned to his shop, hoping that The Name would take the right action.

And indeed, just moments after he reopened the shop, what a miracle, a woman entered the shop asking for a chicken. She had bought a chicken earlier, she told Reb Berish, but on her way home, a cat jumped on her, stole the chicken, and ran away.

Yeah, that was that chicken, the non-kosher chicken! Reb Berish opened his mouth in thankful prayer to the Creator and gave the woman another chicken for free!

That's what happens, you now can see, to men who don't look at women: miracles!

Many miracles, mind you, happen to the righteous. The other day, I read another story in the bulletin: a man got on a bus, where all seats were taken, and he stood next to the door in the middle of the bus. At the next bus stop, a woman got on the bus and stood right next to him. The woman, a Jewess who was not modestly dressed, The Name save us, spoke loudly and laughed heartily, acts that are known to arouse men. Being a righteous Jew, he got off the bus at the next stop. Once he was out on the street, the bus suddenly got into an accident, and one of the passengers was injured and had to be transferred to a hospital. Who was that passenger? The immodestly dressed Jewess who talked loudly, laughed heartily, and tempted the righteous.

That's what happens to Jewish women who arouse righteous Jewish men: accidents!

These are vital lessons to remember, for they will guide a Jew in the right direction.

Yes.

As prayer ends, my host for the evening takes me to Toldos Aharon, the other and bigger of Reb Aharon's disciples, who are known as Reb Ahrelaḥ.

Wow, I can't believe my eyes – a packed place. There are so many *shtreimels* that one would need a national zoo full of sables to make them. Would I like to see something more? I'm asked by a worshipper who introduces himself as Reb Nosson Walles. Yes, of course, why not? We go upstairs, up and up, until we reach a door, which is opened for me by Reb Nosson.

What do I see?

Long rows, one after another, of Reb Ahrelaḥ kids, little Reb Ahrelaḥ, hundreds of them, and they all look at me, a little smile on their faces. So sweet, oh, Lord of Lords! I've never had so many children looking at me, all at the same time, and all are smiling at the sight of a man with rounded red glasses and suspenders, yours truly, a sight that they have never seen before, and they assume, methinks, that I'm a clown.

The images of these sweeter than honey little kids – with white skullcaps that have *chupchiks* (pom-poms) on top, white shirts, rounded sidelocks, and the most heavenly of smiles – I won't ever forget. But if you happen to be in the habit of reading the secular media, all of them are victims of sexual abuse.

Yes. There are those who believe what they read in Sabbath bulletins, and those who believe what they read in the secular media. These two are a perfect match, I think, and they should marry one another.

In any case, Reb Dovid and I walk back to his home, where we sit down to join the kids and the mother, the wife, for the Friday night Sabbath meal. In Jewish tradition, it is customary to have three meals on the Sabbath: on Friday night, Saturday morning, and Saturday afternoon. And he who eats three meals on the Sabbath, the Sages say in tractate *Sabbath*, will be saved from Hell. Yeah!

And now at Reb Dovid's, we are sitting for the first meal of the Sabbath. As tradition dictates, the meal includes fish, chicken soup, chicken, kugel, and *ḥallahs*. The wife, also a convert, has put more food on the table, such as two kinds of fish, many salads, and sweets. The husband, a good German, is busy praying. The food can wait, but God cannot. He prays, prays, and prays. No non-German Ḥasid would pray everything printed in the prayer book, but Herr Dovid does.

Once done praising and beseeching the Lord, Reb Dovid, an honest German, shares with me the most detailed stories about his family, a sad story of a convert.

In the Ḥaredi world, pedigree is everything. If you are a son of a Rebbe, or even a great-grandson of one, it means that your soul is of a higher quality. Blue blood. The greater the Rebbe you come from, the greater person you are.

But before anybody talks about rabbinical pedigrees, the tribe is the umbrella under which any pedigree takes cover. In our case, the tribe is the Jewish people, the Jewish tribe. And the Jewish tribe, so Ḥaredi Jews believe, is above all other tribes, because the Jews were chosen by The Name. As a corollary, all peoples who are not Jews are equal to dogs, donkeys, and elephants. How, then, should a Ḥasidic Jew, or any Jew, treat converts? According to Jewish law, a non-Jew can convert and become a totally kosher Jew, and Jews must never remind a convert that he's a convert. No more a donkey, no more a dog, no more an elephant. It's something equivalent, brace yourself here, to a transgender operation. A man can become a woman, a woman a man, and in Judaism, a dog becomes a Jew. That's the law.

Is this law, specifically commanded to Jews by The Name, being observed? Not really. The excuse for not observing this law, even though The Name personally ordered it, is this: the quality of the soul of an ex-goy, Ḥaredi people believe, is lower than the quality of a Jewish soul, especially if that Jew is a Ḥaredi Jew. The soul of a Ḥaredi Jew, I have been told as a kid, comes from the holiest of places in Heaven, near the Holy Seat of The Name, at the top of the top of the Heavens. There are Seven Heavens, by the way, and The Name sits on His Holy Seat at the Seventh, surrounded by trillions of angels and souls. If you are a descendant of a Rebbe, you shall never forget, your soul comes from *under* the Holy Seat, the highest of the highest of the highest of Holiness.

What all this means, if you follow this logic, is this: The Name can decree whatever He wants, but the Ḥaredim will do what they want. Ḥaredim, if you haven't figured it out by now, are human beings just like you and me, and they are not exactly perfect. This means, in the real world, that in the Ḥaredi environment, a convert is a second-class citizen.

Are you, I ask my hosts, being treated as second class?

"No," they say.

How, then, are you being treated here?

"Third-class citizens," Reb Dovid answers with sad eyes.

This means, sadly, that his children will not, no matter how great and gorgeous they might be, have any reasonable chance of marrying anyone normal from their community. Save for a miracle, and this can happen like any other miracle, if they want to marry anyone from the community, the person willing to marry them would most likely be either chronically sick, much older, mentally challenged, or the ugliest ever created by The Name. And this does not apply just to the residents of this community but to anyone from the Ḥaredi Ashkenazi world.

The Sephardim, Jews who came to Israel from Arab countries, usually cannot marry any Ashkenazi either, unless the Ashkenazi is sick, ugly, very old, or an Ashkenazi who comes from parents who are converts.

This is a sad reality, though Ḥaredi Jews don't have a copyright on this kind of behavior.

The Chosen Ḥaredim, wouldn't you know, are not much different from New York's Progressives, the last cry of the atheist world of our time. The Progressives, who have, regretfully, forgotten that the main pillars of democracy are freedom of speech and thought, that plurality of ideas is to cherish and not despise, view everybody other than themselves as regressive, backward, and a certified lowlife, people who don't merit their attention.

Be that as it may, it's not easy to be a convert in Toldos Avrom Yitzḥok. The wife of Reb Dovid, I find out, goes every Friday night, at the beginning of the Sabbath, to pray at the Western Wall, a twenty-minute walk, and then twenty minutes back, because she doesn't feel comfortable praying in the neighborhood's shuls, where people regard her as a person lower than them, and she feels it.

How could men who spend their entire life avoiding looking at women, without even knowing where in the Bible such a prohibition is written, at the same time ignore an explicit biblical commandment, spoken from the mouth of The Name? The answer: that's life.

One of the children of this family, a young man, a man never treated as equal, is on drugs. "He put things inside him," is how Reb Dovid puts it when trying to explain why this son of his is now asleep in the other room.

Reb Dovid tells me that when he joined Toldos Avrom Yitzḥok, he knew that there would be a price to pay, that he and his family would never be treated as equals. "But I believe that their way of life is the most Jewish way of life," and that's why he decided to be part of Toldos Avrom Yitzḥok. It's unfair, it's cruel, but as Reb Dovid says: "I leave it all to God."

What will God do? Nobody knows but God.

Reb Yeḥezkel, who introduced me to Reb Dovid, introduces me to another person as well, Reb Mordḥe, a man as far from being a convert as can be, and I arrange to meet him after the Sabbath.

Does the Modesty Guard Exist?

Be careful: Satan is hiding under her clothes

It's Sunday, a workday in Israel, and I go to meet an outstanding resident of Mea Shearim by the name of Reb Mordḥe Gutfarb, the second in command of the Ḥaredi community's powerful kashruth authority, known as the Badatz, the highest in its class.

The man, aware of his standing, is dressed like you would expect of an outstanding member of the Toldos Aharon community: white skullcap with a funny *chupchik*, blue-white-striped vest, spotless white shirt, and tzitzit over the shirt.

When I enter his abode, he greets me with a smile and proudly shows me around his kingdom: beautiful paintings all over, painted by his wife, Esther; clothes perfectly folded and geometrically placed in his daughter's spotless room; countless Lego pieces, perfectly ordered and nicely arranged in one of the children's rooms; and a gorgeous silver candelabra in the big living room, where many religious books stand proud in a magnificent bookcase. All in all, a clean, shiny, orderly abode, arranged in great taste and with much love. Reb Mordḥe's wife proceeds to show me a beautiful photo album, with handsome men and gorgeous girls, their children of course. Afterwards, his daughter puts a collection of delicious cakes on the table, cakes that she and her mother baked. The date cake, may I say, is splendid.

This is, simply put, the opposite picture from Reb Dovid's small apartment.

Finally, seated at the big table in the living room, I share with my esteemed host the chicken miracle and the bus accident story that I read in the Sabbath bulletin. Are these stories for real? I ask him. Does he believe them?

He smiles. There are ten million stories written about Churchill, he says to me and asks, "Do you believe them?" The bulletin stories, he lets me understand, were not meant for him or me.

A young man, Reb Mordḥe's son, enters the room.

Does the Modesty Guard exist? I ask, still thinking of my shul visit.

Reb Mordḥe's son, Reb Mordḥe's wife, and Reb Mordḥe himself seem a bit surprised by this question, and all talk, one on top of the other, in reaction to it. The rumors about the Modesty Guard are much bigger than the reality, Reb Mordḥe says. It's not like there's an organization called the Modesty Guard, but there is a man who dedicates himself to this purpose, and if something happens, something out of the ordinary, he gathers a few people to take care of the modesty violators and they, in certain circumstances, beat up the violators. The people doing this Modesty Guard work, the son says, are not the people who excel in studies, but those who are "bored," since they don't study much, and they are the same ones who at night spray-paint slogans like "Zionists are not Jews" on the walls of the neighborhood.

In general, and as far as the people in the present company see it, the Modesty Guard, if it exists, is not much different from what happens in the rest of the world. For example: imagine a couple decides to go naked on the streets of New York or Tokyo. How will New Yorkers and Tokyoites react? Will they let the couple have their way? Of course not. The police will be called, the couple will be taken into custody, or whatever, and charges will be filed against them. And Mea Shearim, according to my hosts, is not that different from New York or Tokyo, except in Mea Shearim, if the couple is dressed in revealing clothes and exchange hot kisses, which to the Ḥaredim is equal to having sex in public, the

Modesty Guard is called in to handle the situation. Is there an office for the Modesty Guard, from which they operate? A small office, the answer comes. How small? Only The Name knows, and maybe not even Him.

Why are the modesty rules so important to this community? Because this is Jewish law, Reb Mordḫe says. Where is that law written? Well, he is happy to show me. He brings a book from his bookcase, Shulḫan Aruḫ, and he reads: "A man must keep distance from women, very, very much. A man is not allowed to look at the beauty of the woman, smell the fragrance of her body, or look at the women hanging their clothes on the clothesline. A man is not allowed to look at the colored clothes of a woman if he knows her, even if she is not wearing them, since the sight might cause him to think about her. He who looks even at a woman's pinky and has pleasure in so doing, it is as if he looked at her private parts."

Oops. And I entertained the thought that Pinky was God's Explicit Name.

The book Reb Mordḫe is reading from, the Shulḫan Aruḫ, is not the Bible or the Talmud. What is it? The Shulḫan Aruḫ was written over four hundred years ago in Zfat (Safed) by the Sephardi rabbi Yosef Karo. To this day, his book is one of the essential books in the Ḥaredi world. Why so? I'm not sure. An ordinary Ḥaredi man will never marry a Sephardi woman unless he has cancer and his days are numbered, but a dead Sephardi's book is held in such high esteem.

Is the Shulḫan Aruḫ right? According to the Bible, the Patriarch Jacob not only looked at women, but he even kissed Rachel long before he married her. Shouldn't we follow his example? Isn't the Pentateuch, which religious Jews believe was uttered by The Name and written by Moses, a holier book than the Shulḫan Aruḫ? I ask. Reb Mordḫe's wife, a scholar in her own right, it seems, replies that Jacob did it before the Torah was given to the Israelites on Mount Sinai. I argue with her. Don't the Sages say, I ask her, that the Patriarchs observed all the commandments long before anything was given on Mount Sinai? And don't the Sages say, I add, that The Name created the world through the words of the Torah, preceding Jacob by thousands of years?

Esther doesn't have answers to my questions, and I take one more slice of the date cake. Oh, Lord of Lords, it's so delicious!

On the fifteenth of the month of Av, as already mentioned on these pages, Jewish boys and girls performed love dances, and The Name Himself, residing in the Holy Temple not far from here, did not mind. On the contrary, He liked it. But that's not proof of anything, I know, because nowhere does it mention that God is Ḥaredi. God, how strange, even likes converts. Perhaps, I'm not sure, we should get the Modesty Guard involved and teach God a lesson once and for all.

I take another slice of the date cake. Oh, Creator of the World, I think that Rabbi Yosef Karo never tasted something so good. If he did, he would no doubt prohibit it.

Reb Mordḥe, a man who also delivers classes in Judaism here and there, shows me more rules in the Shulḥan Aruḥ, just in case I didn't have enough and am curious to know more. Here goes: "When a man first wakes up in the morning, he should wear his clothes while still lying down, so that when he gets up, he is already dressed up and is not in the nude. Don't say, 'I am in my room, who can even see me?' God, the Blessed One, can. As it says, 'The whole of the earth is full of His honor.'"

I don't get this, to be honest. If The Name can see us in our private rooms, it stands to reason that He can see our beautiful bodies under the blanket and under our clothes. Why, then, should we bother to hide our sexy skin from Him?

This is a good question, the kind of questions I asked when I was fourteen, and no rabbi could answer them, except for saying: "What, do you really think that you know better than Rabbi Yosef Karo? That's arrogance, Tuvia! Run away from such questions as one would run from fire!" Another rabbi once said to me: "Questions like these were put in your head by Satan. Be careful!"

In case you didn't know, Satan is an angel who is busy day and night trying to tempt the righteous into more and more and more sexual encounters. A good day for Satan is when more Jews are having sex during that day than on the day before. As you should by now know, Satan hides under women's clothes. That's why, as everybody knows, a woman is the most tempting of all creatures.

In many other cultures, Satan is depicted as the ugliest, most frightening of creatures. Not so in the Ḥaredi world: their Satan is the sexiest, most beautiful female ever created by The Name.

The image of the beautiful *rebbetsen* I met when I walked my first steps in this neighborhood, the wife of the rabbi who claims to study all the time, comes to me now. Is Satan hiding under her clothes?

I ask Reb Mordḥe how many people there are altogether who follow in Rabbi Aharon Rote's footsteps.

All in all, he estimates, the three Ḥasidic courts that follow Reb Aharon's teachings have about twenty-five hundred families: Toldos Aharon fifteen hundred; Toldos Avrom Yitzḥok seven hundred, and Shoimrei Emunim three hundred. If this is correct, there are likely about twenty-five thousand souls of them, given their families' large sizes.

Out of a population of 1.2 million Ḥaredim in Israel, and some say that the number is even higher, these guys are a small minority, but they are much more colorful than the others and more authentic. Most other Ḥasidic courts, for example, are named after Jewish cities, towns, and villages that were decimated during WWII, such as Belz, Gur, Lelev, Satmar, and many others. Not these. They are the followers of Reb Aharon Rote, not the survivors of the long-gone Jewish Diaspora. Their names do not connote death and destruction, crematoriums, and gassing, but a person who wrote books, a learned rabbi, who is today watching them from above, from his kingly seat in the Other World.

I stay for some time with the Gutfarb family, chatting about this and that, and Reb Mordḥe invites me to come for a Friday night meal in a couple of weeks. Judging by the cakes, I expect an excellent meal.

And now that I've met the Gutfarb family, my appetite increases, and I start entertaining the thought of meeting a Rebbe or two. That would be nice, wouldn't it?

The Woman Who Can't Wait to Shave Her Head

And the Ḥasidim who wear Hamas yarmulkes

It's a beautiful, hot day, and I'm walking on Mea Shearim Street. A car passes by, stops, and a man comes out of it. His name is David, I learn, and he is a philanthropist. He is not from this neighborhood, has no beard and no sidelocks, but he has a yarmulke on his head. He is Orthodox but not ultra-Orthodox, kind of Ḥaredi-lite. He tells me that he supports the Toldos Aharon community financially, even though he is not a Ḥasid.

We chat a bit, and he invites me to visit him at his home, outside of Mea Shearim.

I love to be invited, and I accept.

David lives in a magnificent home, which cost him God knows how many millions of dollars to build, and it shows. His living room, for example, has a ceiling so high that thousands of angels could fly in the room, and nobody would notice. As we sit down in the huge room that looks like a very comfy museum hall in Heaven, cookies and drinks aplenty are served on a huge table, and we nosh, drink, and chat.

About what? The Golden Boys.

David tells me that the origin of the beautiful golden and blue coats that the Reb Ahrelaḥ wear, which they consider holy Jewish clothes, dates back to the Ottoman Empire. One day, so his story goes, the sultan's tax collector, making his way from the Galilee to the Holy City of Jerusalem, was attacked by Ashkenazi Jews from Jerusalem. They stole all the money he'd collected over weeks and weeks. When the sultan asked him for the money, the taxman told him what had befallen him. Hearing this, the sultan immediately issued a death sentence on all the Ashkenazi Jews alive in Jerusalem. To avoid certain death, the Ashkenazi Jews started wearing Arab clothes, including a skullcap that looks like "the Hamas skullcap," to hide their Jewishness, pretending to be perfect Muslims.

I love stories like this.

Yes, I know: Hamas was founded in 1987, long after the sultan had gone under the earth, but the story is good, so why argue with a good story?

David also tells me that even the name of the outer garment some Ḥaredi Jews wear over their golden caftan, the jubbah, was coined by Muslims who wear the same coat. I, personally, never met an Arab dressed like a Reb Aharele, but what do I know.

To me, the Golden and the Blue caftans are the sexiest men's clothes ever designed, and I love the yarmulkes with the *chupchik*, be their origin in Hamas or the Hustler Club.

David doesn't see anything sexy about the golden clothes and the people wearing them. As far as he knows, Ḥaredim are not having great sex to start with. There are some Ḥasidim, he tells me, who only rarely have sex. What kind of Ḥasidim are they? The Ger (Gur) Ḥasidim, he answers. He goes to a bookcase in an adjacent room and takes out a book to show me what he calls the Takunnes, ordinances, that supposedly guide this particular Ḥasidic court. Here is a sample of the ordinances: Sexual relations between a couple are allowed only once a month. The sexual relationship must be performed very modestly, with almost all the clothes on, including the tzitzit, in order to tame the man's desires. A man shall not call his wife by her name, and when they are outside their home, he shall not walk together with her.

The book, written by a person outside of the Ger community, does not give the source for these rules. Are they real? Are they practiced? I don't know, but I'm intrigued. I write a note in my head: check if such Takunnes are real.

In any case, David the Philanthropist tells me that he knows the Rebbe of Toldos Aharon personally, and if I want, he can try to arrange for me to meet him in person.

That will be great, I say, precisely what I wished to hear.

I eat, and I nosh more, and as I depart from David, I think: Could such Takunnes exist?

I walk the streets of Jerusalem, here and there, there and here, until I find a Gerer Ḥasid.

I ask the man: Is it true that your Rebbe doesn't allow you to call your wife by name?

"We are a Polish Ḥasidic court," he replies, "and we learned from the Catholics to fear women, but this doesn't mean that we follow all our leaders' commands. We are not in Poland anymore; this is Israel."

Tell me, I ask him, what's your wife's name?

"Oh," says the Gerer Ḥasid, "this is a tough question! Do you have time to wait until I find out? If you do, I'll call my wife, and if she picks up, I will try to get her to tell me her name. Can you wait?"

We both laugh hard.

Yet, there's often a big slice of truth hiding behind a joke, and I start getting ever more intrigued about this Takunnes thing. I will have to find out. I must.

Late at night, on my way back to the hotel, I stop at Uri's Pizza, a place I heard many Ḥaredim swear by. Maybe there I could find a few starving Gerer Ḥasidim, and while they bite into their pizza, they will talk about the Takunnes.

The pizza place is packed with starving Jews, who order pies instead of slices, but not one Gerer Ḥasid do I spot here.

At a table next to me, there are two young blondish girls, around eighteen years of age, both with beautiful, flowing long hair, enjoying their pizza. Excuse me, miss, I ask one of them: Will you shave your head once you get married?

"With The Name's help," she answers, dreamily waiting for the day of staring at her shaved head in the mirror. Both girls, speaking Yiddish with each other, are part of the Boyan Ḥasidic court, they tell me.

Where was the original Boyan? I ask them.

Well, they are not exactly sure. Perhaps, says one of them, in Russia.

As far as I vaguely remember, it's in Ukraine, but I admit that "Russia" sounds a bit more robust.

I write a note for myself, in my brain, to visit the Boyan court.

Meantime, I go out. I'll have to find out about the Takunnes in another place.

The graffiti "Zionists are not Jews," "Zionists are Nazis," and "Zionists are terrorists," stares at me from many a corner. Whoever spray-painted these declarations – even if they are just the handiwork of some bored boys, as I heard in Reb Mordḥe's home – it cannot be denied that anti-Zionism is part and parcel of the mindset of many here, I say to myself. Otherwise, why are the locals not erasing this graffiti?

The Buḥarim neighborhood, where many Sephardim pray daily, is near my hotel, and the next day, I go to visit it. I want to see if the Sephardim also paint anti-Zionist graffiti.

The International Jewish Parliament Convenes at the Pickle Shop

Are you an Ashkenazi or a Jew?

As I enter the neighborhood, something I never did in my younger years, I pass by the Musayof Synagogue. An older Sephardi looks at me, a man of white skin and suspenders, an item he doesn't encounter often. "Are you," he asks me, "an Ashkenazi or a Jew?" To him, white-skinned Jews don't exist. At maximum, people like me are Germans, like the creatures walking the streets of Prenzlauer Berg.

Oh, Prenzlauer Berg, I have almost forgotten thee!

The Musayof Synagogue, I slowly realize, is not just a place for prayers but also lectures. Sounds good to me, and I join a class by Rabbi Mutsafi, as I'm told his name is.

He sits on a nice wooden chair, and his cane, decorated with a silver piece at the top, stands proudly next to him. In his class, he talks about the Rosh Hashanah (New Year) prayer. On the New Year, the Talmudic Sages say, the fate of humans is written, and ten days later, on Yom Kippur, the Day of Atonement, a final verdict is decreed. In between these two holy days, the fate of every human is argued: who will live and who will die, who will be healthy and who will get sick, who will be rich and who will be poor, who will end his life in a fire and who by the sword. On the High Holy Days, soon approaching, all believing Jews ask The Name to spare them from death and grant them life, a good and healthy life. Having this in mind, Rabbi Mutsafi asks: When a Jew asks for life, what life is he praying for? Is it the life in this world, here on earth, or is it the life in The World to Come, in Heaven? The second option doesn't make much sense to me, but I understand that this man doesn't want to lose his cane with the silver top, and he must ask questions, sensible or not.

I leave the rabbi's lecture and walk outside. I check my surroundings and don't see any "Zionists are Nazis" graffiti. Perhaps the Zionist fixation is just an Ashkenazi thing, who knows?

I chat with some people, and one of them tells me that the most important International Jewish Parliament convenes at the nearby Shuk Habuḥarim market every Friday at 11:15 am, at the *ḥamutzim* (pickled vegetables) shop in the Shuk.

Come Friday, I am going to the Parliament.

Yeḥezkel, a talented minstrel, or "*paitan*" in the local lingo, leads the prayer and song for the convention of the Ḥamutzim Parliament. What does the Parliament decide on? Well, on the future of the people in the area. How does it decide? Not in vote but in prayer.

I am elated that I can attend such a significant Parliament session.

A parliamentarian, meaning a person with two legs, two eyes, two ears, and two hands, utters a person's name, Ofer Yoel son of Ḥanah, and the parliamentarians pray for Ofer's success. And successful he will indeed be, no doubt, because the people in attendance, Sephardi Jews, proceed at this very point to drink arak for his success and sing songs to The Name. What do they sing? Great songs. Here goes: "We have sinned against You; have mercy on us." If you don't understand the words, since they are recited in a Sephardic accent, or if you are too busy to think of them, enjoy the melody, for it is very cheerful, and you can imagine it to be a wedding song.

Another "parliamentarian," the son of a famous Sephardi rabbi, Reuven Elbaz, tells me that if I want to meet his father, I should come to the first night of Sliḥot at his father's yeshiva, Or Haḥaim, and his father will sit with me once the Sliḥot service is over for an interview.

Great. Will do.

Yeḥezkel, by the way, also convenes little children in Orel Rachel, a synagogue not far from here, where he distributes sweets to any child who sings better than the other.

I go there.

What a sight! Besides sweets, Yeḥezkel distributes dollar bills. Yes, dollar bills.

Dozens of children sit on the benches in the synagogue, where the name Jehovah, I, H, V, H, is inscribed and printed all around, and he dangles a stash of one-dollar bills in front of the kids, telling them that he who sings the best will get one dollar, hear me out here, DOLLAR. American dollar, the greenest of green of currencies. The kids get excited, each of them trying to top the other in volume, hoping that they will be the lucky owners of the one-dollar bill.

Awesome.

Following the gifts of sweets and cash, a teacher arrives in the synagogue, a rabbi with a long beard. He tells the kids that every request they pray for will be granted during the Sliḥot period (around the High Holy Days), which starts next week. "Heaven opens in the Sliḥot days, and everything you ask for will be given to you. For certain!" Hearing this, they sing at the top of their lungs: "We have sinned against You; have mercy on us."

Very serious words, combined with a cheerful melody, seem to garner no wonderment for the kids or their rabbis.

The tradition of saying Sliḥot, which are penitential prayers and poems, is different for Sephardim and Askenazim. For instance: the Sephardim start the Sliḥot period this coming Monday night, Yeḥezkel tells me, unlike the Ashkenazim, the "non-Jews," who start Sliḥot about two weeks later.

On the street outside, I see a "Zionists are not Jews" graffiti, partially painted over.

What's the story with this graffiti?

The Language of God: Ta, Ta, Ta, Oy, Oy, Oy, Pam, Pam, Pam

"We prefer that people like you, an outsider, don't show up at our tish."

As the Sabbath nears, I walk the streets of the neighborhood again.

Maybe I'll learn something today that I didn't know yesterday.

When I was the sweet boy that I once was, I gravitated toward this place, but now, here again but older, the more I'm in it, the more it confuses me. What in God's name is this place? Why this graffiti all over?

I walk, walk, and walk.

Slowly, I notice the traffic getting more and more sparse until there is not one moving car in sight.

I stop walking and take my time to look at the people once more. When there's no traffic around, only people, my mood changes. There's something tranquil taking shape on the street and in me. It feels good. Sabbath in Mea Shearim, I think now, is one of the things that always made me like the place. It's peaceful – humanity with no machines.

What do I see? What I've seen here before on the Sabbath. Hundreds of women, each showing off a nicer figure than the other, a nicer dress than the other. Modesty shmodesty, these ladies are the sexiest of humanity. Older men, kind and gentle, singing *A gitten Shabbes* to me when they pass by me. Young children, dressed like princes and princesses, strolling around and chatting in a lively Yiddish.

How can one not like these people?

It's all so peaceful, so beautiful, and I fall in love with them again.

I resume walking, blending into the crowd, and as I reach the end of Mea Shearim Street, right next to the shul of the Breslev Ḥasidim, I turn right and walk up the street until I reach the Slonim building. Slonim is a Ḥasidic court that I know nothing about, except that it exists. Some tell me, by the way, that they are not Ḥasidim. Are they Litvaks? Not really, those same people say. So, who are they? Slonimers. Or, as some say, they are Chalmers, meaning Jerusalemites. Go figure.

As I enter the building, I hear singing sounds coming from inside it, and I follow them. The sounds come from deep down in the building, and there I go.

What do I see? I see about one thousand people, mostly on bleachers, their eyes fixated on their Rebbe, the Slonimer Rebbe, an older man with a *shtreimel* who sits at a long table with, I guess, leaders of the community.

Can you imagine what I see here? One thousand men, all with black coats (*bekishes*) and most with *shtreimel*s on their heads, sing in unison. No, they don't sing about sins or forgiveness. In fact, they don't sing about anything at all. This is not the Parliament here. These are Slonimers, and their language is melodies, melodies without words. These are *niggunim*, which can be translated as tunes or melodies. The *niggunim* sung here are long and loud, containing not a single word, and yet full of sounds, all kinds of sounds. "Oy, oy, oy, da, da, da, oh, oh, oh, la, la, la."

That's why, maybe, The Name gave His children tongues, throats, and lips: so that they could sing la, la, la on Friday nights.

There are some other songs sung here, and they go like this: da, da, da. Another one soon starts, and it is: ta, ta, ta. Sometimes it's a combo: Oy, oy, oy, da, da, da, la, la, la, da, da, ah, pam, pam-pam, la, la, la, ah, ah, ah. Interestingly, all the people here, one thousand of them, know where the *la* or *oy* come in the song. One thousand people, a black mass of humans with *shtreimel*s on top, one standing right next to the other, row after row after row, on three sides of the hall and in its middle, known as the Hall of Tishes, Heiḥal Hatishim, and their mouths go: pam, pam, pam, ta, ta, ta. At certain moments, I feel the electricity in the air, when the thousand get into a trance, flying somewhere in the heavens, well above the Seventh Heaven.

"For us," a Ḥasid tells me later on, "this is one of our most intimate moments in life, and we prefer that people like you, an outsider, don't show up at our *tish*. We feel 'naked' during the *tish*; we unite with the rest of the Ḥasidim in the hall, we unite with The Name, and we would prefer to be alone."

A man alone with 999 men.

Privacy notwithstanding, it would be a crime to be in Jerusalem on a Friday night and not be present at this Friday night *tish*. If you come here and see the walls move, as if the building flies high, know that what you are witnessing is not moving walls but the presence of The Name.

Yes, that's what I'm told. And it sounds reasonable. It fits, after all, that a God of no name is worshipped with a song of no words. A match made by The Space.

The Slonimers' caftans are not gold and not blue. They are black. The Slonimers, it seems, don't pretend to be Arab. No Arab, they know, will stand for a full hour singing oy, oy, oy. You've got to be a Slonimer Ḥasid to do that.

Once an hour passes, and everyone is fully connected to Heaven, the Rebbe, meticulously dressed, gets up and makes his way out. The Ḥasidim follow the Rebbe to the exit door and go home.

The hall is suddenly empty, not a single *shtreimel* inside, but The Space is still in the hall. You can hear Him, soundless, and you can see Him, formless.

That's the Jewish God, my friend, and He's presently in Slonim. If you're an atheist, you might argue that no one is present here at all, but Judaism is an abstract religion, and "no one" can be translated as The Name. Yes, I know, you've got to be a Jew to flow with this kind of logic, but if you spend an hour here singing pam, pam, pam, you might get it even if you are a complete goy.

I could stick around and stay for a while with The Space, but I think He's mature enough and knows how to take care of Himself by Himself.

I walk the streets again. "Zionists, your end is near," reads a graffiti on a wall I'm passing by, next to a big announcement for a chance to have all our wishes fulfilled next Thursday evening at the grave of the late Rebbe of Shoimrei Emunim, who promised, so I read, that he'd deliver "gifts" and intervene in Heaven on behalf of anyone visiting his grave on the anniversary of his death, his yahrzeit, which this year falls on the evening of next Thursday. Years back, when the Ḥasidic world started, living Rebbes made miracles; today the dead ones do as well.

That's a significant improvement, I think.

At the bottom of the announcement, I read, buses will be provided to all who would like to receive gifts and have wishes fulfilled.

I shall be there. I want to get a gift. But first off, I plan to have a good cholent tomorrow morning. It's the Sabbath, and on the Sabbath, you've got to eat well.

We Want You Dead. Would You Like Another Portion of Egg Salad?

If you know how to sing Sabbath songs, my dear man, Ḥaredi ladies request your company

On Sabbath morning, I'm invited to the home of Reb Israel Meir Hirsh's sister, who, rumors say, is the best cholent maker in the whole of Mea Shearim.

To get to her from where I'm staying, I must cross many narrow streets, up and down, where people live in utmost proximity to one another, one in the nose of the other. To entertain the passersby, I guess, some people spray-painted very creative messages all around. Here are a couple of them: "Passage for Zionists is forbidden," "We demand: Death to the Zionists," "We demand Holocaust for the Zionists."

What is this supposed to be? Was this written by the sexy ladies I saw last night? If so, are they so mean?

Passing a few more graffitied scrawls, I finally arrive at Reb Israel Meir's sister's home, a simply decorated abode, where the table serves as the main feature of the living room. There are many people in the house. Old, young, middle-aged, male and female, and whatever's in between.

I'm not the only guest in attendance; I slowly realize that other guests are seated at the table – sorry, tables. Yes, yes. The males and females are not sitting in the same room. *Shtreimel*-wearing men here, death-demanding ladies there. But the food, as far as I understand, is the same.

The cholent, what can I say, is outstanding. Even better is the egg salad, which I openly praise.

Upon hearing me praising his wife's egg salad, Reb Shmuel, the man of the house, goes to the kitchen and gets me an additional portion. The non-Ḥaredi Jews shall die, per the graffiti outside, but they get a double portion of egg salad inside.

Strange dichotomy.

I hope there's no poison in my egg salad.

When the food's done, or almost done, the males start to sing Sabbath songs, and the only problem here is this: they don't have a clue about singing. They try, but they fail miserably. This family, I quickly learn, is Litvak, not Ḥasidic, and though the men wear "Arab" clothes, being Chalmers, they don't know how to sing like the Reb Ahrelaḥ, and are as far away from the Slonimers as Heaven is from the earth.

I tell them, God forgive me for being blunt, that the way they sing, sorry, I feel as if I have landed by mistake at a funeral, not a Sabbath table.

And before they have the chance to throw in a line of defense, I start singing, loud and clear.

Suddenly all hell breaks loose. Once the ladies in the other room hear me singing, a miracle happens, a miracle the likes of which has never before happened in Mea Shearim. First the kids, who were eating with the ladies, come to our room, the male room, to see the wonder, which equals in value the resurrection of the dead on the Mount of Olives, and then the ladies show up as well. Oh, how beautiful are the ladies! More tempting than Hillary Clinton and Angela Merkel, Golda Meir and Alexandria Ocasio-Cortez, Annalena Baerbock and Whoopi Goldberg. And they all look at me, these gorgeous ladies, objectifying every part of me, limb and organ, and I'm in Heaven!

None of them, let me make this clear to you, is about to demand my death.

Good.

But there's one little problem, though. No kugel has yet been served – not potato kugel and not lokshen kugel. Where are the kugels? I ask, in total frustration, and the reply comes promptly, without any hesitation: We are Litvaks, not Ḥasidim, and we don't eat kugels.

Oops.

When the Sabbath is over, I make up my mind very fast, I will spray-paint on the walls of Mea Shearim: "We demand: Death to the Litvaks."

Short, clear, neat, and just.

Litvaks, it is known worldwide, like to discuss lofty issues, and at this table, they discuss important issues that have to do with the immediate future of the Jewish people, discussions that cannot be postponed until after the Sabbath. For example: Was, or was not, the Satmar Rebbe, Rabbi Joel Teitelbaum, saved from the

Nazis by the Zionists? The fact is, he was. In the mid-1940s, the Rebbe boarded the Rescue Train, organized by Zionist emissaries, that took him from Hungary under the Nazis to freedom and safety, while his followers who remained in Hungary perished. Were his followers upset at him? No. In fact, and as strange as it might sound, he never forgave his saviors, the Zionists, for saving him, and he dedicated his life to fighting Zionism and Zionists.

But not everybody likes history, and not everybody is convinced by facts. One of the sons of the Rebbetsen of the Egg Salad states unequivocally that it was not the Zionists who saved the Rebbe but the Rebbe who saved the Zionists.

How so?

No answer.

I tell this son about my maternal grandfather, the anti-Zionist rabbi who could have been saved by Zionists, together with his family and followers, but preferred to be with the Nazis.

They were murdered, all of them, in cold blood.

He stares at me, and I look back in his face. Slowly he lowers his eyes, saying not a word, and I leave.

With some other families, the Hirsh family are the flag bearers of the Neturei Karte movement, under whose wing Ḥaredi men in "Jewish clothes" and long sidelocks protest next to major events in different countries, demanding the end of the "Zionist" state. International media organizations often carry photos of these Jews, but how many are the Neturei Karte all together, the world over? If one is to judge by their exposure, millions. But is that so?

I chat with some people in the neighborhood, and they tell me that all together, the Neturei Karte movement counts maybe two hundred families at most. And how many follow the Hirsh leadership? "Five to ten families, most likely five," a young Ḥaredi woman tells me.

Another person, a Ḥasidic man, explains it all to me: "The Neturei Karte people don't work for a living, but the Satmar Ḥasidim in New York support them if they make a lot of trouble in Israel. Demonstrations, graffiti, whatever. The more trouble they make, the more money they get. That's all."

Could it be that the two hundred families, or the five to ten Hirsh followers, are the ones behind the graffiti all over? Maybe. What do I know?

It's time to visit a Satmar shul, don't you think?

Sephardi Jews Would Like to Have Free Coffee, Please

"No studying in the impure Hebrew language"

In the late afternoon, I walk over to the Satmar building, a block away from my hotel, and try to chat with one of the Ḥasidim about Neturei Karte and other related issues, but he's amused. "You seem to think," he says to me, "that my dream is to sit at the head of the table, presiding over a *tish* on Friday nights. No, my dream is different. My dream is to sit at the head of the table, yes, but of a big bank, presiding over financial transactions as the head of the bank. No *tish*; bank."

He smiles, imagining himself having a private bank, all his.

He makes me laugh.

Satmar's main sanctuary is a feast to the eye: a ceiling painted with bluish and azure colors and shades, resembling the sky; a big golden chandelier with many glass droplets, perhaps crystal; an impressive holy ark with a golden crown on top; wooden walls in dark brown, maybe mahogany, with tables and benches of matching brown color. This place cost a pretty penny to construct, no doubt.

Looking around, after about a minute, my eyes spot an announcement: "No study without an overcoat. The use of computers is forbidden in all areas of the building. No studying in the impure Hebrew language."

This reminds me of Reb Yoilish, the Hebrew-speaking trouble-maker who claims he doesn't speak Hebrew.

"Impure Hebrew language." Interesting. I take a photo of this announcement and send it to two Satmar Ḥasidim in New York. Their reactions? The first one reacts with a single word: "Taliban." The second states that the Satmar Ḥasidim in Jerusalem better get the hell out of Israel. Where should they relocate to? Maybe to the moon, perhaps to Egypt, where they all started.

I leave the building and see this sign on the sidewalk: "Women are requested to avoid passing, or staying, on this sidewalk."

A Satmar Ḥasid I talk to tells me that the leaders of his community have gone nuts, sorry.

Moments later, I meet a Ḥasidic Jew who is not from Satmar, and I ask him why the Satmarers are doing this. Is their anti-Zionism so deep? He looks at me, the naïve idiot just arriving from the moon, and says: "No, my dear, this has nothing to do with Zionism, Hebrew, or coats."

What, then, is this all about?

"Sephardi Jews."

What?

"Look, the Satmar building is nice, beautiful, with great air conditioners, beautiful furniture, and it offers free coffee for everybody. But the people in charge had a little problem: they have many Ḥasidim, and the building is often packed, which means that they can't afford to have outsiders coming in. Do you understand?"

What does this have to do with what I asked you?

"The Sephardim have their building, the Musayof Synagogue, a couple of blocks away. There they have no air conditioners, no free coffee, and the place looks awful. So, the Sephardim started coming in to Satmar, taking up the space. To solve this problem, the Satmarers put up the announcement that you saw. Why? The Sephardim know only Hebrew, and many of them don't wear coats. Now, thank God, they can't come in. The Satmarers, you see, couldn't say, 'No Sephardim, please,' because that would be racism. Get it?"

Too complex for me, my dear, and I think I'll get my coffee somewhere else.

I proceed to a restaurant not far away, where they sell super kosher coffee, and take a table next to where three women sit: two Ashkenazi women (a mother and her daughter) and a Sephardi girl. The mother, who comes from one of the most distinguished Ḥasidic dynasties in the area, tells me that she had been sitting home for months and months, spending every waking moment praying to The Name to help her find a suitable wife for her divorced son. Finally, after many tears, The Name helped her, and her son is about to marry this young Sephardi girl. The future wife, the Sephardi girl who is soon to be the Ashkenazi's daughter-in-law, is an amazing woman, intelligent, good, and beautiful, the mother tells me, and adds that she is extremely thankful to The Name for her. Would I like to come to the wedding? she asks. I'm courteously invited, she says, provided I won't take any photos during the wedding.

Why not?

I don't want, she says, that the pictures will circulate all over.

Why so?

She doesn't want, she lets me understand, that everybody will know that her soon-to-be daughter-in-law is a Sephardi. Yes, her son is divorced, and who but a Sephardi, or maybe a convert's daughter, would marry him, but why advertise all over the world that her daughter-in-law is a Sephardi?

"Please don't mention my name," the mother asks me, a request I often encounter in the Ḥaredi world.

Does she plan to go to Sliḥot anytime soon?

I do.

It Takes 3,500 Years for a Soul to Descend from Heaven to the Womb

The story of a rabbi who calls himself a liar, and he is

Past midnight tonight, a Sephardi Sliḥot service is about to take place at the Or Haḥaim Yeshiva, after which I'm scheduled to meet the head of the yeshiva, Rabbi Reuven Elbaz, per my arrangement with his son. Rabbi Reuven Elbaz is one of the more important Sephardi rabbis, especially in the penitent Jews area; the meeting should take place at about 1:40 in the morning.

I go to the yeshiva. And here, lucky man that I am, I will be able to mention my next interviewee by name!

As I enter the hall of Or Haḥaim, a younger rabbi gives a lecture. Gotta study before you pray, I guess. He talks about the origins of human souls. The souls, he teaches us, are coming from the top of the Seventh Heaven. Where is the Seventh Heaven? Well, very far away. It would take, he says, five hundred years for a human being to walk from one Heaven to the other. Five hundred for the height of it, and five hundred years for the width of it. Now, he says, you have to multiply five hundred by seven to get the distance it takes a soul, yours or mine, to travel from the Seventh Heaven to earth to get into the womb of our mothers. And then, he reminds us, it takes not a minute for Satan to lead us astray from the very first minute we are born. How this whole process works exactly, given that pregnancy usually takes around nine months from conception to birth, is something that he doesn't explain. But who cares? The story is excellent.

After this lecture, the hall fills up with people, mainly of the younger variety, and at approximately a quarter to one a.m., Rabbi Reuven Elbaz enters, surrounded by a big group of soldiers. Is a military operation about to take place this morning? I don't know, but Rabbi Elbaz will explain it all when we chat.

Rabbi Elbaz, a man I've never met before this morning, stops next to me to shake my hand. He would be happy, he says, to meet me once the service is over.

I hope he has no plans to meet me with all these soldiers trailing him.

He starts the Sliḥot service.

Part of the Sliḥot reads something like this: We have sinned more than any other nation, we are full of shame more than any other nation. We have committed transgressions, we have practiced deceit, we have betrayed, we have stolen, we have spilled our seed.

The semen thing occupies the mind of Ḥaredi people, Ashkenazi or Sephardi, a great deal. This is not a new issue to Rabbinical Judaism, and the Sages dealt with it as well. Thousands of years ago, they lamented the existence of the penis thusly: "A small organ has a man, starving him when he's satisfied, satisfying him when he is starved."

Religious Jews are not the only ones obsessed with the small organ. One of the main issues of today's most advanced Western societies, where Gay Pride is as holy as Jesus Christ used to be, can be summed up thusly: Where may or may not a man insert his small organ?

But while I'm busy wondering why we are so obsessed with the baby organ, Rabbi Elbaz and the hundreds of students in attendance, not to mention the soldiers around him, are busy with something else: they are busy with telling The Name what big sinners they are, how evil they are, calling themselves robbers, thieves, liars, adulterers, corrupt, criminal – yes, all this is part of their prayer at this early hour of the morning – and they want Him to forgive them despite it all.

Adulterers. Are we?

Could it be that every man here, and in the Ḥaredi community in general, is having sex with married women?

Fortunately, and with Heaven's mercy, this self-incrimination ends at last, and Rabbi Elbaz comes to me again. No, he doesn't come for an interview. No, no. He tells me instead that, sorry, he doesn't want to meet me. Why? Because.

I have to hand it to him: when he prayed just earlier, "We have practiced deceit," he was actually telling the truth. The question is: Is this true about the rest of them and the rest of the Jews? Are Jews, all of them, liars and sinners?

In the Devil's House

How to get ten little Ḥaredim free of charge

How does a sinful Jew start life? To find out, I decide to go to the *ḥeider* of Toldos Aharon, where boys from three years of age get their education. I want to see, with my own eyes, the first steps of the self-proclaimed Jewish devils.

This should be exciting!

Welcome to the House of the Devil.

Accompanied by the man who had first opened the door to the kids for me in this very building not that long ago, Reb Nosson Walles, I start my tour.

The first class I enter, I see about twenty kids, five or six years of age, sitting at tables around the room; the rebbe stands in front, and Lego pieces are all over the floor.

The kids are praying for good weather to come, while praising The Name for creating winds and the dew of the morning.

Yes, they do that.

The rebbe, greeting me with a smile, shakes my hand and talks to the kids, little humans with *chupchik*s at the top of their white skullcaps. For their part, the kids smile when they look at me, trying to figure out this creature, me. Then they smile more.

They look so sweet!

I say hello to the kids and the rebbe, and what follows is this:

The rebbe says to the kids: All of you, say: *Blessing and success!*

The kids say to me: *Blessing and success.*

Rebbe: All of you say: *For him and every one of his family.*

Kids: *For him and every one of his family.*

Rebbe: *In the zḥus of the Tinoikois shel Beis Rabbon* (Thanks to the toddlers in the *ḥeider*).

Kids: *In the zḥus of the Tinoikois shel Beis Rabbon.*

I try to take a photo of the kids with my iPhone, and they look at me, shocked. Reb Nosson tells me that smartphones are forbidden in the community, and the kids are confused at seeing an iPhone in their class. I put the iPhone in my pocket and smile at the kids.

Rebbe continues: *In the zḥus of the Holy Torah* (Thanks to the Holy Torah).

Kids: *In the zḥus of the Holy Torah.*

Rebbe: *May he have a blessed year, a ksiveh v'ḥasimeh toiveh* (meaning that I should be inscribed in the Book of Life).

Kids: *May he have a blessed year, a ksiveh v'ḥasimeh toiveh.*

Rebbe: *And may he never feel any sorrow.*

Kids: *And may he never feel any sorrow.*

Rebbe: *May only the good angels accompany him.*

Kids: *May only the good angels accompany him.*

Rebbe: *Amen!*

Kids: *Amen!*

Rebbe, to me: "I always say: 'Whatever happens, I will never leave the *ḥeider*.' Why? Whatever one needs, the prayer of the pure kids makes it happen. It's an amazing thing!"

I walk over to another class.

This time, I ask the kids to sing. I don't know what makes me say this, but I do.

Fortunately, they flow with me.

The rebbe starts singing, and the kids join. Their song goes like this:

> A father wants but can't, the emperor can but doesn't want. Our Father [God], You want; our King [God], You

> can – have mercy on us, answer us, for we have nothing to show for.

Yeah, again. The bad Jew goes to The Name and tells Him to please have mercy on him, the number one sinner of humanity.

I move on, to see more kids and more classes, on this floor and that – no elevator.

What do I see? Class after class, all angels, different ages, same skullcaps. In some classes, the kids are dancing as I walk in, just for the joy of it, dancing and dancing, while singing praises to The Name and blessings to the guest.

What beauty.

With such a beginning, any wonder these kids grow up to be happy adults, full of humor and laughter? And actors too, actors with costumes, playing Arabs.

If this is the Devil's House, I am a skinny man.

Reb Nosson is not done. Before I leave, he takes me to another floor, where the older boys study.

This floor is not a *ḥeider* but a yeshiva, where teenage boys study the Talmud in pairs, known as *ḥavruses*, meaning study mates. It is refreshing to watch them, each pair in their little world, and so many pairs in one room.

I see myself in them, and it brings back so many memories. Something in me wants to join them, but alas, I'm not a teenager anymore.

Learning by *ḥavruseh*, let me share with you, is a great concept. Of course, you are not likely to encounter *ḥavruses* in a regular college or university, but the method is common in the yeshiva world. It has many benefits, primarily because this way of studying bonds the students to one another and creates a camaraderie between the young men, which can last for life.

This camaraderie is evident not only within the yeshiva walls but also on the streets of Mea Shearim. Wherever you look in this neighborhood, you are likely to see young yeshiva boys congregate together, walk together, and eat together. At times, one student will "suggest" that his sister could be a perfect match for his study mate, and before you know it, another ten Ḥaredim are born.

The great thing about this kind of matchmaking, if you ever wondered, is the considerable savings in matchmaker's fees for both bride and groom.

Leaving Toldos Aharon, I ask myself: Who decided to put in these little people's heads that they must present themselves as a bunch of sinners? Do they really think The Name is so dumb as to believe them? I can buy, though with great difficulty, that the sultan was an absolute idiot and believed that they were Arabs. But do they really think that they can fool everyone, including God?

Perhaps it's a Jewish thing. For close to two thousand years, we have been told by the nations of the world how bad we were, how ugly, and how sinful and deceitful, and it might have rubbed off on some of us, believing the worst about ourselves.

Maybe, maybe not; the only sure thing is this: I must learn more about these people.

When You Walk on the Street, Take Off Your Glasses; When You Bike, Close Your Eyes

Do rich Ḥasidic men look at rich Ḥasidic women?

I contact a young Ḥaredi man and ask him if he has time to sit down with me and teach me the secrets of his being, in case such secrets exist. I don't know him personally; we exchanged phone numbers the other day, when I saw him at a shop, and that's all I know about him.

He says that he would be glad to meet me, and a couple of hours later, we sit facing each other at a kosher – very kosher – Jerusalem restaurant.

I order a chicken dish and Coke Zero; he orders a chicken schnitzel and a regular Coke.

And we talk.

How does a Ḥaredi mind work, I ask the man?

Well, he tells me about himself. He's a Ḥaredi, after all.

He has been married for the past four years, he tells me while biting into his schnitzel, and he didn't have children for the first two years of his married life. Nada. He and his wife wanted to have children very much but couldn't have any for reasons they did not understand. They needed, they thought, Heaven's intervention. So, he took action: he drove to Meron, went to the grave of the Rashbi, and prayed.

Nine months later, a baby was born.

That's part of the Ḥaredi mindset, he explains to me. Heaven and earth are one, and if earth doesn't work out, Heaven must be called to intervene.

The Rashbi that he's talking about is a Sage who supposedly wrote the *Zohar*, arguably the most important book of Jewish mysticism. While nobody will argue the genius of the Zohar, many scholars say that this book was written centuries after the Rashbi passed away. But this doesn't matter. The man facing me, and many Ḥasidim, believe that the Rashbi wrote the Zohar, and they go to his grave, in the northern town of Meron, to pray.

Sadly, no new baby has come out of his wife's womb for the past couple of years, even though the couple desperately wants more babies. Isn't it the time, I ask him as I bite into my chicken, to go to Meron again?

"Good idea," he says, "I think I'll do it."

We both take a *shluk* from our Cokes.

This Jew, who on Sliḥot days and the Jewish High Holy Days will proclaim himself the biggest sinner on earth, presenting himself to The Name as an adulterer, thief, robber, liar, a corrupt person, and a criminal, shares with me his big fights with the small organ, his baby organ.

He takes a little pause from his schnitzel and tells me a story.

Just today, he says, he was riding his motorbike next to Jaffa Street, where, may The Name save us, immodest women were passing by. He didn't want to be tempted by them, and he wanted to close his eyes, but he didn't know how to drive with closed eyes. He didn't want to get into an accident, he says, and for that, he needed his eyes to be wide open, but there were Tempting Creatures ahead of him, not just cars and trucks. Realizing that looking at them might risk his soul, he tells me he made a fast decision to risk his life instead of his soul. What did he do? He lowered his head while biking, looking only at the asphalt, and prayed to The Name to save him from the many vehicles on the road. "You know what happens," he says to me, "when a Jew prays to The Name when he's in danger? The Name listens, and whatever the man asks from the Master of the Universe, He fulfills! I was riding the bike, and all the way through, not one traffic light was red, all were green; this is something that never happened to me before, and I got home safe!"

Wow, wow. It is here we both take another bite from our chicken and toast our Cokes to celebrate the miracle of his survival.

He tells me that there are men in his community who take off their glasses when walking on the street so that they won't accidentally look at women.

I make another Coke toast in their honor.

We continue eating our chicken, hoping that future chicken will not pray to The Name to save them from humans like us.

Do I now understand Ḥaredim more deeply than I did before meeting him?

The next day, I take a taxi to Har Ḥotzvim, to Kiryat Hamada Street, where, rumors say, many beautiful Ḥaredi women work. The taxi driver, an Arab guy, is excited to take me there. He, too, wants to see the Miracle of Beauty. And what a miracle it is! Well-dressed ladies, one after another, can be seen all over, working in different fields, and based on their sexy dresses, they earn a pretty penny.

Will Ḥasidic men working in the area take their eyeglasses off at this sight of beauty?

That's what I want to find out.

Here they are. I spot them.

Dressed in their traditional garb, several Ḥasidic men pass by me, and while talking on their cells, I see them stealing looks at the ladies. Without exception.

Not every Ḥaredi is behaving like the Ḥasid I met yesterday.

Dan Shiftan, you should come here and see the world you don't know exists. Get out of your home – the garbage collection will not run away in your absence – and come here to Jerusalem, the city of the holy and the sacred, and see how many of your hated Ḥaredim work for a living. You'll be surprised.

Leaving the professor aside, do I finally understand the Ḥaredim a bit more? Maybe yes, maybe no, but one thing becomes clear to me: I'm having fun with them. The things I'm doing here, I know without doubt, I wouldn't dare do anywhere else. Would anyone of sound mind, you tell me, take a taxi to see women walking on the street next to an office building?

As a new student of Mea Shearim, what I have just done is perhaps part of being a Ḥaredi, Mea Shearim style. I'm a Yiddish-speaker, after all, and it will always be my grandfather talking with their grandfathers, no matter how dumb my actions are.

But life is not only about having fun, as the daily calls to participate in funerals, loudly delivered on the streets of Mea Shearim, make clear to me. It's time, I think, that I visit a cemetery.

Dressed in Arab Garb, Stoned by Palestinians, Protected by Nazis

From the depth of his grave, the Rebbe will give you a gift

Thursday evening, the date of getting gifts at the Rebbe's grave, the dead Rebbe of Shoimrei Emunim, is here. Buses are ready on Malḥei Israel Street, steps from my hotel, and I mount the first bus.

The yahrzeit, the anniversary of the Rebbe's day of death, is on Friday. Usually, the Ḥasidim go to the tomb during the day, but Friday is also the holy day of the Muslims, and driving to the Mount of Olives requires traveling through Arab neighborhoods. This is a dangerous task for a Jew – even a Jew who's dressed like an Arab – so they come now, Thursday evening. On the Jewish calendar, as we know, the day begins in the evening, and Thursday evening is also Friday.

The bus first makes its way through Jewish neighborhoods and slowly enters Arab neighborhoods.

A smaller car drives ahead of us and is being stoned by Arabs – an everyday occurrence, I'm told, that is rarely, if ever, reported by the media. If we came on Friday, meaning during the day, I'm also told, the stones would be double or triple in number and size. The police, always watchful in this area, decide to take extra precautions and tell us not to wander anywhere on the Mount except for the section of the cemetery they have secured near the Rebbe's grave.

It's incredible to watch the proceedings here: these Ḥasidim, known to be anti-Zionists, can visit the grave of their Rebbe only because the Zionist police, otherwise known as the Nazi police, risk their lives for them.

In any case, we enter the Mount at an entrance near the Rebbe's grave, where several police vans are at the ready to protect us.

The dead Rebbe, the Ḥasidim believe, will fulfill every request of those who come to visit him on his yahrzeit. To be honest, I'm not clear why they don't ask the Rebbe to make sure that no Arab throws stones at them.

The anti-Zionist Ḥaredim, I suspect, are talking big, high, threatening words, but that's just talk. Inside, they are like their little children, little kids who sing for a stranger in the *ḥeider*.

There's a tent next to the police vans, erected earlier by the Ḥasidim, which serves as an intro station to the prayer service that will take place later on by the grave. In it, I see dozens of big trays containing mounds of two different kinds of hot kugels – potato and lokshen. Of course, I take a portion or two of both.

Well, three of each.

They taste heavenly!

Lord in Heaven, listen to my request: make sure these Ḥaredim never die, for who else will make such delicious kugels? Lord, hear me out: even if You decree that I will be stoned by an Arab this evening, I will not regret coming here.

There is a big poster outside the tent containing words that the Rebbe supposedly said while alive: "I will not remain indebted to whoever does for me." In other words: If you come to visit me, in my grave, I'll do something for you. Another line on the poster reads: "Your *kvittel* stays with the Rebbe the whole year."

Having eaten, I get a candle and a piece of paper. The candle is to be lit above the grave, and the piece of paper, the *kvittel*, is to write down what I would like to have in life, how many children I wish for, or just to write down my name and my mother's name, and the Rebbe will take it from there.

The Rebbe buried here is Reb Avrom (Avrohom) Yitzḥok, son of Reb Aharon, the founder.

Little booklets by the grave are available at no charge for those who prefer to pray from written texts.

I read from the first booklet I open: "Peace be upon you, our teacher and our Rebbe, upon you be peace from now until forever; lie in peace and rest, and do not feel sad in the misery of your relatives. The Great King Blessed Be He will fast resurrect you."

Wow, wow, wow!

And here's another prayer: "It is here that I connect my soul and spirit, through recitations of Psalms, with the spirit and the soul of our master, lord, and teacher, Reb Avrohom Yitzḥok..."

The booklets are complemented by additional texts for specific issues, should you choose to use such text. Here, for example, is a prayer for a man looking to find a girl. The text of this specific prayer is interesting. The wannabe married Ḥasid asks The Name to be treated with mercy and be shown to his mate. Why would a man beg for a woman next to the grave of a dead man? There's a strong reason for it, my dear. On the anniversary of his death, listen carefully, the Rebbe's soul hovers above his grave, and any request a Ḥasid makes at the grave will reach Heaven faster than fast when the Rebbe's soul returns to its place in the World to Come.

Is a soul flying over my head at this very moment? I don't know, maybe.

Another prayer text I find here: a prayer for a woman looking to find a mate, a good husband, and a prayer to have children as well.

There are no prayer texts here asking God, Heaven, or the Rebbe for a castle or a villa, a German car, or a honeymoon in the Alps. Only mates and babies.

What's the big deal about mates?

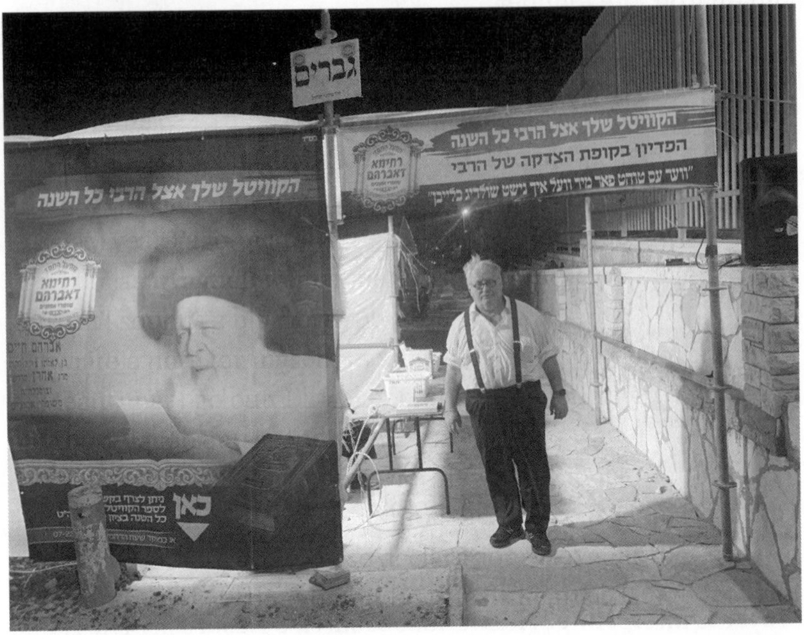

It's big, as the Talmud writes. One day, so tells the Talmud, a wealthy woman asked a Sage: God created the world in six days, and that was long ago; what has He been doing ever since? The Sage replied: Ever since those six days, the Creator has been sitting on His Holy Seat, matching people, one to another. This response surprised her. Since when is matchmaking such a big deal? She, she said, could match between single people – and many of them – in a single day; you don't need to be a God for that. The Sage said to her: You might think that matching is easy, but for the Holy One Blessed Be He, it's harder than the Splitting of the Sea. Hearing this, she took a thousand of her slaves, male and female, and married them off to one another in one evening.

It didn't take long for her to see the idiocy of her act. Once the sun rose again in the early morning, her slaves were bleeding, and their bones were broken, for they were beating one another up all night. Seeing this, she said to the Sage: "There is no God like your God; your Torah is true, beautiful, and good."

I take my time to wander a bit on the Mount of Olives.

It's dark and windy, with tiny stars in the sky and graves on the ground. Grave after grave after grave after grave, dead people all around. Each of the deceased had a story to tell, but all that's left is these graves, their last home, and they are quiet, silent under my feet. I try to imagine them, to give them a face, as a soft wind blows in my face. Are they, the dead, blowing the wind in my face? Is it their souls, flying above their graves, that create the wind effect? For a moment, it seems so, and I don't know if I should be elated or frightened.

Is this what the Ḥasidim feel when they come to pray at the grave of their dead Rebbe?

I walk a bit more, now imagining the Messiah and his white donkey. Somehow – I don't know why – a white donkey fits here; I can see it as part of the landscape. Wake up, Reb Eliyohu, the Messiah will say, and Reb Eliyohu will rise from the dead and, if no Arab stones him to death again, he will go back to Toldos Aharon. And what a welcome he will get there! The best kugels, the most delicious gefilte fish, a tasty *galleh* (a gelatinous concoction made from calves' feet), fried chicken liver with onions, and an ice-cold Coke Zero. Oh, it's been a long time since he last drank Coke Zero! He must be thirsty as hell.

See you soon, Reb Eliyohu, in Toldos Aharon. I'll be waiting for you.

I walk to the bus, rejoining the Ḥasidim on our way back.

What is the depth of the Ḥaredi soul, a depth that stretches from the Holy Seat high in the Seventh Heaven to the graves at the very bottom of the earth? What is it that I left so many years ago and have come back again to look for? A voice within speaks unto me, saying: perhaps this is the "gift" that the Rebbe, Rabbi Avrohom Yitzḥok, is giving you, these very thoughts that you now have, these very questions that you now ask.

As the bus makes its way back to Mea Shearim, I think of the Ḥasidim's strengths.

Their faith is rock solid, and no questions are to be asked. They follow their ancestors' path charted for them, giving them security and purpose. They are a tribe, a tribe on earth and in Heaven, and all their needs will be taken care of, in life and in death. Can anybody beat it? The best a secular person of our day and time can hope for, and for which they fight day and night, is a cool climate one hundred years from now, elimination of national borders, and elimination of the concepts of male and female as we know them. What else have we in the West got? Not one bite of a kugel, not a single "gift" from a grave, and very little happiness.

Yes. The Ḥaredim I've met so far, mostly Ḥasidim, lead a happy life.

They are welcoming, and they have received me, a man who doesn't follow their rules, despite all the offensive graffiti on the walls of Mea Shearim against those who are not religious like them.

They have good, delicious food.

They are together, caring for one another from the cradle to the grave and forever after.

They have Rebbes who pray for them and protect them, even when deep in the ground.

They have a language full of humor, their Yiddish.

And they have music. Their melodies, their ta, ta, ta, da, da, da, oy, oy, oy, and their unique musical interpretation of biblical and Talmudic verses is charming.

Where do these melodies come from? Were they given to Moses on Mount Sinai, together with the Ten Commandments? I don't know. Maybe one day I'll find out, and maybe not.

To top it all, they have music stars, Ḥasidic singers who can melt your heart in the most pleasant way possible and take you on an emotional roller coaster, a ride you have never experienced before.

They are the celebs of the Ḥaredi world.

One of these celebs is a talented singer, a young man who goes by the name of Motty Steinmetz.

When God Loves a Jew, He Finds Him a Parking Spot

"My Soul Thirsts for God, for the Living God."

The Ḥasidim love to sing, sing, sing, and sing, whenever and wherever. On the Sabbath, and you have to see it to believe it, many of the shuls here could successfully compete with any Broadway or West London musical. And when services are done, listen to them singing "*A gitten Shabbes*" to one another. Each Ḥasid has his own tune, and it's almost always delightful.

One of the best Ḥasidic singers I know of, blessed with a great voice and high emotional intelligence, is Motty Steinmetz, a young Ḥasidic singer, about thirty years of age in a seventeen-year-old body, whose songs often play in Mea Shearim stores and the homes of its residents. Motty, born in Bnei Brak, the city of my childhood, would fit perfectly in Toldos Aharon if only he wore the golden caftan, but he prefers living in Bnei Brak, and so, to Bnei Brak I go.

Motty's recording studio, in an unassuming office below street level, is located steps away from the house I grew up in as a child. I take my time to look at the streets of my childhood. It's so different now! In the old days, it used to be a quiet place; we even had an orange orchard next to my home, where I used to pick oranges on my way to and from the *ḥeider*, just so that I could make a blessing, thanking The Name for creating oranges. Today, there are no oranges here. Instead of oranges, I see two girls sitting on a bench, laughing when they see me, a stranger with suspenders in their city. Why would a man, they probably wonder, wear suspenders in the stifling heat of this day when he could wear two or three coats and one big *shtreimel*? To them, understandably, I must be an absolute idiot.

I stare at my surroundings. I can see my father and mother walking these streets. Both are now long dead, but I see them in front of my eyes as if they were alive. And here is me, looking at the walkers, all of them. Here is Ḥaim'ke Kanievsky, the weirdo, and here is Ḥaim Graineman, walking with his head high and his sixteen children following him; they look like a congregation, not a family. Here is Rabbi Gedaliah Nadel, a genius rabbi who made his money selling eggs, and God knows what else. Here is Yaakov Aryeh Alter the Gerer, the future Rebbe of the Ḥasidic court of Ger, walking fast as if demons were chasing him, his head bent down and his long black coat dangling strangely. Here's the German,

Mister Borer, who used to have chickens in his backyard. He died from the coronavirus, I'm told.

I look at them with the eyes of a kid, imagining they are all still here, and I feel like a foreigner. With a few exceptions, my neighbors were of the Litvak variety, not Ḥasidic, and they were cold like the winters of Siberia, even on the hottest days of summer.

A public bus is passing by. On it is a big advertisement, which reads: "Livelihood, Health, Proper Match. Blessing of the Messiah." Below these words is the number to call to gain these blessings, and the words: "May our master, teacher, and rabbi, King Messiah, live forever." The Messiah referred to in this ad is the late Chabad-Lubavitch Rebbe, Menachem Mendel Schneerson, who passed away when Motty Steinmetz was two years old. But according to this ad, he's not dead. He is alive, and he will live forever and ever. Like Jesus Christ.

I go to the studio.

Motty, on a short break during recording, greets me: "Nu, how does it feel to be here, in Bnei Brak?"

This is the studio, he tells me, introducing the place, and today, "the recording is going so-so."

The recording studio contains a recording room, a room next to it, a kitchen, a bathroom, and perhaps some more rooms that I didn't see.

The man is not happy. He's been in the studio for some time, working on a new album, and he's trying hard. But "it's not perfect yet, oh, no." He introduces me to his tech and recording man, David, who happens to be his first cousin. "I record only with him," he tells me.

Also in attendance: Ruvi Banet, Motty's manager, agent, booker, and ten or so other titles, and Ruvi's wife, Naomi, the mama of them all, taking care of them as if they were little children and not grown-ups.

David, a cool guy with sidelocks behind his ears, sits at the computer and records every sound that comes out of Motty's lips. He doesn't just record; he's also Motty's psychologist, kind of. He gently corrects Motty if he feels that the pitch, or whatever, is not perfect, and when he thinks that it's perfect, he tries hard to convince Motty that it's perfect even if Motty believes that it's definitely not.

Ruvi and Naomi alternate standing and sitting, ensuring that everything runs smoothly, that everybody is okay, and that everyone is in a good mood.

You need people like that in life.

Motty, in the recording room, sings lyrics from the Sabbath prayer book, with his eyes closed and his mouth almost touching the mike: "And He, in His compassion, will let us hear for a second time..." He moves his hands as if embracing someone, or something, and then caressing it or him.

David *shokels* (rocks back and forth), like a Ḥaredi in prayer, and so does Naomi, who is invested in every detail. And when Motty recites the words of God, The Name, to His chosen children, the Jews – "I have finally redeemed you, as in the beginning, to be to you for a God" – you feel as if another presence, that of The Name, has entered the room. Motty *shokels* a bit, puts his fingers on his tzitzit, and keeps on singing.

"I was dry before," he tells me when he stops for a moment. "You put me in the right mood, bringing the good muse with you."

He sings again, but this time I feel less taken by him.

I'm not alone feeling this. He feels the same, and he stops the recording despite David telling him that it was perfect, really perfect, more perfect than ever. "It came from my throat, not from my heart," he says.

It is beautiful to see how this young man, whose voice reaches heights you would normally associate with female singers, not male singers, has this capacity to travel to other spheres, other worlds, enter new dimensions, all because he connects his voice to his heart. Hence his ability to take on his listeners, including me, even in a studio, and connect us to something else, to an entity and place deep within us, yet outside of this studio, this city, and this earth. Something heavenly, you might say. He can touch his listeners, including me, in our deeper selves. It's the rare artist who can do this, especially since his songs are not love songs of a man for a woman, or vice versa, songs that can carry us high by igniting our romanticism or sexuality. No, that's not Motty. He doesn't sing romantic songs about great beauties on fabulous horses, but songs about The Name, Torah, and prayer. His beauties, if you need them, are himself. Motty, a bit feminine in look, is handsome, and his manners are superb.

He leaves the recording room and goes to the kitchen to fill up a cup with hot water, which he brings close to his mouth to inhale the hot vapors. You are great, I tell him, speaking of his singing, but he walks away, a bit shy.

The session continues. He reenters the recording room, and he jumps in place, to get in tune with his energies, and goes on singing, now in Yiddish: "*Nuch a mul un nuch a mul...*," "Repeat it, repeat it, repeat it, and one more time, repeat it, repeat it, repeat it..." After jumping, he gets ready to sing another song: "He shields the Patriarchs with His word..." When he was fourteen years of age, he tells me, he heard the Rebbe of Lelev singing this song. When the Rebbe sang it, he gives me the details of what happened then, "an angel was suddenly flying backward, turning white and red. The images you could see there were something, something. When you hear this song, you'll understand."

He sings again, and again he does it beautifully. He's in touch with his feelings, with the words, with his soul, and he's happy like a six-year-old with a new toy. Personally, I don't see any white and red angels, but I didn't come to Bnei Brak to see angels. Nobody goes to Bnei Brak to see angels.

What does an angel look like? I have no idea. I will have to check it at some point, but not now. Now there's music playing: "He shields the Patriarchs with His word. He resurrects the dead..."

Resurrection of the dead. That's part of the faith of a religious Jew, a big part of it.

Motty takes a little break, and when he resumes recording, he sings: "As the heart pants after the fountains of water, so my soul pants after You, God," over and over, but something in him doesn't connect. That mysterious act of connecting to the soul, uniting your vocal cords with an entity flying somewhere in space or inside your intestines, doesn't work. "No, no; I'm not there, I'm not there. I must connect with the feeling, to feel," he says, but it doesn't work. We have to start from the top, he says, hoping to somehow connect with the spirit. But it's hard. That little break that he took before, perhaps, cut his touch with the spirit, the spirit of God, or the spirit of music, and he finds it hard to reconnect, to unite the soul with the mouth, to be in touch with The Name, and only Him. He tries different tricks, like turning off the lights in the recording room, and resumes singing, but God, it seems, has left the room for the evening. Motty can turn off any light he wants, fill the room with any amount of vapors, but nothing will help. The Name, sorry, has left the room.

Motty gives up, leaves the recording room, and we get ready to sit down somewhere else in the city. He has a friend, he tells me, who gave him the keys to his apartment, and it's there that we could sit down for a chat.

We get out to the street, where Motty has his car, a new and shiny white Chevrolet Traverse, and Motty sits in the driver's seat. Soon a bunch of groupies congregate next to the car to take a closer look at this Ḥaredi celebrity.

As we approach the house where we are supposed to have our chat, in an apartment building, the question arises, where exactly can he park the car? It seems that every spot on the street has been taken. Only one spot, we suddenly notice, right by the entrance to the building, a lone parking spot, is empty. "Look, look how the Creator loves us!" Motty says, and in this he reveals his inner strength, the power of the faith. The Creator, The Name, is an entity that this artist is in touch with. Who else, tell me, could take care of keeping this one parking spot empty, the only one in sight, and right next to the entrance? The Name, the one and only, Motty's beloved companion. He, The Name, is the one, in case you didn't get it by now, who got Motty his new American SUV, the shiny car that costs a pretty, pretty penny.

We enter the apartment, and Motty, Ruvi, and Naomi order food, three different kinds of kosher hamburgers times two, plus other goodies. No kugel, no gefilte fish, no *yaptchik*. Burgers. Welcome to America: Chevy and burgers.

We eat, and we chat, washing down our words with a burger.

What do you feel when you sing, what do you see? I ask him. Do you see the Creator in front of you?

"When I sing the words of 'My Soul Thirsts for God, for the Living God,' I look into myself, and my own thirst for the Master of the Universe, and to the path I wish to reach spiritually."

What does it mean, "my soul thirsts"? What kind of thirst is it?

"It is a thirst for the Holy One Blessed Be He. I want to pray better, study His Torah more, you know, all these things."

Words that sound to me mightier than might, now that an American burger is in my belly.

What does the Holy One, The Name, mean for you? I ask him.

"For me, the Holy One is a father and everything. Anything that happens to me, whatever it is, is from the Holy One. Myself, I am part of the Godly Above; He is the one who created me, all the parts of me, the good and the not good, everything that I am. He is the one who brought me here. I am a creature, shaped into being by God's hands."

Kind of a father?

"Stronger than a father. He really knows me from the inside, since He created me."

He looks up to the ceiling, the direction of Heaven, perhaps.

When you talk to the Holy One, do you look up?

"He is all over. His Presence is everywhere. Seeing Him is about concentrating, knowing who is in front of you. His Honor fills the Whole World. I feel alone in the world, facing the Holy One Blessed Be He."

When was the first time you felt a connection to the Holy One Blessed Be He?

"Oh, this is a hard question. You know, you are raised in an environment of faith where you want to be like everybody else. You do what you do because everybody around you does it."

Motty speaks more than just with his mouth; he speaks with his body. He *shokels* when he talks; he moves his hands all over, his eyes sparkle, and his long black sidelocks fly in every direction. We speak in Hebrew, Yiddish, and English, three languages he knows. But his body language is as complex as any spoken language; it's his fourth language and the most interesting one. It's as if every organ in his body wants to express itself, right here and now.

He keeps on talking: "My father is a servant of The Name. I was raised in a Ḥasidic court soaked in awe of Heaven, the Ḥasidic court of Vizhnitz, a court of amazing feelings. Your question, oh, I've never asked myself this question: When was my first time? I have to concentrate on this."

He closes his eyes, covers his face with both his hands, and tries to concentrate.

"I want to think about it. I really want to find this out. I have to go back, go back to know where I was. Oh, this is very hard." He takes his time to think, to recall, to recollect, and then says: "I think that it's in the last few years that I've truly connected." He *shokel*s again, raises his hands high, moving them with immense energy, and in an excited voice says to me that this is indeed a very, very hard question. Not only for him but for every Ḥaredi. "I grew up in a religious environment, my heart totally committed, and your question comes bursting in, a very basic question: In all those years that I have been in this system [of studying Torah and praying], have I ever really faced the Holy One Blessed Be He?"

You have to be a genuine believer, my father would say, to admit your inner doubts. And it's here, like in his comment about the parking spot, that I find the strength of this man, a man who looks a bit like a child, sounds a bit like a woman, a man who touches an untold number of people with his emotional, moving singing. But the secret to his huge success, perhaps, is his deep faith. Instead of concentrating on the burger – which I tremendously enjoy, by the way – this artist is concentrating on when he really faced the Holy One Blessed Be He. It's this, his faith, not just his voice and looks, that he's able to transmit not only to Ḥaredim and not only to Jews but to perfect goyim as well. His song "Tseno Ureno" has thirteen million views, last I checked.

No, he doesn't really know, has no clue, when he first really, but really, connected with The Name, the same Name in whose Name he moves millions of eyes to his mouth. He is totally committed to The Name, totally attached to Him, but he cannot recall when this deep relationship to The Name started for the life of him.

That's okay, even if he himself is not aware of it. Judaism is a highly abstract faith, lacking in imagery, and it's hard to recall when you "started" connecting. *I shall be what I shall be*, said The Name, when asked for His name by Moses the Lawgiver, and Motty clings to the essence of it, and he observes it to the dot.

As far as I understand the Ḥaredi world, he will be thinking of this conversation long, long after I leave him tonight. Ḥaredim talk about rabbis, about commandments, about what is permitted and what is forbidden, but rarely about God. And here I am, asking him about his intimate relationship with God. That's tough, and I understand it.

It is only in the last few years, when aside from his meteoric success, he also faced some tough times, he tells me, that "I live, live the Holy One Blessed Be He."

How do you connect with the Holy One Blessed Be He, aside from the religiously commanded prayer?

He takes his time to think, as if I asked him the most explosive of questions and his life is dependent on his answer. And then he says: "I talk to Him, and I think about Him. A lot of it is thinking. And when something turns difficult, I talk to Him. I say: 'Papa'le.'"

I ask Motty to sing for me a few songs while we sit at the table at his friend's spotless apartment, enjoying the air-conditioned room on this hot day. He promptly complies and, seated, he closes his eyes, moving both hands in various directions, and slowly gets into a trance. From where I sit, it seems that a detachment from reality, via the closing of eyes, enables him to fly to, most likely, the Seventh Heaven.

I hope it will take Motty less than five hundred years times seven to return to us. I close my eyes as well and imagine the hundreds of souls that dropped from the Seventh Heaven at the same time, landing in Toldos Aharon, all of them in the bodies of the sweet kids I met in their *ḥeider*.

I return to Jerusalem. After such a conversation with a Vizhnitzer Ḥasid, I need to go to a *tish* and watch a Rebbe, any Rebbe.

Watching a Rebbe Lick a Gefilte Fish Is Extremely Sexy

Should I hide under the Rebbe's bed on Friday night?

Reb Mordḥe, the man from the kashruth authority that I interviewed earlier on, is back home from a tour abroad, and I'm going to him for the Sabbath meal this Friday night.

Oh, what food this is! One bite of the fish is better than the one before. And the *ḥallah* is genuinely delicious. Yes, there is no egg salad here that I can spot, but so many other goodies that I feel like a king. They know how to eat, these Ḥaredi people. Glatt kosher food, I've good news for you, can be very delicious.

And once the food is done, and the belly feels holy and good, I go to Toldos Aharon. The Rebbe, thank The Name, has come back from his recent vacation, and he's having a *tish* today, where I plan to be for the next hour or two.

It's about midnight, and I see tons of Ḥasidim making their way to Toldos Aharon. They're walking very fast, faster than a space shuttle, and I join them.

The Golden Boys are totally excited and can't wait to see the Rebbe biting into a gefilte fish, a banana, a small red apple – or whatever. They sing, they sing more, and then more, patiently waiting for the banana or the gefilte fish to make contact with the Rebbe's lips.

They sing well, these Ḥasidim. Perhaps not as precisely as the Slonim guys, where the music takes the audience into a trance, but it's more emotional, closer to Motty's style.

A few years ago, I was at a *tish* here but stayed a very short time. The Rebbe was talking, I remember, and his voice was hoarse. I didn't understand a word, and I left. Today I stay for almost the entire spiel, get the swing of it, and enjoy it – and the Rebbe's voice is much clearer. What does he say? Blessings.

Look at his Ḥasidim, the Golden Boys of humanity, how they move as one, one colossal twenty-four-carat gold mass of humanity, shining like a giant diamond several stories high, mighty, energetic, and sexy. Talk of the tempting humans, and they are right here, more alluring than the sun.

In due time, late at night, I leave and am amazed at what my eyes see: the streets of Mea Shearim are packed as if it were a midday Independence Day parade in Manhattan. Where are these handsome people getting their energy from? What kind of concoction have these beauties been drinking?

Yes, I know. Take away their clothes and faith, and they will look like you and me: human animals in a zoo, not the most exciting and beautiful ones. But these people have something extraordinary: The Name, Yiddish, modest clothes, community life, music, food – ingredients that, when combined, set them apart from all others.

And they have something else: the Rebbe.

As I just saw in Toldos Aharon, they cling to him. They love him as if he were their Papa'le, their Tata'le; they admire him as if he were their Turkish sultan; they trust in him as if he were God.

I would like to meet this Rebbe, this Toldos Aharon Rebbe, face to face. I want to see, with my own eyes, what a Papa'le, sultan, and God are made of. I ask David the Philanthropist, the man who sponsors Toldos Aharon, to arrange the meeting for me, if he hasn't yet.

I walk to my hotel.

On the way, in the houses surrounding me, not many are asleep, as far as I can tell.

Friday night, as we all know, is the best time for a husband and wife to unite in a dark bedroom. Are those who are not parading on the streets having fun in the dark at this very moment?

Should I check? In the Talmud, tractate *Braḥot*, there's a story of a Sage who sneaked into his rabbi's bedroom and hid under the bed while the rabbi was "serving" the bed. When he got caught, he said: Seeing how the rabbi is serving the bed is Torah, and I have to learn it. Should I follow that Sage's path and sneak under the beds of some Rebbes in Mea Shearim? I don't think I have the guts to do this, though I entertain the thought.

Yes, there's much to learn on the Serving issue. According to Maimonides, for example, a wife is permitted to her husband, and he can do with her whatever he desires any way he so desires: kiss any part of her and have sex with her any way he wishes to have it, and as long as he doesn't spill his seed outside of her body, anything goes. On the other hand, the late father of Rabbi Ḥaim Kanievsky, who was known as the Steipler, wrote that a man could not have sex with his wife any way he desires unless she gives her permission. He added that he who does not treat his wife with love is a sinner. Now the question is, legally speaking, which of them is right?

From one of the houses, I hear a man singing, a song customarily sung on Friday night before the first meal of the Sabbath. *Welcome, Ministering Angels, Angels of the Most High, Angels from the King of Kings, the Holy One Blessed Be He. Bless me, Angels of Peace...*

I love this song, but I never fully understood it. Who are those angels? Do they really enter the home of every Jew on Friday night? How do they look, the angels? Are angels also serving their beds on Friday nights? Do angels have children, papas, and mamas?

It would be interesting to find out.
Let me try.

You Can Create Black Angels or White Angels; It All Depends on You

The cheapest health insurance in the world: Rebbes

Reb Ḥaim, a follower of the Toldos Avrom Yitzḥok court, honors me with his presence in my hotel. The Jewish New Year is about to start, in a couple of weeks, a time when a man's fate is to be decided, and Reb Ḥaim will go to his Rebbe, who happened to be the brother of the Toldos Aharon Rebbe, and present him with a *kvittel*, the little piece of paper that a Ḥasid gives to his Rebbe, and in this *kvittel*, he'll be asking for a good year ahead. He did it before, he does it every year, and it works, he tells me. The last time he did it was at about this time last year. What did you write on the *kvittel*? I ask him. "My name, my mother's name, my wife's name and the name of her mother, and the names of my children, and I asked for a good year ahead, that I would be written in the Book of Life, and for success in spiritual and financial matters."

Yes, there are people, sad to say, who are written in the other book, the book that details the day of their death and the cause of their death, and Reb Ḥaim wants to be written in the first book. Reb Ḥaim goes to the Rebbe with a *kvittel* not only before the High Holy Days. Sometimes – for example, when any of his relatives are sick – Reb Ḥaim writes a *kvittel* asking for their health and recovery and gives it to his Rebbe.

"I believe in the Rebbe," he tells me. "I believe in a man whose mind is with the Creator every day, twenty-four seven. He is much higher than me, and he can see what I cannot see. When I come to him on the eve of the New Year, on the eve of the High Holy Days, I ask him: 'Can you tell me something that I should undertake for the coming year, something that I have to improve in myself, something that I have to fix?'"

What did you ask the Rebbe last year?

He stops talking, wondering to himself if he should share that personal story with me. I nudge him a bit, encourage him a bit, and finally he talks: Ḥasidim, he shares with me, go to the mikveh before the morning prayer, something he used to do in the past, but in the last year before the previous High Holy Days, he stopped going. The man got lazy, in short. "The Rebbe looked in the *kvittel* and said to me: 'I see on the *kvittel* that you don't go to the mikveh every single day before the morning prayer.'" Reb Ḥaim was shocked, and the Rebbe continued talking, suggesting that Reb Ḥaim take it upon himself to correct this issue and make it his duty to go to the mikveh every day before the morning prayer. How did the Rebbe know that he didn't frequent the mikveh at the allotted time? He saw it in the *kvittel*. Reading the name of Reb Ḥaim and his mother's name, he could connect with Reb Ḥaim's soul, and when he did, he saw that the body carrying the soul, Reb Ḥaim, didn't go to the mikveh before the morning prayer, Reb Ḥaim explains to me. "He can see, looking at the name," he says to me.

Period.

If I have it right, the soul cannot be repaired, or fixed, without the mikveh water in the morning, right before the morning prayer. Yeah. "I'm glad to say," Reb Ḥaim confides in me, "that during this year, I have never neglected to go to the mikveh before the morning prayer, not a single day!"

I should also do this, I say to him. I should go to the Rebbe with a *kvittel* and see what he says to me.

There is only one minor hurdle, I fast find out. The *kvittel* thing, sadly, is not free. “To connect with the tzaddik [righteous man], with the Rebbe, you have to give him something, and once you do that and he gets pleasure from you, this very act creates a connection, through which he can affect you via his holiness,” Reb Ḥaim explains to me. How much does a *kvittel* cost? Well, everybody pays what he can. Reb Ḥaim, for example, gives one hundred dollars to the Rebbe and fifty shekels to the gabbai, the Rebbe’s personal assistant.

Do you really think, I ask Reb Ḥaim, that the Master of the Universe, The Name, will not respond to you if you come to Him directly and pray to Him to help you, and that He will only reply if you go to the Rebbe?

Of course, you can go directly to the Creator, answers Reb Ḥaim, but on occasion, it so happens that a man prays to The Name but his prayer is blocked and doesn’t reach The Name.

What?

Heaven, he explains to me, is sometimes blocked.

I have never heard of this concept before, but life is full of surprises.

I try to understand this concept, and I paint a situation before Reb Ḥaim and ask him for his opinion: I am in the hospital, just before an operation that will determine whether I stay alive or die, and I would like The Name to make sure that the operation goes well. Do I have a better chance that He will help me if I pray to Him directly or if the Rebbe of Toldos Avrom Yitzḥok prays to Him for me?

Well, says Reb Ḥaim, my chances that The Name will make sure that the operation goes well are far better when the Rebbe speaks to The Name on my behalf. No doubt. Why is that? Because of the blockage. What is that? Who is blocking? Why do they block?

It’s here that we get into the angels thing.

Ready?

Here goes: When a Jew commits an *aveireh*, a sin, he creates an angel, a bad angel, or more precisely: a black angel. When a Jew observes a mitzvah, on the other hand, he also creates an angel, but a different kind of an angel, a good angel, or more precisely: a white angel. Now, when a person is in bad shape or a bad situation, such as being on the operating table facing death, all the black angels that the Jew created up to that point run to The Name in Heaven and ask Him to kill that Jew. At this very moment, the white angels, created by the Jew's good deeds up to this very moment, also run to The Name and ask Him to heal the Jew.

This angel thing is becoming complex, I can see. I need patience here.

What's a good deed? I ask.

Well, isn't it obvious? Observing The Name's commandments is one, helping the poor and the weak is another, and studying the Torah, of course. When you study the Torah, every word you utter creates a white angel, as is known worldwide.

But it's even more complex than that.

"Let's say," Reb Ḥaim elaborates for me, "that you make a blessing to God, but you don't think of the words you say, or you say them very fast, the angel you create, as is written in the holy books, is a small or a weak angel."

What does a weak angel mean?

"An angel without a hand or a foot."

That's interesting! How does an angel look, in general?

"As it says in the Book of Daniel."

What does it say there?

"An angel has six wings: two on each side, one below and one up, and each wing covers another part of the angel's body. But he flies with just two of his wings. Something like that."

If I look at a porno magazine, do I create a black angel for every naked woman I look at?

"One hundred percent!"

The porno angels, it is crucial to understand, are terrible news. All black. Very bad.

That's big news to me, but I'm willing to learn.

I gain a lot of knowledge today.

Applying it all in practice, to real-life situations, Reb Ḥaim helps me grasp it a bit more: when I'm lying on an operating table awaiting surgery, the various angels fly to The Name in the World to Come and ask for either my death or my survival. If, The Name forbid, there are more black angels than white angels pleading with The Name about me, the scale on which the angels stand, so to speak, will point at the worst resolution for me. It is precisely here, at this very point, that the Rebbe enters. When the Rebbe joins the white angels pleading for my quick recovery, the scale tilts in my defense, and I'll get out of the hospital healthy like a bull.

A Rebbe, in other words, is like health insurance, only much cheaper.

This all is major news for me.

When I was growing up, no one I knew wrote a *kvittel* in his entire life, and no one went to ask a rabbi for a blessing. But times have changed, I guess, and this ancient tradition, practiced in the old shtetlach (small towns or villages) of Europe, has come back to life. How did this happen? I don't know.

New York, my adoptive city, also changed much. When I first came to New York, there were no Progressives; today the city is full of them. But unlike the Ḥaredim, how sad, no Progressive leader accepts *kvittels*, and if you're sick, sorry.

This idea of a Rebbe joining white angels in Heaven on our behalf, it now occurs to me, could perhaps explain why Ḥasidim are attracted to graves. It makes much sense to ask a dead Rebbe to join the white angels on our behalf, because the dead and the angels are heavenly neighbors. It's like FedEx.

I live, and I learn.

On the streets of Mea Shearim, as so often happens here, a car with loudspeakers announces the funeral service of a community member who has just passed away. This man, if you care to know, will be buried in Har Hamenuḥot, another cemetery in Jerusalem.

The dead man, I understand for the first time, did not die of cancer, old age, COVID, or any other disease or accident. No. He died because there were too many black angels asking The Name for his death, and no Rebbe ran to join the white angels on the scale.

Yes, I live and learn.

The story of black and white angels is very enlightening, perhaps, but I still don't know how exactly the angels look, besides having wings. I'll try to find this out, but before I do that, I want to sit down with a Litvak, one of the self-declared wise Jews who don't walk around with *kvittel*s but with their sharp brains.

A Litvak Explains the Unexplainable

But who has more spirituality, a kishke or a Litvak?

I hear, somewhere out there, a very educated Litvak lives, and he is some kind of a rabbi working in a well-funded foundation in Jerusalem, the Tikvah Fund, which is located near the Central Bus Station of Jerusalem. He is, my dear, the head of Tikvah's Ḥaredi Israel Division, and his name is Rabbi Yehoshua Pfeffer.

I like the name Pfeffer, don't you?

Let's go meet the Pfeffer!

The Tikvah Fund is in a building unlike any of the buildings I've become accustomed to in Mea Shearim. The building is pretty new – it has an elevator, and even some balconies that, what a miracle, were not designed by dust bin manufacturers, like the ones in Mea Shearim. I take the elevator to Tikvah's office, which is also very different from anything one would see in Mea Shearim. The office décor resembles an American office, if you know what I mean. It's that dreary thing, making you feel like you're in a hospital. At the center of the office are desks with computers where various employees work, and around them are private offices for the leaders and managers. Designed according to the modern mindset, the walls and doors of the offices are of see-through glass, giving the impression, or illusion, of transparency.

Rabbi Yehoshua Pfeffer, seated in his glassed office, is a serious academic of the non-Ḥasidic genre, a man whose strongest attribute is not humor but something else, whatever that may be. And so, from the start, I put a serious look on my face and get right to the point. When was the first time, I ask the serious man facing me, that the word *Ḥaredi* appeared, and who invented this word?

The man, a scholar, gives me an answer I can't argue with: "I don't know."

Perhaps I should send him to Reb Israel Meir Hirsh.

I move on. No jokes here. I ask: In the Jewish religious world, they say, "The Name," or in other words, no name. The Christians have a name, even three, Jesus and the Father and the Holy Spirit; the Muslims have a name, Allah; but the Jews, the parents of the monotheistic world as we know it, call their God by no name, The Name. Why?

Unlike other religions, the rabbi opens in response, Judaism is a relationship with God, of living a life in the "Way of God."

You've got to be a Litvak to talk like this, let me tell you.

What's the Way of God? I ask the Litvak.

It's the way of goodness, says he, but "today, that goodness is not revealed."

This Litvak is talking to the wrong person, I say to myself. My very name, Tuvia, means in Hebrew "Goodness of God."

Well, perhaps I still have to be revealed. But I don't say this to him, because you can't talk like this to a Litvak.

In any case, I'm not sure I understand what he's talking about. Seeing my puzzlement, he tries to explain himself: "Why don't we say the name Havayah [Being]? Because His goodness is not revealed." The name of God, Tikvah's Ḥaredi Division head tells me, "represents the goodness of God, and because today we live in a world where that goodness is not revealed, not fully revealed," we cannot say the actual name, and instead we say "The Name."

That said, he insists that the Jewish God, The Name, does have a name, and we know it, but we can't utter it. What's the name?

"*Yud, kay, vav, kay*," which translates into I, K, V, K. And more precisely: I, H, V, H. In Hebrew, in which almost all words have meanings and roots, I, H, V, H, another form of the word *Havayah*, means "being," or something having to do with it.

There are some commentators, by the way, who say that Havayah comes from the Arabic word *hawa*, meaning wind, arguing that since both Hebrew and Arabic are Semitic languages, they share more than it seems at first sight. But, be it as it may – being, to be, wind – it is not a real name. In some prayer books, Ḥasidic and Sephardic, there's a special way to write Havayah, combining the word *Adonai*, meaning "Lord," and I, H, V, H into a single word, giving the reader the impression of seeing with their own eyes the Secret Name of God. The rabbi sitting across from me sees it differently. The Vilna Gaon says, he tells me, "that I, K, V, K means that God is present. Havayah, being. That's His name," says the Tikvah rabbi, adding that "we don't know how to pronounce it." This part, the pronunciation of the I, H, V, H, has not been revealed, he says, looking at me as if what he's saying is so damn simple and how come I'm so dumb not to understand it.

I ask Rabbi Pfeffer to explain himself, to explain to me the reason the pronunciation of I, H, V, H has not been revealed. Idiots like me, what can I do, need extended explanations sometimes.

"The world is not in a state of perfection, enough for The Name to be revealed. God wants to give us His full goodness, and we need to be able to receive that, but we still have work to do to perfect the world, to make it a better place."

That's the reason.

He doesn't say I, H, V, H, but I, K, V, K, exchanging the H with a K, because he believes that saying I, H, V, H, four letters in this order, is not religiously allowed.

I hope that The Tikvah Fund pays him a hefty salary, because, for the life of me, I couldn't come up with such a set of sentences as he did if you put a gun to my face.

But I keep at it. What's the damage, I ask him, if we had the proper pronunciation of the I, H, V, H, enabling us to utter the full name of The Name?

"The damage is that it will be a representation of a perfection that is still absent from the world. And we want to remind ourselves all the time that that perfection is still not with us."

It is at this point that I kind of totally lose it. Why, I ask the learned man, do you think that no other religion has this kind of *kneitsh* (twist)?

Reply: "That's a good question."

My biggest question of the day is this: Why does The Name allow the Tikvah Fund to reveal itself? Don't we have enough problems in the world as it is?

Rabbi Pfeffer is a nice guy otherwise; he's just a Litvak.

As I exit the building, it occurs to me that a visit to Hadar Geula is more spiritually uplifting than a visit to the Tikvah Fund. But I must admit, I gain much less weight when I visit the Fund.

There are people out there, as you might guess, who are more intelligent than all of us, and they can get their hands on the actual name of God or, to be more precise, on the seventy-two names of God, or seventy-two letters of The Name, I'm not sure which. A jewelry store in Jaffa, to cite one example, will gladly sell you a lovely pendant to hang from your bracelet, with the seventy-two names of God engraved on it, for 990 shekels only, free shipping.

Rumors say that there are other people in this Holiest of Cities who can explain theology better than any Litvak. They do it every Thursday night near the Central Bus Station, a walking distance from the Tikvah scholars.

And it's not that hard to find them.

If you walk down the street from Jerusalem's Central Bus Station late on a Thursday night, you'll hear the sound of music, religious music, and smell a strong odor of cholent as your feet move. What's in there? That's the place you can study Judaism 101, Jerusalem style, and it needs no further explanation or introduction. You know, your brain knows, and your heart feels that if you reach the source of the sound and the aroma, you will instantaneously become a devout Jew, even if you were born a pure goy.

That's what I hear, and I trust my sources.

I follow the sound, and my feet take me to a converted kitchen with two Ḥaredi men standing next to huge pots of cholent. The taller of the two asks: How much cholent do you want, a kilo, half a kilo, a quarter of a kilo?

Give me, please, half a kilo with lots of kishke, I say to him.

What's kishke? I'm not sure how to answer this, since a kishke is similar to the I, H, V, H word, a word that cannot be fully explained, other than to say that it is a replica of the food that the most righteous dead Jews eat in Heaven while surrounded by white angels. Full stop.

The cholent man serves me my order. Oh, what a cholent! Oh, Heaven, what a kishke! The best of the best. I get a Diet Coke to accompany the food on its journey into my belly, and as the Coca-Cola slogan goes in Israel, The Taste of Life, it is indeed so.

There are not that many places in Jerusalem where you can find Diet Coke. In Israel, most often you'll find Coke Zero or Pepsi Max. Some Ḥaredim drink only Pepsi Max, while others only Coke Zero. Why's that? Too complex to explain.

A bunch of young men, eating cholent and kishke, drinking Coca-Cola and smoking *shisha*, are making a *zitz* ("sitting"), which in this case means that they sing together religious songs. "I thirst for You, The Name," they sing, as they sip their Cokes.

What a sight!

This is a ritual, I'm told, that is celebrated in many places in Jerusalem every Thursday night. It wasn't in my time, but it is now. A new tradition, a new custom.

Whose Judaism is better, I ask you, the Tikvah's or the Kishke's?

Nothing beats an excellent cholent or a delicious kishke, let me tell you.

And let me also teach you something: he who eats this food on the Sabbath, I know for a fact, creates one thousand white angels who will fight for him every minute of every day until eternity. There's no better way to honor the Sabbath than to eat good food on the Jewish Christmas. That's why tomorrow night, Friday night, I shall join a friendly family for the Sabbath meal.

The Stunning Beauty Who Won't Talk

And the mother who burned her daughter

On the evening that The Name rested, Friday night, I again walk the streets of Mea Shearim and look at the many synagogues, yeshivas, *shtiebels* (small shuls), and shuls all around, and read their names, which I have done God knows how many times before. They are the names of villages, towns, and cities in Europe, Ukraine, Belarus, and Russia, where Jews once lived, until the Nazis and their partners – and the Communists and their partners – got rid of them. The few who survived, especially Rebbes, reestablished the old Ḥasidic courts in the Holy Land, courts that are now kicking with life, Pepsi Max, and Coke Zero.

The history of Jews in the Diaspora is soaked in blood, Jewish blood, be it in York or Rome, Warsaw or Berlin, Bucharest or Kiev. There, the Jews were slaughtered and raped, and yet they celebrate those very lands, cities, towns, and villages, as if those places were paradise on earth, as if Satmar and Belz were holy names. I try to go back to the first days of the Zionist movement, when Jews were called upon to live freely in their own land, and I can see the nightmare that the very idea of freedom inflicted on some of them and their unbearable fear of losing Ger and Auschwitz, Lodz and Lvov. Oh, their hate of the Zionists must have burned in their bones, sending them running into the crematoriums.

Why am I walking the streets now? Because Reb Nosson, the man from Toldos Aharon, has invited me for this evening's Sabbath meal at his home.

Reb Nosson lives in one of those places that most Jerusalemites don't know exist, a house that comes out of a courtyard, inside a courtyard; a place well-familiarized to The Name, but it takes me, a mere mortal, time to find. And when I do, what a find it is! There are several people inside, boys and girls, some shy and others not, and a gorgeous lady with a stunningly beautiful face, which is more or less all the flesh one can see of her. Let me be clear here: she has only white angels in Heaven advocating on her behalf. Not one black angel, I swear.

Knowing how tempting she is, she does not exchange one word with me. Not one. But I slowly find out that this stunning beauty is Reb Nosson's daughter-in-law, and that her husband, a man who doesn't talk much either, is presently studying to write verses of the Bible on parchments, a job I will never be able to accomplish. What I am able to accomplish, if you are eager to know, is to consume diet colas. And, indeed, there are plenty of Coke Zeros and energy drinks on the table. Moishi, a little baby of two years or so, drinks Coke Zero from his baby bottle. I've never seen such a thing before, a little baby with caffeinated diet drinks, and now it occurs to me that maybe I did the same at his tender age, and that's why I drink liters of diet cola every day.

Reb Nosson's wife, an excellent cook, feeds us all, and once the meal is done, and all the white angels you can think of have been created, the adult people at the table will return to the shul, for the *tish* with their Rebbe. At two or three o'clock in the morning, they will come back home, enter the dark bedroom, play a little, and fall asleep. Some will even snore, but that's okay.

On the morning of the next day, they will go to shul again, praying to The Name and singing with the Rebbe. Once the prayer service is over, they will eat the lokshen kugel at the shul, drink diet colas and go back home to eat a full meal with their families and the angels they bred, cholent, and kishke. After the meal, they will learn a bit, creating a few more white angels, and then return once more to shul, where they will pray a little more and study a little more.

Me too. I'm also a learned person and a book reader, in case you wonder.

I open Rabbi Aharon Rote's book, *Shoimer Emunim*, and read:

> And I will tell a story that a trusted person, known to tell the truth, told me. He was at his father's, or uncle's, who was living in some place and was riding with some people who were on a business trip, on a carriage driven by horses, and they were passing through a certain field. Suddenly they heard an embittered wailing sound and loud shouts, women screaming: "Jews, Jews, come, have mercy on us, save us!" They looked around and saw a house standing in the middle of a field, from which the sounds came. Thinking that perhaps a thief had attacked the people inside, they got off their carriage and walked to the house. But no thief was inside, just an old woman and a young woman, and the young woman was lying on a bench, and there was a big fire in front of them. Over the fire was a big pot, and inside the pot were boiling clothes. The old woman didn't say a word. All she did was put her hands inside the boiling pot, take out the boiling clothes inside, and lay the boiling clothes on the young woman's body until the young woman's body burned. The young woman was screaming very, very loud. That done, the whole process repeated itself, over and over and over, every minute the same: taking out boiling clothes and laying them on the body, burning the flesh. The men then understood that what they were seeing was not an event taking place in a human world. They also understood

> that the women were not living women but banished souls in the World of Chaos, where the souls were being punished for acts that took place while they were in human bodies. Once the men realized that what they were seeing was happening in another world, a huge fear engulfed them, and they ran away, all the way to the next village, leaving the horses and the carriage behind. Once they reached the village, they fell on the floor, their bodies weak for several weeks. Only then they recalled that there was no real house in that field and never was. It seems that the young woman was the daughter of the old woman, and that the old woman did not raise her daughter to be modest, and that's why the mother's and daughter's punishment was that the mother would set her daughter on fire.

This story reminds me of the conversation I had with the Litvak rabbi who is gracious enough to stare at his wife while she's preparing chicken dishes, or whatever, and what he told me about the way The Name punishes the sinners: "The suffering in Hell is so severe that no pain exists in This World comparable to it."

Perhaps, it is here that the Ḥasid and the Litvak share a belief.

As for me, it is high time that I finally find out what angels look like.

Fact: Moses the Lawgiver Was Wearing a Shtreimel

Theatrical fireworks at the Lord's Holy Seat in Heaven performed by fiery angels

It's early morning, and I go to a nearby bagel shop to get myself an omelet. As I enter, I see a painting on the wall, a colorful painting, depicting the biblical story of the Israelites' journey from Egypt to the Land of Israel thousands of years ago. In this painting, interestingly, the Israelites are dressed in *shtreimels* and other Ḥasidic garb, and all of them are male. Moses the Lawgiver, in case you wonder, also wore a *shtreimel.*

Who, in his right mind, believes that the Israelites, later called Jews, left Egypt in *shtreimels*? Good question. Another good question: Who, in his right mind, believes that, speaking of Mea Shearim, "There is not one child here who was not [sexually] abused"?

Bottom line: You don't have to be a Ḥaredi to be an idiot. You can be highly educated, secular, and still believe in *bobbe maisehs*, old women's tales.

As for me, after having the omelet, I go to Reb Betzalel, a man rumored to know the Jewish mystical world and all its angels, to teach me everything I don't know. Reb Betzalel was educated in the United States and now resides in Jerusalem with his wife and children, dedicating much of his time to studying the Torah.

His apartment, on the third floor of a residential building, is sparsely decorated with tables, chairs, and a bookcase. On the living room table, prepared especially for yours truly, are muffins, peanut cookies, and beverages. His small children are playing with their toys, and his wife is in the kitchen baking *ḥallah*s.

As is known, the smell of *ḥallah*s being baked in a Jewish home creates the need in humans to discuss God, which is precisely what we are doing.

The first thing to know about The Name, he explains to me, is the *atsmus* of The Name, the very essence of The Name, and then there are various ways in which The Name reveals Himself. It starts with the Or Ein Sof, the Infinite Light, which is the First Revelation of God. You and I exist, he teaches me, but God does not exist. God, he explains, is the True Being; He is the essence, the true existence.

It doesn't make much sense to me, but this is what he says, and it makes tons of sense to him.

The world we live in, he says, if I understand him correctly, is Olam Ha'asiyah, the World of Action. Above that is Olam Hayetsirah, the World of Formation, where the angels live. Above that is Olam Habriah, the World of Creation, where the souls are.

And above that is Olam Ha'atsilut, the World of Emanation, where the Holy Seat of the Lord is. All together: Four Worlds.

I'm interested in Olam Hayetsirah, where the angels live. Who are the angels? I ask. Ḥayot and Ofanei Hakodesh, he answers. These are words that can be translated in different ways, such as Animals and Holy Wheels, Living Beings and Holy Cycles, etc., but no matter what the translation is, it doesn't add much to my knowledge.

He goes on. An angel, he says, is something that The Name created, a revelation of Himself. *Atsilut* is the way He reveals Himself. An angel is something that has a recognition of the Truth of God, and its whole essence is that it wants to become one with God, it wants to cease to exist.

How does an angel look? I ask the man.

As it says in the Bible, he answers, angels have wings and eyes.

Where in the Bible does it say that?

Well, he's not sure.

What else does an angel have, besides wings and eyes?

He doesn't know.

Does an angel have a *bris*? Does an angel use iPhones? Does an angel wear a *shtreimel*? Can one look at an angel, or will he be tempted, exactly like when a man looks at a pretty lady? Are there Ḥaredi angels up there, all suffering from sexual abuse? Do angels like gefilte fish? Is there a *tish* in Heaven, with a Rebbe angel and a thousand Golden Angels looking at him licking a lokshen kugel? Do angels get married to one another? Do angels have matchmakers? Does an angel wear white socks or black socks? Do angels serve their beds? Do they do it in the dark? Can I sneak into their bedrooms to see how they do it? Is an average angel a Ḥasid or a Litvak?

These are but a few of the questions running through my head. Will anybody help me find an answer?

Reb Betzalel tries. He takes out books, one after the other, to find the answers, but no answer is in the offing. Luckily, Google, the Fruit of Knowledge of our day, comes to our aid. It is there that we, together, read the magic words: Book of Ezekiel.

Reb Betzalel hands me the Book of Ezekiel, and we read:

> ...they had the likeness of a man.
>
> And every one had four faces, and every one of them had four wings.
>
> And their feet were straight feet; and the sole of their feet was like the sole of a calf's foot: and they sparkled like the color of burnished brass.
>
> And they had the hands of a man under their wings on their four sides; and as for the faces and wings of them four, their wings were joined one to another; they turned not when they went; they went every one straight forward.
>
> As for the likeness of their faces, they had the face of a man; and they four had the face of a lion on the right side; and they four had the face of an ox on the left side; they four had also the face of an eagle.
>
> Thus were their faces; and their wings were stretched upward; two wings of every one were joined one to another, and two covered their bodies.
>
> And they went every one straight forward; whither the spirit was to go, they went; they turned not when they went.
>
> As for the likeness of the living creatures, their appearance was like burning coals of fire, like the appearance of torches; it flashed up and down among the living creatures; and there was brightness to the fire, and out of the fire went forth lightning.
>
> And the living creatures ran and returned as the appearance of a flash of lightning.

> Now as I beheld the living creatures, behold one wheel upon the earth by the living creatures, with his four faces.
>
> The appearance of the wheels and their work was like unto the color of a beryl; and they four had one likeness; and their appearance and their work was as it were a wheel within a wheel.

In short: pretty scary creatures. No *shtreimels*, no socks of any kind, no sign of gefilte fish, and no smell of any *ḥallah*. And no matchmaker in Mea Shearim, God is my witness, will try in a million years to find a mate for anyone looking like "burning coals of fire." Forget it.

How come, you may ask, a learned man like Reb Betzalel, who is versed in mystical and kabbalistic texts, doesn't know about the Book of Ezekiel, the very foundation of Jewish mysticism?

Because the Book of Ezekiel is part of the Bible, a Forbidden Text.

I know this from personal experience. I studied in a yeshiva, and in the yeshiva, we never read, not to mention studied, most of the Bible. The Book of Ezekiel, like most other Books of the Bible, we did not even open. Nor did we know that, according to the Sages, Ezekiel was a descendent of the biblical prostitute Rahab. Rahab, also according to the Sages, was one of the four most beautiful women in the world. She was so sexy, the Talmud says, that if a man said just "Rahab, Rahab," he immediately ejaculated.

To admit that the Sages wrote such things, when Ḥaredi leaders have long ago decreed that the words "prostitute" and "ejaculate" are forbidden and never to be uttered, is the foundation of blasphemy in the Ḥaredi mindset. Where I studied, reading a book like Ezekiel was forbidden. Yes, we used words such as Ḥayot and Ofanei Hakodesh in prayer because these words are written in the prayer book, but we had no clue what they meant. As far as we knew, Ḥayot was something like wild Sephardi girls, and Ofanei Hakodesh was a Mercedes car with a mezuzah.

Bottom line, and as strange as it sounds: the very people who have made an oath to dedicate their lives to the Torah, be they Litvaks or Ḥasids, have no clue what the Torah says.

It reminds me of the days I studied Talmud in the yeshiva. When we studied tractate *Kiddushin*, I remember, we read that a man can marry a woman through the act of *biah*. *Biah* means sexual relations, but the word by itself generally means coming. In my imagination, since nobody explained it to me otherwise, and I still had not read about Patricia at that time, *biah* was an act of knocking on the door of a woman. I could picture it. I saw myself knocking on a door where a girl lived, and in nine months I would have a baby. And so, in order not to be married at thirteen and become a father at fourteen, I made sure I didn't knock on any door.

When I think of it now, I laugh how naïve a boy I was.

At this juncture, the son of Reb Betzalel comes in from the kitchen with a tiny *ḥallah*, the weight of a regular slice of bread, in his hands, and I ask him if I can buy it from him. For NIS 100, he tells me, he would be willing to part with his *ḥallah*. I give him the money, and he gives me the *ḥallah*, the most expensive *ḥallah* I've ever owned.

Maybe he is naïve as I was about knocking on a door, but he is sure on his way to becoming a very successful businessman.

Will Ḥaredi rabbis ever allow their students to study Ezekiel? Most likely, no. The Ḥaredim, as per their teachings, paint a picture of Heaven where the righteous, often very old rabbis, sit in the Garden of Eden, meaning Heaven, next to The Name, studying the Torah and saying Psalms in His honor. This is not exactly the depiction of Ezekiel. The Court of The Name in Heaven, as depicted in Ezekiel, is full of power, might, and fire, a place resembling an air force base or a submarine platoon, not a yeshiva or a shul, while most Ḥaredi rabbis order their students to avoid serving in the Israeli army at all costs. The Name, they tell them, loves pages, not fire displays, only the Bible has totally different ideas.

Well, it's not up to me to teach these people what to believe in and how to lead their lives. They say that God loves pages, let me join them in a study of the pages.

Yes, that's my next step.

The Belzer Rebbe Is in My Belly

When angels and dead Rebbes unite for the last meal of the Sabbath

Have you ever been to Belz, one of the biggest Ḥasidic courts in Israel?

In Jerusalem, I hear, they have a big center.

I love big, so I go to the Belzers.

What a place these people have! A palace! The king of Jordan would love to have a palace like this.

This Palace of Belz is next to the Rebbe's private residence, a kingly place on its own, a house that will suit any sultan in history.

The main sanctuary, which seems to be a humongous place, is closed when I arrive, but various study and prayer halls are open. I enter the study hall that seems to be the biggest of them, where I see people sitting on benches with open books on their tables.

Some study, some chat, some yawn, and some go quickly over texts without seemingly understanding what they read, all for the purpose of creating more white angels with six wings each.

I sit down, ready to study a page or two.

I open the Book of Deuteronomy, which happens to be on my table.

Here goes:

> When men strive together one with another, and the wife of the one draws near to deliver her husband out of the hand of him that smites him, and puts forth her hand, and takes him by the secrets; then you shall cut off her hand, your eye shall not pity her.

"By the secrets," in case you didn't get it, means by the balls.

And for this, she gets a huge punishment. Does it make sense? I mean, cutting off the hand of the woman just because she wanted to save her husband sounds a little bizarre, doesn't it? Rashi, the leading commentator of both the Bible and the Talmud, explains that cutting off the hand in this case means a monetary fine, if monetary damage can be proven. How do we know that this "cut off her hand" means money and not actually cutting off the woman's hand? According to Rashi, we know this from the wording the Bible is using, namely, "shall not pity." In an earlier text, the words "shall not pity" are also used, Rashi explains, and there it says that it's about monetary matters. Since the earlier "shall not pity" meant monetary, it means monetary here as well.

This kind of Talmudic logic brings me back many years, to my yeshiva years, when I spent an average of ten hours a day studying Talmud.

I chat with some Belzers, and one of them tells me that I should come over on the Sabbath to the main sanctuary, to participate in the Rebbe's *tish* at the Third Meal, right before sunset. It's incredible, he says.

I like incredible, and when Sabbath afternoon arrives, I decide to revisit Belz, to celebrate the last meal of the Sabbath, the one preceding Melaveh Malkah, and one that I have neglected to celebrate thus far.

And so, I go to the Belz Palace, on the way passing by the Palace of the Ger Ḥasidic court, which is even bigger. Can you imagine?

I should go there one day, but not today. Today I am going to Belz.

As I make my way to the Belz Palace, a Ḥasid stops me. "Are you looking for Rabbi Shaul's shul?" he asks. Why is he asking me this question? I have no clue.

Who is Rabbi Shaul? I ask him.

"You don't know? He is the leader of a Ger splitter group. What, you really don't know?"

No, I don't.

"Ger split a while ago, and Rabbi Shaul and his followers daven [pray] right there," he says, pointing at a girls' school.

I'll go there one day, I tell him.

"You should look into this whole issue," he tells me.

I don't know what he's talking about, but I'll go there to find out. Though not today.

Today is Belz. No Rabbi Shaul, no Takunnes, and no Ger.

I enter the Belz Palace's main sanctuary and make my way downstairs, where I see a vast hall with thousands of Ḥasidim, one breathing down the neck of the other.

It's a marvel for the eye, an ocean of humanity.

I'm told the Third Meal of Sabbath will be celebrated in a *tish* format, whatever that means. About twenty-five hundred Ḥasidim are present at the *tish*, which is a number I'm given by one of the Ḥasidim, and all are ready to sing and eat with the Rebbe. The thousands are wearing black *bekishe*s and *shtreimel*s, their eyes focused on one old man, the Rebbe, and for some reason, it all looks to me like a perfect setting for a multi-million-dollar Disney movie.

The meal starts.

This is no movie. This is real.

The Rebbe, sitting at the head of a BIG table covered in a white tablecloth and surrounded by the thousands of men, mostly on bleachers as high as the ceiling, mumbles something over the *ḥal-lah*s, each *ḥallah* about a meter long, but I can hardly hear any sound. The Ḥasidim, miraculously, know exactly what he has just mumbled, and answer *amen* in unison. It's a wonder to behold.

The Rebbe cuts a *ḥallah* with a very impressive long knife, a sword perhaps, and various Ḥasidim, their shoes off, get on the table, take huge slices of *ḥallah*, and deliver them to the Ḥasidim. It's a massive operation, but they do it well. More and more *ḥallahs* are brought to the tables, and more and more slices are being distributed. Then a big plate with compote is brought in, and the Rebbe takes a spoon or two of it into his mouth. The leftovers, known as *shirayim*, are distributed around to the people sitting next to him. Next big plates, of a size I've never seen before, each filled with countless gefilte fish slices, are brought in. The Rebbe takes a bite from one slice, and the rest of the gefilte fishes become *shirayim*. Little bites from the slices are snatched by as many Ḥasidim as possible, and once the little bites enter their mouths, they become extremely happy.

Shirayim means leftovers, but here it means something much more. The Rebbe is a holy man, and if he eats from a plate, the food on the plate turns holy. This means that if I eat from it, even the smallest of bites, holiness from the Rebbe's body will enter my body. Bingo.

This is what I'm told.

I swallow a bite from the gefilte fish. Great! From this moment on, how wonderful, I am a holy man. The Ḥasidim, now holy people as well, and I immediately connect in the umbilical cord of our souls. Together we sing Sabbath songs as thousands of white angels above and hundreds of dead Rebbes below the earth join us in this sound of music. No Disney can create this scene. No way, Jose.

The meal goes on and on, songs and melodies aplenty, the dead and the angels keep on dancing, and when it's over, once the Sabbath ends, I go back to my hotel, light up a cigarette, sip from a cup of boiling Turkish coffee, and it dawns on me what has just happened. From this day on, I realize as I stare at the smoke rings coming out of my mouth, the Belzer Rebbe, I swear, is in my belly via a gefilte fish.

Can anyone ask for more?

Well, the question is this: What happens if the Rebbe dies, God save us?

God Is Alive and Well inside a Ukrainian Grave

White angels roaming the streets of Jerusalem

As Rosh Hashanah approaches, the residents of Mea Shearim are ready, per the text in the High Holy Day prayer book, to confess all the sins, those they did and those they don't even have a clue how to do, begging The Name to forgive them, a community of thieves and adulterers, liars, and cheaters. You know the drill, don't you?

Just as the Sephardim in Or Haḥaim declared themselves sinners, on that interesting Sliḥot evening, so does everyone in Mea Shearim, especially now on the coming High Holy Days.

Who said it's easy to be a Jew? Not me.

Not everybody agrees with me, I admit. Earlier today, the eve of Rosh Hashanah, I was told by a Sephardi Jew that I should read chapter 26, verses 1 through 11 in the Fifth Book of Moses. Why? If I do so, he advised me, "The Holy One Blessed Be He will announce in Heaven: 'I have redeemed all the debts from this man and forgive him all his transgressions.'"

This is the surest, quickest way to guarantee a wonderful year ahead with all the Princesses and Princes of Mea Shearim. Can one ask for more?

Maybe not, but I still get one more thing. I get a message from David the Philanthropist that he has spoken with the people of Toldos Aharon, and the Rebbe will see me after the holidays.

That's excellent!

And before the sun sets, a siren is heard all over Mea Shearim, a sign that Rosh Hashanah is entering in a very, very short time.

Slowly, the traffic ends, and people, not cars, fill the streets.

Fashion-wise, you can tell that this day is different, since many men wear a kittel, a white robe. And for those Ḥasidim who wear *veisse socken*, white socks, it creates a fascinating white reflection, reminiscent of the white angels above.

Are they, oh God, the real white angels?

A kittel-wearing male passes near me. Why are you wearing a kittel? I ask him.

"I'm not sure," he answers.

Can you guess?

He can make up an answer, he says.

Okay, go ahead, I tell him.

"On Rosh Hashanah, we want to look like angels, holy beings."

Not bad, not bad.

Another Ḥasid tells me: "We want to remind ourselves what's at stake on these High Holy Days. A kittel resembles the shrouds that dead people are buried in, and we pray to stay alive."

What different approaches to life!

As I stand here marveling at the white display facing me, a Breslev Ḥasid passes by and hands me a little booklet, *The General Rectification*, ascribed to Rabbi Naḥman of Breslev. The booklet contains ten chapters of Psalms, plus a special prayer for men who, may the Lord save us, spilled their seed the previous night. Spilling the seed, it says in the little booklet, creates massive and frightening damage in all the worlds. In the prayer, the text reads: "I'm tired of being alive, because, oh Lord, I spilled my seed last night."

In case you did not spill your seed last night, the General Rectification is also effective in cleansing your body and soul of other sins as well. Ibuprofen for the soul, in short.

The booklet is given free of charge to any sinner wishing to have it, if you're interested. Breslev, luckily, has a Seed Spillage account with The Name, and He pays all expenses.

The Breslev Ḥasid who gave me the booklet is here, in Israel, but thousands of Breslev Ḥasidim, followers of Rabbi Naḥman, the Rebbe who passed away over two centuries ago, are at present in Uman, Ukraine, I'm told, praying, dancing, singing, and crying at the Rebbe's grave. And a thought comes to me: it's not the end of the world when a Rebbe dies, because dead Rebbes are active in their graves as well. This means that no matter what, I'll always be connected to the Belzer Rebbe via the gefilte fish in my belly.

Hallelujah!

How come I didn't think of it before? I'm such an idiot sometimes.

In any case, another thought comes to my mind: the big Breslev shul in Mea Shearim will have many seats available for the evening prayer, something that most likely cannot be said about most other shuls in the area. Should I go there? Well, of course!

The weather is nice, a cool breeze hits my face, and I'm in Heaven. The weather changes at this time of year, it seems, and I love it. What a difference from just a few days ago, when the earth was burning under my feet, and the sun boiled my head from up in the sky.

Take a look and a listen, my dear, to what transpires here: men in kittels and women in new clothes, tons of little kids and an abundance of older people all mix as one, get busy greeting and blessing one another, and some stop to chat and exchange the latest news: Who got married? Who died? Who just had a girl, and who is next to have a *brit milah*?

The streets of Mea Shearim on the Sabbath and religious holidays, if you haven't figured it out on your own by now, function as the living rooms of the residents here, and it's heartwarming to watch.

I walk, walk, walk, and toward the end of Mea Shearim, where the Breslev building is, I see from a distance hundreds of women packing the streets. What's going on? Is a Ḥasid getting married on the street on the High Holy Day? Was the Rebbe resurrected and showed up in Jerusalem?

When I finally arrive at the scene, I see no groom around, not a single dead Rebbe resurrected. This is not a wedding and no resurrection. What is it, then? The women's section is full, comes the answer, and that's why these women are outside.

I go to the men's section. The picture there is not much better. The main sanctuary is packed, and not just packed. The people in charge of this place have built a metal structure, like a scaffolding, above the heads of the worshipers in the hall, and that's also packed. And so are the adjacent sections and the stairway. As much as I can, I push myself in until the entrance to the main sanctuary. Oh, God! Wherever the eye looks, a Ḥasid stares back at it. Aren't they supposed to be in Uman? Well, tens of thousands have flown to Uman, I'm told, and the crowd here is part of the rest, those who didn't fly.

I join in prayer.

God is not referred to as "The Name" in the prayer service but as Adoinoi (Adonai), which means Lord, or my Lord. Kind of. To be exact, Lord is Adon, and my Lord is Adoni, but the idea is practically the same. Most often, though, the word Adoinoi is not spelled Adoinoi in the prayer book, but I, H, V, H, and pronounced Adoinoi.

Adoinoi, or some variation of it, is the name of The Name.

I mean, not really. But who knows? Nobody.

When praying, Ḥaredi Jews bless God using the Adoinoi name, as in: "Blessed be You, Adoinoi," but when asked if Adoinoi is the name of God, their usual response goes something like this: "The name of The Name is very, very, very..."

Yes, that's part of the game, you might say. It's Judaism 101, and if you don't get it, you better become a goy; it's easier to understand.

Bottom line, if you insist on being Jewish: pray to The Name, to the Lord, to my Lord, to I, H, V, H, or whatever you choose, and it's all the same. Similarly, you can call me Tuvia, Buvia, Y, U, H, U, or whatever you wish, and as long as we never meet face to face and never will, it doesn't matter.

The Jews, including yours truly, keep on praying.

What am I praying for? Well, I flow with the current, and whatever they utter, I utter.

In more detail, here goes: after blessing The Name for resurrecting the dead – when the time comes, of course – they ask God to give honor to His People, happiness to His Land, and joy to His City. Translation: People is the Jews, Land is Israel, City is Jerusalem. And this is the main theme of the prayer, a trinity: Jews, Israel, Jerusalem.

Above this trinity is another trinity, the one that forms the very essence of religious Judaism: Nation of Israel, Torah of Israel, and Land of Israel. In three words: People, Knowledge, Land.

Yet no matter what their lips say in prayer, and as in most other Ḥasidic courts, their very name, Breslev, is a celebration of a place not in the Holy Land but the Jewish Diaspora: Bratslav, Ukraine.

For the thousands of Ḥasidim not here but in Uman, praying at the Rebbe's grave, their trinity is a bit different, consisting of Naḥman, Ukraine, and Uman; that's why they left Israel and flew to Ukraine, because Adoinoi is no longer in the Holy Land but inside a Ukrainian grave.

I leave the shul and stand by the women who pray outside. In my teenage years, I remember, the Breslevers were looked upon as a bunch of weirdos. They used to run around in the wee hours of the morning screaming, "*Katsti b'ḥayai*" (I'm tired of being alive).

I remember hearing their screams in the dark nights on Jerusalem hills and wondering if I should be scared of them or laugh at them. But looking at them now, at the men inside and the women outside, they don't seem to be tired of being alive at all.

Suddenly, as I'm thinking all that, there's a big movement visible from the inside of the building. Countless women are streaming down out of the building, in a scene reminiscent of the Jews' exodus from Egypt; a never-ending outpour of Breslev women, all coming in my direction. Oh, my dear, let me say this: I'm not tired of being alive!

I feel, may I add, like King Solomon.

But the holiday just started; let's see how it continues.

Open Your Faucet and All Your Sins Will Be Washed Away

What happens if you spilled your seed in the previous incarnation?

And it continues indeed. Late in the day on the morrow, I attend a holiday meal in a neighboring community, about a thirty-minute walk from Mea Shearim. I take my place at a table and quickly realize that some people sitting near me are dropouts from the Ḥaredi world. To my left is a young man who used to be part of the Belz Ḥasidic court, and the one next to him used to be part of the Satmar court. Both keep their sidelocks, but their sidelocks are smaller and thinner than the sidelocks of normal Ḥasidim. I guess that even though they have left their communities, they are incapable of making the transfer to another community. I try talking to them, but they are reluctant to speak, and when I look at them closer, I see a layer of sadness on their faces. They don't even eat much, and drink mostly water. Another dropout, at a table next to me, is talking. He shares his hope with those next to him that he will find a mate, a beauty with money in this coming year.

He can dream.

Feeling sad for these dropouts, and unable to cheer them up, I return to Mea Shearim, where the sound of the shofar is heard from every street corner. According to Jewish tradition, the shofar, made of a ram's horn, is blown in synagogues dozens of times each day of Rosh Hashanah. Since Mea Shearim has many synagogues, the blasts are constantly heard while walking the streets. What are these blows supposed to mean? Why are they done? Their purpose is to remind us to repent, a Ḥaredi man tells me. How so? The shofar, so he says, is the Voice of The Name, and the blowing of it is destined to "confuse Satan" on this Day of Awe.

Satan, if true, must be a complete idiot.

It is on this day, the Ḥasid shares what he knows with me, that the fate of every Jew is decided for better or worse; the Heavenly Court is convened to weigh the deeds of every person. And like in any other court, there are judges, prosecutors, and defenders; white angels led by our forefathers, Abraham, Isaac, and Jacob; and black angels, led by Satan, who is also an angel. It is worthy of remembering that Satan is also known by his other name, Angel of Death.

Satan, as is known all over the globe, is the one who is tempting Ḥaredi men with the beauty of Ḥaredi women, and when a man falls into Satan's net and acts on his temptation, Satan, in his other capacity as Angel of Death, approaches the tempted man and takes his soul away.

Fortunately, there's a way to get rid of one's sins and avoid Satan's sword.

How?

Tashliḥ. What's Tashliḥ? Tashliḥ is a process by which Jews throw away their sins, preferably next to an ocean, river, or other body of water. Jerusalem doesn't have an ocean, not yet, but no lack of an ocean will stop a Jew.

I go to Dushinsky, another Ḥasidic shul close to me, to see how they do the Tashliḥ. It's interesting. Countless Ḥasidim, coming from different directions, are pouring in. Some of them run as if they were trying to catch a plane, the last plane, to Mississippi. Once they arrive, they don't go into the shul but congregate next to the entrance. Why are they standing there? I ask a Ḥasid. Well, says he, they have a faucet there. When you have no ocean, a faucet will do, he explains. Brilliant. And there, next to the faucet, they cite verses from the Book of Micah:

> Who is a God like You, Who pardons iniquity and passes by the transgression of the remnant of His heritage? He retains not His anger forever, because He delights in mercy.
>
> He will again have compassion upon us; He will subdue our iniquities; and You will cast all their sins into the depths of the sea.

Is that what they ran for? Don't they have faucets at home?

Be the answer what it may, the main thing is this: the Jews, now that the Tashliḥ is over, are sinless, and their souls are as white as snow. Yet, and despite it all, Rosh Hashanah continues. Why? Rosh Hashanah, you see, lasts for two days. Why does God need an extra day, now that all of His children's sins have been washed by the faucet?

To find out what's cooking on the second day of Rosh Hashanah, I go to the Lelev shul, another of many Ḥasidic courts near me.

As I enter, a few kids walk in my direction, a stern look on their faces, and their eyes are focused on my left hand. What are they doing? Are they planning to throw me out of here? Is a riot about to develop, as I was warned before I even came to Mea Shearim?

I look at my left hand, trying to understand their problem with that hand.

Oh, Lordy Lord: It's my Apple Watch! How come I didn't think of it? Apple Watch, like any computing equipment, is forbidden on the Sabbath and religious holidays.

How to get out of this situation?

Luckily, before the situation worsens, an adult community member offers me a seat and hands me a Maḥzor, the prayer book for the holy day.

Seeing this, the tough kids give me a little smile and move on.

I open the book.

What do I see? A prayer called Tikkun Keri, repairing or rectifying the soul from the damage done by spilled seed.

Lots of men in the area, it seems, are extra busy spilling their seed. Mea Shearim, let me tell you, is packed with stallions.

I read the prayer.

In it, I find out I can ask The Name's forgiveness for "spilling my seed for naught," either through masturbation or accidentally. This request for forgiveness, I read on, is for my most recent spilling of seed, plus any spilling of seed that I have done in the past year, and also all the seed spilling I have done in previous incarnations and, in addition, for all the seed spilling that the rest of the Jews did in the last year.

Wow!

How am I going to pull this off? I hope I don't have to say this out loud.

Fortunately, the Ḥasidim around me are not German converts like Reb Dovid, and they don't pray everything printed in the prayer book. They skip this prayer altogether and, instead, ask God to return to Zion, rebuild His Temple, inscribe all of Israel in the Book of Life, and request that He rule again over the whole world.

Good.

After every few prayer lines, the Lelev Ḥasidim start singing, oy, oy, oy, and some of them begin to dance, then they go quiet, and the Shofar Blower blows the shofar, loud and clear.

They pray: "Instill fear of You upon all that You have made...," and then they burst into song, oy, oy, oh, oh, oh, ta, ta, ta. How lovely! They pray more, sing more, dance more, blow more, and this goes on and on and on. Not to be outdone, the man sitting next to me takes out a little box, a *shmek tabak*, snuff tobacco, and offers it to me. I take a little of it, put it in my nose, inhaling it, a good shot of nicotine. What a celebration!

I love it. Beats the Tikkun Keri a thousand times over.

Yet I have no clue why God needed one more day to have His Chosen Children ask Him for forgiveness when he has forgiven them the day before by the faucet.

As the prayer service is about to end, a man with a long black beard, golden caftan, and big belly who answers to the name Reb Yankev Ḥaim comes to me. He seems a little bit threatening, some kind of an extremist. And then he opens his mouth: "Do you have where to eat the holiday meal?" he asks, and informs me that, if I only want, I'm very welcome to join him at his home. I, a big belly myself, cannot for the life of me say no to a food invitation, and I accept his invite on the spot.

He lives, he tells me, on the third floor, where no elevator or escalator exists. But I should not worry, Reb Yankev says to me, because once the two Big Bellies, he and I, reach the third floor, we will be handsomely compensated by his wife's food.

Let's go!

Despite the three floors, we reach his apartment safely, and his wife, who hails from Australia and looks like a model, cheerfully greets us with a big smile.

Not that long ago, the Australian says, they used to live downstairs, but she wanted to move to the third floor so that Reb Yankev, her big belly husband, would exercise a bit: up and down the stairs.

A big table in the center of the well-lit living room, covered with a snowy white tablecloth, is richly arranged with plates, cups, drinks of all kinds, honey and herring, and everything in between.

Reb Yankev's business, from which he makes money to support the food on the table, is tent rentals; big tents, huge tents, tents for special events where thousands of people show up. As far as I can tell, based on the generous number of various dishes on the table, he has a profitable business.

You must be working quite hard, I say to him, but he doesn't see it that way.

"We don't work for a living," he tells me, speaking of humanity in general. "The money we earn comes from God, not from our work; the work is just a payment for our sins."

Professor Dan Shiftan should be here to hear this.

Reb Yankev loves the Lelever Rebbe from Tsfanya Street (there is more than one Lelever Rebbe, I'm told), and he loves to sing the Rebbe's praises: "When someone new comes to the shul, the Rebbe doesn't ask if the person prayed or studied. No, no, no. What the Rebbe asks is different: Did the person eat already? Should the person be invited to share a meal? Does this new person have a good place to sleep?"

The Australian model, I can tell, has prepared the food with love. Every bit of everything offered here is a delight: fish, meat, *ḥallahs*, sweets; you name it. Reb Yankev, who knows my soul, makes sure that I have a constant supply of ice-cold Coke Zero and keeps telling his children to put a new bottle in the freezer before I am about to finish the old bottle. Coca Cola Inc. and I greatly appreciate the efforts and are extremely thankful.

With my belly full and my heart happy, I finally understand why The Name wanted to have one more Rosh Hashanah day: to make sure we eat well.

Life's good.

Sadly, life's not good for everybody. Some people are poor and can hardly afford great food like I had.

But they should not worry.

Reb Yankev Ḥaim, as I find out a couple of days later, is here to take care of them.

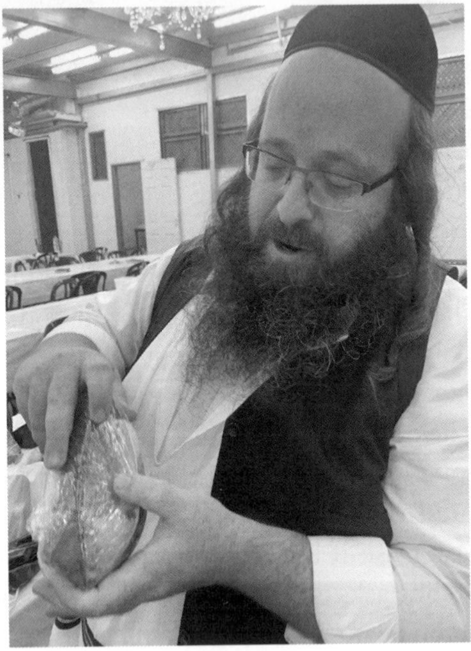

Walking past the Lelev shul, I see Reb Yankev Ḥaim. He has just spent, he tells me, NIS 90,000 buying fish, meat, chicken, candies, cookies, and whatever else he could think of, to be distributed among eighty low-income families, his gift to the needy of his community. Row after row of boxes are all over the place, and young boys walk between the rows with big plastic bags in their hands, filling the bags with one item from every box. Once packed with goodies, these plastic bags are given to different messengers for distribution among the eighty families. To protect the names of the families, this operation is done discretely, and only the messengers know where to drop the bags.

It's an amazing operation, done with a tender love that can bring tears to your eyes, tears of joy that people like this Reb Yankev Ḥaim exist in our world. If you ask me, he should be a Rebbe. Sadly, most likely, he won't. Becoming a Rebbe, just like in many a kingdom of the goyim, is hereditary. As long as a Rebbe has children, nobody outside the family can inherit the throne. And this Rebbe has. In fact, the Rebbe's son is becoming a bar mitzvah next week, thirteen years of age, which means that as of this age, he is a full-fledged "man" and is obligated to observe all the mitzvahs of the Torah. The Rebbe will throw a bar mitzvah party for his son next week and a special bar mitzvah Kiddush on the Sabbath preceding the bar mitzvah, and I'm invited for both events.

Can I say no? No way!

God Speaks Yiddish

A Rebbe agrees to sit down for an interview

It is Friday evening, and I go to Kikar Hashabbat, Sabbath Square, and stand there. The street is full of cars, coming from all directions, but slowly, most of the cars disappear; the ones still moving are taxis driven by Arabs. What Jews do these Arabs drive? The J-Procrastinators, Jews who are in the habit of pushing everything to the last minute.

A few more minutes pass, and the number of taxis is reduced, and those that are still around drive fast, for they don't want to get stuck in a Ḥaredi neighborhood, not able to move once Sabbath enters, in just a few minutes. And then, on Mea Shearim Street, a tall Ḥasid appears, carrying three cartons that generally serve as covers of big boxes, and he drops them on the road. He moves a few steps forward, pushes metal barriers that stand by the sidewalks to the middle of the street, blocking the road for any car wishing to pass. He returns to where he dropped the cartons, stands there like he owns the street, and yells "Shabbes!" as two lone taxis pass by on an adjacent street. A couple of minutes pass, and the traffic lights go off. The Sabbath has entered.

On Sabbath morning, I go to the Lelev shul, arriving precisely when the Torah's weekly portion is read. It's here that I hear God threatening the Jews with awful consequences if they don't keep His commandments. We will be finished, in short. I ask myself: Is God, The Name, really so vengeful that He will kill us all if we do not continuously obey Him?

I'm the only one asking this question, as far as I can tell. The people around me don't bother with any of this at all. They hear the same text, but their connection to The Name is very different from mine. Their God is a Yiddish-speaking God, with whom they connect via the Rebbe. And the Rebbe, as I've already learned, cares more about how much food they have than anything else.

Following the Torah reading, the Lelevers pray to The Name, and I listen. It's the same prayer that the Ḥasidim of Shoimrei Emunim prayed when I was there, and like them, these Ḥasidim have a hell of a time with these same lines.

> Crowds of angels above,
> With Your nation, Israel, below,
> Will crown You, Lord our God,
> Thrice sanctify You together,
> As told by Your prophets:
> And they call one unto the other, saying: Holy, Holy, Holy...

They utter these words loudly, joyfully, and they get into a trance. *Holy, Holy, Holy*, they shout, and they have the time of their lives. Why are these words making them so happy? I have no idea.

They don't ask: How do the angels look? They couldn't care less. Let Ezekiel bother about that, not them in this shul. As far as they are concerned, if I understand correctly, the angels have *shtreimels*, and they fly.

Does anyone need to know more?

They have other things to think about. The son of the Rebbe is becoming bar mitzvah on Sunday, and the Rebbe is giving a Kiddush today, immediately after prayer: herring and kugels, delicacies that none of the angels above have.

I look at the Rebbe's son, the new man, and he behaves in a kingly way. His head is held high, and he looks at the rest of the people as if they were below him. He doesn't laugh; he doesn't talk to anyone but walks around like the king of the castle.

Following the Kiddush, I take a few minutes to sit down with the Rebbe and schmooze with him on this and that, and I ask him if he would be willing to sit down with me for an interview.

"Yes," he says and suggests we meet after Yom Kippur.

That's great. I'd love to sit down with this Rebbe, one on one, and have him tell me what being a Rebbe is.

As I depart, I say to him: Your Ḥasidim love you very deeply.

"I love them too," he replies.

By Sabbath's end, the season's first rain falls following the rainless summer months in Israel. It's only a drizzle, yes, but rain, nevertheless. Mea Shearim, the One Hundred Gates, is getting wet, yet the people, as usual, assemble outside to talk, to chat, to schmooze, to discuss. Last I check, they are still out at three o'clock in the morning. The light in the living room of the streets is still on.

I go to sleep, and on the next day in the evening, I go to the bar mitzvah of the son of the Lelever Rebbe. The Ḥasidim, for whom the bar mitzvah celebration is a holiday, wear their Sabbath and holiday clothes, *shtreimel* and caftan, in honor of the event. The shul, the home of the Ḥasidim, is packed. In one section of the shul, the little children stand; in another, the singles; in yet another section are the married men with the *shtreimels*. The Rebbe and his son, with the elders of the community, sit on an elevated platform, presiding over us all, and in the back is the orchestra, made of one singer, who will get us all to sing for the duration of the evening.

The Ḥasidim come here to eat, drink, sing, and celebrate with the Rebbe and his son, the Prince of Lelev. There is gefilte fish and all kinds of fish aplenty, plus chicken and lokshen kugel, because food, after all, is the engine of life, and this Rebbe likes his Ḥasidim fed.

The Ḥasidim, happy as if this evening were their private wedding party, move their bodies right and left, jump in place in unison, and go wild. Everybody knows everybody else, and it seems as if all of them are one family. At a certain point in the evening, while singing and shaking with them, I feel as if I've gone into someone's bedroom, staring at their most private of private spaces. It feels good, by the way.

And as the evening progresses, various Rebbes, such as the Dushinsky and the Karliner, show up. They sit next to the Rebbe and his son for a short while to show their solidarity with the Rebbe and his Ḥasidim and then move on to make room for other Rebbes.

The various Ḥasidic courts of Mea Shearim, it occurs to me, might not always intermarry, but since most of them speak Yiddish, dress similarly, and are chased by the same Satan, they form one umbrella tribe, a world unto its own, a world of *shtreimel*s and "Arab" caftans, of *tiḥel*s and *kvittel*s and kittels, Coke Zero and Pepsi Max, loudspeakers announcing funerals, and a world where white and black angels are created faster than the speed of light.

I had a bar mitzvah too. It took place in Bnei Brak, at the Vagshal Hotel. Many rabbis came – some of them were the most important in the land at that time – and my rabbi predicted that when I grew up, I would be the biggest rabbi in Israel. It didn't happen, not yet. You never know, it might happen one day.

Later this week, a bird whispers in my ear, the various Ḥasidic groups of Mea Shearim will jointly welcome new residents to the area: chickens.

Yes, you heard that right. The chickens are coming!

What's Mightier, a Mea Shearim Rooster or an Iranian Atomic Bomb?

Nothing beats drinking wine while staring at a photo of an old Litvak

If you give a donation to an organization called Vaad Harabbonim, the Board of Rabbis, you will have a good year ahead, I read on a big poster hanging near Sabbath Square, signed by Rabbi Ḥaim Kanievsky. I was under the impression that God decided life and death issues, but perhaps I was wrong. If this poster is correct, the one deciding these issues is Ḥaim Kanievsky, not God. Unless, of course, the real name of The Name is Ḥaim Kanievsky.

Funnily, someone presents me with a bottle of wine, called Wine of Salvation, that has the photo of Rabbi Ḥaim Kanievsky on it. He who drinks from this wine, as you probably guessed on your own, will find salvation.

Rabbi Kanievsky is a Litvak, not a Ḥasid, and I wonder why the people here, mostly Ḥasidim, believe in him.

Go figure.

A few steps away is a huge truck carrying thousands of live chickens, and it slowly makes its way toward me. Traffic immediately stops when the truck tries to maneuver into a parking spot, and drivers of passing cars blow their horns, creating sounds that could split the heavens into pieces. As far as I can tell, the chickens have no clue why they were brought in the thousands to a place where a male is not supposed to look at a female, while their males like to parade naked on the truck, not to mention look at every naked female chicken. What did these chickens do before they came here that there are so many of them on this huge truck?

We are in the Mea Shearim world, and in this world, no truck, not to mention a huge truck, comes for a visit for no reason.

So, what are the chickens doing here?

These chickens, lo and behold, will save the residents of this area from annihilation. Yes. These chickens have more power than an atomic weapon.

Everybody in this country has heard from many Israeli leaders, year after year after year, of the horrifying possibility that one day, sooner or later, Iran will bombard this little country with atomic weapons, and the Jews living in it will evaporate from the face of the earth in minutes.

No, this is not going to happen.

Why?

Chickens.

The Persians may try to shoot a gazillion nuclear missiles into Israel, but none will land in the homes of this Yiddish-speaking society, because the slow-walking little chickens on the truck will stop the fastest, largest, and mightiest missiles from infiltrating the community.

How so?

That's where the Kapparot (Atonements) come into play. What is Kapparot? Well, people die because they have committed sins, thereby creating too many black angels, but if people can come up with a formula to get rid of the bad angels, they will stay alive. One way of getting rid of those angels is, as mentioned, making Tashliḥ by the faucets of Dushinsky. But not everybody knows where the faucets are, and that's how the chickens come into the picture. It is possible, tradition says, to transfer one's sins onto a chicken, kill the chicken, and thereby transfer one's death sentence decreed by Heaven onto the chicken. Simply said: If you spilled your seed, say hello to the chicken.

That's why we have the chickens here between Rosh Hashanah and Yom Kippur when one's fate is written and signed. All you have to do is buy a chicken for NIS 45, hold the chicken in your hand, swing it above your head, and say this text three times: "This is my exchange, this is my substitute, this is my atonement. This chicken shall go to death, and I shall have a good, long life and peace."

This is precisely what the people here are doing, and I'm watching them, partly in disbelief and partly in awe.

The males do the Kapparot with a rooster, the females with a hen. I have no idea, sorry, what transgender people are supposed to choose, a rooster or a hen, but perhaps they can get a transgender chicken somewhere, maybe in California.

Once the Kapparot are done, people go home with their chicken, which they will bring to the butcher later on; once it is ready to be cooked or grilled, they will give it to the poor or eat it themselves.

Some prefer to have their chicken slaughtered on the spot, a wish they can materialize for an additional NIS 35.

A non-Ḥaredi walks by, and he's shocked at the inhumane treatment, so he says, of chickens by the Ḥaredim. He can't grasp that all these thousands of chickens will be slaughtered. Is he a vegetarian or a vegan? No. He eats chicken, he says, but how can any human being even dream of slaughtering such a friendly creature?

Yeah.

Most religious Jews, however, do their Kapparot with money, not chicken, and instead of saying, "This chicken will go to death," they say, "This money will go to the poor."

In Mea Shearim, many families prefer the chicken, because the children love it.

I watch dozens of these children as they watch the chickens. They look at the chickens from this angle, from the other angle, from the top, and from the bottom. They want to know how chickens are made and whether they are Jewish or Arab.

Of course, if you're an adult who doesn't like chicken, or if you're allergic to chicken, and you have missed the Tashliḥ, you always have one more option: drink the Wine of Salvation. And if you can't get your hands on this bottle, there's one more chance for you: pray good on Yom Kippur. Yom Kippur is coming, my friend. Get ready!

Beware: Don't Snap a Photo of the Taliban Ladies

Got coronavirus? Come to shul!

A news item flashes on my iPhone: Riots erupt in Mea Shearim as the police try to enforce a demolition order issued by the Jerusalem municipality against a large sukkah built illegally. Cops are clashing with rioting Ḥaredim, I read on.

I rush to the address given in the news item. Finally, I have some riots to watch!

Once I arrive at the location, I see not even a shadow of a cop, only a bunch of young onlookers who have come here to see a free show; they must have read the same news item I did. The police were here before, a young Ḥasid tells me, but once they were presented with papers verifying that the construction of the large sukkah met safety standards, they left.

I stick around, walking here and there.

Something looks weird, I suddenly notice. The graffiti that proclaimed the Zionists are not Jews, the Palestinian flags, and the "We demand: Death to the Zionists" has been painted over with white paint.

Almost all the offensive graffiti I saw not long ago was black over white, and I wondered what was under the white. Now I get it: there must be a group, or a person, who spray-paints hate messages all over and another group, or person, who paints over them.

I keep walking, noticing more white paint over hate graffiti, street after street.

I ask people to explain this to me, and I get different answers. Some say that there are two groups, each made of two fifteen-year-old kids, who have nothing better to do than painting the neighborhood walls. Others say that "crazy Neturei Karte men," who get money from Satmar Ḥasidim in New York, spray-paint the hate messages and that the municipality paints them over. Who is right? I don't know. But both say that this cat and mouse game has been going on for years, and nobody is paying any attention to the graffiti and the paint. It would be nice, I say to myself, if somebody painted chickens on the walls.

As I continue to walk, it dawns on me that the faces of the people on the street are becoming familiar to me, and my face is becoming familiar to them. "Have a good year," some say as I pass by them. "Good to see you, Tuvia," others say. And there are also those who approach me with: "When are you going to come to our shul again?"

They are welcoming me, I feel, in their big living room: the streets.

Tomorrow evening is Yom Kippur, when the people of this community will go to shuls and beg their Father in Heaven, The Name, to sign them in the Book of Life; to have enough food on their tables in the year ahead; that the singles will get married;

that the barren women will get pregnant; that the sick will heal; that the Messiah will come; that the Temple will be rebuilt; that all the Jews of the world will move to Israel; and that, finally, they will see their grandparents again once they rise from the dead.

But now, on the evening before Yom Kippur, the shops in Mea Shearim are open, and thousands of people are shopping. They buy everything: food, plastic plates, decorations for the sukkah, books, snuff tobacco (I buy one too!), and new clothes. Here, in a store I'm passing by right now, whose windows are covered, I take a little peek and see Ḥaredi women buying festive gowns and some of them, Taliban ladies, buying new burqas. What are they thinking, these Taliban? I ask myself. Why would anyone need a new burqa? Can one tell the difference between one burqa and the other? Are they trying to be more tempting to the men? I keep on walking. A group of burqa and hijab ladies passes by me, and I snap a photo of them. "Erase the picture!" one lady yells at me. Yeah, yeah. She is afraid, I guess, that I will advertise her photo, a mountain of black, on a porno site.

And here's something nice. One of the stores is playing an adorable song in Yiddish, "Der Rebbe Iz Do" (The Rebbe Is Here), which goes like this (translated into English): "The Rebbe is here, the Rebbe is here, the Rebbe is here. At every gathering of Ḥasidim, the Rebbe is here. At every gathering of Ḥasidim, the Rebbe is here. At every gathering of Ḥasidim, the Rebbe is here. When the student says that the Rebbe is here, then the Rebbe is here. When the student says that the Rebbe is here, then the Rebbe is here. When the student says that the Rebbe is here, then the Rebbe is here. The Rebbe is here, the Rebbe is here, the Rebbe is here."

What brilliant lyrics!

At midday tomorrow, I hear, the Slonimer Rebbe will be having a *tish*. I have been to Slonim before and was impressed with their melodies. I make up my mind to go to Slonim.

I try to convince a Slonim Ḥasid to stand next to me in case I need some explanations. He's an older man, friendly and warm, and he says to me: "I have no problem sitting with you at your home or your hotel and chatting with you for as long as you like. But if you come to Slonim and approach me, I will ignore you. We don't like foreigners in Slonim."

By midday of the morrow, I go. My two feet and two eyes are good enough for company.

Oh, Slonim! The last time I was in Slonim, they had a *tish* in the basement. Today, they're doing the *tish* on an upper floor, a much bigger hall, because there are many more Ḥasidim around this time, many of them in the back, standing. Two thousand, three thousand, The Name knows how many. Imagine Carnegie Hall packed with sardines. And this mass of human flesh is ready to shoot prayers faster than Iranian missiles.

At the moment, they are not singing, because the Rebbe is speaking. What does he say? Allah knows. He speaks in a low voice, with no loudspeaker connected, and the thousands are "listening" to him. What is this? A Ḥasid approaches me, telling me that he can find me a seat. When a guest comes to be with us, he says, we should honor him.

Are you sure that you are a Slonimer Ḥasid? I ask him, wondering that he even approached me.

"If I were a Slonimer," he answers, with a big smile on his face, "I wouldn't welcome you. Slonimer Ḥasidim are elitists who think everybody else is below them. I used to be a Slonimer Ḥasid, but I am no longer."

That's life.

The Rebbe talks.

He talks, talks, talks, talks, talks, but I can't hear a single word. Elitists like to speak, I guess, even if nobody can hear them. As for the Ḥasidim, they don't seem to mind. Perhaps the wind that comes from the Rebbe's mouth as he talks has the same effect as the *shirayim* of the Belzer Rebbe or any other Rebbe, and holiness passes from his mouth to them.

Some people in the crowd wear masks on their faces. Why are they wearing masks? I ask the ex-Slonimer.

"They have coronavirus," he answers.

They really shouldn't be here, the Ḥasidim and I know, since the coronavirus is highly contagious, but who am I to say? They are Slonimers; I'm not.

After a long while, a Ḥasid finds it worthy of putting on a loudspeaker, and the voice of the Rebbe is finally heard. Well, almost. The sound is very low, but at least Heaven can comprehend what he says, and more white angels will be created by him to protect him on Yom Kippur.

After a while, thanks be to the Holy One Blessed Be He, the Rebbe stops talking, and the singing starts. This time they sing lyrics, words, not just oy, oy, oy. What are they singing? Well, here goes: "Our sins are countless, the level of the crimes we have committed reaches the sky."

When they sing these words, as you probably have already guessed on your own, they are not crying or weeping, The Name forbid; they just sing, happily, as if they were praising themselves about how great and how gorgeous they are.

Some of the songs are in Yiddish. For example (in translation):

> A Yiddene [a Jewish woman] came to the *tatte* [father], of blessed memory, and she was crying very hard. The father, of blessed memory, asked the woman, "Why are you crying?" She answered, "Because I have headaches." The father, of blessed memory, said to her, "When a person is crying, the headaches are getting more painful." To which she replied, "How can I not cry when my only child will face a court hearing tomorrow, and who knows if he will win the case?"

This refers to Yom Kippur, which starts tomorrow, meaning this evening, if I have it right.

When the Slonimers are done, I go to the *tish* of the Rebbe of Toldos Avrom Yitzḥok.

I like these folks.

When I enter, I see the Rebbe eating gefilte fish. Bon appétit.

I would love to be a Rebbe! Imagine me eating gefilte fish, and thousands of people can't wait to lick from the same fish that my tongue touched.

Outside, on Mea Shearim Street, I meet a taxi driver and he asks me if I would like to meet the "most extreme anti-Zionist," the rabbi of Toireh v'Yireh. "I'm his driver," he tells me, "and I know him. He's a real fanatic, but he's sweeter than honey."

The driver is a secular Jew and a Zionist. But who cares?

The clock, my dear, is ticking. Yom Kippur is about to start. Are you ready?

When Lilith Meets Palestine

Will I have a Mea Shearim baby of my own?

As Yom Kippur, that holiest of days on the Jewish calendar, is about to enter, I go to the Lelever shul for Yom Kippur's first service, Kol Nidrei. A little kid, looking at the way I'm dressed, head missing a *shtreimel* and body missing a kittel, approaches me. "Why are you here?" he asks.

What are you planning to do on Yom Kippur? I ask him in Yiddish.

"Pray," he answers.

I plan to pray, too, I say to him. He smiles, greeting me heartily. Another kid, who remembers me from my earlier visit, approaches me and starts singing next to me, inviting me for a dance.

These kids of Mea Shearim, who sometimes look like tough kids, are awesomely sweet.

What does Lelev mean? What's the origin of this name? I ask a Ḥasid standing with an open book next to me.

"It's a place in Poland, Lelów," he answers.

How big is that place?

"It's a little village. It has three main streets and five regular streets. That's it."

How they get from that little place several Lelev Rebbes is anyone's guess.

I take a seat, waiting for the service to start. Various people, meanwhile, come over to wish me a good and prosperous year ahead. What a difference between them and Slonim!

The Lelever Rebbe, sitting on a nice chair, doesn't talk, at least not now; he's just sitting. At times he stands up, then sits again, and he's praying. His presence is felt everywhere, because the Ḥasidim keep looking at him.

The service, I'm told, won't start before the Rebbe tells them to start. For the time being, they sit, doing nothing special. Some read books, others chat, and some go out to enjoy the cool air of Jerusalem, celebrating the end of the hot days.

There are some Lelevers who, at this juncture of inaction, mumble lines from the *Zohar*, the mystical book that they believe was written by a holy Sage about two thousand years ago, though most likely it was written by a Spanish Jewish maverick about seven hundred years ago, as already alluded to on these pages. But nobody here, as far as I can tell, will agree. How could a Sephardi Jew, after all, write such a brilliant book?

I check what they're reading. The *Zohar* text speaks of the Shḥinah, which is supposedly the feminine side of God, and Lilith, believed to be the sexual partner of the Angel of Death. I'm not sure what this all means: Does it mean that The Name has a wife, or that He's transgender, God forbid? Does it mean that the Angel of Death, Satan, spends his time playing love games while killing people? To the people here, I think, none of this matters. It's a text that they have been told is holy, and that's good enough for them. The only issue that matters is this: The Name, they pray, will make sure that the Angel of Death doesn't reach their doors throughout the year. Lilith, shmilith, who cares. If getting Satan out of their lives requires uttering a few meaningless sentences, so be it. Do climate change activists understand the nitty-gritty details of climate, any climate? Do all those human rights activists of the secular West who are fervent supporters of the Palestinians even know where their beloved Palestine is on the map?

Climate shmaimate, Lilith shmilith, Palestine shmalestine. Same thing.

Time moves, and when Lilith falls asleep in Heaven, the Rebbe motions to his Ḥasidim that they can start the prayer service, and they do.

After the traditional annulment ritual of personal oaths, the prayer following it gets heavy. In it, like many other Ḥaredi Jews that I have seen before, worshippers are proclaiming themselves before The Name in the worst of terms, accusing themselves of the worst crimes. Some of the crimes they are confessing include prostitution and incest, crimes they have been confessing, year after year, since the day they knew how to hold a prayer book. They, including the little children, recite this text because it's written that they have to recite it, and being that they are Ḥasidim, they add a little melody while they recite it. It's funny to watch. The Litvaks, as I remember from my youthful days, take this text very differently. They say the words aloud, in complete seriousness, and when you hear them declaring themselves prostitutes, you believe them, and the only question you have is this: Who would pay for such screaming prostitutes?

Reb Yankev Ḥaim watches it all from the back, me included, and he's happy. Happy that the Rebbe is healthy, happy that the community exists, that the family functions well, and happy that I pray.

May we all be inscribed in the Book of Good Life, I say to Reb Yankev Ḥaim and many other Ḥasidim as I leave the shul at the end of the service, and they wish me the same.

"You never know what the future holds for you," a Lelever lady tells me outside the shul. "It's all in God's hands, and I bless you that by next year at this time, you'll have a baby of your own, that by next year you will be walking these streets with a baby carriage."

Come to think of it, I wouldn't mind having a little Mea Shearim kid, tough and sweet, as a son.

The streets are quiet, and very few people are present. This is a day of prayer, introspection, and a day of standing before the King, The Name, confessing that they all are sex offenders, cheaters, sinners, thieves, and pretty much brainless. This is not the day of parading on the streets with your most precious clothes showing everybody how beautiful, handsome, and sexy you are. Nope. This is not the day for that. Wait a day or two, and then you can parade again. Not today. Today, nobody is eating. Today, there's no gefilte fish, no kugel, and no cola of any kind. Today is a fast day, a prayer day, and a saying "I'm so bad" day.

Yom Kippur prayers end with the prayer known as Ne'ilah, closing, in which religious Jews ask God to erase death from the face of the earth. Ne'ilah, which many consider to be the most important of prayers, is the prayer before closing, meaning before the Gates of Heaven close, before the Heavenly Court retires – the last chance to make sure that we will stay alive and healthy, in this year.

And for this prayer service, I choose to go to the Ger center in Jerusalem and join the Gerer Ḥasidim in prayer.

The Palace of Ger at the Bottom of Hell

Turn off the lights, put on your clothes, and have fun in your bed

The Ḥasidic Court of Ger, established well over a century ago in the Polish city of Góra Kalwaria, is known as one of the stricter Ḥasidic courts and is reportedly the largest Ḥasidic court in Israel. Their center in Jerusalem, on Yirmiyahu Street, led by the Rebbe Yaakov Aryeh Alter, my strange neighbor when I was a kid, can hold thousands upon thousands of Ḥasidim under one roof. Architecturally, at least from the outside, the center looks like a mighty palace, evidence of the vast financial resources this Ḥasidic court has. Reportedly, and as David the Philanthropist showed me in that book of his about the Takunnes, Ger couples are not allowed to have sex more than once a month, can't call their wives by name, have to be dressed when they do have sex, can't do this and can't do that, but they are allowed to pray, and I go to pray with them.

There's no way I can even estimate how many people are present at this Ger Palace, but a person I met on the street told me that twelve thousand men were attending services in the shul. How many women? I don't know. All I can see in front of me is males.

The hall of prayer is a combination of two halls – one is the old one, and the other is the new one. There's a partial wall in between them, and I can't see all the worshippers, but it seems that what I see in front of me is just half of the worshippers. Amazing!

As I'm standing in the shul, looking at the huge mass of people, a middle-aged Ḥasid, who looks like a bully, comes my way and, speaking in English, loudly demands to know: "What are you looking for?" This is the worst welcome I have received in any shul or community thus far. Ḥasidim next to him hear this but say not a word; they just look at me, the foreigner on their turf.

I have to take action before this bully orders me out. I answer him in Yiddish: You are a Jew, I'm a Jew too, and together we will pray.

Hearing me speak Yiddish, which like many other Ger Ḥasidim he doesn't speak, though he might understand, his bully nature softens, and he asks: "Do you need anything?"

No, I say. From you, I need not a thing.

He walks away, defeated.

The service goes on.

The worshippers pray and sing. Like other places I've visited, there is no connection between the horrible words of self-incrimination uttered and the melodies sung. Still, nobody is paying attention to this dichotomy other than me.

Following the self-incrimination and songs, they say this:

> I remembered, God, and I groan,
> When I see every city standing tall,
> And the City of God at the bottom of Sheol.

Are they for real? Have they not seen this gorgeous building they are in at this very moment, this Ger Palace, or are they blind?

And, just to understand them better, does the capital of Pakistan look better than Jerusalem? Or, for that matter, does Washington, DC, look better than Jerusalem?

In their defense, and being that they are keepers of the Takunnes, humans who are rarely allowed to engage in the pleasures of the flesh with their spouses, and of course forbidden from spilling their seed at any point in life, they might indeed feel like they're at the bottom of Sheol.

That said, the singing is terrific. And since the cantor can hardly be heard, as no loudspeakers are allowed on Yom Kippur, different sections in the audience sing at slightly different times, and the sound emanating from one section vibrates into the other section, and vice versa, resulting in sound effects that feel like magic.

But every good thing, as is known, comes to an end, and when the prayer service is done, Yom Kippur is over. Gone. Done.

When this happens, everybody sings, "Next year in Jerusalem," as if we were in Singapore right now.

We are in Jerusalem, and this little song was obviously written when Jews lived as far away from here as possible. Yet this is a tradition, and nobody is fighting tradition. It's a tradition that says that man is not allowed to look at women, it's a tradition that says that converts and their children can marry only the sick and the retarded, it's a tradition that says that eating gefilte fish touched by a Rebbe's tongue is holier than Mecca, it's a tradition that says that the dead will rise, it's a tradition that says that a prehistoric donkey is still alive and kicking, and it's a tradition that says that Jerusalem is ruined to the ground, all in ashes.

Yes, I know. Ḥaredi Jews, their brains sharpened by the Talmud, will argue that "Next year in Jerusalem" means in the "rebuilt" Jerusalem, the "real" Jerusalem, the Jerusalem that will be built only after ten million eagles, carrying all Diaspora Jews, have landed in the Holy Land, and the white donkey has entered the city gates. And at that time exactly, as everybody knows, the climate will be perfect, all cars will be electric, half of humanity will live on the moon, there will be no border between nations on either earth or moon, except for Palestine, and most people will be transhuman, no more just transgender, and they will choose to be cats.

Hopefully, may I add, now that Yom Kippur is over, all Ḥaredi Jews will have an excellent year ahead.

Not precisely, sadly.

Just a couple of hours from the passing of Yom Kippur, a car drives in Mea Shearim, a loudspeaker over its roof, announcing the death of a righteous Ḥasid and asking people to join in the funeral this evening, now.

Soon, when the next Sabbath comes, the Ḥasidim of Mea Shearim will go to their shuls to hear Moses's last words before he, too, dies; that's the Torah's weekly portion for the coming Sabbath.

Luckily for them, no Ḥasid in Mea Shearim, so far as I can see, occupies his time thinking about such things. The engine that drives my neighbors is happiness, music, Rebbes, and kugels. And with such good food on the table as they have, is there any time left to ponder sad questions? Definitely not. So, let's celebrate and sing. The biblical holiday of Sukkot, the Feast of Tabernacles, is soon upon us, in four days. Celebration is in the air; it's time to be happy. Yet again. During Sukkot, I heard a rumor, even Gerer Ḥasidim are allowed to have sex. So put on your clothes, turn off the light, and have a good time.

Are those Ḥasidim who have split from Ger also planning to have a good time?

I'll have to find out.

The Fake, True Story of the Brothel on Tsfanya Street

In Yiddish, yes can mean no

Since the shops have been closed for a long time, a full day on Yom Kippur and half a day on the Eve of Yom Kippur, people are starving. Or at least this is the way it looks. Shopping on the day after Yom Kippur requires patience, more patience, and ever more patience. The stores are packed as if no food has been available for at least twelve years, and everybody has a smile on their faces once they leave the stores with huge bags that require a truck to carry or at least a big taxi.

Instead of going to shop, I would prefer to chat with a Rebbe. I call Reb Yankev Ḥaim and ask him how the interview with the Lelever Rebbe can be arranged. I remind him that the Rebbe agreed to sit down with me for an interview after Yom Kippur.

"I don't think," answers Reb Yankev Ḥaim, "that he was thinking when he said that to you."

That's news to me. Could you ask him if he wants to give me an interview or not, I suggest to Reb Yankev Ḥaim, and let him decide?

"I will ask him and let you know," he says to me in Yiddish, which means he won't. In Yiddish, you see, yes lives very well together with no, and a blessing could mean a curse and vice versa. For example, *yimaḥ shmoi*. *Yimaḥ shmoi*, which means "may his name be blotted out," can also mean "what a brilliant man!" As in "I love that *yimaḥ shmoi'nik*!"

Anyway, time is moving fast, and another Sabbath enters soon, much sooner than I expected.

What should I do, where should I go?

I have been to a Toldos Aharon *tish*, but I've never prayed with them, at least not for a full service. Isn't it time? Besides, I want to meet the Rebbe of Toldos Aharon, and if David the Philanthropist is right, I will meet him after the holidays. In such a case, it might be beneficial to see how he handles a prayer service, as I might learn something about him.

If I get to meet the Rebbe of Toldos Aharon, and I won't know until it happens, it would be a huge, huge feat. In fact, he's the number one Rebbe that I want to meet. Who would not want to meet the leader of the Golden Boys?

To Toldos Aharon I go.

The place is much more packed than the last time I was here. Ḥasidim are occupying every conceivable inch in the place. They are standing here, standing there, and standing in between, as if they were popping out from inside the walls. The only place where they can theoretically put more people is on the ceiling.

I push myself in, and, miraculously, my body lands inside.

Almost all the people around me are "Arabs," which means that gold is the leading color here. I, for one, have no golden clothes on me and, no big surprise, some kids soon gather around me to watch the interesting creature. To them, no wonder, I look like an animal from the zoo. I ask one of the kids: *Voos macht a Yid?* What is a Jew doing? In Yiddish, this means, How are you?

They get confused by the Yiddish coming out of my lips and quickly conclude that I'm a Jew like them, just naked.

They move on, prayer books in hand, and disappear in the crowd, pushing everybody around.

The prayer service goes on.

"And You are trusted to resurrect the dead," the worshippers say to God.

When, exactly, did He promise them to do so? I ask some people, but they can't give me any source for such a promise. Of course, they are not the only ones who can't quote the source for the basics of their belief. Ask an average Christian where Jesus Christ is mentioned in the Old Testament, which they believe to be the case, and most likely, you will get a bewildered look in response.

Yet, if I remember correctly, the source for the "promise" according to the Talmud in tractate *Sanhedrin*, is a verse in Exodus, "And I have also established my covenant with them, to give them the land of Canaan." Why does it say "them" and not "you"? the Sage, Rabbi Simai, asks. It is God's promise, he answers, given to the ones who will be resurrected. And that's the proof that resurrection is mentioned in the Five Books of Moses. Maimonides, for one, disagrees. Other sources, such as some verses in Isaiah, Daniel, and Ezekiel, met a similar fate when some rabbis said that the prophets didn't mean it literally.

Promise or not, the evening's prayer service, which takes about forty minutes in any other ordinary synagogue, takes two hours here. The Ḥasidim of Toldos Aharon pray slowly, uttering every word clear and loud, allowing their minds to fly high above the clouds of doubt, combining awareness and imagination that bring them into unity with Heaven above, while lovingly guided by their pilot, the Rebbe. They fly high and higher, secured in their holy aircraft, and there's no room for questions on the plane. According to Rebbe Aharon Rote, investigating what is true and false in matters of faith will lead people to a bottomless pit. A striking example of this concept can be found in Reb Aharon's book, *Shoimer Emunim*, in which he deals with imagined, fake stories about various Rebbes, stories that tell of miracles performed by this or that Rebbe. He writes that doubting the truthfulness of such stories, even if the stories are indeed fake, is the root of heresy.

And when the service is finally over, the Rebbe stands on an elevated platform by the Holy Ark, faces his Ḥasidim, and like a fatherly king says to them, in Yiddish, Have a good Sabbath.

Like children to their papa, they look up to him and are grateful that he is there for them.

The evening seems to be over, but suddenly, a bunch of men in gold start moving the tables away and bring in the bleachers, many of them. What's going on? The Rebbe, it turns out, wants to do his *tish* now, instead of around midnight, as is usually the case. This change of the hall from a shul to a *tish* hall with Ḥasidim on bleachers takes but a few minutes, and when it's done, the *tish* starts. This means songs, more songs, and more songs.

At some point – I don't even bother to check what time it is – the *tish* ends.

I go to my hotel room, and I read a bit.

The leading article on the internet site of *Haaretz* today is about mental, physical, and sexual abuse in a Ḥaredi yeshiva a few minutes' walk from where I am. I don't know anything about that yeshiva, but the Ḥaredi children and teenagers I saw today were smiling, happily singing, and overall, in an excellent mood, dressed in the shiniest and cleanest of clothes, very well taken care of and plentifully fed. If journalists or writers looks for dirt, they can find it in any community of people. Why are these people, the people of Mea Shearim, singled out as the worst of all?

Haaretz is not alone in its obsession with the Ḥaredim of Mea Shearim. A lovely woman I happened to meet the other evening said to me that "the Ḥaredim of Mea Shearim" were constantly visiting prostitutes, day and night. How did she know that? Her mother, she told me, used to live on the same street as my hotel, and one floor above hers was occupied by two ladies, a Ukrainian and a Russian, both top-class prostitutes. Day and night, she told me, the staircase was constantly busy with Ḥaredim going in and out of the Ukrainian and Russian's little brothel. I don't know if her story is true, but even if it is, does this mean that "the

Ḥaredim of Mea Shearim" constantly visit prostitutes? Were all Ḥaredim, including all the Rebbes in the area, running up and down the stairs of the Ukrainian and Russian Garden of Desire?

You can argue, and I'll admit it to you, that even if this lady's story and conclusion are fake, they are still true according to Reb Aharon's principles.

A gitten Shabbes.

Tomorrow, if no Ukrainian or Russian prostitutes divert my attention, I shall visit the other Ger folks, the ones who split from the Palace.

The Rebbe Carries a Pistol to Protect Himself from the Ger Ḥasidim

Have you heard of the Real Estate Rebbe?

On Sabbath afternoon, after failing to find the Ukrainian and the Russian, I go to visit the Ger splitter group, a few minutes' walk up the road from the Ger Palace.

Who are the people of the Ger splitter group? I don't know much about them, except that they are people who once followed a Rebbe, a mighty Rebbe, but one day decided not to follow him anymore, forming a new Ḥasidic court, kind of, and knighting another person as their Rebbe, even though the new Rebbe prefers to be called "Rabbi" or "Rosh Yeshivah" instead of "Rebbe," which of course he is, as far as my mind grasps it. His name is Rabbi Shaul Alter, and if I'm not mistaken, he is the cousin of the Gerer Rebbe, Yaakov Aryeh Alter.

It will be interesting to see this group.

Led by Rabbi Shaul Alter, the group was formed two years ago, from what I understand. Rabbi Shaul, known as a great thinker, used to be an admired rabbi and head of the Ger yeshiva until the Palace Rebbe closed it down at some point. The Palace Rebbe also changed the course of study in the Ger institutions, from *iyun*, meaning in-depth study of the Talmud, to *bekiyus*, meaning studying without depth, delegitimizing Rabbi Shaul in the process.

Members of the splitter group convene at a girls' school, Bais Yaakov, on Saturdays and Jewish holidays when the school is closed. They are, in a word, homeless.

Let me see them.

I walk in and see about two hundred Ḥasidim sitting at cheap tables, eating herring. The place is so poorly decorated that it makes me wonder what these people feel now that they have left a rich Rebbe and gotten themselves under the wings of a poor one.

Not to worry, I'm told. Rabbi Shaul Alter has already raised millions of dollars, and a new building will soon be available to them.

Sounds good, at least for them.

The two Ger communities, the Palace guys and the splitter group, together number 13,500 families, a Ḥasid tells me, which would make it well over a hundred thousand people, since the average family size is quite significant.

How are the families divided between you and them?

"They have thirteen thousand; we have five hundred."

For some reason, the word *Takunnes* suddenly flashes before my eyes.

Tell me something, I ask the man, is it true that the Ger Ḥasidim have Takunnes relating to the relationship between a man and a woman?

"Did you mean to ask if we have Takunnes relating to the relationship between man and God?"

No, between man and woman.

Another Ḥasid is eavesdropping on the conversation and intervenes, saying about the Ḥasid I'm talking with: "You shouldn't talk to him about this. He's not married, and he doesn't know anything."

Well, I say to this new guy, can you answer the question?

"Yes, I can," he says, but abruptly, he stops talking.

Can you answer my question?

"I don't know what to say."

Tell me what you know, if you don't mind.

"Why do you want to know?"

I'm a curious man.

"I don't know what to say."

Why is it so hard for you and your friend to answer such a simple question?

"Because we are Polish people, and Polish people don't answer questions."

I've got news for you. I'm Polish too, a pure Pole, and what you just said about Polish people is offensive to me, as a Pole, and to you, if you're indeed a Pole.

At this juncture, another Ḥasid comes in, an older Ḥasid. He wants to know what the discussion is about. Do you guys, I ask him, keep the Takunnes?

"The children of Yaakov Aryeh Alter certainly don't," he answers, referring to the children of the Rebbe. "As for the rest, I don't know. Nobody can keep account of what people do in the privacy of their homes."

Does this mean that those Takunnes indeed exist?

"Yes."

Sex no more than once or twice a month, no calling the wife by name, no walking on the street together with the wife, etc.?

"Yes. But it doesn't mean that people observe these Takunnes."

What does it mean, then?

"The Takunnes are for people who want to have Takunnes. I don't follow them."

Both Ḥasidic groups, the one in the Ger Palace and you in the girls' school, are Gerer Ḥasidim. How do you differentiate between the two?

"They are Ger Nadlan [Real Estate], and we are Ger Torah."

Ger Real Estate? What does that mean?

"Ger Nadlan is led by a merciless thief who calls himself Rebbe, a corrupt man who is obsessed with money and power. He is not a Rebbe but a businessman. He can't even read, not to mention being a scholar. Why do you think he closed the yeshiva of Rabbi Shaul? Because Rabbi Shaul was admired too much for the Rebbe's taste; he was afraid that the Ḥasidim would follow Rabbi Shaul instead of following him. He also changed the study method in all Ger institutions because he has no depth. He doesn't care about the Ḥasidim; he wants them dumb. He's a moneyman, not a holy man. He is a multimillionaire, having real estate properties that cost millions upon millions, and he collects millions in donations every year from his Ḥasidim, supposedly for worthy causes, but all of it goes to his private pockets. For some time now, he has been trying his best to torture us, torture our children and our families, and we are happy that he's no longer our Rebbe. Upon his order, the children of those who went with Rabbi Shaul were thrown out from the Ger schools, Ger *ḥeider*s, and Ger yeshivas. The new Ger group, where we are now, is called Ger Torah because we care about the Torah, not about real estate."

If what I hear is correct, I have found the formula for how to have thousands of admirers follow me: order people to avoid sex and make them empty their pockets for me. In other words: take away from people their natural desires and channel the power behind those desires to love you to death instead.

Genius.

When the Sabbath is over, the Ḥasidim gather around Rabbi Shaul, their new Rebbe, clinging to him like babies to their mama. It's touching and saddening at the same time. Without their new Rebbe, they would be lost, and nobody would accept them.

I approach Rabbi Shaul and ask him if he would mind giving me an interview. "I would rather not," he says to me, "but you can talk to the Ḥasidim, and they will talk to you."

Outside, in the front yard, one of the Ḥasidim does exactly what Rabbi Shaul suggested. He tells me how vengeful his old

Rebbe, Yaakov Aryeh Alter, the Nadlan Rebbe, became after the split. The Rebbe's followers gathered around the homes of those who split, demonstrated against them, calling them murderers, and demanded that they leave their homes. It was awful, he recalls. He is grateful, he tells me, that Rabbi Shaul did what the Radzyner Rebbe did well over one hundred fifty years ago and split from Ger.

Wow. The Radzyner Rebbe? Is he talking about my great-grandfather? Yes, he is.

It takes me time, but then it hits me: I'm walking here into my own family's past. Who would have imagined!

Yes, over a century and a half ago, and before becoming a Rebbe, Rabbi Yitzḥok Meir Alter, credited as the founder of the Ger court, was a follower of Rabbi Menaḥem Mendel of Kotzk, known as the Kotzker Rebbe. After being crowned to replace Menaḥem Mendel, following the latter's death, Yitzḥok Meir moved to Góra Kalwaria, Poland, and thus Kotzk became Ger. My great-grandfather (more exact: great-great-grandfather), the Radzyner Rebbe, split from Menaḥem Mendel, leaving the Kotzker-slash-Ger Ḥasidic court on the Jewish holiday of Simḥas Toireh (Simḥat Torah) to establish his Ḥasidic dynasty of Izbica, to where he moved because of the hostility he faced from Menaḥem Mendel's followers. His son, who followed his father as the second Rebbe, relocated to Radzyn, and the Izbica Ḥasidic court soon became the Radzyner court. It is told about his son, the third in the line of the Izbica-Radzyner Rebbes, that whenever he traveled anywhere, he had a pistol with him. When asked why he needed a pistol, he reportedly replied: "I need it as a protection against the Ger Ḥasidim."

The Radzyner Rebbe of old and Rabbi Shaul of today have split from Ger, and both suffered from hostilities mounted against them.

It's funny. Leaders of Ḥasidic courts are usually determined by heredity: if you come from a Rebbe – that is, you're the child or grandchild of a Rebbe – you become a Rebbe. This means, strange as it sounds, that I could become a Rebbe too, at least theoretically speaking. What kind of a Rebbe would I be, with a pistol or without? Well, with a machine gun, perhaps. I have to outdo the former Rebbe, after all. But as of now, I know one thing: I'll have to dig deeper into the Ger story. In the meantime, I return to Mea Shearim.

Could You Donate a Burial Plot, Please?

How to sell a five-shekel fruit for two thousand

The night moves slowly in Mea Shearim, and stores are open all over when the Sabbath ends. Here is a jewelry store, and it's packed, and here's a ladies' fashion store, also packed. And when clothes shopping is done, building the sukkah gets started – for those who haven't done it yet.

There are hundreds of sukkahs being built in the area these days, one for each family, and big sukkahs for various Rebbes, synagogues, and Ḥasidic courts. A sukkah is temporary housing for the seven days of the Sukkot holiday, and each of the sukkah builders likes to decorate the sukkah differently. Hence, sukkah decorations: all over the place, a gazillion kinds of sukkah decorations are being sold. Glittering balls, photos, paintings, and all kinds of other tchotchkes that defy description.

"In my view," Professor Dan Shiftan told me, "the Ḥaredim are the number one threat to the Jewish people." And he called them "parasites." Are these people parasites? Are these beautiful ladies with their handsome golden husbands threatening the Jewish people?

Not that everybody is shopping or building. There are those, Dan Shiftan Ḥaredim, who are schnorring. There are always schnorrers here, just as there are all over Manhattan, but there seem to be more of them on the eve of the coming holiday. Shoppers and schnorrers always go hand in hand, but the schnorrers here are a bit more creative than the schnorrers of New York. Here, they have more panache. "I'm collecting money for a bride who is getting married next week, and she has no money for the wedding. Can you help? Your donation will hasten the coming of the Messiah," is an example. "Give me a few shekels, and The Name will save you from death" is another example. Don't be surprised if somebody here approaches you asking you to help him purchase a burial plot on the Mount of Olives.

In the wee hours of the morning, when the shoppers and builders are finally asleep, the police arrive in Mea Shearim. As you might guess, they are here to take down a big sukkah for safety reasons. It is in the same place I visited a few days ago, where riots were reportedly taking place. Yes, the builders had papers signed by engineers testifying to the safety of the sukkah, but those engineers, it turns out, had no authority to sign anything. Save for a few young men, who must always make sure that they spill no seed at any time and are ever looking for activities to take their minds off women and little organs, nobody else comes to protest this demolition.

And when the sun shines on a new day, the shoppers return.

They buy more, more, and more.

One interesting item that people buy in droves at this time of year is Arba'at Haminim, the Four Species. They are esrog/etrog (*Citrus medica*), lulav (palm frond), *hadas* (myrtle), and *aravah* (willow). On Sukkot, every Ḥaredi takes these four together in his hands, shakes them, and waves them in this direction and that direction while uttering a special blessing, a practice supposedly first performed in the Holy Temple that is performed ever since. On these days, in every corner of Mea Shearim, you see people buying this species or that, paying between fifty shekels to thousands of shekels for them. Motta Brim, my neighbor, shows me the esrog he bought, a huge esrog.

How much did you pay for it? I ask him.

"I got a discount," says he.

How much did it cost you after the discount?

"NIS 1,800. The real price is 2,000."

The real price of esrogs should equal that of lemons, ten shekels per kilo, let's say. But that's not the way it works when it comes to esrogs. How much an esrog costs depends on the street smarts of the seller.

If you want to know who the next millionaire in Israel will be, you should come here and observe the esrog sellers. The future tycoon sells his esrogs like this: He randomly picks an esrog from a box, puts it aside, and when a well-dressed man shows up looking for the nicest esrog, he tells him that all the esrogs in the shop are good, even excellent. When the wealthy buyer asks, as he usually would, if the seller doesn't, just by chance, have something better to show him, the seller answers: "Well, I have one that I picked for myself, that's true, and it's the finest of the esrogs one can find, but that's for me. I can show it to you, but I'm not selling it." A long back-and-forth haggling then ensues, and by the end of it, the esrog exchanges hands for thousands of shekels.

When the wealthy man goes, happy to Heaven with his purchase, the seller picks another esrog from the box randomly, without even looking at it, and waits until another well-dressed man enters.

I keep on walking, marveling at the wits of the future tycoons, when I get a call from a Ger Ḥasid asking if I would like to meet him at the home of an affluent man this evening, have a good meal, and chat. I say yes. I will never say no to a good meal.

"I'll pick you up," he says.

The Rebbe Owns My Testicles, and Sometimes He Squeezes Them

All married women have the same name: "Pss, pss, pss"

As I arrive at the affluent man's home, whose identity I didn't know before, I'm surprised to see him, for this man is also a very famous Jerusalemite. And as I enter the living room, I'm told: his name, and the names of the others who are present, are not to be made public.

What is this all about, and why was I invited?

I don't know, not yet.

On the table, I see, are expensive-looking cheesecakes and chocolates, artsy-looking cakes, plus coffee, tea, and Coke Zero. There are three men at the table, one man I met before and two that I have not.

It is agreed that I not disclose any description of the house or any other identifying information.

That's the price for top cheesecakes, I guess.

What would you like to eat? the host asks me.

Omelet, I say.

I don't know how this word came out of my lips, but it did.

In minutes, a miracle omelet, the likes of which has never been seen by the human eye, reaches my mouth. This miracle omelet,

let me testify here under oath, is the best omelet that has ever reached any human mouth since the Six Days of Creation.

A miracle! And after this miracle, let me tell you, I wouldn't be surprised at all if Abraham's white donkey were to enter this very room, with the Messiah on top of it, and eat the kingly cheesecakes and princely cookies, slice by slice by slice.

My dear white donkey, it's a pleasure watching you swallowing the white cheesecake and the white chocolate cookies. What a beautiful white display.

Oh, what an omelet!

I don't know what it is with me in this land, but almost everywhere I'm invited, the food turns out to be amazingly good. In New York, where some of the richest people in the world live, the food is almost always tasteless.

When I have eaten my omelet, the people at the table start talking.

All three are Ger Ḥasidim, they tell me, and all started life with the Palace Rebbe, the Nadlan Rebbe, but in their hearts, they are part of the other group, the splitter group. One or two of them may have made the transition to the other group, but I'm not sure. These three, after all, are very secretive people.

In any case, they teach me their lingo. The Palace Rebbe's court is "Old Ger," and the splitter group is "New Ger." "New Ger," I admit, is a much better term than "splitter group," which has a negative connotation.

They talk.

"I love the New Ger, but I can't be part of them," the younger of them says.

Why not?

"I will try to explain this to you."

Please do.

"My heart is in the New Ger, but my testicles are in the Old Ger."

Your testicles?

"Yes. You see, in the Old Ger, you are assigned a guide when you get married, and this guide is responsible for you."

What is the guide doing with you?

"He guides me in the most intimate."

Explain, if you don't mind.

"Before I got married, the guide had a long talk with me. He told me that after my marriage, I will have to sleep with my bride, my wife, and that while having sex with her, I must keep my clothes on, including the tzitzit, and that I should do the intimate act very fast, to make sure that I don't enjoy it. He said that having intimate relations is an ugly part of life, but nature is not perfect, and this is the only way to get children. I can sleep with my wife twice a month, at a maximum, he said, and I should never call her by name."

How do you call her if you need to call her?

"Pss, pss, pss."

Once you got married, did the guy verify with you that you indeed followed his guidance?

"Yes. We met after my first night with my wife, and we kept on meeting for the next four years to guide my sexual life."

Were you looking forward to your meetings with him?

"No."

How did these sessions with him make you feel?

"Horrible."

How did your wife feel?

"Horrible."

Is there a time when you are allowed to call your wife by name?

"No. But after having the first child, I could call her Ima, Mom."

When you said that your testicles were in the old Ger, what did you mean?

"The Rebbe owns my testicles. For real. And he squeezes them whenever he wants."

How come?

"The Rebbe of Old Ger, Yaakov Aryeh Alter, is a cruel, merciless Rebbe. The Name doesn't mean anything to him. As he sees it, he owns all the properties of Ger, and no one else should have access to the Ger court's money. He owns everything because he *is* everything. Yes, there is one God, and it's him, not The Name, not the God of the Bible. Yaakov Aryeh Alter doesn't care about Jews, religion, or Judaism. He cares about himself, and the Ḥasidic dynasty, which also means himself. And if you disagree, he knows what to squeeze."

What does it mean that he owns everything? The Palace, for example, belongs to the community, doesn't it?

The oldest of the three chimes in: "As Yaakov Aryeh Alter sees it, it doesn't matter if this or that property is registered in the community's name, because in any case, all that it means is that it belongs to him. The Ḥasidim, the people, also belong to him. In the old, actual Ger in Poland, in Góra Kalwaria, there was a feudal system, where the people, all people, belonged to the Polish lord. And because they belonged to him, everything they owned also belonged to him. Same with Yaakov Aryeh Alter. He learned from the Polish goyim of old."

Do you mean to say that God, the God of the Bible, doesn't feature in this system?

"Nowhere," says the younger one, and the other two agree.

"Some of us," says the third Ḥasid, "are afraid to leave the Old Ger. Getting the children thrown out of the institutions, where they study and where their friends are, could be very traumatic for them."

The younger Ḥasid says: "The way he sees the world, he is the Rebbe, the Leader, and if you don't obey him, he will take revenge. No mercy."

Are you telling me that he is not worried at all about damaging the future of the little kids, who might never recover from the experience of being thrown out?

"He will keep his kingdom and his feudal objects at any cost," says the older Ḥasid.

You three portray a man of no values, no principles, no heart, and no Judaism. A cruel man. Do you really mean it?

All present answer in the positive.

Can I get another omelet? I need an omelet, one more omelet.

Yes, I can, and in minutes, I get it. And this one, miracle of miracles, is even better than the one before.

They keep on talking about the horrible Rebbe and his battalion of enforcers, whom they call Kozaks.

It's a strange experience to derive so much pleasure from a delicious omelet in your mouth at the same time as hearing horrible stories entering your ears.

Once my second omelet is done, all securely placed in my stomach, I tell them of my experience while visiting the New Ger: I looked at the people there, I tell them, and they looked to me like people who went through a trauma.

The younger explains: "They *are* in trauma, still, and The Name only knows if they will ever recover. The Ḥasidim in the Old Ger are different; they have power and a God. On the Sabbath, for example, the Ḥasidim in the Old Ger's big building don't wear their *spodiks* [a certain kind of *shtreimel*] during prayer. Do you know why?"

No.

"Because the *spodiks* are high, and since there are so many people in shul, the *spodiks* might prevent the Ḥasidim who are not in the front row from seeing their God, Yaakov Aryeh Alter –"

They are praying to him, then?

"Who else do you think they pray to?"

Up to now, I thought that Ḥaredi Jews were the happiest people on earth. But from what you are telling me, it seems that the Gerers, the biggest Ḥasidic group in Israel, are people who are either enslaved to a cruel lord or mentally impaired, depending on which Ger they belong to. Did I get the picture right?

They look at me, at each other, and then back at me, and then the host asks: "Coffee?"

Yeah, I'll have coffee.

"Would you like something grilled? We can make you an excellent steak!"

No, thanks. Coffee, for the time being, is enough.

"You have to understand," one of the three says, "that most of us don't keep the Takunnes. And, actually, many of us celebrate sex like no one else."

After the pictures of horror and terror you painted for me, how could any of you celebrate?

"We take it all in stride. No matter what happens, we keep our sense of humor."

Sense of humor with such Takunnes and throwing kids out of school?

"Of course. We are Jews. We have the best sense of humor! We invented humor."

They laugh.

"Humor comes from suffering, and the more we suffer, the more we laugh."

I pour myself a cup of Coke Zero, and they ask me if I want to take some bottles of Coke Zero with me. We have enough, says the host.

I drink the Zero and pour myself yet another cup.

One day, hopefully, the testicles of the Ḥasid will come back to him. I drink to that.

Strangely enough, the song "Der Rebbe Iz Do" comes to my mind. It plays in my ears, only now it feels very different, having an opposite meaning: the Rebbe is here, holding your testicles – and he will squeeze them if he feels like it.

The "Rebbe," I live and learn, can also mean something horrifying.

As I get up to leave, the younger of the three offers to drive me back.

"We'll be in touch," he says. "Next time we meet, we'll have something for you. Recordings and videos."

I'm looking forward to getting them.

The Messiah Will Arrive on a Saudi Arabian Airliner

A match made in Heaven: Ḥaim Kanievsky and Greta Thunberg

Shop till you drop, goes the American saying, and by daylight, the Mea Shearim people practice it with zeal: gowns, kugels, bracelets, milk, watches, butter, socks, cakes, *tiḥels*, olive oil, and sukkah decorations.

The sukkah must be decorated very nicely because very, very important guests will be coming to visit the sukkah of every Jew every day of the Sukkot holiday, seven days in total. Each important guest, it's worthy of remembering, will stay in the sukkah for twenty-four hours. Yes. Who are the guests? The Patriarch Abraham, the Patriarch Isaac, the Patriarch Jacob, Joseph the dream interpreter of the Egyptian king, Moses the Lawgiver, Aharon the Priest, and King David.

In the future, certain Ḥasidim hope, the holiday will extend for one more day, for one more sukkah guest to show up: Yaakov Aryeh Alter, the God of the Kozaks.

I have a sukkah, too, built for me by the hotel owner.

Isn't it lovely?

I pour myself a cup of Vietnamese coffee, which is one of my favorite coffees, and think about my strangest childhood neighbors, two men whom at the time I thought desperately needed a psychiatrist: Ḥaim'ke Kanievsky and Yaakov Aryeh Alter, two

bizarre fellows. How did it happen that these two, these and not others, have risen to the highest levels of the Ḥaredi world? One is at the top of the Litvak world, the Prince of Torah, and the other is at the top of the Ḥasidic world, leader of the biggest Ḥasidic court, God of the Kozaks. How did that happen?

Thousands of miles from Mea Shearim, across the oceans, where the most advanced societies of the First World live, hundreds of thousands of supposedly sound-minded people follow a teenager named Greta Tintin Eleonora Ernman Thunberg, known as Greta Thunberg, or simply as Greta.

According to published reports, Greta, diagnosed with Asperger syndrome and OCD (obsessive-compulsive disorder), has no academic degree of any kind and is no climate specialist of any sort. Yet, like the rabbis Ḥaim Kanievsky and Yaakov Aryeh Alter, she is a Princess of Science and the Goddess of the Atheists. Ḥaim and Greta, methinks, will make a perfect couple.

Is there something in the human psyche that chooses to be led by the strangest of us?

About a twenty-minute-walk from me, up the road, is the Boyan synagogue. I remember something about Boyan. What was it? Oh, yeah, the two lovely girls I saw the other day in Uri's Pizza, and one of them was waiting for God's help to have her hair shaved once she gets married. It would be nice to see her one more time, I think. She looks much better, wouldn't you know, than Ḥaim and Yaakov and Greta combined.

Up the road I go.

The holiday of Sukkot will soon be ushered in, and slowly the stores close, and cars draw to a halt. The Ḥasidim, dressed just like on the Sabbath, start parading their tempting bodies on the streets for all of us to desire.

Let me, I say to myself, pray with the Boyaners.

The Boyaner building is big and impressive, with a cute dome on top.

The prayer hall, which I enter via a metal stairway, is big. There are hundreds of Ḥasidim inside, dressed in *shtreimel*s and black *bekishe*s, all praying, welcoming the holiday of Sukkot. Unlike some other synagogues of similar size that I visited in the area, the man leading the service can be heard – and he's pretty good.

The prayer service is relatively short, and at its end, the Ḥasidim go to wish the Rebbe "*A gitten yom tov*," a happy holiday, while he stands near the Holy Ark like a statue, not moving a limb. Afterwards, the Ḥasidim go out to the street, waiting for him to pass by on his way home. They want to see him one more time. They love to be close to him, their papa, their leader, the leader of their tribe, the Boyaner tribe.

What is unique about the Boyaners, and what differentiates the Boyaners from any other Ḥasidim? I ask a Ḥasid. "Of all the Ḥasidic courts in existence, we are the gentlest because our Rebbe is."

Can you give me an example of what being gentle means?

"Look at the Rebbe, and you'll see a gentle man. Did you see him?

Yes, I did.

"Didn't you see how gentle he is?"

Not really, sorry.

"Okay, I'll give you an example: when the Rebbe eats soup, he never bends his body down to eat it. He eats the soup while sitting straight. You should see it!"

Do you have another example? The example you gave me is a bit weak.

"Oh, there are so many examples that it's hard for me to think."

One example, if you can think of it.

"No, there are just so many of them!"

How much does he affect your life? For example, if he tells you to do something, would you do it?

"Sure!"

Do you have an example?

"My son wanted an organ. I went to the Rebbe to ask him if I should buy him one. The Rebbe said I should, and that's what I did: I bought the organ."

An organ? That's a big thing, isn't it?

"No, not that kind of organ! I wouldn't buy him a church! It's a small organ, electronic."

It's time, I think, to speak about something more important than organs. Donkeys, for example.

Tell me, I ask, do you believe in the resurrection of the dead?

"Of course!"

When the Messiah arrives, on the donkey of the Patriarch Abraham –

"No. The Messiah will not arrive on a donkey."

I heard that he would!

"No, no. The one who will arrive on the donkey of Patriarch Abraham is the Prophet Elijah, who will march in with the donkey three days before the Messiah's arrival, to announce to the people that the Messiah is on his way and that everybody should get ready."

Oops. If he's right, I've been wrong all along, confusing the Messiah and Elijah, the biblical prophet, for months now!

And how will the Messiah arrive in Jerusalem? I ask my new teacher.

"What do I know? Probably on a plane."

Flying from where?

"This I don't know."

So Elijah will come on a donkey, followed by the Messiah on a plane.

"Yes."

On the Saudi Arabian airline, Saudia, maybe?

"It's possible."

Tell me something, where are the women praying this evening?

"This evening, the women's section of the Bayan synagogue is closed."

There goes the Uri's Pizza girl and her shaved head.

"Bayan," the Ḥasid explains to me – he pronounces it "Bayan" and not "Boyan" – "is a kingdom." The Bayaners' specialty, he says, is that they regard their court as a kingdom. Boyan, which is related to the Ruzhin Ḥasidic dynasty, is a kingdom, in keeping with the Ruzhin dynasty's description of itself. This kingdom, by the way, is not a kingdom like, let's say, the British monarchy, but something much bigger.

How did Boyan (Бояни), a village in Ukraine, grow to be bigger than London, England's capital?

"Kingdom is also a kabbalistic concept," he says, and that can be found only in a little shtetl.

I have no clue what he's talking about, but I let go. They want to call it Kingdom? That's fine with me, as long as I don't have to pay them any taxes.

Does the Kingdom have unique traditions?

"At prayer times, when all of us gather to pray in the shul, the Rebbe usually davens [prays] alone, in a room next to the Holy Ark."

Why does he pray alone?

"Because that's what you do in a Kingdom. Did you not see the Rebbe's *shtreimel*? It points upward like a dome. That's a sign of a kingdom."

Do the Boyaners also have Takunnes, like Ger?

"We had Takunnes in Bayan too, but the Rebbe canceled them. But let me tell you something: from the perspective of the relationship between men and women, the best Ḥasidic court is Toldos Aharon. They are the most open. Look at their couples walking on the street, and you will see how happy they are with each other. They are romantic, sweet!"

I can't wait to see the Toldos Aharon Rebbe, if indeed I get to see him.

I follow the Boyaner Rebbe as he goes home from the synagogue and watch the men and the women standing on the street to catch a glance of him – just as British citizens would do if they knew that a king or queen would be walking out on the streets of London.

The Rebbe walks fast, and no interaction occurs between him and the Ḥasidim. But the Ḥasidim are elated.

I hear some of them talking about how great the Boyaner Rebbe is, and I ask a Ḥasid: What's the accurate pronunciation of your Ḥasidic court? Is it Boyan or Bayan?

"It should be Boyan, but people say Bayan."

Some, I'm told, say Biyan.

Interesting. The girl from Uri's Pizza didn't know the origin of the Boyan court, and here I have Ḥasidim who can't pronounce Boyan. I'm curious if they know more about Ger than they do about Boyan. I ask the Ḥasid: What do you know, in case you do, about the Gerer Rebbe, Yaakov Aryeh Alter?

"He breaks up families. If your son, for example, prays with Rabbi Shaul, he will be thrown out of the community, and you must cut off all your ties with him for good. You must deny your son. Yaakov Aryeh Alter is an idiot. He is not like our Rebbe."

With prayer and Rebbe Watching done, I walk with one of the Ḥasidim, Motta Brim, the guy with the expensive esrog, to his mother's home, which is across the street from my hotel, to eat the holiday meal in their sukkah, with him, his mom, and his extended family: brothers, their wives, and their children.

What a family! The children, his nieces and nephews, look like gorgeous flowers, each with a smile and the manners of princes. And if you say to yourself that I generalize in my observation about the kids here, similarly to what the *Haaretz* journalist did in his opposite characterization, listen to this: a thirteen-year-old girl, sitting opposite me, spent the day reading. She read two books, cover to cover, totaling nine hundred pages, in a single day. Yes.

Motta's mother, Hendel Esther, is the family's matriarch, and she rules over the house. She is the queen, and her family is her kingdom. And when the men sing holiday songs, she sings with them. Normally, Ḥaredi women don't sing in the presence of men who are not part of their family, but she doesn't care. She is as Ḥaredi as they come, but nobody will tell her what to do in her own home. It's a marvel to watch. From time to time, she recites verses from the Bible, giving her commentaries and teaching her children and grandchildren in the ways of the Lord. Here, in this sukkah, in her home, she is the Rebbe, and what she says goes. She is the queen, and this is her kingdom. And all admire her. She is a woman of biblical proportions, only she doesn't wear any *shtreimel*.

The food, no need to say, is superb.

Say whatever you want to say about Mea Shearim, but your taste buds will not be able to deny the outstanding culinary magic of its residents.

And the more I stay with the people here, I wonder again and again and again: What did these sweet Ḥasidic people do to the Christians of the world, to the Europeans, that they slaughtered and raped them for centuries on end?

Beats me.

Got a Problem? The Ḥasidim Got a Crane!

It doesn't matter if God exists or not. Just believe!

The next day, lucky me, the Boyan Ḥasidim celebrate the Simḥas Beis Hashoeivah as part of a multi-day celebration during the holiday of Sukkot. The Boyan Ḥasidim will celebrate in a giant sukkah built for Sukkot near their shul. The celebration will last two days, with two thousand people joining today and two thousand others joining tomorrow. There are too many Ḥasidim for them all to fit in the sukkah, and Boyan needs to split the congregation.

I go there.

The song "And you shall rejoice in your holidays" is heard loud and clear from streets away, and Ḥasidim in the hundreds are rushing to secure a spot at what promises to be a packed event.

As I arrive, I see the Rebbe sitting on one side of the giant sukkah, surrounded by the thousands of Ḥasidim on bleachers on three sides of the sukkah, and all are protected from the elements by the sḥaḥ (often made of tree branches, loose wood, or bamboo sticks), high above their heads.

The Rebbe sits at an elevated table, and four gabbais stand near him, ready to serve this holy man in whatever he needs. In the middle of the sukkah, there is a table around which important people sit, and there are additional chairs close to the table for less important people.

The orchestra is playing, the Ḥasidim sing and dance on the bleachers, and I join them on the bleachers, my first time ever on bleachers.

I feel like a real Ḥasid, in his twenties or so.

All eyes, two thousand pairs of them, are focused on the Rebbe.

The older of the gabbais hands the Rebbe a cake, and specially assigned Ḥasidim walk on the ground with boxes of sliced cakes to distribute to the thousands. Even those Ḥasidim standing at the top of the bleachers, kissing the roof, should have a cake. The Rebbe makes a blessing and eats from the cake, and the thousands follow. When the Rebbe eats, the Ḥasidim eat as well.

The same gabbai proceeds to pour wine for the Rebbe, and at the same time, wine is distributed to the thousands. The Rebbe makes a blessing and sips from the wine, and the Ḥasidim follow. When the Rebbe drinks, the Ḥasidim drink as well.

The Rebbe, with the kingly *shtreimel* on his head, the center of which points upward, sits mostly motionless. But then he gestures with his right hand to the Ḥasidim on the right side, the sea of *shtreimels* on the bleachers at right, and they gesture in return, with their right hands, just like him. When the Rebbe greets, or whatever this gesture is supposed to mean, the Ḥasidim greet as well. Then he moves his hand in the direction of the people facing him, and they greet him with their right hands. Then he greets those on the left, and that sea of *shtreimels* greets him in the same manner.

It's fascinating to watch.

Der Rebbe iz do.

I witness this relationship between Rebbe and Ḥasidim, marvel at its interesting visual, and am trying to decipher its essence.

The prayer lines "You have chosen us..." are sung solemnly, and the thousands sing together in a solemn voice. The same lines repeat themselves, now to a slightly happier melody, and the thousands shake from right to left on their bleachers, a bit livelier. Then the same lines repeat themselves, again, only now to a very happy tune, and the thousands get elated, jumping up and down, down and up; the bleachers shake, and the music is roaring like a zoo full of lions.

The music subsides at some point, then stops altogether, and the Rebbe gives a sermon. His manner of speaking is monotonic; this man doesn't get easily excited in life, I think. The ideas he presents in his sermon are almost none. It seems that he doesn't have much to say, and this is not lost on the Ḥasidim, about half of whom start yawning. Finally, thank Heaven, the Rebbe finishes his sermon, and the music starts again. The Ḥasidim go wild, jump on the bleachers like there's no tomorrow, and stare at the Rebbe constantly. They love him, admire him, need him, and worship him. To them, it seems, the Rebbe can do no wrong, even if he's boring them to death. Perhaps, as far as I can judge, they are imposing an image on him, making him be what they want him to be, what they desire him to be, what they wish him to be, what they would love him to be: their Good Lord.

Der Rebbe iz do.

These people are united by music, dress, traditions, and Rebbe. To them, the Rebbe, if I interpret it right, is not a man, a person, but holiness. The Rebbe, in a way, is an extension of The Name. Maybe, even, The Name is an extension of the Rebbe. As one Boyaner tells me: "I don't know if The Name exists, and it doesn't matter if He exists or not; I believe that He exists, and that's good enough." The Rebbe, at least, exists in front of his eyes, and he loves it.

Der Rebbe iz do.

Suddenly, a section of the sḥaḥ roof detaches and is hanging by a thread. A few Ḥasidim try to fix the problem, fearing that the sḥaḥ will fall on people's heads. They find somewhere a couple of long 4 x 4s and try to push the sḥaḥ upward, but the sḥaḥ is stubborn and won't move. Then, miracle of miracles, a crane comes in – God knows where the Ḥasidim found it – operated by a Ḥasid, and a few Ḥasidim jump on it, and in minutes – God knows how they pull this off – everything is fixed. These are the Ḥasidim. Nothing stands in their way. Got a problem high up? They've got a crane. If, for whatever reason, you need a submarine, rest assured that these Ḥasidim would find and operate it for you. Now a crane was needed, and they got it. And they know how to operate it. Because if anybody knows how to operate a crane or a submarine, it's the Boyaners.

It's amazing.

The music continues throughout. Music is the air of Ḥasidim, and when they sing, they can perform miracles.

How do they do it? Don't ask.

After a while, the Rebbe leaves, and I leave as well.

Boyan is not the only Ḥasidic court in Mea Shearim celebrating a Simḥas Beis Hashoeivah; many others do too. Including, happily, Toldos Aharon.

The next evening, I go to celebrate once more.

Can You Give Me Your Smartphone and I'll Break It for You?

Welcome the Łódźer Rebbe, Me

Mea Shearim Street is packed, and cars can hardly move. There are so many people walking all over that you can't tell where the sidewalk ends and where the street begins. Where are all these people going? To Toldos Aharon's Simḥas Beis Hashoeivah. Their event, everybody in Jerusalem knows, is the best in all of Israel.

But there's one little problem: there are a lot of Toldos Aharon Ḥasidim, and their numbers are growing so fast that they have no place for the multitudes of outsiders who want to join them. In fact, the managers of Toldos Aharon put announcements in the Ḥaredi media asking people not to come. But people do. How can they give up on such an event? Yet once they arrive, their entrance is blocked. There's no room. Luckily for me, a big shot by the name of Reb Shmuel, whom I happened to meet at some point, hands me an entry ticket.

I am in.

Unlike at Boyan, there are very few bleachers here, mainly for kids, and the Ḥasidim dance on the floor, not on bleachers. How many Ḥasidim? Gazillions of them. Who are they? They are the golden ones, and they know how to move on the floor. Oh, they move! They are happy, very happy; they sing, loud; they jump, high; they run, fast; and they don't stop, ever on the move. It's a sight to behold: endless gold in constant motion, like a flowing river of gold, a gushing sea of gold, a roaring ocean of twenty-four-carat gold.

This is, let me share with you, the best dance party in the whole of the Middle East.

"Do you know," asks a man standing next to me, "how much the Rebbe's *shtreimel* costs?"

No idea.

"Twenty-six thousand dollars!"

Now we're up to $26,000. If I ever become a Rebbe – either a Radziner Rebbe, or I might find myself another Polish city in which Jews have been killed, maybe Lodz (Łódź) – I'll get myself a *shtreimel* like this.

"Would you like to eat something?" one of the Ḥasidim asks this Lodzer Rebbe.

Yes, of course.

He takes me to a courtyard outside, an area packed with people who eat instead of dance. I get a big plate of noodles, the Ḥasidic kind, and I feel I'm in Heaven, together with the Prophet Elijah. All that's missing here is a donkey or a Saudi plane.

After a while, I go out to the street, trying to move. It's not easy, I find out. There are so many people out, moving in the direction of Toldos Aharon.

Staring at the mess in front of me, I think of the taxi driver, the one who spoke so warmly about the rabbi of Toireh v'Yireh. Why don't I go to see Toireh v'Yireh now? I ask myself.

Good idea.

I walk the inner streets of Mea Shearim, those very narrow streets, and make my way to Toireh v'Yireh, a group of people rumored to be the biggest troublemakers of Mea Shearim, folks who like to break everything that doesn't fit their religious agendas.

Is that true? I don't know.

On my way there, I'm approached by a little Ḥasidic kid who asks if he can use my phone to call his dad, whom he lost in the crowd. Of course, I say to him, and hand him my iPhone.

This is not what he expected. On seeing my iPhone, the kid runs as if from fire.

In this kid's community, they don't use smartphones, at least not in public. Here, as in many other Ḥaredi communities, they use kosher cellphones. You can make a call, accept a call, but you cannot, The Name forbid, use the internet, where, Heaven save us, one can see women. Oy vey.

I reach Toireh v'Yireh, and I walk in.

It's small. Toireh v'Yireh might be known, it might be famous, but it's small. All in all, there are maybe two hundred people in attendance. No comparison to Toldos Aharon. Still, the people in this Toireh v'Yireh have more energy than the average crane. And their kids, what can I say, they have more energy than the fastest Arabian horses. And when they see me, these kids, over twenty of them approach me, forming a circle around me. Who are you? they ask. What's your name? Why do you have a ring on your left finger? Don't you know that rings are only for ladies, not men? Would you mind, please, taking your ring off? What is it that you have in your shirt pocket? Is that a smartphone?

Yes, it is, I tell them in Yiddish.

"Why don't you get rid of your smartphone?"

I can put it in my pants pocket if it bothers you.

"You can give your smartphone to us, and we'll break it for you!"

I need my smartphone for my job.

"What's your job?"

I'm a writer.

An adult watching this tells the kids: "He needs the phone to make a living, and it's therefore permitted."

They accept the ruling.

I address the kids, asking them to tell me what they have learned today. Once they answer, I ask them to recite for me, by heart, the text they have been studying in the last few days. The kids, hearing my request, in their kind of Yiddish, start reciting the texts. It's amazing to watch, listen, and realize how educated these kids are. These little kids, I guess between eight and twelve years of age, recite, by heart, entire pages of complex Talmudic texts, word for word. How do they do it? Not only do they do it, but they also do it while smiling, with a shine in their eyes and pride in their hearts.

Oh, God, could human beings be more cute, sweet, lively, or educated than these kids? Even The Name, I can tell, is proud of them today.

They are all here, of course, to celebrate the Simḥas Beis Hashoeivah.

What is a Simḥas Beis Hashoeivah? It is connected to the Temple, the holy place that once was, but no more. Once a year, when the Temple was still standing, water was drawn from the belly of the earth and splashed over the altar. That's when the first Simḥas Beis Hashoeivah took place. To remember this, Ḥaredi Jews observe the Simḥas Beis Hashoeivah, the celebration of drawing up water, hoping that the Third Temple will soon descend from Heaven.

The fact that the location of the Temple that once was is a mere five-minute ride from here gives this celebration special meaning.

There was another Sukkot custom during the Temple days: priests circling the alter with the lulav. These days, religious Jews rotate the bimah with their Four Species while reciting the prayer, "Help me, oh, God; save me, oh, God; and please make me successful."

This custom is called Hoshanot (or Hoishanes), and my presence will be welcomed in Toldos Aharon, I am told via a message to my iPhone in the wee hours of the morning, at exactly noon tomorrow. The person who sent me this message also has an iPhone, or another kind of smartphone, both forbidden in his community.

Well, these Ḥasidim are not Germans. The smartphone might be forbidden, but it doesn't mean they can't have one. Prohibitions, especially in Yiddish, sometimes mean anything but prohibitions. What do they mean, then? Nobody knows exactly, but everybody is hoping that when the Messiah arrives, he will explain what the word *prohibition* means.

In any case, I reply: I'll come.

These Jews Think They Are Jordanians

Death to the Zionists!

At noon, on the dot, I'm in Toldos Aharon.

The place, no surprise, is packed. Dressed in gold, each man holds his Four Species high and proud. The shul looks like a brilliant color display: gold and green.

The placement order of the congregation's members for the service is visually brilliant. Children are at the center, on the floor; around them are tables for the older folks who want to sit from time to time; the rest, about 90 percent of the people, stand on bleachers, divided between the married and the singles. And since each group is dressed differently, the visual effect is stunning.

I take my place between the children and the elders, watching the children's fashion today. Almost all of them are dressed in three-quarter-length pants and black socks. A few are with white socks, which means either that they are from different Ḥasidic courts or that they are from the family of the Rebbe, as one person explains to me, who are groomed to become a Rebbe one day in the future. To be a future Rebbe, I guess, you need to be trained in putting on white socks.

All people around me have black leather shoes; I have sneakers. I also have an Apple Watch, and the children look at it intensely.

They think, perhaps, that Satan is hiding inside it. I let them believe what they want.

The Rebbe leads the prayer, a prayer that goes slower than the fattest elephant, and he shakes his greenery, which he holds with both his hands, moving them up and down, right and left, front and back as if he were chasing someone away, maybe Satan and maybe an imaginary beautiful Ḥasidic girl. Though he prays very slowly, his shaking is exceptionally energetic, full of power, and more intense than a jackhammer. At times it seems as if he's trying to dig into a heavy concrete wall with his lulav, pushing harder, harder, and harder.

He prays: "Help me, oh, God; save me, oh, God; and please make me successful." When the Rebbe is done shaking the Four Species, the Ḥasidim follow up by doing the same.

After about an hour or so, the thousands of Ḥasidim start moving. They must circle the bimah, one by one by one by one, as tradition dictates.

The clock on the wall shows one hour earlier than it is. "This is Jordanian time," one Ḥasid explains to me, because "we don't use Zionist time." These Jews, don't you know, are Jordanians. I check the time in Amman on my iPhone, and it's the same as in Jerusalem. But who cares? It sounds good, creative, and a bit anti-Zionist.

No matter what the actual hour is, the time moves slowly.

Why do they shake the lulav and the other three species with it? Some say that this is done to send away evil spirits; others say this is done to remind The Name that the same way these Four Species need water to grow, so do His children, the Jews, need plenty of rain to survive. If the second reason is correct, The Name must be a little deaf or slow in understanding, and that's why they shake the species so much.

Once the prayer is over, I go out.

It's raining outside, the second rain this year. The Name, you could say, got the message.

I get some groceries, drop them at the hotel, and move to Lelev. I haven't heard from them in a while and wondered if they preferred that I come no more. But all's good, as it turns out. Reb Moishe, a nice Lelever Ḥasid, invites me for a Sabbath meal at his home following the evening prayer.

Who else is in the shul? Reb Yankev Ḥaim. Did the Rebbe tell you when I can sit down with him for a chat? I ask him.

"Not yet," says he, but once he has the Rebbe's answer, he will relay it to me.

Yeah, yeah.

The prayer service goes fast this evening, much quicker than any prayer at the Reb Ahrelaḥ, and Reb Moishe and I walk to his home for the Sabbath meal.

He was the Rebbe's study mate before the Rebbe became a Rebbe, he tells me, but now the ex-friend is a holy man, his leader, and he will follow the Rebbe everywhere and anywhere. How does it go from being a friend to becoming a follower? I ask him.

He doesn't understand my question. "He is the Rebbe," he says to me, and that's it.

What makes a Rebbe? I ask him.

This, he says, is something I will probably not understand, since I don't have a Rebbe.

Could he try to explain it?

Well, what is there to explain? A Rebbe is a Rebbe, period.

We soon reach Reb Moishe's home, and I am seated next to his grandchildren, little kids.

Oh, boy, these little kids are something! Curious, bright, and sweet, all combined into one.

They want to know everything about me, the stranger at the table. I tell them that I'm a journalist, immediately igniting their imagination.

One of them asks: How do you become a journalist? And another wants to know, Can I become a journalist too? They have more questions, of course, as the evening progresses: Did you interview a prime minister? Can I interview a prime minister? How do you get to interview a prime minister – do you have to show him a press card? If you have a press card, can you meet anybody you want? Can I get a press card too? And so on, and on, and on.

I look at them, listen to them, and ask myself: Will these inquisitive kids ever ask, What makes a Rebbe?

On the streets outside, there's new graffiti. "Death to the Zionists," and "Zionism = Holocaust."

Got it.

The holiday continues.

Why Can't Reform Jews Have Good Food?

To avoid getting sick, take off your clothes and stand naked facing the moon

The next day, I go to lunch in Baka, quite a distance from Mea Shearim, join an American Progressive rabbi and her family, and get a perspective on Mea Shearim from a safe distance.

Women in Mea Shearim rarely join men in public social activities, including religious activities such as prayer in the synagogue. Ḥaredi women who like to pray either do it at home or, if they prefer to go to shul, pray in the Ezras Noshim (Ezrat Nashim), a place designated for women in the shul, usually above the men's section – which is why I personally have limited access to the women in the community. But no woman functions as a rabbi in the Ḥaredi world. There are those who are known as a *rebbetsen*, a term usually meaning the wife of the rabbi, some of whom advise women in the congregation on matters spiritual and psychological. Some *rebbetsens* are also in charge of the community's finances, wielding immense power. In Reform Judaism, on the other hand, there are more female rabbis than female congregants.

The woman I'm visiting today is such a rabbi. A Reform rabbi, male or female, has almost nothing in common with a Rebbe. A Rebbe is hereditary, meaning if you are the son of a Rebbe, most likely you will be one as well. The children of Reform rabbis, on the other hand, are often not even religious. In fact, some Reform rabbis I met in the past don't believe in God to start with. Many Reform rabbis, by the way, don't differentiate between Jew and non-Jew or between believer and non-believer, and they may regularly support this or that Palestinian cause.

I'm seated at the rabbi's sukkah, which in this case is a bit of a depressing place, and the food at the table, may I say, is fit for flies and rats. It has very little taste, if at all, though it's healthy. There's no Coke Zero here, Diet Coke, or Pepsi Max. There is no carbonated liquid of any kind, to be exact. But you can have pure water, if you wish, right from the faucet. Do you want cholent? Not here. Do you want gefilte fish? They have little bites of it, but it tastes like a reformed gefilte fish, nothing any Jew from Mea Shearim would even recognize. There are salads here, vegetable salads, fried peppers without anything, and all kinds of environmentally friendly foods, meaning no meat or chicken and none of their derivatives.

There's something big missing here, beyond just food or environment, and it's called "soul." What is a soul? The Ḥasidim have it, and you feel it every minute you are with them. It's something that connects you with the heavens, with angels, and with The Name, even if The Name doesn't exist. That soul, be it what it is, is what connects me to the Reb Ahrelaḥ, for instance. It's something that precedes us, them and me, long before either of us was born. It's that "Jewish" thing that they and I share, a history and a fate that form the core of what we are, a relationship – sometimes a bit bizarre, I may add – to The Name. This Reform rabbi and her husband don't have it, not a trace of it. They don't even have – sorry for coming back to food – a potato kugel here.

They are, in short, a waste of time.

I go back to Mea Shearim.

My neighbor Motta, spotting me on the hotel's terrace, asks me: Where have you been today?

I was invited for a meal by a Reform rabbi, I say.

"How was the food? Pretty dry, ah?"

Yes.

"They have no taste."

The man is right.

Motta invites me to his sukkah for a nosh.

When visiting a Ḥasidic family that you already know, the rules change. Women, for instance, often join the table and participate in discussions with the men, since now we are a "family." Similarly, in Motta's sukkah, at his mother's home, women are present, and they talk to me, a man. Across from me is a lady fifty years of age, and she is already a grandma, a very happy grandma, who looks not a day above forty. One of her children puts eight different cakes and cookies on the table, all of which she baked. I bite into them, and I immediately know that she will never be a Reform rabbi. Her daughter, a beauty, is married to a handsome man, and I am told exactly how this couple met. "We prayed for three days, twenty-four hours each day, and at the last minute, we found this man, my son-in-law."

God only knows how many hours the man prayed.

Tomorrow, by the way, is Hoishaneh Rabbeh (Hoshanah Rabbah), the last day of Sukkot, a day with its own rituals. For example, holding several willows and beating them on the ground or other solid surfaces. Why that? Well, it turns out that even though the fate of every creature for the rest of the year has been signed on Yom Kippur, the signed verdict has not yet been delivered to the proper location in Heaven. This means that there is still a chance for those signed for a lousy year to change their terrible fate and reverse the judgment; a new verdict, a good one now, will be placed where all the verdicts are kept in Heaven. Therefore, it is a custom to greet each other on Hoishaneh Rabbeh with the blessing "*A gitten kvittel*," which means, "May you have a good paper." What does it have to do with the willows, you may ask? Well, beating the willows mercilessly causes all sins to disappear, and you will have an excellent year.

Try it.

Another custom I read in a Ḥaredi publication is Minḥag Hatsel, the Custom of Shadow. This custom is fascinating, though I don't know how many people follow it. It goes like this: On the evening of Hoishaneh Rabbeh, you go out, anywhere the moon is visible, and you take off your clothes – all of them – and then look at the shadow of your body by the light of the moon. If the shadow is clear, this means that you are going to have a fantastic year. On the other hand, if the shadow is not clear, you must get dressed fast and start praying very hard, begging The Name to change your bad fate. If the shadow made by one limb or another, let's say, your right hand, is unclear, this means that you are going to get hurt on that limb during the year, maybe even lose it all the way. Solution: pray.

If you see your neighbor standing on the street naked, now you know what he's doing.

Do Ḥaredi people, in general, believe in it? On my street, at least, no one is standing naked.

On Hoishaneh Rabbeh, how fitting, I meet a German acquaintance who lives in Israel and chat with him on issues very close to his heart: Ḥaredim. What about Ḥaredim? He hates them. Who gave those people, those Ḥasidic Jews, he demands to know, the right to have streets free of cars on the Sabbath? I want to know, in response, why he doesn't go back to Germany to enjoy the cars over there, since he's so bothered by the Ḥaredim here? This upsets him, as you might imagine. He is also very, very upset that Ḥaredi women cover their hair. I, in response, send him to Prenzlauer Berg, where he can have his women dressed to his taste. This upsets him even more. He doesn't want to correct the Germans; he wants to fix the Jews. Period!

He is upset, he is angry. And now he wants to know why Ḥaredi women can't sit next to their husbands in the synagogue.

It's funny to watch a German, who is not Jewish, and an atheist on top of that, getting so upset at a synagogue's seating order of Ḥaredi Jews.

I can't blame him, to be honest. His friends, secular Israeli Jews, speak the same way about the Ḥaredim, and most likely, he picked it up from them.

On the streets outside, "Death to the Zionists" and "Zionism = Holocaust" have been painted over. They are no more, at least for now.

Tomorrow is Simḥas Toireh (Simḥat Torah), in which the last chapters of the Five Books of Moses are read in the synagogues. The Name shows Moses the Land of Israel, a land he will not enter, and Moses dies. He is buried, says the Bible (in Deuteronomy), "and no one knows his place of burial to this day." No Jew – or German – will be able to pray at his grave. God, it is clear, doesn't look positively on people who pray at graves. Yet many Ḥaredim do precisely that. Why? Because.

Grave or not, get ready for the next holiday!

How to Purify the Bodies of Dead Jews

Do Rebbes give interviews?

On the holiday of Simḥas Toireh, Happiness of Torah, a celebration of the fact that they have read the whole Torah in the course of the year, religious Jews celebrate the Torah more than any other day. In synagogues, the Torah scrolls, containing the Five Books of Moses, are taken out from the Holy Ark in what is called Hakufes (Hakafot), and their carriers dance with the scrolls in big circles. Everybody in the congregation joins in the circles, dancing, singing, eating, drinking, and having the time of their lives.

I am at the shul of the Karlin-Stolin Ḥasidim, just steps from my hotel, watching the Ḥasidim as they dance with the Torah scrolls in their arms. The scrolls, each pretty heavy, have beautiful silver crowns on top of them, accentuating the respect these people have for the writings of their forefathers.

And soon, a Ḥasid approaches me, asking if I would like to dance with one of the Torah scrolls. Well, of course. I like to try everything. Promptly, another Ḥasid takes off his tallit and gives it to me, since carrying the Holy Book requires, by tradition, to have a tallit on. I put on the tallit, take the scroll, and dance with the Ḥasidim, encircling the bimah in a holy dance. A few little children are standing by the bimah, and every time I pass by them, they bend down and drop hot kisses on the scroll. Kiss after kiss after kiss, as if the Torah scroll were the most delicious of cookies.

It occurs to me that what I'm holding in my hands, the Torah scroll, is the basis of Judaism. Along the ages, Jews risked their lives to protect the Torah scrolls. If a fire started in a synagogue, for example, Jews would run into the burning building to protect the scrolls, just like the one I'm holding. According to the Sages, the Five Books of Moses were uttered by The Name and written by Moses, meaning that the real author of these five books that I'm now holding, if one is to believe the Sages, is The Name. And, just a reminder, without the Five Books of Moses, there would be no Judaism, no Christianity, and no Islam. No wonder these kids kiss the scroll so passionately.

Once I'm done and outside on the street, walking in no particular direction, several people stop me to chat. "Why don't you come to us for the Hakufes? Come tomorrow morning. You'll love it!" "Why don't you come to us, at the big Ger? Come tomorrow; it will be amazing!"

A few steps later, two Ger Ḥasidim, followers of the Palace Ger, stop to chat with me. "How dare Rabbi Shaul," one of them demands, raising his voice at me, "split the Ger Ḥasidic court when the Rebbe is still alive? That's an unheard-of crime! He who follows Rabbi Shaul is a participant to murder, a murder of a living, kicking, successful Ḥasidic court!"

Both are impeccably dressed, as if they were on their way to a modeling job, in tailored Ḥasidic clothes that probably cost as much as a new Mercedes.

It's amusing to watch rich people getting so upset because not everything in life goes the way they want.

And so, when morning arrives, I make my way to a shul where followers of Rabbi Shaul daven to celebrate the morning Hakufes with them.

This is not a Ger shul, neither the Nadlan nor the Torah, some tell me when I start chatting with them in Hebrew and English.

But when I switch to Yiddish, they change their tune. Yes, most of the people in this shul, they now say, are Ḥasidim who split from the Palace Rebbe. "We are a Ḥasidic court in the making," one of the Ḥasidim tells me. Another one adds: "What we are doing these days will affect not only the Ger court but the rest of Judaism. This is major!"

Shulem, a man who strikes me to be around fifty years of age, works in a Jewish burial society, and he shares with me his life story. "Immediately after my Sheva Braḥot" – meaning the week-long celebration of his wedding – "I told my wife: 'I want to join the burial society.'" She was shocked, but eventually, "she joined the burial society as well."

How long after the Sheva Braḥot did she join the burial society?

"Thirty years later."

This man has a funny bone.

What does this Shulem do as a member of the burial society? Many things, he says, including the Taharah, purification. What's purification? "I get the body of a dead man, my wife does the same with women's bodies, and I take off his clothes, or whatever else he has on his body, and I wash him with soap. Then, using a hose, I empty the food from his intestine so that he's totally clean, inside and out. Then I, with the help of others, put him on a special mat that we can drop and hoist, and we immerse the body in the mikveh. We hoist the body, dress it with shrouds, and spread sand from the Holy Land over the body."

Sometimes, he tells me, he knows the people whose bodies he purifies, and it's not easy to do. The worst, he says, is to purify the bodies of children. That's tough emotionally. All told, he's happy he's doing it. He even tries to make a joke out of it. "In this job, the client never comes back asking for a refund."

Do you think of the day when you will be purified? I mean, did you arrange a burial plot for yourself?

"Yes, I bought a plot."

Where?

"Mount of Olives."

How much does it cost?

"I paid $18,000."

That's all?

"I don't know how much it costs today. I bought my plot twenty years ago."

I came here to hear about the New Ger and their Rebbe, but I'm spending my time talking about the dead. Luckily, at last, the herring arrives, the cholent, the kugels, the brandies, sweets of all kinds, Coke Zero and Pepsi Max.

"If you are going to write about us," a middle-aged Ḥasid shares his wish with me, "you will write nice things. Right?"

I'll write what you say to me.

"Thanks."

How do these people know that I'm writing about them? They must have heard from The Name, as far as I can tell.

Not everybody in this shul is a follower of Rabbi Shaul, and this I find out once I'm outside.

A five-minute walk from the shul, a Ger Ḥasid, who was in the shul with me, approaches me. "Now," he says, "you have to go to the big shul, talk with the real Ger Ḥasidim and pray with them. You can't make up your mind if you listen only to members of Shaul's group."

I thank him for his advice, and we part ways.

I keep walking.

Where to? God knows.

I'm spending my days in this holiday season going from one shul to the other, from one prayer service to the next.

What are shuls and prayers all about? Most often, they have to do with the Temple. After the Temple, the center of Jewish worship, was destroyed, Judaism faced the danger of being wiped off the face of the earth. Hence the shuls, a brilliant invention of the rabbis who came up with it. A shul, they decreed, will function as a replacement for the Temple – until it is built again. And the prayers will, for the time being, replace the Temple's animal offerings.

Thus was Judaism saved.

But I have a question: Prayer replaces the sacrifices, the shul replaces the Temple; does the Rebbe replace God?

I think that I should see a Rebbe, personally. I would like to stand in front of a Rebbe, look into each other's eyes, and have the Rebbe explain to me what a Rebbe is.

"Don't set your hopes high," a Ḥaredi journalist who works in the Ḥaredi media tells me. "Rebbes don't give interviews. Forget it! We have tried it many times and always failed. It's not going to happen. Change your plans."

Perhaps he's right, but I still hope that I'll get to meet the Toldos Aharon Rebbe.

And if David the Philanthropist is right, I should meet the Rebbe soon.

God's Name Revealed: Yaakov Aryeh Alter

Give me money and I will resurrect your dead relatives

When the holiday is over, the people of Mea Shearim are not eager to say goodbye. Come evening, many of them do Hakufes Shniyes, Second Hakafot. Don't bother to figure out in what Book of Moses they found this additional holiday. But why not have one more evening of fun?

The Ḥasidim, all stripes of them, pack the local synagogues, and some fill the streets as well, as they dance wildly while carrying the Torah scrolls. Some, like those of Breslev, drive around with big vans while dancing on top of their vans, with blaring music – "From the mouth of God, from the mouth of God, may all Israel be blessed" – and distribute booklets for men who spilled their seed and regret it.

Some, sadly, will never spill any seed anytime soon.

A car drives on the streets of Mea Shearim at this very moment, announcing the funeral of yet another Ḥaredi, who returned his soul to Heaven and whose body will be buried in the Mount of Olives. It will take another thirty-five hundred years, as you already know, for the soul to come back to where it came from, the Seventh Heaven.

Meantime, the Second Hakafot are soon over. But the funerals go on, and the story of Ger continues.

One of the three Ger Ḥasidim I met over that delicious omelet invites me to his home. He plays for me, among other things, an audio recording of his conversation with the son of the Palace Rebbe. This relates to Simḥas Toireh of two years ago, and in the recording, the Rebbe's son warns him of what will happen to any Ger Ḥasid who dares to celebrate the holiday with Rabbi Shaul and dance with the Torah scrolls with him. The Rebbe's son says: "Whoever celebrates Simḥas Toireh with Shaul Alter tears himself off from Ger and will be thrown out from the community, from all its *moisdois* [institutions, such as yeshivas and *ḥeiders*] and *shtiebels*. This will be announced tonight in all the *shtiebels*."

This is a threat, as brutal as such threats come, to anyone who simply goes to Rabbi Shaul's shul for one evening: he will be thrown out of the community, and his children will be thrown out of their schools. Just being in the presence of Rabbi Shaul, known as one of the most prominent scholars of Ger in the past, merits a divorce, with all its ugly consequences.

My host tells me another story. On a Friday night two years ago, just before the split between the Palace Rebbe and Rabbi Shaul took place, Rabbi Shaul went to pray in the Palace, accompanied by another person. In the part of the prayer when the Rebbe traditionally faces the Ḥasidim, one of the Ḥasidim claimed that the person accompanying Rabbi Shaul was at that very moment looking at Rabbi Shaul instead of the Rebbe, which is a severe offense against The Name, and immediately that person was taken out and beaten up ruthlessly for quite some time.

On the eve of Simḥas Toireh, he tells me, Rabbi Shaul decided to celebrate Simḥas Toireh with his followers outside of Ger, thereby splitting from Ger. According to his followers, Rabbi Shaul chose Simḥas Toireh to do the split in keeping with the same time frame, Simḥas Toireh, that my great-grandfather, the founder of the Radzyn dynasty, split from Kotzk-slash-Ger, to create his own court.

I think now of what I was told the other day, that when I speak in Ḥasidic Yiddish with the people here, "it's not you and me talking, but your grandfather and my grandfather talking." And now it feels so much like it. Rabbi Shaul's grandfather and my grandfather are uniting, splitting from Ger and meeting hostility.

My host has some good news to share as far as he's concerned. Rabbi Shaul and his people don't have to pray anymore at the girls' school but have their own shul now.

That said, he plays for me a video of a speech by one of the Rebbe's lieutenants. Speaking of the Rebbe, Yaakov Aryeh Alter, he says: "A word of the Torah: The Rebbe, that's God."

If I ever wondered what a Rebbe is, here is the answer. The Rebbe, at least the Ger Rebbe, is God. Period.

I think I should go back to the Tikvah Fund and tell Rabbi Yehoshua Pfeffer: I know God's name. I found out. His name is Yaakov Aryeh Alter.

Nice name for a God, by the way. Very creative.

Yet, as surprising as this might be, the Gerer is not the only one making such a claim. Rabbi Eliezer Berland, a controversial figure with thousands of followers, reportedly said the same. According to the newspaper *Haaretz*, Rabbi Berland said: "The Tzaddik [righteous one, another name for a Rebbe] is not a person at all. He is the Holy One Blessed Be He [God] Himself who descends in the form of man."

And it is him, of course, who is the Tzaddik.

Rabbi Berland, accused of committing sexual offenses against his followers, including rape, and defrauding them of vast sums of money as well, under bogus promises of curing the cureless and resurrecting the dead, is not the best company to be in. But the two leaders, Yaakov Aryeh and Eliezer, might enjoy each other's company.

As for us, mere mortals, the Sabbath is soon upon us. And with it, my dears, the gefilte fish, the kugels, the cholent, the kishke, the *galleh*, the *gehakte leber*, the strudel, and the brandy.

And a little Torah reading.

Moses the Lawgiver has died, as was read in the shuls, and it's time to restart the cycle of weekly Torah readings from the very beginning, from Genesis. It's there where the Bible tells the story of Adam and Eve, how they walked naked in the Garden of Eden until they committed the first human sin, a sin that made them aware that they were naked. Being ashamed of being naked, they covered their sexual organs. With their organs covered, temptation rose, and Adam slept with Eve.

At this point, if I have learned anything here in Mea Shearim, Adam started wearing a *shtreimel* and Eve a *tiḥel.*

Nice.

But don't expect a *tish* this Sabbath, my dear, at least not in Toldos Aharon or Boyan. The Boyaner Rebbe, I hear, left Jerusalem to rest somewhere else in the country. The Toldos Aharon Rebbe, his gabbai tells me, also left Jerusalem for some time to rest somewhere. Other Rebbes might have done the same, and I don't even check.

And what about the Ḥaredim, the rank and file? Are they also resting?

Not really.

Come to Vizhnitz, Stand with the Boys and Experience It

How to make sure that your soul does not burn for eternity in boiling excrement

Tomorrow, Sunday, ten thousand Ḥaredim, so I hear, will gather in a big arena in the city of Elad, a city that prides itself as the City of Yeshivas, for the V'Shinantom event. What kind of event is it? From what I've been told, V'Shinantom is an organization that gives award certificates to men across various sects of the Ḥaredi world who were tested in multiple tractates and proved broad knowledge in them. It's like what I saw in Shoimrei Haḥoimois a while back, but on a much larger scale.

Motty Steinmetz will perform, in addition to some other singers. His manager, Ruvi, is heading the music band that will accompany the singers.

I go to Elad.

The event takes place in an arena outside the residential areas, where thousands of people, primarily young, sit on plastic chairs, facing a big stage that emits blinding lights, where Ḥaredi leaders and musicians are to share space.

The seating arrangement of the audience is not designated, and people sit where they choose. What do they choose? Litvaks sit with other Litvaks, Ḥasidim sit with other Ḥasidim, and Sephardim sit with other Sephardim.

As the event starts, a rabbi asks the men, who sit at a big table facing the stage, simple questions, but they don't have the answers. They can repeat pages by heart, perhaps, but not much more. If the Ger Rebbe, Yaakov Aryeh Alter, were here, he would be embarrassed, as his system of studying the Talmud is looking totally ineffective on this V'Shinantom stage.

Luckily, after long embarrassing moments, a few men have a few answers, though not always correct.

A speaker comes to the podium. "They want to destroy the Torah," he shouts, not bothering to give any details of who "they" are, but it's good to have an enemy, I guess, and nobody asks any questions.

The star of the evening, Motty Steinmetz, enters the stage.

He starts with merry songs, which are okay, but I think he could do better.

It is when he drops the merry and goes for the emotional, especially in the song "In my heart, I will build a tabernacle to glorify His name," that he catches my heart. Images of the Holy Temple in Jerusalem, as Ḥaredi people believe it used to look, are projected on the screen, and Motty does what he knows best: sucks us into his world.

A procession of the Who's Who in the Ḥaredi world follows, each leader sitting for just a few minutes on the stage. So many Ḥasidic, Litvak, and Sephardi leaders that even I am impressed.

And then Rabbi David Batsri, accompanied by his son, mounts the stage, where he is introduced as a holy man.

David Batsri is a man I've met more than once, and I know him to be a crook who squeezes thousands of shekels from the poorest of people, promising them to "repair their souls," souls that have become defected by Spillage of Seed. He tells them that unless they pay him and his son exuberant sums of money, they will burn for eternity in boiling excrement in Hell. If this Batsri is called a holy man, and no one on the stage is protesting, I guess they are as holy as he is.

The event, combining songs and speeches, lasts for over four hours, and it's a bit messy. Each Ḥaredi group in the audience wants to have their songs, and there's little unity between them. And when the singing and speeches are over, the thousands leave for the waiting buses outside to take them back home. Only then, as the people go, the awarding of the certificates starts, with no audience. This is strange. The whole event was for them, in their honor, but they are pushed into the dark as if they were having kosher marital relations.

So be it.

As for me, I sit down with Motty Steinmetz for a little chat in one of the back rooms of the arena.

"After our last meeting," Motty starts, "I thought a lot about what you asked me, and it bothers me because I said things to you that I don't feel were right."

I have expected this, and I listen to him.

"I feel that in the past few years, my connection to the Master of the Universe advanced. But saying that I was not connected with

Him until that day is not true. What I want to tell you is this: I was always connected to The Name. Like any Jew, I go through different stages in life, some up and others down. There were times in my life that were difficult, especially when I went through the divorce from my first wife when I had to digest what just happened to me, but I was always connected to The Name. Yet, yes, in the last few years, my connection to The Name has strengthened. But I always had it. I remember praying the Sabbath morning prayers in Vizhnitz as a young man. What a connection to The Name! The Sabbath morning prayers lasted four hours! Oh, you have to come and experience it! Hear the prayer. Stand in the middle, with the yeshiva boys. Inside."

At Shoimrei Emunim in Jerusalem, the Sabbath morning prayer lasts five hours!

"Five hours? Well, we are not in a competition."

He goes on: "I believe that The Name is ever-present in us, sustaining us every second of our lives. For example, when I have a performance and feel that my voice is not very good, I say: 'Master of the Universe, You are in control of everything, and I have complete faith that You can renew my voice, make it the best it can be.' You know, it works!"

He's sweet. I never doubted his faith; on the contrary, I thought that admission of spiritual highs and lows testifies to genuine faith, but he feels the need to clarify his thoughts.

"Ruvi said to me," says Motty, "meet him [me] after the event and tell him everything you want, so I did."

He and Ruvi and Naomi. As always. Ruvi and Naomi are the papa and the mama, and Motty is the child, and the three were just having a lovely outing together. The child went to the stage, and papa and mama made sure that he's happy, playing nicely and having the time of his life. Later on, perhaps, they will buy a big pizza for the child and eat together.

"What do you think of the event in general?" Motty asks me before I depart.

Elad, I tell him, is not Mea Shearim.

The event in Elad, at least for my taste, lacked spirituality. It takes a Litvak to think that this event was inspiring, but if you ever tasted the joy of a gefilte fish, you know that Elad will never be able to compete with Mea Shearim.

Yet, I'm intrigued about his Vizhnitz, and I make up my mind to go there during this journey.

As of now, I return to Jerusalem, to Mea Shearim.

What's new here? It's quieter than during the holiday season but still very alive. Funerals go on, making Shulem and his colleagues busy; the wall painters of Mea Shearim keep at each other with black letters and white paint, and the two courts of Ger keep the fight alive.

A draft document, which seems to have been overseen by leaders from the Palace Ger, is sent to me by one of Rabbi Shaul's followers. In it, the writer admits that physical violence was exercised against the followers of Rabbi Shaul.

This is good for history, he says to me, in case Ger Nadlan folks deny it years later.

For the moment, I'm going to sit down with Motta, my neighbor, and have him tell me everything he wants about his Rebbe.

Your Daughter Is Pregnant!

A gefilte fish can bring you closer to God

Motta is having a cup of black coffee at his mother's home, and I join him.

We sip from the bitter water together and chat about the most pressing issue of our time: Rebbes.

What is a Rebbe? I ask him.

Quoting a particular Rebbe, a man I never heard of, Motta says: "There is a rabbi of a country, of a city, or a synagogue, and then there is a 'miracle rabbi,' a Rebbe. From a Jewish religious perspective, the country rabbi controls a country; the city rabbi controls the city, and the synagogue rabbi controls the synagogue. A Rebbe controls himself, and that's why people follow him."

What's a Rebbe for you?

"For me? Everything."

What does this mean?

Speaking about his Rebbe, the Boyaner Rebbe, Motta says: "I dream about him, and I live him. I think of him, and I pray for him. And he prays for me too. The energy that I have, the power that I have comes from him. I live with him in me all the time. Not only I. My father of blessed memory, who was older than the Rebbe, felt similarly toward the Rebbe; he felt him every minute. My mother too. She feels him, his strength, all the time, and it gives her the capacity to go on. She was in the hospital for a few months, and two months ago, her situation deteriorated; she was hanging between Heaven and earth, and we thought she wouldn't survive. We went to the Rebbe, and he said: 'She will come back home and stand on her feet.' Even I, with all my faith, didn't believe it. But a day later, her situation drastically improved, and she was released from the hospital."

Hendel Esther is out of the hospital, correct, but she can't stand on her feet, not yet. After catching the coronavirus a few months back, she became sick and has not recovered. She needs a wheelchair, and an oxygen tank is next to her all the time.

How do you think the Rebbe knew that your mother would be out of the hospital?

"I don't know. Either because he prayed or because he felt it."

What is a Rebbe?

"A connection to God."

In other words, if you connect to the Rebbe, you connect to God.

"Exactly." Every human has something Godly in them, only the Rebbe has more of it, Motta tells me. He loves the Rebbe, he says, and in general, "I'm attracted to righteous people."

When you look at him, do you see something Godly?

"Exactly, exactly. But this doesn't mean that he's God; what it means is this: his Godly soul, it's so clean that the Ray of Light from Heaven shines stronger and brighter on him, and therefore we can see it."

When you say that you love the Rebbe, does it mean that you would like to kiss him?

"No. I love The Name. Can I kiss The Name? No."

What do you want to do when you see the Rebbe?

"I want to be connected to him."

What does this mean?

"Spiritually, I want my soul to connect to him."

Do you eat *shirayim*?

"Yes."

Why?

"We believe that what the Rebbe eats is like the sacrifices in the Temple. When a pure man like him eats, the food that he leaves behind, the *shirayim*, is like the *shirayim* of the Temple sacrifices. Like in the time of the Temple, when the Jews ate the *shirayim*, what was left of the sacrifices from the Altar."

What do you feel when you eat the *shirayim*?

"It gives me life."

Meaning that you are closer to God after eating gefilte fish from the Rebbe's plate?

"Yes."

The Boyaner Rebbe, Motta tells me, became a Rebbe at the age of twenty-five. But Motta knew him since the future Rebbe was thirteen years of age and was highly impressed with him. Starting when the future Rebbe was sixteen, Motta was taking personal care of him, including taking care of his food daily, until the future Rebbe was married, at twenty-one.

Motta is a visual artist, and he shows me some of his paintings, primarily modern and abstract. He is very talented and competent, as far as I can judge, and next month, he will have an exhibition of his art somewhere in the city. If I want, he'll send me all the details.

I don't know if I'll go, but I am happy that his peers appreciate his art.

From time to time, Motta tells me, he goes to the Rebbe with a *kvittel* and a *pidyen*. What's a *pidyen*? It's a bit of a complex idea, but it can be summed up in one word: money. How much money is a *pidyen*?

"Depends on the person and how much the person can give."

How much did you give last time?

"One hundred shekels."

Did you put the money in his hands?

"No. The *kvittel* I give him in the hand, and the money I put on the table."

Why give him money?

"I don't know how to explain it."

Can you try?

"When you give a Rebbe money, it gives him the power to help you."

How?

"How? This I don't know."

What Motta does know is this: "Whenever I pray to The Name, I remember the Rebbe, my late father, and my grandparents; I imagine them in front of me, then I connect with the Rebbe, and I know that my prayer has a much better chance to be answered."

This happens when he prays outside the Boyaner shul or when the Rebbe is absent. When the Rebbe is present while he is praying, he tells me, he prays to The Name, saying Blessed be You, Lord our God, while his eyes are fixated on the Rebbe, because the Rebbe is the conduit through which the prayer goes to The Name.

I ask Motta: assuming that the beauty of a woman, if she happened to be beautiful, is Godly, would you understand me if I pray to God while looking at a stunning lady? After all, the same as you do, looking at the Rebbe while praying to God, I too can look at a stunning lady and have her beauty, her Godly beauty, serve as my conduit to the Lord. Am I making sense to you? I ask him.

"Yes," he answers, to him it does make sense if I do that, but he prefers to look at the Rebbe while praying.

Motta, besides being funny and artsy, is also a handsome man. I ask him: Should a man make sure the room is dark while he has sexual relations with his wife?

"If the wife is ugly, yes," answers the funny man.

Motta's brother, Bentzi, lives nearby. He's not a painter but an artist, nevertheless. What's his art? *Shtreimels*. Yeah, Bentzi is a *shtreimel maḥer*, as they say in Yiddish. In simpler words: he is a *shtreimel* artist.

As I enter Bentzi's home, where his office and "factory" are, he shows me to my seat in the living room, as he goes to the kitchen to bring some sweets and drinks, I assume. But when Bentzi comes back, it's not a cola and cookies he carries but a hot dish, a real meal. Mashed potatoes, cooked vegetables, and schnitzel. His schnitzel, may I say, is the best schnitzel I ever had. Really. As for the mashed potatoes, this comes from the Garden of Eden, where Adam and Eve had the time of their lives. He offers me wine as well, a wine that he makes. The wine, he tells me, he makes for the Rebbe, but he leaves a little for himself. Lucky me, I have it too.

While he knows how to cook and make wine better than most, he doesn't have a clue how to operate a computer, he tells me, and he doesn't follow the news either.

"Why do I need to read the news and know that in America fifty people died in an accident, that people got sick, and other problems like that? What do I need that for? Why do I need all the tumult in the world in my head? If you wake up in the morning and hear about all the world's problems, your heart starts aching, and you get into a bad mood. Why would you need that? Live your life, get up in the morning and say good morning and Moideh Ani, enjoy your home, your family, and you'll feel good. That's the way people live here."

People outside say that the women here have a pretty bad life. The men rule over them, they say, and these women can't do what they want.

"Go look at the couples of Toldos Aharon, the extremists of Mea Shearim. See those couples walking on the street and tell me what you see. You'll see how happy they are together!"

I have heard that line before, and it is true, at least from what I have seen. I also remember that I was quite impressed with Rebbetsen Leah of Toldos Aharon on my first days here. And so far, during my months-long stay here, I have not seen any proof that the women of Mea Shearim are less satisfied with their lives than the women of, say, Berlin. The main difference between these two ladies is this: Mea Shearim ladies have Rebbes, Berlin ladies have Greta.

Tell me, Bentzi, what does the Rebbe mean to you?

"Life."

What does it mean?

"I don't move a single meter without the Rebbe. Everything that I do in life, I ask him first."

Give me an example.

"Everything. If I should accept a job, anything to do with medical issues, which people to meet –"

Did you ask the Rebbe if you could meet me?

"I thought of that, I thought to ask the Rebbe if I should talk to you, but when my mother heard it, she said: 'I say to you: You talk to him!'"

The mother says, Bentzi obeys. She is, I can see, above the Rebbe.

To him, Bentzi tells me, "The Rebbe is the best mediator between me and the Master of the Universe. You don't go to court without a lawyer, you don't do a business transaction without a lawyer, and I do the same. This is the way I was raised."

I still don't fully grasp the Rebbe concept, I tell Bentzi, and nudge him to help me out here.

Bentzi tries harder. What makes a Rebbe, Bentzi says, is the followers. They are the ones who give the power and the ability to the "Rebbe" title bearer to be a Rebbe and to connect to The Name.

This reminds me of an old Ḥasidic tale that every Ḥasidic Jew knows, and it goes like this: Once, a Ḥasidic Jew, in the middle of the night, woke up his wife, Ḥanneh Dvosheh. "Ḥanneh," he said to her, "I just had a dream, a wonderful dream, and you won't believe it. I'm so happy, Ḥanneh!" "What's the dream?" Ḥanneh Dvosheh asked him. "I dreamt," he said, "that I am a Rebbe, a big Rebbe with a thousand Ḥasidim!" She looked at him, at her good-for-nothing husband, and said: "Don't wake me up in the middle of my sleep when you dream that you are a Rebbe. If a thousand Ḥasidim dream that you are their Rebbe, then wake me up!" And immediately, so the story goes, she fell asleep again, while her husband stood in the corner of the room, crying like a baby.

Bentzi goes on. When he asks the Rebbe about a possible match for one of his children, let's say a guy for his daughter, "The Rebbe can tell me how the guy looks, what character he has, and everything about the guy, without ever seeing that guy before. The Rebbe knows everything about the guy based just on the name of the guy and the name of the guy's mother."

I wonder how this works, how the information is transmitted to the Rebbe from God, when all the Rebbe gets from the Ḥasid is the name of the Ḥasid and his mother's name.

"It's something on the scale of prophecy, of Ruaḥ Hakodesh [Holy Spirit]."

The Talmudic Sages say that after the Destruction of the Temple, the power to prophesize was given to the idiots. Are you saying that your Rebbe is an idiot?

"No, no, it's not a prophecy."

His son, listening to our chat, offers his explanation: "It's a help from Heaven."

Go figure what that means.

"I went to the Rebbe the other day and gave him a *kvittel*," Bentzi tells me. "On it, I wrote the names of the people of my family and their mother's name. That's it. The Rebbe looked at the *kvittel* and asked about my daughter: 'What month is she?' He smiled, and then asked me, 'She didn't tell you?' I was very surprised, because I didn't know anything about it. I went out, called my daughter, and said to her, 'Is it nice?' She asked, 'What's the matter?' I said, 'You have news, but you don't tell me?' She was surprised; she didn't know. After we talked, she went to the doctor, took a test, and the result was positive; she was pregnant!"

Why don't we do this: I'll go to the Rebbe with a *kvittel*, on which I'll write my name and my mother's name, and I'll see what the Rebbe says. Can I do it?

Bentzi's son immediately objects. I cannot do this, he says. It's not right. It's not right at all!

I say to him: If you are afraid that I'll find out something that you don't want me to find out, then, it seems to me, you doubt the Rebbe more than I do.

Bentzi agrees. The Rebbe is smart enough to handle me, he says, and holy enough to avoid falling into any trap.

That said, Bentzi tells me that I have to make an appointment first.

Can he make the appointment for me, I ask him?

Well, he gives me the name of the Rebbe's gabbai and his telephone number. I should call him, he says, tell him that I was in Boyan at the Simḥas Beis Hashoieva and that I want to give the Rebbe a *kvittel*. I can tell him that I got the number from the family of Motta and Bentzi, and everything will be good.

What if it doesn't work out? I ask.

I should call Motta, Bentzi says, and he'll take care of it.

Settled. I can't wait.

And now that we've gotten through all that, let's talk about *shtreimels*, I say to Bentzi. When did the *shtreimel* start?

"Oh, what a question. Well, the *shtreimel* didn't 'start.' The *shtreimel was*. Based on the research that I've done, the *shtreimel* was the hat that everybody, not just Jews, was wearing. Historically, most Ashkenazi Jews lived in countries where the weather was cold, and everybody, not just Jews, wore a *shtreimel* to get warm. There are stories, I'm not sure about their authenticity, that at some point there was a decree forbidding Jews from wearing *shtreimels*, and that as a result, some Jews, like the Ger Ḥasidim, made their *shtreimels* bigger than the normal *shtreimel*, while other Jews made theirs smaller – so that they wouldn't look like the gentiles – but everybody had *shtreimels*, Jews and non-Jews. If the story about the decree is true or not, I don't know."

I like this man, straight to the point; no *bobbe maisehs*. Reb Yoilish Krois should learn from him.

And now, some specs: The *shtreimel*, Bentzi tells me, requires 100 to 140 sable tails. It can be made from the tails of other animals, but usually, it's made from sables.

What is the word "*shtreimel*," and where does it come from?

This Bentzi doesn't know. He's not the only one who doesn't know. I asked many Ḥasidim the same question, and to date, none had an answer.

You never asked yourself what "*shtreimel*" means? I ask Bentzi.

"There are many questions that I never asked," he answers.

Every *shtreimel*, if it's any good, is made to order. It must fit exactly on the head, since it's heavier than typical hats. Some Ḥasidim, he tells me, like their *shtreimel* heavy, while others like it as light as possible; some want this width, others want another width; some want their *shtreimel* with a crown (the thinner part on top), others don't.

Someone told me that the Rebbe of Toldos Aharon has a *shtreimel* that costs $26,000. What kind of *shtreimel* is that?

A $26,000 *shtreimel*, Bentzi says to me, doesn't even exist. Whoever gave me this figure has no idea about *shtreimels*. Some *shtreimels* are expensive, those made from pine martens, but nowhere near such a figure.

How much does the *shtreimel* of the Toldos Aharon Rebbe cost? Do you know?

"That *shtreimel* is beautiful. It's made from tails of Baummarder [pine martens], and it costs around $10,000."

Getting a *shtreimel* done takes a lot of work; I find out when Bentzi takes me to another room, where his little "factory" is. He shows me different kinds of tails: Canadian, Russian, and God knows what else. Sables and martens in different stages of the process: the tails, you see, must be soaked, stretched, colored, and glued before they turn into a *shtreimel*.

It's fascinating.

If I become a Rebbe, the Lodzer Rebbe, I will have my Ḥasidim buy the same *shtreimel* as the Toldos Aharon Rebbe has. Yeah!

Which reminds me: the holidays are over, and I should know by now if I'll get to meet the Toldos Aharon Rebbe. I contact David the Philanthropist, and he gives me the numbers of the Rebbe's people. I send a message to one of those people, and he tells me that soon he'll let me know.

I'm waiting.

Excuse Me, Are You in Touch with the Holy Spirit?

Make sure that your children aren't anywhere near this Torah scroll

Back in my hotel room, I read a document sent to me by one of Rabbi Shaul's followers. The document is a letter containing a set of questions sent by an individual to Rabbi Shaul, in printed format, on which Rabbi Shaul wrote his answers with a pen.

The man writes to Rabbi Shaul about a story that he heard, asking if it's true. The story is about a young girl healed from a sickness, and the healing could have come through Rabbi Shaul's intervention. Is that true, he wants to know? Rabbi Shaul answers him that God healed the girl, not him. Another question: Should I, asks the man, always ask the Rabbi what to do? No, Rabbi Shaul answers. The man goes on: Is Rabbi Shaul, he asks, in touch with the Holy Spirit (Ruaḥ Hakodesh)? No, Rabbi Shaul answers, sorry.

The Boyaner Rebbe, I learned earlier, is in touch with the Holy Spirit, but not Rabbi Shaul.

Good to know.

The story of Ger, Yaakov Aryeh versus Shaul, doesn't end. It's been brewing for some years, and who knows what its future will bring. It's a story about a Rebbe, a Rebbe of the largest Ḥasidic court of our time in Israel, and what happens when some Ḥasidim don't want to follow him anymore. This story touches the very core of the Ḥasidic movement, at the heart of the Ḥaredi branch of Judaism and the nerve center of faith. And it puts the "Rebbe" concept up front, projecting a magnifying light on the very essence of a Rebbe. And my question is: Will the Ḥasidim, any Ḥasidim, dare to look at what the light reveals?

There's another question: Can a man who says that the Holy Spirit does not speak from his mouth overwhelm a man who sees himself as a God?

The Saga of Ger continues.

There's an Inauguration of a Torah Scroll this Wednesday late in the afternoon in the city of Ashdod, celebrating a new Torah scroll donated to a shul of the New Ger, those who follow Rabbi Shaul. An Inauguration of a Torah Scroll often entails a dance-and-song procession from the donor's home to the shul, in honor of the Torah and the donor. The followers of the Rebbe, Yaakov Aryeh, want to make sure that no Ger Ḥasid or child of a Ger Ḥasid from their camp, Heaven forbid, sees the procession and, Heaven save us, enjoys it. For this reason, they have added extracurricular activities for the schoolchildren at the exact time of the scheduled procession, to guarantee that no child sees any dancing or singing follower of Rabbi Shaul. In case the child can't come to the extracurricular activities, the parents must make sure that their child is at home, not anywhere else, and sign a special note, to be delivered to the teachers on the next day, that their child was indeed at home during the hours of the procession.

They are obsessed.

Life, of course, is not just Ger. I call the Boyaner Rebbe's gabbai, per Bentzi, and leave a message for him, saying that at the advice of the Brim family, which is the family of Motta and Bentzi, I would like to come to the Rebbe and give him a *kvittel*.

I hope he answers. Will he? Well, it probably depends on how much the Rebbe's gabbai trusts his own Rebbe.

Meanwhile, I am invited to a Sheva Braḥot for Itsik, the guy who, months ago, introduced me to Reb Yeḥezkel Lefkovits of

Shoimrei Haḥoimois. Itsik just got married to a lovely lady, and I am delighted to see him again on his happiest of days.

I go. Besides Itsik, I don't know anybody around, but the food is good, the Pepsi Max is also good, and even the cookies are good. What else is new? These people know good food.

One of these people is Rabbi Nota Schiller, the dean (or *rosh yeshivah*) of Ohr Somayach, a yeshiva geared for *baalei tshuvah*. As far as I know, this man founded Ohr Somayach together with my late rabbi, Berel Schwartzman, when I studied in Mea Shearim.

I would like to meet this man in private.

Would he meet me?

I ask him, and he says that he'd be glad to meet me later on.

Rabbi Nota's specialty is *baalei tshuvah*, the penitent Jews. And if I understand correctly, the kind of *baalei tshuvah* he deals with are educated folks, college students or those who already have academic degrees. This type of *baalei tshuvah* is worlds apart from the *baalei tshuvah* in Breslev, and none of them is expected to marry a Taliban.

Rabbi Nota is the perfect person, I say to myself, to ask my old questions about Messiah ben David, Abraham's white donkey, and the resurrection. If anyone, he should know these issues best.

"Later on" soon arrives, and I mount a white taxi, not a white donkey, and in due time I reach my destination, the Ohr Somayach yeshiva.

When in the Toilet, Don't Think of Women

An Arab cabbie dreams of Ḥasidic women begging him for sex

The yeshiva is one big complex, and the architecture is modern. The study hall features an impressive bookcase, whose upper shelves, those that can be reached only by giants, have light fixtures in them instead of books. There are big windows all around, behind which are eye-pleasing Jerusalem-stone walls, and the place broadcasts peacefulness and tranquility.

Rabbi Nota and I meet in his small but comfortable office, and he offers me grapes, chocolate rugelach, and a cup of Taster's Choice coffee. No, he doesn't have Turkish coffee, for he's not an Israeli; and he doesn't wear a *shtreimel*, for he's not a Ḥasid.

I make a blessing on the coffee, and we are ready to talk.

I ask Rabbi Nota: A Ḥaredi Jew prays three times a day for the resurrection of the dead. Can you tell me the details of what will happen before the resurrection? The donkey, the Messiah, the Prophet Elijah. Is it, by the way, the Prophet Elijah who will be coming on the Patriarch Abraham's white donkey, or is it the Messiah who'll be coming on the donkey?

"We don't have a vivid clarity. We find different positions in the Saying of the Sages and in later commentators about the different stages of what's going to happen when the Messiah comes. I wouldn't attempt to give a graphic picture of something that I don't have clarity on."

I heard two versions. One version says that Messiah ben David will come riding on Patriarch Abraham's donkey, to the Mount of Olives, stand near the graves and say: "You, son of this one and that one, wake up!" And they will rise. Another version I heard claims that the Prophet Elijah will come to Jerusalem, riding on the Patriarch Abraham's donkey, three days before the Messiah arrives to proclaim his arrival ahead of time and urge people to repent their sins. Do you know these versions? Is either of them correct?

"I don't pretend to understand them fully well."

But what is the written text, prior to understanding it –

"We have a premise that the literal text is the beginning of trying to understand, and you have to decode the literal text."

Certain writings of the Sages, he says to me, are written in a special way "in order to communicate ideas and concepts that have to be transmitted from generation to generation but to cloak them in a sense of mystery that only people who are deeply, deeply trained in learning and have achieved a certain level can access them. So, you have extraordinary things that are described –"

It is obvious that Rabbi Nota is not a Ḥasid but a Litvak. He speaks in measured tones, doesn't get excited, and his vocabulary is different.

I ask Rabbi Nota to give me the sources of the stories, since I would love to at least have the correct version, whatever the text's more profound meaning. I want the text, the original text, and wonder if he knows where the text exists.

In response, Rabbi Nota tells me that he will make a list of the sources and send them to me.

Good.

Life is good. In the next few days, I hope, I'll get to enter the Boyaner Rebbe's abode with a *kvittel*, get to meet the Lelever Rebbe for a chat, and get the list of sources from Rabbi Nota. Not to mention the Toldos Aharon Rebbe, which for me is the most important, because I like the Golden Boys and the Tempting Girls of Toldos Aharon.

In any case, I ask Rabbi Nota if, in the meantime, he remembers who is the one riding Abraham's donkey – Messiah ben David or the Prophet Elijah?

"I don't know," he says, and then adds: "I don't think it is to be taken merely simply literal. There is a literal meaning which has significance, but there is also a symbolic meaning, and you can't separate one from the other."

Is the resurrection also symbolic?

"No. Resurrection of the dead is something that will happen."

Why would you say that the story about the process to resurrection is, if I understand you correctly, allegorical, while the story of the resurrection itself is real?

No, he doesn't agree with my interpretation of his words. "Allegorical," he says, "usually means to the exclusion that the simple literal text is not true unto itself."

That's what I understood from what you said –

"No. When we say that [the text is not to be taken literally], we mean both. What is the relationship between the allegorical and the literal? This I don't know."

Oh, God, this man is such a Litvak!

So, the resurrection is not allegorical, and when the Messiah comes, this process will start on the Mount of Olives? I ask the Litvak.

"Yes, this is part of the basic Thirteen Principles of Faith."

When the Messiah raises the dead, how will they come up?

"Sorry?"

How will the dead rise once they are resurrected? Let's say, here was buried an eight-year-old and there an eighty-year-old – what happens when they rise? Will the eight-year-old and the eighty-year-old be of that same age?

"No idea."

What he does know, he tells me, is that the righteous will be the first to be resurrected.

He adds that he knows one more detail, which relates to the physical. When a person is buried, his body decomposes, but one part of the body, part of a bone known as the *luz*, never decays. This part, the *luz*, will enable the dead to resurrect.

Sounds strange? Perhaps, and Rabbi Nota is trying to explain it a bit better. "When dealing with mystical categories," he teaches me, "it's counterproductive to pretend that we understand them fully. Let me give you a premise: I believe that it's a mitzvah to try to understand the maximum you're going to understand rationally; on the other hand, I think that there's nothing more rational than understanding the limitations of our reason."

Let me ask you: If we are going in that direction and say that whatever the religious text says about resurrection is somewhere between allegorical and reality, could we also say that whatever the religious text says about the past – such as the story about the Splitting of the Sea (the parting of the Red Sea by God, according to the Bible, that enabled the Israelites to escape their Egyptian enslavers) or the giving of the Torah at Mount Sinai – is also somewhere between allegorical and reality?

While my argument is logical, no religious person would toy with accepting it; if they did, they would say goodbye to their faith in no time. Understandably, therefore, what I just said is a tall order for Rabbi Nota to accept. How does he get out of it? Using his linguistic talent, he immediately finds a way out.

"I think that the terminology is problematic. We are not saying that it is, in fact, somewhere between allegorical and reality. We say, 'My ability to understand it and to relate to it is somewhere between –'"

Can we say that same thing about the past?

"No."

Why not?

Well, we go back and forth for God knows how many times, reaching no agreement but loving the process. This process, for the uninitiated, is what "studying the Torah," Litvak style, means. It is this kind of back-and-forth debating and analyzing, the most enjoyable part of my time in the yeshiva world, that Yaakov Aryeh Alter finds threatening to his kingdom and would have none of.

My youth comes back to me now as I sip the last drops of the Taster's Choice. We didn't talk about The Name in my yeshiva days, God forbid, though we analyzed all other texts and issues to death. When I tried to do it, to talk and study about God, either through reading the Bible or, for example, Maimonides' philosophical composition *Guide to the Perplexed*, I was told that such was forbidden. Then as now, it seems, Ḥaredi Judaism toils hard not to grasp what its faith is. Of course, I would be very impressed if the Boyaner Rebbe meets me and finds out, based on just my name, that I'm pregnant or some other surprise on such a scale.

That said, and in defense of the Ḥaredim, even the brightest of philosophies is not foolproof. Often enough, people use philosophical argumentations to reach the most ridiculous of conclusions.

Whatever the case, Rabbi Nota, my dear Litvak, is an excellent debater, and I enjoy every minute with him.

Before departing, I ask Rabbi Nota, whose main aim is working with *baalei tshuvah*, for the most common motive that drives people into the arms of religion. "There is definitely more psychology in life than there is philosophy. People's philosophies are functions of their psychologies," he answers.

The man is brilliant.

We bid each other farewell, and when I'm back in Mea Shearim, I eavesdrop on a kid, about three years of age, praying to The Name from the balcony of his home. His prayer: "You bestow knowledge upon man and teach mortals understanding. Bestow upon us from You, wisdom, understanding, and knowledge. Blessed be You, Lord, Who bestows knowledge." Does this kid understand what he's saying? Most likely not, but it doesn't seem to bother him. And maybe, just maybe, when this kid grows up, he also won't care much about who rides the white donkey.

I feel a bit exhausted due to too many doses of religion, and when Friday night comes, I leave Mea Shearim, and in just minutes find myself at the intersection of Jaffa and King George Streets. It is there that I meet Ayman, a Muslim taxi driver, who's working on the Sabbath. There aren't many passengers to drive on this day, and Ayman takes it slow and is eager to chat. Yes, he says, the Ḥasidic Jews are not supposed to drive on the Sabbath, but some do. "You see the taxis here?" he asks, pointing to a number of taxis waiting for clients, "that's for the Ḥasidic Jews."

Do they take taxis on Sabbath?

"Some of them. They come here, take off their skullcaps, enter the taxi, and sit down."

Where do they go?

"Nowhere. They ask me to drive them, no address, just drive, and teach them all kinds of things."

What things?

"The young of them, they don't know what to do with their wives, where to put their penis inside the woman, and they want me to explain this to them. Some are gays; they ask me to masturbate them. Sometimes the ladies come because they want a man, a man like me, to sleep with them."

And you sleep with them?

"No. I'm a Muslim, and they are Jews, and I don't want to break their families. Are you German? You write for *Der Spiegel*, right?"

Why do you think that I write for *Der Spiegel*?

"You look like *Der Spiegel* type."

As far as I can tell, no Ḥasidic woman is anywhere near looking for Arab taxi drivers.

When I tell of my encounter with Ayman to a young Jew, he laughs. "Palestinian men have more sex with sheep than with women. What do they know?"

It would be nice to put this guy and the Muslim driver in the same room or taxi and eavesdrop on their conversation. It would be hilarious, I'm sure.

Up on Jaffa Street, I go to visit a small Sephardi synagogue. On the walls all around, I see various illustrations containing the I, H, V, H combinations in different colors, each in a different design or font. There is a Sabbath bulletin on the table, and in it, there are various sections. I turn the page to the Pinat Halaḥah, meaning Jewish law corner. In it, I read that when a man uses the toilet, he should not think about the Torah. Unless, it stipulates, his mind makes him think about women, and the only way for him to stop thinking about women is by thinking about the Torah, then he is allowed to think about the Torah even in the toilet.

Good to know.

And now that I met a cabbie, I think it's time to meet a politician.

What's the connection? I don't know. It just occurred to me. Don't ask.

Future Husbands of Taliban Ladies Try to Set People on Fire

A hot coffee mixed with a hot kiss in the most extreme of synagogues

I go to meet MK Uri Maklev, the man who studied in the same *ḥeider* I did in Bnei Brak (called Tashbar) and is today one of the hardest-working members of Knesset, representing the non-Ḥasidic part of the Ḥaredi party, United Torah Judaism.

There is a flyby of four military aircraft, including an Israeli Air Force F-35 and a German Luftwaffe Eurofighter over the Knesset, just as I arrive at the gates of the Israeli parliament. The exactness with which the squadron flies above my head, with two of the planes being flown by the Israeli and German Air Force commanders, is awesomely impressive.

I enter the building.

The Knesset, a place I've visited many a time in the past, is strangely quiet today. I can hardly spot a soul anywhere, but Uri is in. This man works around the clock.

His office in the Knesset is similar to an office of members of the Bundestag in Berlin, meaning it's not grandiose, but it's functional, and he welcomes me with chocolate waffles, Coke Zero, and crackers. He is bald, has a stubble beard, and a big black yarmulke on his head; he wears a white shirt, a grayish tie, and a chronograph watch. Behind him is a bookcase for primarily religious books, a window, and a display shelf for, I think, awards that he received over the years.

The word *Ḥaredi*, he tells me, was probably first coined by a German Jewish community before WWII.

Reb Israel Meir Hirsh, were he here, would explode. I have no idea how Rabbi Yehoshua Pfeffer would react.

I have been living in the Mea Shearim area for a few months now, I tell the MK, and I find them very welcoming people. Yet, to the average Israeli, the Ḥaredim are the worst of mankind, creatures who hardly deserve to be called human. Who is wrong here, I or they?

"People from the outside," Uri answers, "say 'Ḥaredi,' but they don't know what it means. I met a forty-year-old journalist who lives in Tel Aviv, and she told me that I was the first Ḥaredi she ever met in person. For her, Ḥaredi was someone from behind the mountains of darkness."

Still, why is it that the Ḥaredim are viewed so badly?

As far as Uri sees it, the reason for it lies with a small group of Ḥaredim who spoil the field for everybody else. He says: "The Ḥaredi world comprises many groups and subgroups. There is one small, tiny group that has no leader and is aggressive, violent, and dangerous, and they are located at Ohel Sarah [in Mea Shearim]."

I write a note in my brain: Go to Ohel Sarah.

Outside of Ohel Sarah, so says MK Uri, the Ḥaredim are wonderful people. Most of the foundations that help the needy and the sick in Israel, MK Uri tells me, were created by Ḥaredim, and these foundations help all the needy, Ḥaredi or secular. The Ḥaredi world, he says to me, has done more about social issues than any other group in Israel.

Will he, I ask him, desecrate the Sabbath to save the life of a secular Jew?

He's bewildered that I even ask such a question. "Of course," he says, "no doubt!"

It would be interesting to have Reb Yeḥezkel Lefkovits sit here and see how he feels about this MK.

Not only would the Ḥaredim desecrate the Sabbath to save the life of any Jew, MK Uri tells me, but they would also be kind to secular Jews in much less extreme circumstances. If anyone from a Ḥaredi family leaves the fold, he gives me an example, the family will be on their side, embracing them no matter what.

"I was an eyewitness to this when a father came to Rabbi Elioshiv [the late leader of the Litvishe branch of the Ḥaredi world] and asked him if he could tell his daughter, who left the fold, to leave the house. He said to the Rabbi: 'The behavior of my daughter is deteriorating; she is the oldest of my children, and her influence on them is very bad.' When Rabbi Elioshiv heard this, he said to the father: 'Put your other children in yeshivas, and let your daughter stay home.'"

To the best of my memory, this behavior did not exist when I was part of the Ḥaredi world.

MK Uri tells me more: "The head rabbi of a certain yeshiva came to Rabbi Shteinman [another late leader of the Litvishe branch of the Ḥaredi world] and asked Rabbi Shteinman to allow him to expel from the yeshiva a student he considered problematic, a student that he felt he couldn't have in the yeshiva anymore. Rabbi Shteinman said: 'No, let him stay.' So, the head rabbi let the student stay, but the situation got worse. He went back to Rabbi Shteinman and said to him: 'This student is destroying the other students. I must expel him. It's either him or us.' Rabbi Shteinman asked: 'Did you do everything you could to help him?' 'Yes,' said the head rabbi. 'I did everything I could, but nothing helps. If this student stays, he will destroy the yeshiva. May I expel him?' Rabbi Shteinman asked: 'What's his name?' 'Yaakov,' the head rabbi said. 'And what's his mother's name?' Rabbi Steinmann asked. 'I don't know,' answered the head rabbi. At this, Rabbi Shteinman was shocked, saying to the head rabbi: 'Are you telling me that you didn't pray for a boy like that?? That you don't even know the name of his mother?'" (In the religious world, when praying to The Name for other people, one has to mention the person's name and the name of that person's mother.)

Sitting with MK Uri Maklev brings me back to my childhood in an intimate way. We knew each other as kids; I knew his father and uncle, and he knew my father and mother. Looking at him, I see him in my mind's eye at the age of seven, the kid he once was, and I see myself next to him, at the same age. It's a memory mixed with reality, for he and I are here, in the flesh. Oh, if we could only walk back the years and be seven again!

Coming back to Mea Shearim, there's a huge tumult just outside my hotel. The street is louder than on any other day since I came here. It seems that the municipality, or whoever, has left two old garbage containers somewhere in the area, the small ones, and now some Ḥaredim emptied them on the street to make it impossible for public transportation buses of the Egged company, one of the biggest in the country, to pass through. A few other Ḥaredim push the containers away from the road, but when an Egged bus approaches, two Ḥaredi demonstrators stand in front of it, not allowing it to pass. I join the protesters to see it all up close. Suddenly, a guy takes a cardboard box, sets it on fire, and throws the burning box under the bus that can't move, hoping that the bus will be set on fire, together with the passengers in it.

Who are the passengers on the bus? They, too, are Ḥaredim, but for the demonstrators here, it doesn't mean a thing. If the people on the bus burn alive, that's okay with them.

Other Ḥaredim, angry as can be at what their eyes witness, run under the bus, take out the burning box, and forcefully push away those standing in front of the bus, allowing the bus to pass.

This scenario repeats itself over and over and over, bus after bus after bus after bus.

The group that's creating the troubles here, I quickly notice, comprises three adults and about ten kids, and they are bitterly fighting a much larger Ḥaredi group who have had enough.

The image of two groups of Ḥaredim fighting each other is bizarre, but it might testify to the conflict between a small violent core and the majority of the people. "They are destroying the good name of our neighborhood," a Ḥaredi woman tells me, speaking of the demonstrators.

Thirty minutes pass before two police squads finally show up. "Nazis!" some of the kids shout at an approaching bus, obviously believing that Egged drivers were the ones who murdered six million Jews during the Holocaust. Go prove otherwise.

The police take a look at the mess and drive on. They conclude that there's a better way to handle this mess. And indeed, another twenty minutes go by, and the Egged buses are rerouted outside this area.

It takes but three men and ten kids to make an entire neighborhood look like a bunch of aggressive, violent people.

It's by chance that I saw this just after I met Uri, but it certainly illustrates the point he made about a small core of troublemakers. Years back, while visiting the area, MK Uri Maklev, according to media reports, was attacked by a bunch of "Sikrikim" (Sicarii), the name by which the local troublemakers are known. However, the troublemakers here are not Sikrikim, whatever Sikrikim means, but Sephardi *baalei tshuvah*. If these three men ever get married, the thought comes to me, their wives will most likely be Taliban. A match made in Heaven.

In the meantime, Rabbi Nota, true to his word, sends me the list of sources.

I read it.

Yes, it is now confirmed: it's the Messiah who will show up riding on the Patriarch Abraham's donkey, not the Prophet Elijah.

Not bad.

How will the Prophet Elijah show up here in Jerusalem? I'm not sure, but perhaps he will come on a Saudia flight from Egypt, then ride on an Egged bus to the Holy City, provided that three Sephardi *baalei tshuvah* don't set the bus on fire before it reaches the Holy City.

As for the Boyaner Rebbe: I'm still waiting for a response.

Will it ever come? I'm not sure, but meantime, I'm going to Ohel Sarah, the headquarters of the Sikrikim, as I have been told, and the place that MK Uri Maklev described as violent and dangerous.

It takes me some time to find the place, which is on a narrow side street, and when I do, I eagerly walk in, excited to meet the troublemakers of the area. I imagine them to have batons, a stash of big rocks, and maybe a knife or two, plus a collection of Palestinian flags.

There are two people inside. Are you the Sikrikim? I ask them. "Who are you?" they ask.

A man looking for Sikrikim, I answer.

They laugh. "Where are you from?" they ask.

From the world, I answer.

The younger of them, sitting in the back, says: "Would you like a cup of hot coffee? I can make you one if you have time."

No rocks, no flags, no knives. Just coffee.

I sit down with him and ask him to tell me what he does in life.

He studies, he says.

What are you studying now?

"Genesis."

I look at the book next to the cup of coffee to see what this Dangerous Man is reading. The chapter he's reading tells of the Patriarch Jacob dropping a hot kiss on beautiful Rachel at the very instant he sees her.

Yes, yes. I admit: hot coffee and a hot kiss can be very dangerous.

Time to move on.

Who Is a Bigger Idiot, the Litvak or the Ḥasid? Both, Says the Litvak

Two young Litvaks spend their nights dreaming of blonde Germans

The sun rises on a new day and, per the old request made by David the Philanthropist, the gabbai of the Toldos Aharon Rebbe informs me that this week I'll be able to meet the Rebbe in private. The Rebbe is not in Jerusalem these days, but I'll be able to see him wherever he is during the week.

The Boyaner Rebbe, on the other hand, cannot be accessed while he, too, is on vacation, but with Heaven's help, I'm told, I'll be able to meet him when he's back. When will he be back? Heaven knows, but if I understand Yiddish correctly, he'll return to Jerusalem with the Prophet Elijah. I also send a message to Reb Yankev Ḥaim about meeting the Lelever Rebbe, and he says he'll let me know. This means, in Yiddish, that he will not.

And while I'm waiting to meet this Rebbe or that, I wonder what today's Litvaks think of Rebbes in general.

To find the answer to this brilliant question, I mount an Egged bus that will take me to the Ḥevron Yeshiva in the Givat Mordeḥai neighborhood of Jerusalem.

When I was a sweet boy walking the streets of the greater Mea Shearim, Ḥevron was just steps from my present hotel. But no more, because life moves on, and yeshivas too.

So be it.

I take my seat on the bus, and before long, my feet stand right in front of the Ḥevron Yeshiva.

What a difference this Ḥevron is from the old one! This Ḥevron looks gorgeous. A little garden with olive trees and other greenery welcomes my eyes as I look at the complex around me. On the left is a vast study hall, in the center is a big dining area, and to my right are the dormitories. Hundreds of students are walking around, dressed in white shirts and dark pants, chatting with one another or talking on their cell phones. Most are constantly moving, and some are spending quality time with their cigarettes, blowing kosher smoke into the holy blue sky above.

One of the students, who probably thinks I've come here to study the Talmud, asks me if I would like to learn with him. Without hesitation, I say yes, and together we enter the study hall. Fifteen hundred boys are studying in the yeshiva, he tells me, and though he loves his time here, he would love to meet a "match," a girl, and get married already. He's twenty-three years of age, an age considered "old" by the standards held in this place on earth.

How much does it cost to be a student here? I ask him.

"NIS 1,200 a month, which includes tuition, food, and accommodation," he answers.

That's what I paid the other day for one night in a Tel Aviv hotel. Not bad.

The students, who study daily from the early morning hours until late in the evening, with an afternoon break, are slowly coming back to the study hall from the break, taking their places on the many benches here and studying together in groups of two, *ḥavruses.*

This semester, the students of this yeshiva are studying Tractate *Baba Metsia*, and my new study mate and I are no exception. We start at the top of the tractate:

> Two people are holding a garment. This one says, "I found it," and that one says, "I found it"; this one says, "All of it is mine," and that one says, "All of it is mine"; this one takes an oath that he does not have ownership of less than half of it, and that one takes an oath that he does not have ownership of less than half of it; the garment will then be divided between the two of them.

The first time I studied this tractate, I was five years old, if I'm not mistaken, and here I am back at it. Am I five again? I wish!

The student, a very nice guy, and I study for half an hour or so, discussing every iota of what we have just read, debating the meaning of it all, when more students join us, asking me what I do in life and how life is outside of their big yeshiva.

Dinnertime is approaching fast, and my study mate says that he would gladly drive me to any restaurant I fancy and offers to bring along one of his friends to join us in the eating and the discussion.

His friend, a cute young man, shows up, and we drive to a super kosher restaurant twenty-five minutes away.

We order chicken, *gehakte leber* (chopped liver), chicken liver, mashed potatoes, and Coke Zero.

And we chat.

Both guys tell me that their primary purpose in life is to "study Torah."

Why?

"Because the Bible says, 'This book of the law shall not depart out of your mouth, but you shall meditate therein day and night.'"

What is the book of law?

"The Torah," the first guy explains.

Where is this verse in the Bible?

"In Psalms."

I correct him. This verse, I say to him, is written in the Book of Joshua, and I suggest that we see the context of it. I open the book on my iPhone and read a few verses to him from it:

> Moses my servant is dead; now therefore arise, go over this Jordan, you, and all these people, unto the land which I do give to them, to the children of Israel.
>
> Every place that the sole of your foot shall tread upon, to you have I given it, as I said unto Moses.
>
> From the wilderness and this Lebanon even unto the great river, the river Euphrates, all the land of the Hittites, and unto the great sea toward the going down of the sun, shall be your border....
>
> This book of the law shall not depart out of your mouth; but you shall meditate therein day and night.

These verses are said to Joshua, I say to them, in the context of conquering the Land of Israel. What do these verses have to do with you, two young men eating chopped liver in Jerusalem?

But the Sages say, they argue with me, that these verses mean that we, Jews, must dedicate every moment of our lives to the study of the Torah.

No, I tell them. You know, or should know, better. There's one opinion like the one that you just mentioned, but several other opinions oppose such an interpretation.

Here they get confused. Very confused. They, as it turns out, don't know why they want to dedicate their lives to the study of the Torah to start with. Both have gone out on dates, but neither felt attracted enough to the girls they met.

Which girls do they dream of in the dark of night on their beds? I ask them.

Well, the answer is simple: When nobody is around to see or hear, the girls they dream of are blonde Germans.

The chicken liver, by the way, is excellent. It's a bit burned on the outside, delicious inside, and it comes with fried onions. It's heavenly, let me tell you, and it goes down very well with the cola. Trust me.

What do you think of Ḥasidic Rebbes? I ask my co-eaters.

This is a very easy question for them, and it doesn't take an extra second to answer. "He who follows a Rebbe," they say, "is an idiot."

Why?

Well, only idiots follow Rebbes, they say. Period.

If I get sick, I was told when I was a kid, the first thing I should do is pray to The Name to heal me. Now, I ask them, if you get sick, what are the better chances that The Name heals you, is it if you pray to Him directly, or is it if Rabbi Ḥaim Kanievsky prays to Him on your behalf?

My study mate of today says that, definitely, his chances that The Name would heal him are far greater if Rabbi Kanievsky prays for him.

Hearing this, I tell him that if the Ḥasidim are idiots, he is no less of an idiot.

His friend, looking at both of us, agrees. "My chances that The Name heals me," he says, "are greater if I pray to Him directly."

There's a reason for his divergent opinion, he explains to me. "I moved a few steps astray from religion, but I hope that I find a girl who is more righteous than I am and, hopefully, she will bring me back to have a stronger faith." When this happens, and he gets sick once he's more righteous, he, too, will prefer that Rabbi Ḥaim Kanievsky pray for him.

Well, first off, he will have to find a blonde German more righteous than him. When he does, she would probably be an atheist or a Christian, and I would love to be with them when he places a call to Rabbi Ḥaim Kanievsky to pray for him.

What happened to "He who follows a Rebbe is an idiot"?

We chat about it for a couple more hours, by the end of which they conclude that everybody is an idiot, be it a Ḥasid, a Litvak, or whatever.

Once the chickens are finally done, I bid the Ḥaredi blonde-seekers goodbye and call the gabbais of the Toldos Aharon Rebbe, Rabbi Dovid Kohn, asking again to meet him.

Call me tomorrow, one of his gabbais says to me.

The next day, I do.

"Come over," the gabbai says.

Over to where? this idiot asks.

"Beit Meir."

Where in Beit Meir?

"In the shul."

Where's the shul in Beit Meir? Do you have the address?

"When you come to Beit Meir, you'll see it."

I don't know Beit Meir, a moshav (town, village) founded as a religious-Zionist settlement, and I have never been there. All I know is that Beit Meir, with a population reported to be fewer than 750 people, is a thirty-minute car ride from Mea Shearim at this time of day. I should be there, I'm told, around six p.m.

At five p.m., I leave Jerusalem and reach Beit Meir at five thirty.

Where's the shul? I ask the first person I see.

"Which one?" he answers.

Oops, I have no idea. He doesn't know either, but trying to help, he points to a road ahead of us and says: "There are two shuls over there, one Ashkenazi and one Sephardi – check them out."

A Conversation with the Rebbe of Toldos Aharon

The Rebbe speaks, uncensored, and drops a bombshell

The landscape in the Beit Meir area is as gorgeous as they come, especially now when the sun starts setting. But I have to go to the shul and leave the bewitching landscape for tourists. And that shul, I find out, is the Sephardi one. Why is the Rebbe going to the Sephardi and not the Ashkenazi shul, given that he's Ashkenazi? I don't know. Perhaps he thinks that a man dressed in "Arab" garb should join the Sephardim, whose grandparents lived in Arab countries. In any case, this shul is small, a tiny little place compared to the big Toldos Aharon in Jerusalem.

Well, this is Beit Meir and not Jerusalem, and the Rebbe is here for only a few days, for a much-needed post-holiday rest, and for this occasion, smaller is better.

As I stand in front of the Sephardi synagogue, before walking in, one of the Rebbe's Ḥasidim approaches me.

"You must have very good connections!"

Why do you think that?

"To get a private audience with the Rebbe, you need good connections. I heard that you are a journalist."

Well –

"Don't tell the Rebbe that you're a journalist!"

Why not?

"If he knows that you're a journalist, he won't talk to you."

And if the Rebbe asks me what's my profession, what should I tell him?

"Do you do something else for a living?"

I do theater in New York.

He looks at me as if I had just told him that I'm a donkey rider on the moon.

I'm also a writer; I write books.

"About what?"

Sadly, it happens to be about anti-Semitism.

"Are you for or against?"

You mean to ask which side of the anti-Semitism I am?

"Yes."

I'm against.

"Perfect! Tell him that you are writing books against anti-Semitism – he'll love it!"

I'm happy to hear that.

Once the afternoon prayer service is over, I enter the synagogue. The Rebbe sits near the front wall, where leaders sit, next to a table of sorts, as a couple of Sephardi residents are preparing to approach him for a blessing, a blessing from a holy man.

The Rebbe, Dovid Kohn, about seventy-five years of age, is dressed in a long white scarf, glasses, and Ḥasidic garb. His white beard testifies to his age, but his face is soft, and his gleeful eyes are focused on the people around him.

A young man approaches the Rebbe with a question: He would like to study the Torah, but he has a job. Can the Rebbe bless him?

I don't know what kind of a blessing this man is looking for but, as far as I can see, this man would like the Rebbe to tell him that he doesn't have to work, and perhaps the Rebbe will give him a blessing that will facilitate money dropping from Heaven directly into his pockets. If the Third Temple can drop from Heaven, why not a few shekels into a Sephardi pocket?

The Rebbe's response?

"You have to work," the Rebbe says to him. "People have to work, and if you want to study, you can do that too. After you wake up in the morning, wash your hands, say the morning prayers, and eat something, you can study a little. After you've done that, go to work, do your job, and in the evening, once you've finished your work, pray the evening prayers, eat, and make yourself time to study. You can do both: work and study."

That's it. No manna from Heaven, just the sweat of your brow.

Professor Dan Shiftan should be here to hear this.

A man with a newborn baby approaches the Rebbe. He wants his baby to be blessed. The Rebbe puts a hand over the baby's head and mumbles a prayer.

Then come I.

I give the Rebbe a *kvittel*, that little piece of paper, with my name and the name of my mother on it. What secrets will the Rebbe uncover, I wonder? Will he, like in the story of Reb Ḥaim, whose Rebbe is the brother of this Rebbe, find out that I didn't go to the mikveh in the morning? Will he, like the story Bentzi told me about the Boyaner Rebbe, tell me about some pregnant relative, a lady who doesn't yet know that she's pregnant?

Let's see. I'm very, very curious!

The Rebbe takes the *kvittel*, looks at it for less than two seconds, folds it, and leaves it on the semi-table by his side. He blesses me that I should have a good life and make a good living.

Thanks.

I tell the Rebbe that I am the great-grandson of the first Radzyner Rebbe. I could be a Rebbe too, I say to him, though obviously, I have chosen not to become one.

"You can still be," he says.

He could join my rabbis, from my bar mitzvah, who dreamt that I would be the rabbi of the land.

Yeah, yeah. I missed my calling.

The Rebbe, I fast realize, is in love with my family. "Oh! The Radzyner Rebbe," he tells me, "was a holy man! All the Radzyner Rebbes were. I have their books; I studied them, holy books, brilliant books. What holy people they were!"

Excellent!

And now that we've established a Rebbe connection, I get a little excited about the possibility that I, yours truly, will maybe, maybe become a Rebbe one day soon. So, I ask this Rebbe: What does it take to be a Rebbe – does it take a special person to be one, and how does one know that he is destined to be a Rebbe?

"To be a Rebbe, you have to be a person with an inner need to help others, to think of the other before you think of yourself."

This Rebbe, obviously, doesn't know me. Have you ever seen, my dear, an author or a journalist who thinks of others before he thinks of himself?

Well, true, I can be the first.

Let me think about it. Meantime, I continue my chat with the Rebbe.

A Rebbe, the Rebbe elaborates, is not just a rabbi. "A rabbi must have a *smiḥeh* [rabbinical ordination certificate] and say what the *halaḥah* [religious law] is; he has to know the Talmud and the commentators. A Rebbe has to know the people; a Rebbe has to care for the people, a Rebbe has to lift the people spiritually."

Does it take a special soul to become a Rebbe?

I don't know how this question crossed my lips, since I have no clue what a "soul" is, not to mention a "special soul." The Rebbe, on the other hand, seems to understand my question better than I do, and he confirms that, indeed, it does take a special soul to become a Rebbe.

What kind of soul?

"A person who has it in himself to gather the people around him and lead them right, to lift their spirituality: a person who wants to help people."

Oh, Lord, this gets too complicated for me. Am I that person? Can I be?

I ask the Rebbe: When did you know, if you did, that you would be a Rebbe one day, that you have the capacity to be a Rebbe? When was the first time that you realized it?

He tells me that at the time, before he became a Rebbe, there were disagreements in the Ḥasidic court of his father about who would take the leadership after the father's passing, he or his brother. In the end, both became Rebbes. He became the Rebbe of Toldos Aharon, while his brother established another court, a much smaller court, the court of Toldos Avrom Yitzḥok. But he always knew, from early on, that he would be a Rebbe one day.

When did it occur to you?

"When I was a kid. When I was a kid, I felt the need to care about the other kids, and I tried to help them. Then I knew that this is what I had to do when I grew up, that this is my mission."

This Rebbe is very different from me, I can tell. When I was a kid, I dreamt of becoming the Secretary General of the United Nations. Why? Being a Ḥaredi kid, what did I know? I thought that the Secretary General of the United Nations meant the King of All Nations. So, why not me?

I don't tell the Rebbe about my UN dreams, but I ask him, out of curiosity: How old were you when you had this thought, four years old?

"Not four, but around that age, a little older. A small kid."

What is the most challenging part of being a Rebbe? I ask him, still toying with the idea of, maybe, maybe, maybe, becoming a Rebbe after all, if I can get a thousand Ḥasidim to follow me.

"You have to think about others, not about you."

This Rebbe, I see, has never heard of Yaakov Aryeh Alter, the Ball Squeezer of Ger.

In any case, what I want to know more than anything is the *kvittel* thing. If I am to become a Rebbe, how am I going to pull off the *kvittel* thing? So I ask the Rebbe: I just gave you a *kvittel*; in it I wrote my name and my mother's name. That's what Ḥasidim do. What is it about?

"Nothing."

Can you read anything in my *kvittel* besides my name?

"No."

What will you do with my *kvittel*?

"You saw; I took it from you and left it here."

That's it?

Well, yes.

I can't believe that he says this, that a *kvittel* is just a piece of paper and no more, in effect saying that the Ḥasidim who give *kvittels* to Rebbes, while parting from their cash in the process, are nothing but fools. But there you go, the man said it.

Perhaps seeing my "disappointment," he adds: "In the old days, there were Rebbes who could look at a *kvittel*, read the names written on it, and see all kinds of things. But such Rebbes don't exist anymore."

I like this man, and I move on.

I've been to Toldos Aharon a few times and was impressed with your Ḥasidim. What is the most important part that makes Toldos Aharon be Toldos Aharon? I ask him.

"Faith. That's the most important. To have faith."

Faith, yes. What about Jews who don't have faith? There are people, secular Jews, who have no faith. What do you think of them? And what do you feel about the Zionists? What will you do if they come to Toldos Aharon?

"If they come to fight us, what can we do? But if they don't, what is the question? We will welcome them with open arms. Of course. We are all Jews!"

There is much hatred between various Jewish groups, sometimes within the same group. Why are there so many fights between Jews?

He looks at me, the Radzyner Rebbe's grandson, deep into my eyes and says: "Those who hate don't think of the others; they think only of themselves. They are not doing what the Radzyner Rebbe did, what the holy Radzyner Rebbe did. The Radzyner Rebbe had a fire in him, and he did everything he could for his Ḥasidim."

As great as the Radzyner Rebbe was, it obviously didn't pay off. Look what happened: the Ḥasidic court of Radzyn no longer exists; it's dead. Is that the reward for the Radzyner's faith?

"The Radzyner Rebbes, like any other people, came to the world to repair their souls. And they, of the very few, did it; they completed their mission. Other Rebbes, other courts, did not, and that's why they are still with us."

This Rebbe is one of the bravest Rebbes that I know of. To say that a *kvittel* means nothing, the same *kvittel* that hundreds of thousands of Ḥasidim around the world swear by and live by, is nothing less than heresy in the Ḥasidic world. In addition, the *kvittel* is one of the main sources of income in many a Ḥasidic court, and if he belittles the *kvittel*, he will need many David the Philanthropists to replace it. Do they even exist?

I look at this old man, a man with the fire burning in his soul, a fire that won't soon be extinguished, and I chat with him a bit more about this and that, and when the time arrives for me to go, I bid him goodbye.

And I think: Toldos Aharon is a wonderful Ḥasidic court because their Rebbe is a wonderful man. But what will happen after he's gone? What will happen if that son of his, that "London" rabbi, the lame husband of Leah who has no time to talk to people because he's so righteous, assumes power? He could turn this great Toldos Aharon into an army of hooligans, just as Yaakov Aryeh Alter is doing to his court.

Well, that's life.

And now that the sun is long gone, darkness filling the little town – a village, to be more precise – I breathe the clean air and the cool temperatures. I sit down on a bench at the bus stop nearby, light up a cigarette, stare at the clear sky above, and write down my impressions.

A car with two Reb Ahrelaḥ inside stops by.

"Where are you going?" asks the Ḥasid sitting in the passenger's seat.

Jerusalem, I say.

"Would you like a ride?"

Yes, thanks.

I mount the car, and before I know it, I'm back in my Jerusalem hotel.

These Ḥasidim drive fast.

And I'm left to think on my own: If the *kvittel* is nothing, but the Ḥasidim still believe in it and still view it as one of their most cherished foundations of faith, does it mean that Reb Israel Meir Hirsh was right when he told me that "the whole Ḥaredi world is one big idol worshipping"?

While thinking, I get a message from a Ger Ḥasid, one of the three Ḥasidim that I met a while back. He says that he wants to talk to me face to face, to pour out what's in his heart. Would I have time?

Yes, I do.

The man must be suffering, trying to unload his pain in the hope that it will be easier to handle.

The Rebbe Is in Your Bed

The Ḥasid who did not spill his seed for a decade

The Gerer comes to my hotel, dressed in the Ger garb, the long black coat, and we sit down to talk over a cup of Turkish coffee and peanuts.

He tells me that he is against the Rebbe, Yaakov Aryeh Alter, and he hopes that Rabbi Shaul Alter will be successful.

Well, this I know. This, after all, is the same man who told me that the Rebbe owns his testicles.

I start with small talk. How many Ḥasidim in the Palace Ger, the Nadlan Ger, are faithful followers of the Rebbe? I ask the man.

"Depends on what age they are and how safe they feel financially. If you are over thirty-five and have a good job, there's nothing the Ger court can offer you."

But they are still there. Why?

"I'm still there, not because I want to be there. If I left, my brothers wouldn't talk to me; as for the rest of my family, they would be forbidden by the Ger activists to talk to me. In some Ger neighborhoods in Israel, if you are caught praying in the shul of Rabbi Shaul, you must leave your home. Many Ger Ḥasidim live next to each other, and if we change loyalties, we cannot stay in the neighborhood. If you pray at Rabbi Shaul's, you can't enter the Old Ger shul anymore, and your kids are thrown out from their schools. And nobody will do business with you. In some cases, those who left or were about to leave, their kids would not join them at their new shul, splitting the families. A new organization was established recently by the Old Ger to turn these kids against their parents. And when the kids turn against their parents, the organization calls them heroes, making the kids feel proud that they disobey their parents."

What is the origin of the split between the Rebbe and the Rabbi?

"Officially, Rabbi Shaul left Ger two years ago, but the beginning of the conflict between the two opposing camps started years earlier."

What was the reason?

"By order of the Rebbe, Yaakov Aryeh, all classes in Ger institutions were canceled."

When?

"Twenty years ago."

Because of the *iyun* and *bekiyus* issue?

"Yes. The Rebbe said, 'In Poland, the Ger court didn't have classes, and we don't need them here either.'"

No classes? How are the students studying in the Ger institutions?

"They study without classes. They recite the Talmud, page after page after page after page. No analysis of anything."

For years, Rabbi Shaul was the most influential teacher in the Ger court, if I understand right. How did he take this new order?

"He lost his job. There were no classes to be given anymore. He sat home and studied alone, all those years. The students, who now had no classes anymore, had to adjust. The Rebbe, Yaakov Aryeh, destroyed the elite of the Ger institutions, the highly respected Ger institutions."

If I understand you, this issue was out in the open for many years, yet there was no split. How did the split happen?

"Dovid Mendel Berliner, who lives abroad, had a major real estate dispute with the Rebbe. One day he came to Israel, to participate in his daughter's wedding, and what followed was horrible. Hordes of Ḥasidim stood outside the house where he was staying in Jerusalem and shouted: 'Thou shalt blot out the remembrance of Amalek from under heaven; thou shalt not forget it' [from Deuteronomy], equating Berliner with Amalek, the Bible's most bitter enemy of the Jews. They also shouted, referring to Berliner: 'May his name and memory be erased!' It came to the point that Berliner couldn't leave the house. When that happened, Rabbi Shaul published a letter of support for Berliner, referring to him as 'my friend,' and urged that the violence, which he termed 'terror,' against Berliner stop. 'These acts of terror, violence, and shaming are the opposite of what our sacred Torah and our holy Rabbis have taught us,' he wrote. This letter was viewed in the Ger court as a rebellion against the Rebbe, and the next time that Rabbi Shaul came to Ger (Old Ger) to pray, the person who was with him was beaten within an inch of his life."

How did the split affect you personally?

"When I was young, the Rebbe was everything for me! I was proud of being the Rebbe's Ḥasid. Not only that, but in my eyes, he was very nice-looking!"

Is he still nice-looking in your eyes?

"No."

What is he for you now? How does he look?

"A monster."

This "monster" still has tens of thousands of people following him. What makes people go for a monster?

"His biggest asset is his silence. He hardly talks and, using silence, he creates an aura around him that makes him extremely powerful."

Silence? That's all?

"Through the Ger Takunnes, he controls the sex life of his Ḥasidim. You are his slave. He resides in the most intimate rooms of your heart. He is present in your bed when you have sex because your testicles belong to him. When I believed in him, my testicles belonged to him. And when you come to him, standing in front of him, he can make you miserable in four minutes of his silence!"

If I'm not mistaken, the sex Takunnes are part of Rabbi Shaul's camp as well, aren't they?

"From the beginning, when these Takunnes first took shape years ago, they were meant to be taken as ideas, something for a Ger Ḥasid to aspire to, not something to practice, and that's how the people behind Rabbi Shaul see them. But for Yaakov Aryeh, ideas don't exist. He is not a man of ideas; he is a man of deeds. He has no ideas. He hardly gives speeches, because ideas are not part of his personality. For him, the Takunnes must be enforced in practice. And in Old Ger, they enforce these Takunnes. You have a guide, a man older than you, and you have to share with him what happened last night in the bed with your wife."

Where do you stand today, religiously speaking?

"Yaakov Aryeh made me doubt everything."

Doubt what?

"In the Ḥaredi world, the system is this: no questions are allowed. But because of Yaakov Aryeh's hard interpretations, because he owned my testicles, I started doubting and asking questions. And for me, that's the end of it."

What do you mean, don't you believe in God anymore?

He looks at me, shaking his head. It's hard for him, a Ger Ḥasid dressed in all the required garb, beard, and long sidelocks, to utter the words, the horrible words: I don't believe in God. I give him his space and let him handle it his way, no pressure.

After a few minutes, the man speaks: "I can't honestly say that I believe in God. I was told to be mindful not to spill my seed from the age of nine. For me – I can speak only about myself – that was very difficult. But I kept the rules. I did my best not to spill my seed for the next decade. But then, one day, after asking questions, I realized that the seed issue was invented by a rabbi in Poland a few hundred years ago – that it was not a prohibition given to Moses on Mount Sinai, as I was taught. I wanted to scream!"

You support Rabbi Shaul. Why?

"As I see it, Rabbi Shaul breaks to pieces one of the most corrupt Ḥasidic courts in Israel."

Why do you care? You don't even believe in God.

"I am a believer and I am not a believer, at the same time. The Judaism of Yaakov Aryeh is a Judaism I don't believe in. The Judaism of Rabbi Shaul is a Judaism I want to believe in."

I have a question for you. I've been in the Mea Shearim area for a few months by now and have gone to shuls of many Ḥasidic courts. Usually, I'm very well received, but not in Ger. When I went there, a Ḥasid approached me and, speaking in English, raised his voice at me: "What are you looking for?" None of the Ḥasidim around protested his behavior. Is there a reason for it?

"Yes. Old Ger is a cult, not a court. They look at you, and they say: From this man, the way he's dressed, something bad will come. They know that something is rotten in them. They hide it, but they fear that a stranger would see it."

If I remember well, you told me the other day that the Rebbe is a merciless man.

The man sitting next to me, spiritually and psychologically broken, seems shocked at his own words. "No," he says to me now, "the Rebbe is not a merciless man. He just thinks differently."

When I met you and your friends that evening, you said that Yaakov Aryeh Alter is a "cruel, merciless" Rebbe.

"What he does is merciless, what he does is cruel, but he's not a cruel man. I want you to understand that. There is a difference. He's not cruel or merciless."

If I understand this man right, at this very moment, the Rebbe is squeezing his testicles, and he tries to be less critical of the Holy Squeezer.

I saw a video clip, I say to him, given to me by one of your friends, in which Yaakov Aryeh is referred to, by one of the Old Ger leaders, as God: "A word of the Torah: the Rebbe, that's God."

"No, no. Those words were not meant in this way. Yes, they were said, but it is a *vort* [literally, "a word"], an illustration of a concept, not real."

What's the concept?

He doesn't know.

He is the one who told me that the Ḥasidim in the Ger Palace must take off their *spodiks* so that everybody can look at the Rebbe, at God, when they are praying. But now, being squeezed where it hurts, he tries to be nicer to the Squeezer.

The man facing me is crying for help. His past was robbed from him, and if he doesn't act soon, his future will be robbed from him for good. And he is scared.

He gets up, shakes my hand, and I watch him as he walks out, a broken spirit dressed in black garb, getting ever smaller and smaller the further he walks until he disappears.

What are the options this Ger Ḥasid has if he chooses to leave? What are the options any Ḥaredi has if he decides to leave his community?

An ex-yeshiva student invites me to join him and his wife for the coming Friday night's meal. He lives in Jerusalem, away from Mea Shearim.

I accept the invitation.

Honoring Sabbath with Cannabis

Why are Sephardi rabbis honoring a pedophile?

My host and his wife, a young couple in their early twenties, observe the Sabbath and keep kosher. They live in a beautiful apartment in an artsy part of town, and their Sabbath table is covered with food: salads of all kinds, wine bottles, *ḥallahs*, meat, fish, and a fresh chocolate cake as well. In case I'm interested, they also have special cookies: cookies infused with cannabis, about two dozen of them, nicely arranged on a big tray. Before the Sabbath started, they tell me, they had a wonderful time together filled with weed. "We had a pre-Sabbath joint," is how he phrases it.

Cannabis, I can see, has replaced the young man's Talmud. Yes, he has the whole set of Talmud at home, but he's too busy with cannabis to read it. He is lost, and so is his wife.

Yes, he made a complete switch sometime in the past, becoming secular and saying goodbye to God, but it didn't last long. He came back. Not all the way, but a little. He observes Sabbath with cannabis and welcomes Sabbath with a joint.

What else does the young couple do? Not much.

But they have a dream.

What's the dream?

To live in Switzerland.

Why Switzerland?

Well, why not?

For how long?

They don't know; they will think about it during their next joint session together.

These two people, they let me understand, come from well-to-do families and have everything one can dream of. They have found love, they have money, they have a nice house and an expensive car, as they tell me, but they don't have anything else. They have no community, except for other cannabis lovers, and street cats. They feed street cats; that's their passion.

What do they strive to achieve in the future? I ask them.

That's a bit tricky. What they want to achieve in life cannot be phrased in words. It's spiritual, out there, between the cats and the cannabis.

As I take a bite from the fresh chocolate cake, I notice a street cat walking in. Cats, as far as I know, are not big lovers of kosher chocolate cakes, but I shall not worry about the cat. The wife, noticing the cat, immediately rushes to feed it. She grabs a bag of cat food, a commercial-size bag that could feed twenty thousand cats, from which she feeds this one cat. When you are on weed, I see, a cat looks like a lion, and a commercial-size bag looks like a wallet. Later in the evening, they will go to bed, and maybe a street cat will join them.

A gitten Shabbes.

Before Sabbath ends on the next day, I decide to go to the Lelever shul to see if I can get to meet the Rebbe without making an appointment. But the Rebbe is not present, just a few lonely Ḥasidim having a herring.

As I walk out from shul, I see a Sephardi Ḥaredi man rushing to a poster glued on the wall across the street. He tears the poster down in pieces and throws them on the sidewalk.

What are you doing? I ask him.

"Why are you getting involved?" he shouts at me in anger.

Because you are making garbage in my neighborhood, I shout back.

He doesn't answer. Instead, he gets angrier and throws more pieces on the sidewalk. When I tell him to stop, right now, he runs away.

I walk over, pick up the pieces, and reconstruct the torn poster like a puzzle. What is it about? It's an announcement, letting residents know that a private Ḥaredi court concluded that two Ḥaredi rabbis, brothers, had committed sexual offenses against yeshiva students. The two rabbis, Yitsḥak and Moshe Tufik, leaders of Be'er Yehuda Yeshiva, a yeshiva with a gross of close to six million shekels a year, stand accused of committing "severe aggressions" against dozens of students in the past few years, the kind of aggressions that "cannot be written down," a Ḥaredi code for sexual offenses, including pedophilia. In the ruling, the court prohibits community members from sending their children to Be'er Yehuda Yeshiva, a yeshiva of three hundred students.

The story, though, doesn't end there. Less than a week ago, the wedding ceremony of Yitsḥak Tufik's son took place, attended by top Sephardi Ḥaredi rabbis. What were they thinking?

This sexual abuse story, I read, has been going on for three years already. Three years ago, Rabbi Yitsḥak Tufik signed a letter in which he promised never to be alone with students. As it turned out, however, according to this Ḥaredi court's findings, a court made of top Sephardi Ḥaredi rabbis, Rabbi Tufik did not and does not keep his promise.

Instead of a story about a Rebbe, I got a story of pedophilia.

What an exciting way to start a new week.

Do I need to see another Rebbe? Not really. I already satisfied my "Rebbe curiosity" by sitting privately with the Toldos Aharon Rebbe. But if I can get one or two more Rebbes, why not?

פסק דין

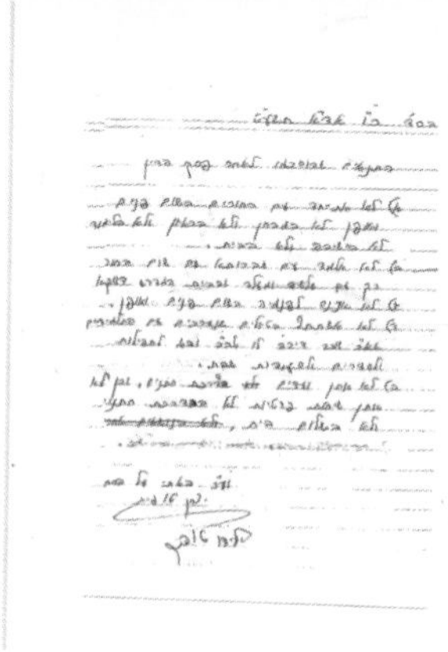

On the way back to my hotel, I see Motta. Can you get me an audience with your Rebbe? I ask him. I just want to give him a *kvittel* and see what he says. Motta answers that he'll do his best and talk to the people taking care of such requests, recommending that they make this possible.

Well, we'll see. If not a Rebbe, I might find another interesting story on the way. Hopefully, not another pedophile.

This Sephardi Rabbi Is So Holy, His Eyes Have Never Seen a Woman

An Ashkenazi rabbi arrested as a suspect in a murder case

I have no idea why, but my feet drag me to Rabbi Berland's community the following day. His followers live east of Mea Shearim, in the Morasha neighborhood, across from where Mea Shearim Street ends.

As I enter his neighborhood, coming from Mea Shearim, there are two very interesting buildings on my right and left: a Polish monastery, "Dom Polski," on the right, and the "Representation of the Romanian Orthodox Patriarchate at the Holy Land" on the left. That's the two countries I come from, so to speak: my father was born in Poland, my mother in Romania.

Welcome home.

I keep on walking. Is this the place of Rabbi Berland's followers? I ask a young man.

"Yes," says he.

Is Rabbi Berland in the area today?

"No."

Where is he?

"In the north."

Vacationing?

"No. He is under house arrest."

Why?

"You don't know?"

No. I don't live here.

"Where you from?"

All over.

"Where's that?"

Berlin.

"Oh."

Why is Rabbi Berland under house arrest?

"We gave him money to pray for us, and he took it."

What's wrong with that?

"That's an excellent question! Listen to me: one day, all the Jews will open their eyes and see what a holy man he is!"

Sounds promising.

"Yes. Have a wonderful day."

One more question: What kind of Ḥasidim are you?

"We are Breslev Ḥasidim."

Like all other Breslev Ḥasidim?

"We follow the Tzaddik, Rabbi Berland."

Factually, Rabbi Berland is not under house arrest but is spending his time between a jail and a prison, on different counts. In addition to the money issues, the authorities suspect that he was involved in the murder of two people some thirty years ago, a murder case that was reopened not long ago after new evidence came to light, according to police.

But the followers follow.

Not surprising, though. One of the basic foundations of the Breslev court is what their Rebbe, Naḥman, once said: "Not asking questions is the essence of faith."

A couple walks ahead of me. He is dressed in black Ḥasidic garb, and she is dressed in a cross between a Jesuit nun and a Muslim Brotherhood woman.

Excuse me, I ask her, are you a follower of Rabbi Berland?

"Yes," she answers.

I ask: Are you dressed like this on the orders of Rabbi Berland?

"No," she replies. She just likes to dress like this, she says, giving me a shy smile.

I walk to the shul where Rabbi Berland prays when he's not under one or another sort of arrest and find a group of men in attendance. They don't pray or study. What do they do? They eat soup. You can worship The Name, I learn, by eating soup. You slurp that soup in honor of the Lord, and nobody can say that you're less righteous than any other Ḥasid.

I try speaking to them in Yiddish, and they just shake their heads and have more soup. It takes me time to realize that with one exception, none of them understand Yiddish. They are *baalei tshuvah*, the kind of folks Reb Yoilish Krois would rather get out of the area altogether. One of these days, perhaps, he will hang Palestinian flags here as well. That would be fun.

Unlike Rabbi Berland, Reb Yoilish Krois, as far as I can tell from visiting him, doesn't make money off people who come to him. Some prominent Rebbes, on the other hand, make a pretty penny from their followers, and their estimated personal worth runs in the millions. In an article about the wealthiest rabbis in Israel published by Mako, one of the top Israeli news sites, about ten years ago, the Belzer Rebbe's estimated worth was 180 million shekels, the Gerer Rebbe's 350 million shekels, and Rabbi David Abuhatzeira's 750 million shekels. The figures are most likely much higher now, but this list hints at the money side of being holy.

Rabbi Abuhatzeira, known as Admor, another term for a Rebbe, is a Sephardi Rabbi who lives in the northern city of Nahariya, about three hours' drive from where I am – a long schlep. But I say to myself: I want to see a man who beats the Gerer Rebbe, the biggest Ḥasidic Rebbe in Israel. And the good part is, visiting this particular Rebbe doesn't require an appointment.

But should I do this? I ask a man I meet on the street, whom I don't personally know, to tell me his thoughts about Rabbi David.

"He's holy, he's pure," he says, his eyes shining with delight as if he has just seen the most gorgeous lady on the planet, maybe even the biblical beauty Rahab.

How do you know? And what does "pure" mean? I ask the man.

"He never looked at a woman," he answers. "Never. When women come to him, he doesn't see them. Women who want his blessing or advice can come, but they stay outside. They leave a piece of paper for him with their requests, and a gabbai takes it from them, but the Admor doesn't see them. He doesn't look at women. His eyes have never seen a woman. A holy man!"

This Admor, it dawns on me, is the most Progressive man in the world, for he never looks at women with thirsty, desiring eyes. Nope. He doesn't sit at cafés, sipping Italian coffee or Arabic tea while his eyes get busy staring at every inch of passing women's bodies. No. He is good, and he should run for office as the Progressive candidate in the USA, the Green Party in Germany, or Labour in Britain. Period.

"Rabbi David's vision is so deep that his eyes penetrate where normal human eyes cannot," another person tells me.

Wow!

The Price of a Blessing: From 20 Shekels to 50,000 Shekels

A man gets rewarded in the World to Come, a woman gets rewarded in This World

I am told that Rabbi David is on Abir Yaakov Street in Nahariya, so I take a train from Jerusalem to Nahariya to see him. Once I get off the train, I ask a fellow rider if he knows where Abir Yaakov Street is.

"Going to Rabbi David?" the man asks.

Yes, I say, surprised that he figured out where I'm heading to.

"Anyone who comes to Nahariya asking for Abir Yaakov Street is looking for Rabbi David," he tells me.

His name is Itsik, and he is a Nahariya man. Itsik didn't come here to meet the Admor, but he did go to him in the past.

Why did he go?

"I went to him when I had a big money problem. I had a lot of debt, and there was nothing I could do to repay it, and no money was coming in. I was down, at the very bottom. I was drowning. I went to Rabbi David and told him my problem. I don't know what to tell you, but money started flowing in my direction a few days later. Listen: Abir Yaakov Street is a bit of a walk from here; why don't you take a taxi? There's a set price from the station to the Admor: NIS 15. It's worth it."

I take a cab and tell the driver to take me to Abir Yaakov Street. "To Rabbi David?" the cabbie asks. "That's NIS 15."

Good.

He drops me off by Abir Yaakov Yeshiva on Abir Yaakov Street. "The Admor receives people in the yeshiva," he tells me.

I walk in.

About fifty people are ahead of me in a big hall full of books, tables, and chairs when I arrive.

Is there a line here? I ask a man sitting in the back, also waiting to see the Admor.

"No lines here," he answers.

Do I have to take a number?

"No."

Am I after you?

"There is no before and no after."

What do you mean?

"Don't worry. Just sit down."

How long is the wait?

"Nobody knows, except for the Admor."

Where is he?

"Inside."

Where?

"You can't see him from here. Sit down."

What happens after I sit down?

"Rabbi David is a holy man. He knows you are here without seeing you. He communicates with your soul, and he knows you are here when you enter the building. If he wants to see you, in the flesh, he'll call for you. Where are you from? Do you live in the area?"

I live abroad.

"Which country have you been to before you came to Israel?"

Germany.

"He knows that."

Who does?

"Rabbi David. He knows everything. He already knows everything about you through your soul when you come in. He is a holy man. He knows that you came from Germany."

Where should I wait?

"Take a seat. Anywhere. If he wants to see you, he will call for you. Whenever he wants to call for you."

I sit down on the first empty seat I find.

On the table next to me is a book. I open it and read: "*Ish* [man] is with an *i*, *ishah* [woman] is with an *h*; together, *i* and *h* is the name of God. *I*, the man, is getting rewarded in the World to Come; *h*, the woman, is getting rewarded in This World."

What is this?

I get up and take a seat closer to where the Admor is, at least where I think he is.

"Why do you sit here?" the gabbai of the Admor asks me. "Go back to where you were before."

I do.

Two minutes later, the gabbai calls me, a big smile on his face, and says: "You can go in now. May the Lord bless you!"

He shows me to a corridor, where a few people stand in line. We are the selected folks chosen to see Rabbi David first. A few steps ahead of us, behind a little stand, wooden in part with plexiglass on top, I see the Admor, standing, and people pass by. They stop for a couple of seconds, asking for a blessing or advice, and move on.

How does this work? I ask a man who stands before me. "Write your name, or a request, on a piece of paper, and when you stop by Rabbi David, you give it to him."

This is a *kvittel*, I realize, just like the Ḥasidim when coming to see their Rebbes.

Do I have to give him money? I ask the man.

"No. Unless you want to."

How much?

"From NIS 20 to NIS 50,000. Any amount you want to give him is good."

How much do you give?

"NIS 100."

I do the same thing I did when visiting the Toldos Aharon Rebbe. I write my name and my mother's name on a piece of paper and wait my turn to see this Rebbe.

Once my turn comes, I give Rabbi David the *kvittel*, together with an NIS 50 note. He takes the money and puts it in a box next to him. The *kvittel*, on the other hand, he holds in his hands.

There are people behind me, who have God knows what kind of troubles and problems, and I can't take too much of the Admor's time. I better come up with a question, whatever question, on the double. What am I going to ask him? I decide to be "original," and I say thusly to him: I am in Israel to write a book about the Ḥaredi world. Does the Rabbi have any advice or blessing to offer?

Brilliant, isn't it?

He looks at me, smiles, and puts a finger on my first name in the *kvittel*, Tuvia. "Your name is Tuvia," he says, offering one more smile. "What does 'Tuvia' mean? Look!" He points to each of the Hebrew letters of my first name and says that each letter of the name is an abbreviation of words about the book. What are the abbreviated words? In Hebrew, they stand for: "The book will do very well."

Nice. Definitely worth my NIS 50.

And now that I have visited both Ashkenazi and Sephardi Rebbes, I feel that I have achieved one of my main goals: to experience the life of the Ḥaredi at its most intimate, being in the presence of an almighty leader.

Surrounded by Sephardi followers of their leader, I am reminded of Rabbi Reuven Elbaz, who stood me up on the first day of the Sephardic Sliḥot at his Or Haḥaim Yeshiva. Should I make another attempt to ensure that he doesn't want to see me?

Tomorrow, a bird whispers in my ears, Rabbi Elbaz will serve as a mohel (circumciser), performing a *brit milah* (circumcision) on an eight-day-old baby boy at a venue in Jerusalem. There's no better place to meet a hiding old rabbi, if he's indeed hiding from me, than next to the foreskin of a baby boy, when it is being cut off.

Tomorrow comes, and I show up at the venue.

A Rabbi Hiding behind the Foreskin of a Baby

The Prophet Elijah appears, but the rabbis are afraid to talk to him

Food aplenty is offered in the venue's courtyard before any baby's foreskin is cut. Schnitzel fingers, Moroccan cigars (pastry filled with minced meat), fried potato pastries, orange juice, various cola drinks, and a host of other goodies are ready for the arriving guests. The guests nosh and drink, drink and nosh, nosh and drink.

I join them: schnitzel, potato pastries, cigars, and a bottle or two of Coke Zero. Why not? I light up a cigarette, smoke it until done, and chat with other smoking guests.

After some time, and once all smokers have had their addiction fully satisfied, we are invited inside the hall for the circumcision event, where tables have been arranged beforehand for the meal that will follow the circumcision.

The sandek, the man holding the baby during a circumcision ceremony, sits down with the baby on the Seat of the Prophet Elijah, the prophet known to attend every *brit milah* there is. Yeah. Rabbi Elbaz, looking happy for his date with the baby, enters. He puts down his mohel's kit next to Elijah's Seat and opens it.

Guests form circles around the two men and the baby, ready for the show to start when the newborn will be transformed from a mere human into a Jew.

First, Rabbi Elbaz organizes his kit. In it, there are knives, scissors, a *brit* shield (a tool to ensure that the mohel doesn't accidentally cut off more than needed), some powder, an ointment, a few gauzes, and Listerine. I always thought that Listerine was a mouthwash, but obviously, it has more uses than one.

As he arranges his mohel kit, Rabbi Elbaz looks at me and smiles as if he's delighted to see me.

That's a good sign, isn't it?

Rabbi Elbaz then moves his head a little bit and continues to smile at me.

Happy days are ahead!

And he starts the circumcision.

As he cuts the baby's foreskin, blood gushes out of the baby's penis. Looking at the blood, he asks an aide for wine. The aide offers him the wine in a silver cup, and Rabbi Elbaz takes a sip from it, then bends down and sucks the blood from the baby's penis. Then he spits the blood into the silver cup.

The baby is crying.

The sandek, a famous Israeli rabbi by the name of Yitzchak Dovid Grossman, says: "May all of us soon be present on the day of the Prophet Elijah's coming when he will proclaim the imminent arrival of the Messiah. Amen."

"Amen," the crowd replies.

I'm not sure why he is looking to meet the Prophet Elijah on some future date when the Prophet Elijah is already here, sitting right next to him, on this very seat, the Seat of the Prophet Elijah. I also don't understand why he's talking to the guests about the Prophet Elijah when he could speak to the prophet directly.

Well, I guess I don't understand everything. Does anybody?

Rabbi Elbaz cleans his knife, throws away the gauzes with the blood, puts on new gauzes where the blood is still coming out. He sprinkles powder, applies some ointment, and covers the baby with diapers. As for the Listerine: I don't see him using it.

The baby stops crying.

As the crowd sings and prays, happy as can be, Rabbi Elbaz turns to me.

"What did you write?" he asks.

I have not written about our chat, if this is what you mean, I answer him, because you and I have not sat down to chat yet. Would you like to meet?

Rabbi Elbaz doesn't answer. Instead, he makes a circular motion with his right index finger, as if I were a deaf-mute who communicates in sign language.

What do you mean? I ask him.

He does not answer.

And that's it.

I get intrigued about the man and check him out in some databases, where I find that a few years ago, he was convicted by an Israeli court for "facilitating bribes and conspiring to commit a crime," for which he received a suspended prison term of eight months and was fined NIS 120,000. He appealed to the Israeli Supreme Court, and his fine was increased to NIS 250,000.

Well, there you go.

I sit down at a table, eat more, drink more, and chat with fellow diners, mostly Sephardim, about Rabbi David from Nahariya. "He is a holy man, the most righteous of all alive," one of them tells me. When hearing that I met him the day before, one of my new dining friends tells me: "You are the luckiest man in the country!"

I'm happy to hear that. I swallow another Zero and slowly leave.

A car announcing the imminent funeral of another great man greets me as I return to Mea Shearim.

Jews are born; Jews are dying. The Prophet Elijah is busy collecting foreskins of the newly born, and Messiah ben David will soon be busy doing resurrections at the Mount of Olives.

A group of *baalei tshuvah*, all Sephardim, each holding a huge sign denouncing the use of smartphones and non-kosher cellphones of any kind, marches up and down Yeḥezkel Street, right next to my hotel, singing and shouting, getting on the nerves of everybody alive. It's interesting how they do it. They stop marching when reaching a store that sells cellphones, occasionally point their fingers at the store owners, often shout, and always keep their eyes closed, so that they won't see, The Name forbid, women. They do this every day, on this street and that, per the command of their rabbi, an Ashkenazi man, who believes that Sephardim can be more productive marching on the streets than sitting in a yeshiva and studying. Some of these *baalei tshuvah* are former convicts, prone to violence, and at times when they encounter a Ḥaredi man with a smartphone, they beat the hell out of him.

In addition to these guys, there's an organization called Rabbinical Committee for Communication Matters, known in the Ḥaredi world as a "mafia" without real rabbis behind it, and it often uses violence to force store owners to sell phones that it, and only it, certifies as "kosher." Just a few days ago, they got a bunch of men to demonstrate outside a cellphone store in Bnei

Brak, vandalized the place, and promised to come back unless the owner would give in to their demands.

That's life, and so it goes on, and ain't nobody going to change the course it takes. Unless, of course, the International Jewish Parliament in the Shuk Habuḥarim's pickle shop decides that enough is enough, and the majority of its parliamentarians vote to change this course once and for all.

The holiday season is long over, but this does not mean that people are not busy, I learn as the days go by. Circumcisions, bar mitzvahs, weddings, and funerals are just part of the daily routine of the Ḥaredim in Mea Shearim. There is also the mikveh, the prayers, the Sabbaths, the *tish*es, the Rebbe visits, and the Torah studies – to name but a few Ḥaredi activities.

Studying the Torah, in-depth or not, is a major issue. Here, for example, is what I just read on one Ḥaredi site: "When a man dies while studying one of the Talmud tractates, and has not finished the tractate before he dies, it is written that after he resurrects, the Talmud tractate will remind him on what page he stopped and ask him to finish it." Yeah, books have personalities, and mouths, and they talk more than Rabbi Elbaz will ever do.

Their busy lifestyle, not to mention all the *gmaḥ*s around, make Ḥaredim have a more satisfying life than the rest of us. Though their employment rate, according to just-published reports, is less than the average Israelis', women at 83 percent and men at 46 percent, they are a happy bunch of people. Based on statistics released four or five years ago, the latest statistics that I could find on satisfaction rates, 98 percent of Ḥaredim report being satisfied with their lives, higher than any other segment of the society, and only 11 percent of them say that they feel lonely, the lowest percentage of any group surveyed by Israel's Central Bureau of Statistics.

The Ḥaredim, reported to be close to 13 percent of Israeli society at this writing, are living the good life. Many of them, especially the Ḥasidim (not counting a few specific courts, such as Ger, for example), speak Yiddish, a language that unites them more than most anything else. God Himself, let me make it clear to you, speaks Yiddish. Yes. And if you didn't get it yet, let me reiterate: When these Ḥasidim talk, in Yiddish, about the Patriarch Abraham's donkey, the great resurrection, or the Prophet Elijah flying all over, not to mention the white and black angels, there's no point in asking them for exact details. Being exact will do you good if you live in Stuttgart and work for Daimler, not if you live in Mea Shearim and work for God.

Some of the Sephardi Ḥaredim, those who want to be seen as closer to God, break their teeth trying to communicate in Yiddish. It's not easy for them, because Yiddish is also a lifestyle and a prism through which its speakers see the world, but those Sephardim try. For example, at the *brit milah*, some of the Sephardim I chatted with threw in Yiddish words here and there. But the Yiddish they tried to speak was so bad, it was painful to listen.

Simply put: you can download a set of strict Takunnes into a Yiddish-speaking Ḥasid's head, but not much of it will stick there. The Ger Ḥasidim, speaking little to no Yiddish, are a different story. Hence their big fights and strict behavior.

"There's someone in Hatzor HaGlilit," I get a message, "who would like to talk to you about the Ger issue."

Should I accept the invite?

The Best Way to Find a Mate: Hang a Scarf on a Tree Next to a Grave

American Jews who care about transgender and proper Halloween dress: read Psalm 15

Hatzor is in the north, and I wonder if I should schlep myself north again, but my curiosity gets the better of me, and I go.

As I enter the town, I see two Ḥasidim walking. Are you for the Rebbe Yaakov Aryeh Alter or Rabbi Shaul Alter? I ask them.

They stop their walk and stare at me as if I were a white donkey, al-Buraq, or some other figure who is not human. They say nothing and then walk away.

I walk to the man who wants to talk to me.

I enter his house, sit down at the table, and his wife walks in. The husband tells her that her presence is not needed now; he can talk to me on his own. But she sticks around, saying that she wants to make sure he doesn't speak badly of the Rebbe. He tells her that if she sticks around, keeping watch on every word coming out of his mouth, he won't be able to talk. Hearing this, and not wanting to embarrass her husband, she leaves the room.

She goes to the next room and hides behind the wall separating the two rooms so that she can hear everything even if we don't see her. It takes her husband one second to realize what she's doing, and again he tells her that under such scrutiny, he won't be able to talk. Would she please go somewhere else in the house?

She finally does.

What is she so worried about?

Go figure.

The man sits down and talks. He recounts the story. Rabbi Shaul, the cousin of Rabbi Yaakov Alter, was the *rosh yeshivah*, the head of the Sfat Emet Yeshiva, until the Rebbe closed it down and changed the way the Ger Ḥasidim study the Talmud.

Good. I know this story already.

Who's right and who's wrong in all this? I ask him.

No answer.

I have come all the way up north, I realize, to hear nothing.

Okay. Let's talk about the Takunnes. What's your opinion about them? Are you for or against? I ask the man.

"If you tell people not to look at the pink elephant in the sky, the next thing they will do is look up in the sky for the pink elephant," he says.

What are you trying to say?

"Denying humans anything makes them crave it even more."

Can you be more precise?

"Psychology and emotions are two elements in humans that connect them between their bodies and souls. The Takunnes are designed to control the psychological and emotional parts of the human."

That's as far as this man is willing to go. After all, I've got a brain, and I have to conclude on my own where he stands.

Well, let me try to get this man to utter his thoughts in clear words. I say to him: If I understand you correctly, you are totally against the Takunnes. Correct?

The man refuses to answer. His tongue is stuck somewhere inside his mouth and won't move.

I try another question: Does Rabbi Shaul also ask his followers to follow the Takunnes?

"No. Rabbi Shaul said specifically that the Takunnes were designed for a specific time in the past and are no longer valid."

Do you, then, support Rabbi Shaul?

No answer.

The image this man projects, whether he is aware of it or not, is of a man living in constant fear of what the Ger Ḥasidim will do to him or to his family should he dare open his mouth. He lives in terror, paralyzed and confused, craving to act but having no guts to do so.

As I'm getting ready to leave his house, he tells me that I should follow the legal proceedings to be played out before an Israeli court, based on a complaint brought by Attorney Shlomo Elbaum against the Rebbe's followers, including the Rebbe's son, Shlomo Tsvi Alter.

I don't know what he's talking about, but I'll look into it.

Not far from Hatzor, in a deep valley called Amuka, lo and behold, is the gravesite of the Sage Jonathan ben Uzziel. So, at least, they say.

The weather is excellent, and it's a perfect opportunity for me to see the place once more.

The Talmud says about this Sage that while he was studying the Torah, birds that were flying above him were "immediately burned." Why did they burn? Because, some commentators say, angels from above would be coming down to earth to hear him study the Torah, and their fire burned the birds alive.

So be it.

It is said – could be true and could be not – that if you are lonely in life, meaning a single person, you come to Amuka, pray, leave a little piece of paper with your name on it on the grave, and in twelve months, you will be lucky in love.

The late Gerer Rebbe, Pinchas Menachem Alter, the father of Rabbi Shaul, sent his unmarried followers to Amuka to "burn the birds in their heads." There's a double pun here, and I like it.

Amuka today, I'm told, is one of Israel's top five holiest sites. How did it get such an honor when in my time almost nobody showed up there? I don't know.

Once I arrive at the grave's parking lot, something that wasn't around back then, I must pass through a special pathway from the parking lot to the grave. The pathway is divided by a fence that covers the view of those walking on the other side of the fence; one side is for women, the other for men.

God forbid that the eyes of any of the men who are looking for a woman should see a woman.

It is bizarre, but it makes life more interesting, doesn't it?

This fence wasn't in existence when I was the sweet lad I once was, but now that I'm a grown-up, the people in charge here want to make sure that I don't see any women.

Makes total sense.

I enter the grave area, which is surrounded by captivating green hills and cedar trees. There's a partition here too, in the middle of it; one side is for men, the other for women, so no man can be tempted by any woman and, The Name save us, spill his seed over the "*luz*" of the Sage.

Over the grave, there are see-through plastic pockets for the lonely singles looking for a match on the other side to leave their written mate requests for the dead Sage to take care of.

Oh, Lordy Lord.

There is a tree next to the grave. On its trunk and branches, look, there are many scarves hanging – too many to count. What are they doing up there? They were put there by lonely women who believe that if their scarves are there, next to the grave, the Sage Jonathan will not forget them and will work double hard to find them a match.

Does any of this have anything to do with Judaism?

Halloween, a very non-Jewish holiday, is in a couple of days. According to *Encyclopedia Britannica*, Halloween "seems to have developed mostly from Christian feasts of the dead."

Back in the United States, the powerful Jewish NGO the Anti-Defamation League (ADL) is governed by Progressive Jews nowadays. And for whatever reason, they are getting very busy with Halloween.

In an official statement in honor of Halloween, the good Jews from New York bitterly criticize "girl costumes" that "predominantly focus on dresses and being pretty." They decry the impression they have that girls' superhero costumes "include skirts, instead of the more practical pants for crime-fighting."

Yeah, that's New York these days. Women should not be dressed in pretty clothes, God forbid. I think that my Reform rabbi from Jerusalem would love this.

Yeah, yeah.

The ADL statement goes on, in a tone sadder than the funeral announcers of Mea Shearim: "Costumes marketed to older girls emphasize attractiveness and sexual appeal."

Oy vey, vey, vey.

To them, no doubt, the fence and partition in Amuka, separating men and women, are not high enough.

How we got to the point that Ḥaredim and Progressives – Jewish God-fearers and Jewish atheists – are so fearful of any sign of female prettiness is beyond me.

The ADL Jews go on to say: "Many Halloween costumes perpetuate gender stereotypes and exclude those who don't conform to traditional gender norms, especially those who are transgender, non-binary or gender non-conforming. Be mindful that you may have students who feel excluded and marginalized by the overly gendered way Halloween costumes are marketed."

These American Jews, always trying to be more righteous than the goyim, should join the Taliban of Jerusalem. It is in the Taliban women that they will find kindred spirits.

To date, as far as I know, the ADL has not issued any advice regarding grave tours.

On the other hand, the map-publishing company Carta has published a *Carta's Guide to Tombs of the Righteous in the Land of Israel.* It is 496 pages in total and includes graves of all kinds and sorts to visit, plus advice on what chapters in Psalms to recite when the need arises.

Here goes: If you are unemployed, recite Psalm 41. If you encounter thieves, recite Psalm 16. If you have pain in your shoulders, Psalm 3. If you have bad desires, Psalm 69. If demons chase you, Psalm 15.

ADL people, I think, should recite Psalm 15.

I move on to another gravesite; this one is in Zfat (Safed), a few kilometers up the road.

There's a limousine ahead of me, a VIP limo service for Ḥasidic American Jews who come to the north of Israel to pray in Zfat, a city known for its abundance of graves, dead rabbis, and dead kabbalists.

The limo is parked near the entrance to the Old Jewish Cemetery, while its American tourists are praying at a gravesite – reciting, perhaps, the pre-assigned Psalms chapters in *Carta's Guide*. Their driver stands ready to drive them once they are done with their grave-praying, and I have a little chat with him.

Why don't you pray with them? I ask the driver, an Orthodox Jew.

"That's paganism."

What's paganism?

"Praying at graves."

He tells me that there is an impressive number of famous Jews buried at the Old Cemetery, including Rabbi Yosef Karo, the Holy Ari, and many more.

At what grave are your Ḥasidic tourists praying now?

"Bat Ayin."

What's Bat Ayin (literally translated: Daughter of the Eye)?

"I don't know. It's a grave that's becoming more and more popular. Six years ago, when I started doing grave tours, there was a maximum of six buses coming here on the anniversary of the Bat Ayin's death, which is next month. Now, seventy buses come. And it's becoming more and more popular every year."

What is the grave good for?

"To protect you against losing your eyes," he says, laughing.

No, really, what is it good for?

"What are you asking me for? What do I understand about pagan worship?"

Once your American Ḥasidim are done with the grave, where are you driving them next?

"I don't know. They have a list of graves, and I drive them where they ask me to drive. I hope to do this all night."

What?

"I get paid by the hour. Every grave is money for me. Thank God there are so many graves in Israel!"

Aided by Carta's grave book, I find out that the Bat Ayin grave is that of Rabbi Abraham Dov of Ovruch, Ukraine (died 1841), the author of a book called *Bat Ayin* (often rabbis are named after their books).

Despite what the driver joked about, the reason people come to this grave – the real reason – is different, as I learn from another person: the Ḥasidim coming to pray at the Bat Ayin grave are looking for a match, and they believe, just like those going to Amuka or the Western Wall, that if they come here, a spouse will follow.

Well, that's life.

Once back in Jerusalem, I see big posters inviting the lonely souls to come and pray at the Western Wall this coming Saturday night to find a match.

I already went to one such gathering some months ago, and I'm not planning to go again. Yet I stare at this poster, and it makes me think.

Ḥaredi men have their heads covered with a kippah, aka skull-cap, aka yarmulke. Why are they wearing a kippah? The source for the kippah wearing, as far as I know, is in Tractate *Kiddushin*, where one Sage, by the name of Huna, is quoted as saying that he covered his head because of the "Holy Presence above my head." And I'm thinking: If that's the reason the Ḥaredi Jews wear a kippah, why would these people need to go to the Western Wall, where the Holy Presence is said to reside, to pray for matches in Her Presence? The Holy Presence, after all, stands or sits right on top of their heads. If they want the Holy Presence to help them find a mate, why don't they stand next to a mirror, stare at the top of their heads, and say a prayer?

I'm not done yet.

Fact: A Sheep Says "Amen" to a Rabbi

Fact: A dead man will resurrect the other dead

Did Jews indeed cover their heads with a skullcap in Talmudic times? Not really. A few individuals might have, but the rest of the Jews did not. In fact, as late as the eighteenth century, such a custom did not exist, and even the Vilna Gaon (1720–1797), the ultimate rabbinical authority of the Ḥaredi Litvaks to this day, specifically ruled that there's no prohibition at all against being bareheaded (with minor exceptions, such as during prayer).

The Litvaks, supposedly the most intellectual of the Ḥaredi world and people who say that they follow the path of the Vilna Gaon to the letter, seem to be neither in real life.

As for me, when I'm outside my hotel room, I wear a kippah in Mea Shearim, signaling to my neighbors that I respect them, and they appreciate it.

Right now, at this very moment, I'm taking a walk with a black kippah on my head.

A Ḥaredi Jew, also wearing a black kippah, approaches me. "I heard," he says, "that you are writing a book about Ḥaredi Jews. Is that true?"

Yes, I answer.

"What is there to write about us?" he wonders.

I meet people, I talk to them, and I write down what they say, I answer him.

"Do you ask them questions?"

I try.

"What kind?"

Different ones.

"Do you ask them what they believe?"

Let's say.

"Do you ask the tough questions?"

Like what?

"What is God?"

What do you think?

"About what?"

What is God?

"This is tough."

What do you think?

"I don't know."

Do you believe in God?

"No question!"

Who is He? What is He?

"This I don't know."

Thanks for sharing.

"Have a good day."

He walks away.

I find this encounter very interesting. Don't you?

Because my adoptive neighborhood is a closed neighborhood, many of its people know that I'm here to write about them. Some Ḥaredim stop me on the street to share their ideas of what I should write, some send me messages, and others invite me to their homes.

A Sephardi Jew sends me a message. Here goes: Our Rabbi, Rabbi Yitsḥak Yosef, has made a blessing, and a sheep standing by answered "Amen."

How am I supposed to react?

Sometimes I'm invited by Ḥaredim who live outside of this neighborhood. For the upcoming Friday night, for example, I'm invited by a Chabad-Lubavitch couple, who live some distance from Mea Shearim, for the traditional Sabbath meal.

Chabad-Lubavitch is known as a missionary Ḥasidic court, with representatives ("emissaries") around the world. It is a court that, to an extent, shares more with Breslev than with any other court. Both don't have a living Rebbe and follow a dead one, and both are missionaries who spend much of their resources turning committed atheists into ardent believers.

In due time, I arrive at the couple's home.

Luckily, the woman of the house is a great cook, and the man pampers me with expensive whisky. Who can ask for more?

My host sits at the head of the table, and behind him, on the wall, is a big photo of the late Chabad Rebbe, Menachem Mendel Schneerson, who passed away in New York in 1994.

Well, "passed away" is debatable. Yes, there was a funeral, and his gravesite, a place known as the Ohel, stands tall in Queens, New York, but not all agree that he passed away for real. Some of his followers believe that he never died and that the dead body carried during his funeral procession in 1994 was not his body. He is, they say, the famous Messiah ben David, and what happened with him is that he went into hiding. At the end of his hiding, so they say, he will reappear, resurrect the dead, and redeem Israel. Period. Other Chabad Ḥasidim, who frequent the grave and pray there whenever they can, believe that even though he died, he is still the Messiah and that he will raise the dead and redeem Israel. Both sides, in other words, are confident that he is Messiah ben David.

My hosts belong to the latter group.

So, the Rebbe is the Messiah mentioned in the Talmud? I ask them.

"Yes," says the man.

Let me understand: the Talmud says that the Messiah will come and resurrect the dead, correct?

"Yes."

Now, if the Rebbe is dead, how can he resurrect the other dead?

"Righteous people, it says, will be resurrected before the Messiah arrives."

Where does it say that?

"In the sources."

Who else will be resurrected from the dead before the Messiah arrives?

"The Rebbe."

Just him?

"Yes."

How many photos of the Rebbe do you have hanging on the walls of your home?

"Three."

I look at the photo behind him.

I have seen this Rebbe's face on the walls of every Chabad Ḥasid I've ever been to in the past. The Christians have Jesus, they have Schneerson, and everybody is happy.

The Ohel (tent in Hebrew) is a structure over the Rebbe's grave, busy around the clock. Those who cannot visit the Ohel for one reason or another can write to the Rebbe on a sheet of paper via post or online, and their letters will be delivered to the Rebbe. The Rebbe, rest assured, will read your letter and act on it. How exactly does this process work? Beats me.

There are some Chabad Ḥasidim, I was once told, who don't believe that the Rebbe is the Messiah, but I haven't seen them yet.

I enjoy being with this lovely couple, who are excellent hosts, but I miss Mea Shearim. Yes, I do.

A Conversation with the Rebbe of Shoimrei Emunim

Who is God? What is God? What is a kvittel?

Come Friday of the following week, I join the Ḥasidim of Shoimrei Emunim. Months ago, I prayed with them on a Sabbath morning and tremendously enjoyed their lokshen kugel; why not repeat the formula?

First things first: prayer. Like the last time, the Ḥasidim of Shoimrei Emunim pray very, very, very slowly. They enunciate every syllable, and every word takes forever to utter. Unlike last time, I decide that this time I will do it exactly as they do, schlepping out a word as slowly as I can.

Doing is believing.

When I utter the words so slowly, even words that I know by heart, they suddenly take on a different meaning. It's like eating ice cream. You can do it fast, and you can do it slowly, but if you take it slow, lick calmly, your taste buds react differently, and you enjoy it much more. When these Ḥasidim read, and I join them, as slow as can be (from Psalms), "Mightier than the thunder of the great waters, mightier than the breakers of the sea...," I imagine the endless sea, hear the thunder, sense the mighty breakers of the sea, and the words give me a different feeling. Never before have I seen those images as clearly as I do now; never before have I sensed and heard them as I do now. It is amazing.

The service takes a few hours, of course, but it's beautiful to discover something so simple and so basic: to imagine, hear, and sense what your mouth says.

Shoimrei Emunim is much smaller than Toldos Aharon, notwithstanding that they share the same grandpa. How many families are part of this Ḥasidic court? Reb Mordḥe told me that Shoimrei Emunim has three hundred families, but it might be an exaggeration.

The Rebbe and his family live upstairs, and I'm invited to join them for the Sabbath meal.

Oh, this will be interesting! I would love to see how the Rebbe relates to his wife, children, and whoever else will be there.

I go upstairs.

The house is lovely, spotless, and the floor, which I think is made of marble, is shining. There's a beautiful chandelier hanging from the ceiling, a big table, and chairs in the middle of the living room, and little kids with shiny, smiling faces to welcome the guest, me.

I stand by the window and look out, and what I see are other houses, and they are so close that I can almost touch them with my fingers. In this neighborhood, I noticed ages ago, some houses are so close to one another that there's very little privacy left. No one in his right mind, let me make this clear to you, would even dream of having a little brothel here, that Garden of Desire, with the Ukrainian and Russian beauties. Oh, no!

I take a seat at the table and wait to see how the evening will unfold.

Where's the Rebbe? He is not in yet.

Two of his sons-in-law, impeccably dressed, and a few more kids enter.

No women in the room. None. Nada.

The Rebbetsen, in the adjacent kitchen, prepares the evening meal.

Men, I'm told, will be sitting in this room and the women in another room.

Yeah, we're not going to be joined by any lady here. No garden, no desire. Forget it. No temptations.

The Rebbe enters, and in less than a minute, he leaves.

Why did he leave?

Oh, he's not going to be sitting with us, I'm told.

Doesn't he eat? Well, he'll eat at the *tish*, in a few hours from now, with the Ḥasidim.

What will he be doing till then?

Studying.

Since he became a Rebbe a few years ago, I'm told, he doesn't eat with his family.

Downstairs, he has a room, I'm also told, where he studies, eats, and sleeps. The man, in short, is a saint.

There's no Rebbe in the room, but there's food, all made by the Rebbetsen. And what food it is! The gefilte fish, for a start, is the best of its kind that ever reached my mouth and soul. Blessed be Shoimrei Emunim!

With the gefilte fish done, more food arrives: a most delicious soup, made with holy waters; chicken, most likely sold by the righteous Reb Berish; potato kugel, made for angels; and other dishes from the Garden of Eden, not the Garden of Desire, with a recipe written by Adam and Eve.

Yes, I can imagine it. Adam, the first human being ever, according to the Bible, sitting at one end of the table in the Garden of Eden, dressed in a $26,000 *shtreimel*, and his wife Eve, sitting across from him, dressed in a glittering white *tiḥel*, eating this same food.

What a paradise!

And as Adam and Eve sing Sabbath songs, in Yiddish, The Name comes by to drink brandy, the special Israeli 777 brandy, with the two creatures He created. Oh, what a vision! Welcome

Papa'le, welcome Tata'le, they say to Him, and He smiles at them, and gives them a little *shmek tabak* to sniff. Oh, what a beauty!

Back on earth, the sons-in-law ask me for my impressions so far.

You are, I tell them, the biggest Zionists I've ever met.

This surprises them. How can I say such a thing? Don't I know that they are the most ardent anti-Zionists?

Look, I tell them: you're not the only Ḥaredim in the world. There are Ḥaredim in Manchester and London, New York and Antwerp, and many other places. Those Ḥaredim suffer from anti-Semitism, and I know this for a fact, but they hardly ever rise up against their tormentors; they are quiet like fish. On the other end of the world is you. You spend enormous energies against the "Zionists," spray-paint slogans and curses against the government and the other citizens of this country, mainly for no reason.

Over there, abroad, your brethren suffer violence and abuse from their neighbors but say not a word. Over there, they are afraid to open their mouths, because they know they are guests in someone else's country. Here, you have no fear. Why don't you have any fear? Because here, you feel that you are in your home, in your land, the lord of the manor, amongst other Jews, amongst your brethren. Are you not, look in my eyes, the biggest Zionists there ever were?

They listen. "Interesting," one of them says, as the other nods in approval, adding: "Perhaps you're right." They never thought about it in these terms, they tell me, but now they do.

We chat for another hour or two, and after a good portion of delicious super kosher nondairy ice cream, I leave. But not for long. Come Sunday evening, I write a *kvittel*, my name on a piece of paper, and return. This time, for a private audience with the Rebbe.

Some Rebbes might be hiding or procrastinating, but not the Rebbe of Shoimrei Emunim, Shloime Rote.

Yes, I called his gabbai earlier in the day, and he said: "Can you come at nine o'clock in the evening?"

And here I am.

The Rebbe, Shloime Rote, sits at his study room, at the head of a long table, as I enter.

First off, I thank him for inviting me for a Kiddush a few months back, when I took my first steps in Mea Shearim, and tell him that the lokshen kugel I ate at his shul on that day is the best I ever had.

He remembers me, he says, and I'm surprised that he does. Yes, his congregation is not that big, but he must meet many people daily, and I'm not the only one he has seen since then.

In any case, I say to him: not only the kugel, that unforgettable lokshen kugel, was the best, but the gefilte fish I had on Friday night is the best gefilte fish anyone ever made! The Rebbe's wife, your wife, is the best cook in the world!

Historically speaking, I'm probably the first person in the history of Ḥasidic Judaism to come to a Rebbe and chat with him about kugels and gefilte fishes, but why not?

"Why didn't you come yesterday for the Sabbath morning meal?" he asks.

Well, I say to him, even if I came, you wouldn't be sitting at the table, as you didn't sit at the table on Friday night.

That's true, he says. "I don't sit at the table with my family. I eat with the Ḥasidim and with the yeshiva boys, but not with the family." He is blessed, he says to me, to have a wife, a *rebbetsen*, who understands his dedication to his Ḥasidim. His wife is American, he tells me, whose mother tongue is English, but he didn't want his children to learn English, and English is not spoken at home.

Why not?

"English is an impure language; it's a language of non-Jews."

We communicate in Yiddish, and that's the language spoken in his home. Why that?

"Yiddish is a Jewish language!"

Yiddish is an old German dialect, and it's basically German at its root. Not exactly a Jewish language.

"Yiddish is not German. If you speak Yiddish with a German, he will not understand you."

Not exactly true. If you speak Yiddish with Germans, they will understand most of what you say to them. Yiddish is the daughter of German, if you will.

"Do you understand German?"

Yes, I do.

He looks at me, and I hand him my *kvittel*.

What will he do with it? I ask myself.

He takes it, looks at my name, and puts it on the table.

I just did, I tell him, what I think that Ḥasidim do: give the Rebbe a *kvittel*. Does the Rebbe have anything to say to me? Does the Rebbe see anything in the *kvittel* beyond just my name?

"Generations ago, Rebbes would get a *kvittel* and see worlds in it. Not today. All I see is your name. No Rebbe today can look at a *kvittel* and see anything in it other than what's written on it."

This Rebbe, just like the Toldos Aharon Rebbe, says to me that a *kvittel* is nothing. It's incredible to hear, and it's courageous of them to say this. However, I have a question: If you know that the *kvittel* is just another *bobbe maiseh*, why do you accept it?

"Sometimes, if the Ḥasid believes it, the Master of the Universe does miracles," he answers – in Yiddish, of course. In other languages, what he says is this: What do you want me to do when an idiot comes to me with a little piece of paper? Should I tell him not to be an idiot?

This reminds me of the fake miracles that I read in his grandfather's book, and I say to him: if I'm not mistaken, the Rebbe's grandfather wrote in his book, *Shoimer Emunim*, that doubting fake stories about miracles done by Rebbes is heresy. Is that what it is?

"I don't remember the exact words – my brother knows the book *Shoimer Emunim* better than I do – but I think that the book refers not to fake stories but exaggerated stories. Sometimes, when a story changes hands, being told by somebody who heard it from somebody who heard it from somebody, it's not the same story anymore. It's not fake; it's exaggerated. The idea is this: it doesn't matter if the story about a particular miracle performed by a righteous Rebbe is true or not because, in any case, the righteous Rebbe would have been able to perform even a bigger miracle than the one told in the story."

These lines are totally convincing when said in Yiddish.

In other languages, what this Rebbe just said means the following: all the stories about the Rebbes who have performed miracles are as accurate as any of the tales in *One Thousand and One Nights*.

Yes, yes, it now occurs to me that this Rebbe was right when he said before that "Yiddish is not German." He's right. Yiddish and German are two different languages, having almost nothing in common. Yiddish is, my dear, the language of God and His Chosen People. Period.

Yeah.

It is at this moment that I find it proper to raise my most significant criticism of the people of Mea Shearim: faith. I have been in Mea Shearim for quite a few months by now, I tell the Rebbe, but for the life of me, I don't get what the people here believe in, and I don't think that they get it either.

He asks me to explain myself.

Here's an example, I say to him: they say that they dedicate their lives to studying the Torah, but they don't. The foundation of the Torah – and no one will dispute it – is the Bible, the very book that they don't study, the very book that they don't even know.

He knows this to be true, and he won't argue it, but in defense against studying the Bible, he says: "The biggest heretics are the ones who study the Bible."

Period.

If I get him right, a Jew who does not want to be called a heretic should follow this rule: do not study the Bible but cherry-pick Talmudic sayings against looking at women.

For his part, the Rebbe goes on to remind me that "one of the most learned Sages, the Sage Elisha Ben Avuyah, did ask all the questions, and as a result, he stopped believing in God. Altogether." From that time on, after he stopped believing, Elisha was so despised by the Sages that when the Talmud speaks about him, it does not mention him by name but refers to him as "Aḥer," meaning "other."

And God is not mentioned by name either, but let's not talk about that.

For my part, I keep on: not only do the people here not study the Bible, but they also have no clue about the very essence of their faith.

He asks me to explain myself.

They believe, as I'm sure the Rebbe does too, that after their passing, and if they observed God's commandments while in this world, they will go to Heaven. And I ask them: What is Heaven? What will be in Heaven? Is Heaven something real, something that you can see and feel, or something else? They have no clue.

"This is not a question. The Talmud discusses it in detail."

And what does the Talmud say?

"There is a disagreement between the Sages about it. But why do you ask this question? Would you also ask, What is God? Who is God?"

He calculates, obviously, that I would never ask such a question and that if I don't ask this question, I shouldn't ask other questions either. Instead, I say to him: Not a bad question! The Rebbe has a good question, and I'll ask it: What is God? Who is God?

He looks at me, the strange kugel and gefilte fish eater that I am, and says: "The Master of the Universe is the very essence, the very being of everything. He created the whole world with the breath of His mouth, with words coming out of His mouth.

He said, 'Let there be,' and it became. That's who He is, and that's how He created the world."

Why did He create the world, by the way?

"Because He is a King, a Master, and a master needs to have people around him."

According to Judaism, the world was created about six thousand years ago. Also, according to Judaism, God is infinity, and He existed infinite years before the world was created.

Now, let me ask you this: If you are right, and God created the world about six thousand years ago because He wanted to have people in His kingdom, or whatever, why did He wake up only six thousand years ago to create a world and not an infinite number of years earlier, trillions of years earlier?

"This is a question that you are not allowed to ask!"

His gabbai opens the door and says that somebody is waiting to get in.

"I'll be brief," the Rebbe says to the gabbai.

In the few minutes that are left, he tells me that he knows that God exists because he has seen the miracles of God and personally experienced them. It was a miracle, he says to me, that he found the millions of shekels that it took to build his house here, above the shul, supported by the sale of a house that he owned in Bnei Brak. Initially, when he assumed the Rebbe's seat, following the passing of his father, he stayed in a small room in the shul while his family lived somewhere else, and it was extremely difficult for him and his family. But The Name helped him, and he doesn't doubt His existence for a second. His house, he gives me another example, was built without the required construction permits, but the city's inspectors didn't notice the construction until the house was complete, even though they were walking in the neighborhood God knows how many times during the construction. Isn't this proof of God's existence?

His faith is right, his Ḥasidic court is right, and even the Ḥasidic world's traditionally most bitter enemy, the Litvaks, now admit that the Ḥasidim are right, he tells me.

"When the Ḥasidic movement was established, the Litvaks fought them. For almost two centuries, they fought us with all their might, preaching against Rebbes and the very idea of Rebbes. The fight was bitter, but today they have their own Rebbes, go for blessings and advice, and follow their Rebbes. Ḥasidism has won. We won!"

As I get up, ready to leave, he says to me: "I never left this country."

You must be a big Zionist, I say to him, the leader of a community known to be extremely anti-Zionist.

"I am the biggest Zionist there is," he replies.

Yes, you are, I say to him.

I like this man.

I go out, breathing the fresh air of the Jerusalem evening, cool and calm. Ever since I've been here, and except for a couple of troublemakers, there have been no demonstrations on the streets, not a sound of anger but many sounds of joy, and I've been welcomed more than I dared to hope in my wildest dreams. Perhaps, following Murphy's Law, violent demonstrations will flare up in Mea Shearim just after I leave. And who knows how the story of Ger will end, and how much more violence will transpire between the two camps. It can happen. Everything can happen. I never believed that I'd live to see violent demonstrations in Midtown Manhattan, but just over a couple of years ago, New York City burst into rage and fire, looting and bullets.

As I walk, looking at the people around me, human all, I think of the story I read in the *Shoimer Emunim* book about the mother and her daughter and the infinite torture they went through, and still go through, in a house that never was.

Is the story true? Did it happen? Did the two women ever exist? Does it matter?

And, as I continue to walk, I think of New York.

In New York, as already mentioned on these pages, we are not supposed to say "he" or "she" anymore if we want to be accepted by the elite of our culture. There's no he, and there's no she. Man and woman are binary, and he or she who says "he" or "she" is a bigot, a racist, a fascist, a chauvinist, a homophobe, a xenophobe, and one hundred other titles reserved for the lowest of the low. A Nazi, in short. These days, if you are a writer, a singer, a director, a moviemaker, a philosopher, or whatever, and somebody out there comes and says that thirty years ago, you improperly touched them, you are immediately pronounced guilty. Whatever you authored, a book or a film, a song or a theory, is no more to be read, sung, or seen. It's called Cancel Culture. And if you drive a diesel car, if you dare, you are selfish, an egoist, a murderer, and as close to a Nazi as can be. And oy to you if you smoke a cigarette instead of marijuana. In today's New York, the Puritans tell us to join the fight for gay rights, transgender rights, Black rights, colored people's rights, women's rights, children's rights, and animal rights. These Puritans, whose Messiah is Greta and whose Chosen People are the Palestinians (yes, they love Palestinians), tell us that if we don't join the fight, we are racist, misogynist, chauvinist white bastards. They, the famed New Yorkers, the people whom, years ago, I chose to be part of, don't have a white donkey and will never have it. For them, you see, riding a donkey contradicts fundamental animal rights.

Who makes more sense to you, you tell me: the Ḥaredi people of Mea Shearim or the non-binary people of New York?

I pause to read a big obituary announcement put up on the boards and walls of Mea Shearim by Toldos Aharon, which mourns the passing of Esther Malke Steinberger, a woman who was laid to rest on the Mount of Olives. Is she related to Eliyohu Steinberger, the father-in-law of the man who returned his soul to Heaven on the very first day I arrived in Mea Shearim?

As I reach Tsfanya Street, I see Reb Yankev Ḥaim driving his car. He's been away for some time, he tells me, and he invites me to come over to his home next Friday night for the Sabbath meal.

I, as usual, immediately accept.

"I hear that you and Motta Brim have become friends; is that true?" he asks me.

How do you know that I even know Motta? I ask him.

He smiles and drives on. There's an old man in the neighborhood, who lives alone, and Reb Yankev Ḥaim is going to keep him company for a while. One day he feeds the needy, the next he entertains the lonely. That's him.

Late at night, or you might say early in the morning, at 4:22 a.m., the muezzin is heard. Yes, this is Jerusalem: Ḥaredim here, Muslims there, One Thousand and One Nights, one white donkey and one white Buraq, and I'm done for the day.

A Miracle: A Rebbe Comes to Visit, but He Didn't

What's the difference between Ḥaredim and Catholics?

Day follows night, and I make some calls.

I contact the Boyaner Rebbe's gabbai and tell him that I would like to meet the Rebbe.

"This week is going to be tough," he says to me. "Call me next week, and I'll try to arrange it."

I contact the Lelever Rebbe's gabbai and tell him the same. He'll get back to me today, he says.

The day goes by, but the Lelever doesn't call.

The next day, I call him again.

"I'll call you back in two hours," he says.

The two hours go by, and then some, and he doesn't call.

So, I call the gabbai of the Lelever Rebbe yet again.

"Call me in half an hour," he says.

Half an hour later, like a Swiss clock, I call. The gabbai doesn't pick up. This is my last call to him. I don't have to torture a man who can't say yes and can't say no.

Meantime, surprise, a Rebbe comes to visit me in my hotel. We chat about this and about that, and before he leaves, he says to me: "This is between you and me; nobody should know we met. I was not here."

No problem.

The Rebbe, I see, is afraid.

Two more hours go by, and I get a message from a yeshiva student I don't know. He asks if I wouldn't mind coming to his yeshiva now that I have been to Ḥevron.

How do you know that I went to Ḥevron? I ask him.

"I heard from a friend who studies in Ḥevron," he answers and adds: "Don't tell anybody that I invited you; no one should know that I have internet access."

Okay, I respond. I'll try to come next week. What's the address?

He sends me the address. His yeshiva, Netivot Ḥoḥmah, also known as the Wolfson Yeshiva, is in the Orthodox neighborhood of Bayit VeGan, in Jerusalem, and I consider going there sometime next week.

The student is afraid of his rabbis, and the Rebbe fears his followers. What a world.

I go for a walk near Sabbath Square, when a man I don't know comes by and taps me on my shoulder. "It seems to me that you have come back; you are one of us again," he says.

Is he right?

A lovely Ḥasidic girl, fourteen years of age or somewhere near it, passes by me. She stops to look at me, deep into me. Is her name Rachel?

Am I losing it? I hope not, but just in case, I make up my mind to take a short break from Mea Shearim. Where to? Jaffa Street. On Jaffa Street, as all of us know by now, immodest women are walking on the street, God save us. They are the reason, I read in a holy book the other day, that the Messiah has not arrived yet.

Yeah.

In one of the numerous outdoor cafés in the area, and while sipping Italian coffee (yes, they have it in this country as well), I meet a historian who tells me that he is a religious Jew who is currently dating a German lady. The moment she converts to Judaism, he lets me understand, he'll marry her.

Does she want to convert?

"She's more Jewish than me," he responds.

As I sip more of my Italian, I ask the man to draw me a picture of society in the middle of the eighteenth-century Kingdom of Poland where the Ḥasidic movement was founded. I suspect, I tell him, that the Ḥasidic movement, made of people of flesh and blood, was influenced by the culture surrounding it. Is my assumption correct? I ask him.

"There's no question," he answers, "that Jews were influenced by the external culture."

And what was the external culture like, let's say in Eastern Europe, in the eighteenth century?

"Eastern Europeans at the time were traditionally pretty superstitious, pretty illiterate, and pretty primitive."

Let me see: we are talking about the period when serfdom was still around, and a big part of society was made up of peasants. They believed in God, didn't read the Bible, reached God via an intermediary – the priest – and believed in miracles. Correct so far?

"Yes."

The Ḥasidim believe in God, don't read the Bible, reach God via an intermediary – the Rebbe, living or dead – and believe in miracles. Correct?

"Yes."

Can I conclude that the Ḥasidic movement is a copy of the Catholic movement, only in Yiddish and minus Jesus?

Because he's a religious person, this comparison is something that he finds hard to digest. He gives me a long lecture about Catholic versus Orthodox Christianity, Poland versus Ukraine, and everything in between. But when everything is said and done, we are back at square one, and he finally agrees: the Ḥasidic movement, at its roots, is a copy of the culture surrounding it centuries ago, only in Yiddish and minus Jesus.

I sip a bit more of my Italian.

There was a time in history when the Litvaks said this same thing about the Ḥasidim. But nowadays, once they have adopted the Ḥasidic way of rabbi worship and created their own Rebbes, and don't question anything, there is no difference between the two except, as you already know, for the humor that the Litvaks are still lacking.

Oh, Lord, this is what happens, having thoughts like these, when a man goes to Jaffa Street, where ladies walk about immodestly.

I take the last sip of my Italian and walk back to Mea Shearim as quickly as I can.

Oh, my Mea Shearim: it's nice to be here again, where the sweet boy I once was still lives.

And on the Sabbath, when God's Bride arrives, to Reb Yankev Ḥaim I go, to enjoy the pleasures of the Sabbath: out-of-this world herring and onion salad, accompanied by Glenlivet eighteen-year aged whisky – and that's just for a start.

"Did you meet Rabbi Meileḥ?" Reb Yankev asks me.

Who is Rabbi Meileḥ? I ask him.

"If you don't know Rabbi Meileḥ, Rabbi Elimeleḥ Biderman," he says, "you have to restart your whole journey into the Ḥaredi world. How can you not know Rabbi Meileḥ?"

Rabbi Meileḥ, it turns out, is an important man in many circles. What is he about? No, he's not a Rebbe, though he is connected to the Ḥasidic court of Lelev. What is he? He is a *mashpia*, an Influencer, and he has many followers. On the coming Monday evening, I read in a Ḥaredi media outlet, he will have a big event in the hall of the Boyaner building not far from me, and thousands are expected. What is the event about? It's the anniversary of the Bat Ayin, Daughter of the Eye. Yes, that man who's buried in Zfat, whose grave has become one of the holiest places in the land. It turns out that Rabbi Meileḥ is responsible for making that gravesite so popular. Are all the thousands planning to come looking for a mate? The Bat Ayin, Rabbi Abraham Dov of Ovruch, had a mate, but he had no children, making it a perfect opportunity for Rabbi Meileḥ to be his champion.

As for me, I can't go to Rabbi Meileḥ's event on Monday because I'm going to meet Ḥaya, a follower of a rabbi sitting in prison, on that same day. Sorry.

She Died, but Her Rabbi Resurrected Her

The Romanian nun feeds me Palestinian cookies

Ḥaya used to be secular, as secular as they come, served in the Israeli army, and was dating an Austrian man, not Jewish. But she's no more secular, and no Austrian should even dream of dating her. Today she's religious, as religious as they come, and she thinks the world of Rabbi Eliezer Berland. To be more exact, she believes in him. For her, he's everything. He is like Moses the Lawgiver, and it says in Exodus, she teaches me, that the Children of Israel "believed in the Lord and His servant Moses." It's written, no questions asked.

Ḥaya tells me that it all started with an accident when she was serving in the Israeli army. The accident was so severe that she was clinically dead for about twenty minutes. Her soul, she tells me, departed from her body and flew up to Heaven, to the Heavenly Court. There her fate in the Other World was to be decided: Would she go to Paradise or Hell? The Heavenly Court, just like any court down on Earth, was in session, and as the judges were to decide her fate, one of the judges took the gavel, banged on the table, and said: "Her time is not over yet. She must be returned to earth, to life." The Heavenly Court accepted the judge's opinion, sending the soul back to earth, and she was resurrected.

She remembered the face of the judge who decreed that she be returned to life, she tells me, but for years, she didn't know who he was. Until she met Rabbi Eliezer Berland. It was him! It was he who sat on the Heavenly Court, ordering her soul to reunite with her body yet again. Him. No other. No doubt. And she became religious and a follower.

There are women, I say to her, who testified that Rabbi Berland sexually abused them, and he's serving time for that. Are they all lying?

"You know why they said that?"

You tell me.

"Because Rabbi Berland gave those women money to say that."

To say that he sexually abused them?

"Yes."

Why would any man pay women money to accuse him of abusing them?

"Read the Book of Isaiah, chapter 53, verse by verse, and you will understand."

Does the prophet write about Berland? Wow. Let me see. I read some of the verses.

> But he was wounded because of our transgressions, he was crushed because of our iniquities; the chastisement of our welfare was upon him, and by his wounds we were healed....
>
> He was oppressed, though he humbled himself and did not open his mouth; as a lamb that is led to the slaughter, and as a sheep that before her shearers is silent; yea, he did not open his mouth.
>
> By oppression and judgment he was taken away, and with his generation who did reason? For he was cut off from the land of the living, for the transgression of my people to whom the stroke was due.

> And they made his grave with the wicked, and with the rich his tomb, though he had done no violence, nor was any deceit in his mouth.

Okay, I get it. And truth be told, Rabbi Berland's followers are not the first to use Isaiah to bolster their arguments on issues of faith. Along the ages, Christianity used, and still does, the same verses to explain away the suffering of Jesus Christ, a dying God on a cross.

Ḥaya goes on. "As it says in Isaiah, Rabbi Berland suffers for us, to save us. He wants to be indicted; he wants to go to jail, to suffer more, for us."

And that's why he admitted abusing the women?

"Yes."

He has also been implicated in the murder of two people.

"He asked his followers to go to the police and say that he was involved in the murder. And he admits it. He does it all for us. He suffers for us, as it says in Isaiah."

He never abused any woman?

"Never! He is a holy man! Do you know how many people he saved? Who saved me when I was at the bottom of the bottom? The Tzaddik. He saved thousands of Jews. Many people owe him everything they have."

Not only that, she says, but Rabbi Berland is "a descendant of King David."

How do you know that?

Well, that's simple. The other day, she tells me, Rabbi Berland signed his name thusly: "Eliezer, Son of David."

Bingo.

She gives me a booklet, a collection of chapters from Psalms as arranged by the Tzaddik, which will help me in times of need. A gift. "Come back any time," she says, right before I leave.

A few steps down the street from where we meet is the impressive building of the "Representation of the Romanian Orthodox

Patriarchate at the Holy Land," just across the street from Mea Shearim. I saw this building last time I was in the area, but now I try to go in.

A gorgeous nun, Mother Nicolaida, opens the gates for me and lets me in. Dressed in beautiful modest clothes, as if she were a Ḥasidic woman, she welcomes me with a smile and an apology. What is she apologizing about? Her dress, she says, is dirty, because she was taking care of the dog just before I came in, and she feels terrible welcoming a guest with unclean clothes. I don't see any dirt on her clothes, and say that to her, but she still thinks that she's very dirty.

Why does she need a dog? Because some people in the area have tried to damage the building, which serves both as a church and a monastery, she tells me. A few months ago, she adds, someone tried to set the place on fire, and recently, someone tried to jump the fence into the building at night.

Was he an Arab or a Jew? I ask her.

"A Jew," she says.

Well, good excuse to have a dog.

She lets me into the church, a gorgeous church with painted walls and many an icon and lots of gold all around, and I sit down on one of the few chairs in the church. Orthodox Christians, I learned a while ago, prefer not to sit in service.

Have you ever fallen in love? I ask the nun.

"Yes, with Jesus."

That's it?

"After you fall in love with Jesus, who is so perfect, no man will match Him!"

Across the street from her are the Breslevers. They love Rabbi Naḥman, and she loves Jesus. Both Jews, Naḥman and Jesus, are long gone, dead, but their followers keep following them.

I like Romanian people, I tell her. Maybe they are not as perfect as Jesus, but they get close. My mother, I share with her, was born in Romania.

Hearing this, the gorgeous nun immediately feels an affinity with me and starts conversing in Romanian.

Sorry, I tell her, but my mother never taught me the Romanian language.

"Why didn't she?" she asks.

It's a long story, I say to her, but she wants me to tell her the story anyway.

Well, I say to her, trying to be concise, this is why: When the Romanian Fascists eventually lost power, she wanted to go back to her home, but her parents were no longer alive, and a Romanian family had taken over their house. Her neighbors betrayed her, and the pain was too much to swallow.

She looks at me with her two beautiful eyes and excuses herself. She leaves the room, and when she comes back, she comes with a tray with fresh Palestinian cookies, the semolina kind, and water to honor the Jewish guest.

We chat a bit more, and when I'm about to leave, she hands me a copy of a painting, the Virgin Mother and Baby Jesus on a background of Romania, a gift. To help me, I guess, in times of need. "Please come again," she says.

I walk on the street and look at the people around me, an act that I have been doing for months by now, and I can't shake off the thought in me: that nun and the Ḥasidic women on the street are so much alike. In looks, manners, belief, thought, and dress.

I keep on walking, and a car driving on Mea Shearim Street approaches me, its driver waving to me. Who is he? Reb Yeḥezkel Lefkovits.

I wave back.

I recall what he said to me when we met, God knows how many months ago: "We are Jews because we were born Jews, and we have to be Jews."

If he gets to meet Nicolaida, I suspect, he would be surprised at how Jewish she is.

A small world, within just a few steps, and everything is in it. And everybody. Except for Rabbi Eliezer Berland. He is not here; he's up there, chairing the Heavenly Court as we speak.

The day is long, as the days often are, and I go to Motti's restaurant, which is just a few minutes' walk from here.

I order chicken soup and chat with a Ḥasid about the white donkey. I ask him: Why do you think that The Name created this donkey on the Six Days of Creation?

"No," he says. "The donkey that was created at the end of the Six Days of Creation, right before the Sabbath, was not Abraham's donkey but Balaam's she-ass," referring to the biblical story of a prophet named Balaam who was about to curse the Jews but ended up blessing them after his donkey opened its mouth and spoke to him.

Well, what can I say? The donkey story is getting too complex for my taste. Did you know, by the way, that Nicolaida's beloved, Jesus Christ, also entered the Holy City of Jerusalem riding a donkey?

Sadly, I have no donkey. I take a taxi to Bayit VeGan, to the Wolfson Yeshiva.

On the way, I call the Boyaner Rebbe's gabbai. He doesn't pick up. I call again, and again, and again. The man doesn't pick up.

His loss.

He's not the only Rebbe in town.

I can meet others.

A Conversation with the Karliner Rebbe

Why the Boyaner Rebbe is a smart man

Why do I want to meet another Rebbe? Well, I can't stop wondering about one of my little discoveries, that of the *kvittel*. The *kvittel* is a major part of the Ḥaredim's core belief, encompassing an unshakeable trust that the Rebbe (or the rabbi, in other instances) can read deep into their souls and see their fate when he reads their names in the *kvittel*. Yet the Rebbes of Toldos Aharon and Shoimrei Emunim said to me, in the clearest of words, that they can't read anything in those *kvittel*s. Would other Rebbes say the same?

One Mea Shearim resident, a brilliant guy who is deeply connected to the Karlin-Stolin Ḥasidic court, suggests going to the Karliner Rebbe. If we come early on an evening when he accepts his Ḥasidim, he says, the Rebbe will see me.

Perfect.

We drive to see the Rebbe in Givat Ze'ev, near Jerusalem, where he lives and where he has a Ḥasidic center (in addition to the one in Mea Shearim).

In a waiting room, right before the Rebbe's room, there is a big table, many chairs, and holy books for those who want to study or pray before meeting the Rebbe. On the table, at its center, there are pens and papers for the Ḥasidim to write their *kvittels* if they have not done that yet.

I take a piece of paper and a pen and write my name and my mother's name.

There are about thirty Ḥasidim in the room presently, and they are doing the same. Some take a lot of time to write their *kvittels*, some do it faster, but all eagerly wait their turn, as if their lives depended on it, to have the Rebbe read their *kvittels*. Some of them are very tense, probably worrying about what the Rebbe will discover about them.

I walk in.

The Rebbe, Boruch Meir Yaakov Shochet, looks at me, and immediately a smile spreads over his face. He says: "You live in Mea Shearim, you came here from Germany, and now you are here."

Wait a sec. How do you know all that, Rebbe?

"If you want to believe that I can see things when people just come in to see me, you are welcome to believe so. But I'll tell you how I know: I read about you in the papers; there were a few articles about you. What brings you in, Tuvia?"

I'm trying to meet some Rebbes because I have questions.

"Which Rebbes have you met so far?"

I met the Rebbes of Toldos Aharon and Shoimrei Emunim, I saw Rabbi David Abuhatzeira, but the Boyaner Rebbe didn't want to see me.

"He is a smart man!"

Thanks.

We laugh.

When the laughter dies down, I give the Rebbe my *kvittel*, and he takes it. I say to him: Now that I gave you my *kvittel*, what do you see on it, besides my name?

"I don't see anything."

He laughs, and I do too. We laugh, laugh, and laugh.

Yes, there's nothing to a *kvittel*. Only if I want to believe in it, if I'm naïve enough to believe in it, I'm welcome.

There you go. The third Rebbe in a row to say the same thing.

Yet his Ḥasidim write their *kvittels*, wanting him to connect with their souls, and he can't tell them to stop. They won't take no for an answer. Period.

I spend twenty minutes with him, telling him of my experiences in Israel, and we laugh yet again. This Rebbe, whose court counts roughly two thousand families, is one of the friendliest Rebbes I've met.

I like him, but it's time I meet some Litvaks.

God Wants Ḥaredi Litvaks to Be Poor

A Yiddish-speaking camel enters a yeshiva

I have never been to the Wolfson Yeshiva, and if not for the little message that I got from the Unknown Student, I wouldn't even know that it exists.

But it does, and as I inquire about the yeshiva on my way there, I'm told that it is one of the finest Litvishe yeshivas in the land.

That's good.

I reach the yeshiva and enter its grounds, a big yard in front of the study hall, and start chatting with some of the students, who wonder what brings me to their yeshiva. I have no idea if the guy who asked me to come is among them, and he doesn't introduce himself if he is.

I tell the students that I'm an author writing about the Ḥaredi world and that I'd love to interview them. Hearing this, they invite me to come in.

We enter the study hall, and I sit down in the first seat I find, in the front row, where their rabbis usually sit. And soon enough, a rabbi shows up. He looks at me as one would look at a camel inside a brothel, wondering what a creature like me is doing in a holy place like his, and in an area reserved for rabbis. I greet him in Yiddish, a language he understands but cannot speak, and he doesn't know how to communicate with me. He sits down, two seats to my left, and opens a book. He probably wants to say something to me, but what can a Litvak who doesn't speak Yiddish say to a Yiddish-speaking Jew? Not much. He bites his lips, his face showing the first signs of frustration and anger, and it is evident that he would like my presence to evaporate at once.

His students, mindful of their suffering rabbi, ask me if I wouldn't mind sitting with them outside, at the entrance to the study hall.

Okay, I say.

I walk outside, and five of them join me.

In no time, another twenty or so join, all wanting to know what the non-camel Yiddish-speaker is doing in their yeshiva. And soon, another group of students shows up, keeping a little distance, and they stare at me as if I were an exhibition piece planted in their yeshiva by the Israel Museum.

The students around me all talk, each contributing a question or comment, and each building on a question or comment their friends have just made.

They want to know, they tell me, why I really, really showed up here of all places.

I came to learn about you, I say to them.

"Learn what?"

What's your *shnit* (specialty)? What is it, for instance, that this yeshiva offers that you won't get in another yeshiva?

"Why do you want to know?"

Well, since I'm writing about the Ḥaredi world, and since I'm here, I'm intrigued about what makes you different.

"Did you go to other yeshivas?"

Yes, I did.

"And what is their *shnit*?"

I don't know. I didn't ask them.

"Why then are you asking us?"

Every place I go, I ask different questions, whatever comes to mind. If I asked everybody the same, I'd be bored.

"You went to the Ḥevron Yeshiva, right?

Yes, I did.

"Did you ask them about their *shnit*?"

No, I didn't.

"Did you figure out their *shnit*?"

I have to think about it.

"What did you ask them?"

Other things.

"Why do you ask us about our *shnit*?"

It just came to me.

"What's the reason this came to you?"

I have no idea. It just popped out of my brain.

"So, when you came here, you didn't come to find out about our *shnit*."

I did not.

"Then why did you come here, to us?"

I got a message from one of you asking me to come.

"From whom?"

I can't say his name, but as far as I know, he could be one of you.

"If you find out about our *shnit*, will you write it?"

Perhaps.

"Will you write positively about our *shnit* or negatively?"

It depends on what the *shnit* is.

"In general, will you write positively or negatively about the Ḥaredim?"

I don't know yet; I will have to think about it.

"But what do you have on your mind?"

I'm trying to find out.

"How do you do that?"

I talk to people.

"Are you like all those journalists who go to Yoilish Krois, and he tells them that the graffiti against the Zionists on the streets of Mea Shearim is just because the residents want that no *baalei tshuvah* will come to live in the neighborhood...?"

I heard that from him.

"Then you are like them: you go to Krois and Hirsh, and you'll write about how crazy we are."

Not exactly. I talk to many people, many. I actually live in Mea Shearim.

"You live in Mea Shearim?"

I do.

"Why Mea Shearim? There are many Ḥaredi neighborhoods outside of Mea Shearim too! Why don't you live here, in Bayit VeGan?"

Well, I'm here now. Am I not?

"Oh, that's true. How do you like us so far?"

You seem to be a nice bunch of fellows.

"What's nice about us?"

Don't you think that you are nice?

"The question is: Why do you think that we are nice?"

And so it goes: on and on and on and on. I came to interview them, but in the end, they interview me. Great!

And they have questions up the wazoo.

They are, in a word, Litvaks.

We talk for almost two hours, and I love every second of it.

As we chat, two more rabbis pass by, and each of them stops to look at this strange encounter between their students and me, and then moves on. Judging by the expressions on their faces, they are not happy, but they say not a word. "This is the *shnit* of our yeshiva," one of the students tells me. "In this yeshiva, the rabbis let us be who we are. Yes, there are red lines, as there are in any institution, but if we don't cross those lines, the rabbis here won't get involved."

That's good. The older students, he proudly tells me, can even study the Bible if they want.

Wow!

Of course, being that these guys are Litvaks, someone must sharply disagree with the explanation I was just given – and that someone, it so happens, stands right near me and says, "The reason the rabbis didn't say anything when they saw us talking to you is different!"

What's the reason?

"They have no guts!"

I like these yeshiva guys, and I enjoy their never-ending questioning.

Still, I miss that one thing that the Ḥasidim have, and they don't – and you know what that is: a sense of humor. I don't know why, but the Vidui, the confession prayer on Yom Kippur, jumps into my mind this very second.

The text of this prayer is the same for both Ḥasid and Litvak, but the delivery is a study in opposites.

The Litvak beats his chest for each offense he confesses to having committed, starting with *Oshamnu, bogadnu, gozalnu, dibarnu doifi* (We have trespassed, we have betrayed, we have robbed, we have slandered), etc. He beats his chest so hard that by the time he's done with all the offenses, it's a miracle if he doesn't have a huge heart attack in the process. The Ḥasid, on the other hand, does it differently: he beats his chest for each offense, confessing to the same horrible deeds, saying the same words, though in Ḥasidic accent, but he sings in between. Here goes: *Ushamni*, ta, ta, ta, la, la, la, oh, oh, oh, *bugadni*, ba, la, ba, la, ba, la, da, da, da, ya, ya, ya, *guzalni*, pam, pam, pam, oo, oo, oo, li, li, li, li, ma, ma, ma, mu, mu, mu, *dibarni doifi*, yom, yom, yom, tam, tam, tam, tam, tam, tam, la, la, la, la, pom, pom, pom.

The Litvak, raised to seek knowledge and reason, understands that if he confesses to such horrific deeds, *Oshamnu, bogadnu, gozalnu, dibarnu doifi*, etc., and is asking forgiveness for them, he must take them seriously. He beats his heart as hard as he can, hoping that if his body is in pain, The Name will forgive. The Ḥasid, raised to sing and enjoy his faith, understands that there is a text that he must read because that's the tradition, and he will even beat his heart, though lightly, and hope that if he sings loudly enough and beats lightly enough, he will create enough white angels to protect him in time of need.

In any case, believe it or not, before the day is over, I go to meet one more Litvak, this one from a different yeshiva. We meet at his home, where most of his furniture is made of plastic. The man is not rich.

He tells me of the horrible "animals" roaming the land, the Zionists, who steal all the money from the Ḥaredi people, may The Name strike them all and kill them, he says, and may they all go to hell once they are dead.

How did the Zionists steal your money?

"Yeshiva students used to be paid by the government for sitting in yeshivas and studying Torah, and now a new Zionist government has been installed in Israel, and they have cut our pay by two-thirds. Shame on them!"

The Ḥaredim don't like the present Israeli government, which they consider anti-Ḥaredi. One of the people they dislike the most in the government is Yair Lapid, son of the late Tommy Lapid, the leader of a now-defunct political party regarded as anti-Ḥaredi. "Look who is in the coalition," my Litvak tells me. "Yair Lapid!"

Without resorting to names, let me ask you: the previous government was also made up of Zionists, and they gave you a generous Torah subsidy, or whatever it's called. Were you thankful to them, to those Zionists?

"The Zionists, no matter which Zionists, never gave me anything; that's totally false."

Who then gave you the money, before the new government was installed?

"The Name."

Let me understand: before these Zionists cut the two-thirds, it was God Who personally deposited money in your bank account, straight from Heaven, into your checking account. Is that so?

He looks at me, the idiot that I am, a man who lacks the brains to understand the simplest of issues: "Are you telling me that you support what the government is doing? You know what? It doesn't matter. It is the will of The Name that we see clearly how cruel the Zionists are, how they steal our money, and this theft brings us closer to The Name. The less we have, the closer we get to Him."

Does God want you to be poor?

"Yes, as the Sages in the Sayings of our Fathers teach us about the best way to study the Torah: 'Eat bread with salt, drink water in small measures, sleep on the floor, lead a life of suffering.'"

Then, it's God Who doesn't want you to have money, not the Zionists. What's your problem with them?

"They don't believe in God!"

If this Litvak had a little sense of humor, he would know how senseless his arguments are.

I try to find out in the Israeli media about the money issue, and what pops up in front of my eyes, the hottest news of the hour, is this news item: contrary to earlier reports, it says, Rabbi Eliezer Berland denies any involvement in the murder case, and he is to be released from jail soon. However, for other crimes, he'll return to prison, from which he'll be released a few days later as well.

I wonder what Ḥaya would say, now that her Heavenly Judge is being released.

It is with this latest news that my days in Jerusalem are soon ending.

They Are Ready to Die for Their Faith, but What Is It?

A dead man, covered with a tallit, at the entrance to Jerusalem

On my last Sabbath in Mea Shearim, as the community celebrates the eight-day-long Ḥanukah festival, I walk the streets of the neighborhood one more time.

Look, my dear, look at this family walking together right in front of me. Do you see them? All the siblings are dressed in similar clothes, similar cuts, similar shapes, similar colors, and they look so gorgeous!

What can I say?

The more time I spend here, the more conflicted I am. I like the people very much, but for the life of me, I don't understand them. They are kind, pleasant, warm, and funny, and I can't get enough of them, but what in the world do they believe in? Yes, they told me, over and over, and I understand, linguistically, every word they say to me, but I don't get the logic of it. When I dig deep into their faith, the faith that forms them as a community and as individuals, they get stuck trying to explain what they really, deeply believe.

The truth is, I suspect, they don't know their faith, even though they are willing to die for it. They wait for a white donkey to appear one day, but they go silent when I ask for the details. They pray in synagogues, "You are Holy, and Your Name is Holy," but the only name they know is no name. Three of their finest rabbis bravely declared, when I talked to them, that *kvittel*s mean nothing – not to mention Rabbi Shaul, who specifically says to everybody who wants to hear that he doesn't communicate with any Holy Spirit – but their followers firmly believe otherwise. Deep down, do they really believe that going to graves makes any sense?

Their main purpose in life, they say, is to study the Torah, but they wouldn't read most of the Bible, which is the foundation of the Torah. Year-long, they spend every waking moment they have blessing the Lord and praying to Him, but on their holiest day, they present themselves in front of their Lord as incest-driven liars and thieves. They have turned Judaism into a faith of modest clothing for both men and women, but when I ask them for the origin of their unique clothes, they give me bizarre tales about a Russian tzar, a cat's tail, a Turkish sultan, and a mother who tortures her daughter with boiling water. If this is not enough, they think that Satan hides under women's dresses and the Holy Presence rests over men's heads, and if the two meet, oy vey, Satan will win, not God. No, I don't have anything against Ḥasidic fashion – I think it's the sexiest fashion there is. But they don't think that.

Yet, and on the other hand, which group of people does make sense? Are the conservatives in the United States making any sense? Many of them are religious Christians waiting for Jesus, whom they believe to have risen from the dead, to show up again as their Messiah. Does this make any sense? Does it make sense that God would kill His son, His only son? He died for us, for our sins, the believers say, as if God could not have forgiven them their sins unless His son was bleeding on a cross. And if indeed Jesus rose three days after being crucified, after dying on a cross for their sins, as they believe, what was the point of having him dead for just three days? And of course, if he has indeed risen from the dead, where has he been hiding for the past two thousand years?

And then we have the Progressives. Do American or European Progressives make any sense? If they believe, as they say, that everybody is entitled to their opinion, why can't they tolerate anyone who disagrees with them? And why are they so much into sex issues, teaching us day and night what we are allowed to say or do or look at or think and whatnot as if they were devout Mormons? Since when, pray I, is it the prerogative of Progressives to meddle in people's bedrooms as if they were the Gerer Rebbe?

Do Muslims make any sense? If Allah wanted to talk to Mohammed, why did He have to fly him around on al-Buraq? Couldn't He chat with him over a cup of Turkish coffee in Mecca?

Do those Japanese who chat with the spirits of the dead day in and day out make any sense? Do the Aboriginals of Australia make any sense when they worship a mountain? Do the Hindus, who worship cows, make any sense? Do Western gays and lesbians, who are in love with Gazans – the biggest enemies of the homosexual community – make any sense?

Bottom line: perhaps none of us makes any sense.

These are my Sabbath thoughts.

Yes.

And then the Sabbath ends, and cars fill the streets again. The funerals resume. One after another, two funerals are announced this evening within one hour.

But not all is sad. It's Ḥanukah, a festival of light and hope.

I go to the Reb Ahrelaḥ to join the festivities with them, because everybody tells me: if you are in Jerusalem on Ḥanukah, you must go to the Reb Ahrelaḥ.

The shul is packed. I feel like a sardine in an airtight, hermetically sealed metal box. This is not an exaggeration, nor a depiction you might be told by a claustrophobe strolling on Manhattan's Fifth Avenue, but an exact description of reality. I can't move a hand; the *shtreimel* of the person standing behind me rests on the back of my head, my belly pushes against the back of the person in front of me, and there's no way I can move my feet unless I push myself out of here like a bull in a rodeo arena, an option that I won't consider.

I don't know if I will survive this event without causing damage to this or that part of my body, and I don't know if I'll be able to breathe much longer under such pressure, but I'm not leaving.

For the first time, flesh pressing against flesh, bodies intertwined, I'm one with these people, Ḥaredi Jews wearing golden caftans and sexy white socks.

That's Ḥanukah in Toldos Aharon.

Ḥanukah, as described in *Encyclopedia Britannica*, "commemorates the Maccabean (Hasmonean) victories over the forces of the Seleucid king Antiochus IV Epiphanes...and the rededication of the Temple [in] 164 BCE.... According to the Talmud, when Judas Maccabeus entered the Temple, he found only a small jar of oil that had not been defiled by Antiochus. The jar contained only enough oil to burn for one day, but miraculously the oil burned for eight days until new consecrated oil could be found, establishing the precedent that the festival should last eight days."

The Rebbe, whom I met quite a few weeks ago, enters the main hall of Toldos Aharon with a big menorah and slowly puts it down on the table. He starts to light the menorah, but it takes him forever to do it. I have no idea why, and the Ḥasidim don't care a bit. They have time, and they don't mind standing glued together for another forty hours, watching the Rebbe trying to light a menorah. This process usually takes four to seven seconds, but it takes an eternity here.

Finally, thanks be to The Name, eternity ends, and the Rebbe successfully lights the menorah. He sits down on a chair, facing the light coming from the menorah, and prays. What is he praying? It's between him and The Name. He's praying and praying and praying; this man has all the time in the world. He is not going anywhere from here, and at this hour, the early hours of the evening, he anyway has nothing better to do. The Ḥasidim, with their mouths closed, stare at him and enjoy every second of it. As far as they are concerned, let him pray until the Messiah arrives.

What do they see that I don't see? What do they experience, and why do they enjoy it so much?

After the Lord knows how long, the sign is given from the gabbai, or whoever he is, standing next to the Rebbe, and the throng of Ḥasidim start singing. What do they sing? Melodies of longing, though they don't say what they are longing for. It's: Ya, ya, ya, la, la, la, na, na, na, da, da, da. After some time of this, they go, Yo, yo, yo, lo, lo, lo, di, di, di, ti, ti, ti.

And so on and so on. The Golden Boys are having a good time.

Whatever these Goldens aspire to, and I'm not sure what it is, they seem to achieve it at some point, or at least part of it, and they move on to sing a happy song. This one is about the story of Ḥanukah; it has words, and it tells the story of how the Greeks, centuries ago, gathered against the Jews and defiled the Holy Temple, but then, miracle of miracles, the Holy Temple was recaptured, and the sacred light shone all over.

Tightly squeezed among the Golden Boys, surrounded by gold and engulfed by the magic of the menorah, I find contradicting images from the past five months running through my head at high speed: from the Ninth of Av fast to the Ḥanukah festival, from the day that the Temple was lost to the day it was recaptured, a story of tragic loss that ends in miraculous gain. And between these two extremes, there was I, walking and sleeping, eating and dancing, chatting and praying, and interacting with anyone and everyone my eyes, feet, and mouth met.

The many images from the past few months, one impregnating the other, form a circle of images in my mind that constantly negate one another, yet at the same time complete one another.

Do I now know more than I did five months ago? Do I now understand these people?

Perhaps, maybe.

Who are they?

First off, people. Just like you and me.

And then they are unique.

Yes, my dear, you too are unique, only their uniqueness is different from yours.

How so?

Try being them for a day or a year, and you might grasp it.

Their human desire for the flesh, coupled with the prohibition for spilling the seed, is channeled into a longing for The Name, and this is what makes them tick.

When the Ḥaredi Ḥasidim pray on Sabbath, welcoming the Bride, they recite a text that is both spiritual and sexual, a he and a she, God and His People, making them intimately delve into a relationship driven by the sexual and consummated by the spiritual.

In the words of the *Zohar*:

> Just as they unite above in One, so too does She unite down in the Secret of One to be above with them One to One. The Holy One Blessed Be He will not sit on His Seat of Honor above until She joins in the Secret of One. Like Him, to become One in One. And here we have explained the Secret of "the Lord is One and His name is One." The Secret of the Sabbath: the Sabbath unites in the Secret of One, so that the Secret of One may dwell on her.

Dressed in their finest, serving as witnesses and participants to a marriage between the Sabbath Bride and The Name, every Sabbath they enter a realm that no words can describe, yet they are totally consummated by it.

And sometimes, not only on Sabbath.

On this holiday, when they are here now, staring at the light and watching their Rebbe praying, uniting with The Name, they serve as witnesses to a relationship consummated between man and God.

They see it. They are the living witnesses to it.

And what worthy witnesses they are! Their golden caftans, fur hats, and white socks are holy clothes that suck the holiness into their bodies. Their dress is not Arab, and no tail of any cat is on their heads. Their clothes are holy, and every part of them is sacred. The married among them wear white socks, the singles wear black socks, as I can now see when sandwiched between them. The yarmulkes, the white yarmulkes with the *chupchik*, were handmade for them, they tell me, by their mothers, wives, and sisters. All holy.

They, all this mass of human flesh encircling me, are uniting, just as on Sabbath, "in the Secret of One," and this, their behavior, forms the faith, a bubble of being, you may call it, that in its essence always desires, ever longs, but never physically achieves.

In it, in this tight bubble, there is no room for questions. How could there be? Can you question "Yo, yo, yo, lo, lo, lo, di, di, di, ti, ti, ti"? Can you deny the holiness in your clothes, gorgeous clothes that so nicely protect your naked skin?

This Secret of One is spiritually visible when the Rebbe spends so much time impregnating the menorah with the fire in his hands, or when the Belzer Rebbe touches the gefilte fish that his Ḥasidim rush to swallow. You can see the menorah with your eyes, but you can't touch the sacred fire with your fingers; you may know of all the gorgeous ladies out there, but you cannot spill your seed even once; you can have a thousand questions, but you can't ask even one. And as long as you don't look, spill, and ask, the tension within you will be released only at the gate to the Lord, a gate wide open at this very shul.

You might say that all of the above will perhaps explain the male side of Ḥaredi existence, but what about the female side of the equation? Don't they, 50 percent of Ḥaredi Jews, count for anything?

The answer is: they count, and entirely so.

It's called the Secret of One. Just like The Name, who unites with the Shḥinah above, the feminine Holy Spirit, so do the male Jews unite with the female Jews, and all together, unite in One. All of it – God, Shḥinah, and the two sexes of the Jews – is One. There's no man by himself and no woman by herself, no Rebbe by himself and no Ḥasidim by themselves, no God by Himself and no Shḥinah by Herself, but all of them are One. You and I think that there are men and there are women, but no. Men and women are one. And that's why it's crucial to have a "mate," because otherwise, there's no man and no woman. And even they, by themselves, don't exist separately unless they are united with Heaven. But this is not the end of the story either. Man, which includes the woman, is not separate from the angel, and the living are not separate from the dead. It's all one. The Secret of One.

This bubble, carefully constructed, can burst and die if one of its ingredients is missing. Look at a woman who is not your wife, spill that seed, ask one question, and it's all over.

This, you might be inclined to say, is perhaps Ḥasidic Judaism, but no Litvak will subscribe to it. Well, they do. As the Shoimrei Emunim Rebbe said to me: "We won."

As they see it, I finally understand, clothes, both of men and women, cover the flesh and bring out the soul. Yes, yes, yes. I finally get it, I finally get their obsession with clothes, with modesty – why the "modesty" issue is so important for them, and why they don't stop reminding everyone to be dressed modestly. To cover the body and celebrate the soul is the essence of their being. Period. Full stop.

Over twenty years ago, at about this time on the Jewish calendar, my mother of blessed memory returned her soul to Heaven and was buried in this Holy City of Jerusalem. When I came to this city, it was around the anniversary of my father's death, and now it's around the anniversary of my mother's death.

How fast time moves.

It is on the eighth day of Ḥanukah, the last candle already lit, that I make my way out of Jerusalem, out of Mea Shearim, and go to Bnei Brak, the City of the Ḥaredim, known as the City of Torah, the city in which I was conceived.

I'm now ready, I feel, to visit the place that first formed me.

There's bumper-to-bumper traffic on the broad road at the entrance and exit of Jerusalem, and on the side of it, where no cars go, I see about one hundred Ḥasidim walking fast in a group. Leading them are four Ḥasidim carrying a stretcher, on which is a dead body covered with a tallit. This must be a funeral procession, but there's no hearse or other car in front or behind them. Just a group of men carrying the dead body of a friend.

I've never seen anything like this, people carrying a dead body on the street, and it's frightening. It reminds me of my first day in Mea Shearim, of the car with a loudspeaker mounted on its top, announcing: "The funeral of the pious rabbi..." This is, my dear, how such a funeral looks.

Emergency! This Is Your Last Chance to Find a Mate!

If you can't find a girl in a grave, come here!

It is still the last day of Ḥanukah when I arrive in Bnei Brak, the city of my childhood. The days of Tzefania Hotel are over: welcome to Hotel Aristocrat in Kiryat (Kiryas) Vizhnitz, Bnei Brak. How did such a word, Aristocrat, enter the lexicon of Ḥaredi Bnei Brak? Beats me. When I was a child, I didn't even know the meaning of the word Aristocrat, much less how to spell it.

I reserve a suite at the Aristocrat because I can't find any other hotel in Bnei Brak, a city not known for hotels. Lucky me, Aristocrat is located less than ten minutes' walk from my childhood home.

I park my suitcases in the hotel and walk over to my past, to the sweet baby I once was.

I see no Patricia on my way and no Taliban. Are there no Taliban in Bnei Brak?

Across from my childhood home is the Ḥazon Ish Synagogue, also known as the Lederman Synagogue, where I prayed to The Name often on weekdays. In my time, it was a small synagogue, nothing to brag about size-wise, one floor only, but today it's big, wide, and impressive. And lo and behold: on the second floor, right at this very minute, shortly before eleven p.m., there are all kinds of people carrying big cameras. Is a wedding taking place over there? A funeral? I walk up the stairs, and when I reach the second floor, I see the place packed with people. And all they're doing is praying. No wedding, no cakes, and not even a funeral. What is it? It's a special prayer, an emergency prayer. What's the emergency? At this very hour, I read in a brochure given to me, the Gates of Heaven are open to accepting our prayers. The worshippers, aware that it is a matter of time before the Gates of Heaven close shut, have gathered here to conduct an emergency prayer. What kind of an emergency? A find-your-mate emergency.

These people, no doubt, are unlearned idiots. Don't they know that if you want to find a mate, you must go to a grave in Amuka, a tomb in Zfat, an Ohel in New York, and the Western Wall? Don't they know, by the way, that Heaven promised to accept requests only on the Sliḥot days? Don't they know that they must drink from the Wine of Salvation if they want God to fulfill their wishes?

Who's behind such an ignorant act? Who's organizing this prayer? I ask myself.

I read in the brochure that Rina shel Torah, an organization under the leadership of a man living next to the synagogue, Rabbi Ḥaim Kanievsky, is the organizer of the event.

Interesting.

Rabbi Kanievsky even announced, I read, that he planned to attend the prayer, though obviously, he didn't make it. At his age, ninety-four, perhaps he isn't looking for a match.

But his followers are; they're looking for mates in Lederman's.

Wait, wait a second! Wasn't it Rabbi Kanievsky himself who had already promised to take care of all the singles who sent in their names by one thirty p.m. on the eve of Tu b'Av, the Fifteenth of Av, when the Gates of Heaven were supposedly opened for the single Jews looking for a mate?

Well, there's a reason Ḥaredim are not supposed to ask questions.

Rina shel Torah also announces that a "Secret Prayer" will take place today at the grave of the Ḥazon Ish (an admired Litvak leader who returned his soul to Heaven in 1953), an act sanctioned by Rabbi Ḥaim Kanievsky, who said: "I also go to pray there."

The people around me, I assume, are pleased to know that no effort is being spared to find them young girls.

I watch the lonely souls of Bnei Brak, men looking for women, males who are not allowed to look at females, and wonder who are those idiots who say that Ḥaredi women suffer under the yoke of Ḥaredi men? The suffering Ḥaredim, my dear, are the males, the men, those born with a *bris*. And if you don't believe me, come join me here, and see for yourself.

Dressed like Litvaks, which they are, they look 180 degrees different from the Golden Boys. They have no *shtreimels*, no caftans, and for the life of me, I can't tell what color their socks are, because they have full-length trousers that cover the socks. They have hats, boring ones, and black jackets that are similar in cut and design to the attire of the average European bookkeeper, only of a lower quality. These lady-hunters are supposed to be, at least in their minds, intellectual and much better versed in the Talmud than any Ḥasid in the land. Which is, as far as I can see, debatable.

The Talmud, if they really knew it, deals beautifully with matchmaking, but they seem not to know it. Here's what the Talmud, in tractate *Sotah*, writes: "Forty days before a child is born, an echo comes out of the sky and declares: 'The daughter of so-and-so will be married to so-and-so.'" In other words, my dear worried single men, your girls are out there somewhere already, and you don't have to bother The Name at this late hour. He gave you your gals, my dear Litvaks, long before you were born, and they're certainly not here, because here you are surrounded by men only.

And brochures, more than just one.

There are two kinds of brochures that the worshippers get. One contains various chapters from Psalms plus various prayers, and the other lists names of people, identified by their first names and the first names of their mothers, who are looking for mates. The listed people, I'm told, would like the lonely worshippers who are looking for a mate for themselves to ask The Name to find mates for them as well.

Just in case, and since the Gates of Heaven are open for a short time only, people wishing to have children or buy a home have submitted their names as well, asking the miserable and lonely congregants to mention their names too when beseeching The Name for mates.

Cameras roll, and the service starts one hour before midnight, eleven p.m. sharp.

I read the prayer texts for finding a mate, one geared for a boy looking for a girl, and the other for a girl looking for a boy. They are identical, but for one significant difference. The girl is praying for a handsome man, while the boy is begging for a good girl. Yeah, I remember this from the old days: You can say "handsome man," but you can NOT say "beautiful girl." Why can't you say it?

Because if you say "beautiful girl," you might imagine a beautiful girl, and, Lord save us, spill your seed.

So, if you're a man praying to God to find a girl, please don't say Beautiful Girl. If you want, you can say Good Girl, because "Good" is not known to cause the seed to spill.

Yeah.

Honestly, I pity them. A Ḥasid who doesn't have a mate at least has excellent kugels; these Litvaks have nothing, just brochures.

The evening of the Lonely Souls goes on.

In between the prayers for Handsome and Good, a rabbi makes a speech. He tells the worshippers that the Lord accepts tears, many tears, and asks them to cry to Him, show Him how hurt they are, and how much suffering they're going through.

They listen, they accept, and the tears follow.

I look at the young men. They are crying, they are shouting, and they *shokel*. It's touching to see this, to see so many lonely people, men who have never touched a woman and are dying to do it already.

The Story of the Lonely replicates itself one level higher, in the women's section, where women are begging Heaven to find them handsome men. But theirs is a much smaller crowd, and some of them are mothers of young men, praying for the sake of their sons.

Prayers and gatherings like this did not take place in my time. But times are a-changing, I guess.

Unlike yesterday, these worshippers are not dancing and are not singing. The people here are not Ḥasidim; they are Litvaks. The Ḥasidim sing, the Litvaks cry.

For a moment there, when looking at the people and hearing them cry, one could think that today is the fast of the Ninth of Av, not the festival of Ḥanukah. Only Litvaks, wouldn't you know, can take a happy day and turn it into a crying day. That's talent.

Why would Rabbi Kanievsky and Rina shel Torah come up with this idea of turning Ḥanukah into a match worship day of tears and cries?

Let me see if I can find out.

The Haters and the Terrorists Join in Prayer

The dissonance between students and rabbis, at the time when the Ḥaredi world opens a little and the Free World closes a lot

The Yale of the Litvishe yeshivas, so I've heard many a time, is the Ponevezh Yeshiva in Bnei Brak. I'm sure they would dispute this in the Ḥevron Yeshiva in Jerusalem, because nobody is better than them, but we are now in Bnei Brak. Bnei Brak decides for itself who is best and who is not, and no yeshiva outside the City of Torah may compete for The Best title.

In any case, I'm going to Ponevezh, established in Bnei Brak by Rabbi Yosef Shlomo Kahaneman when the Holocaust was still raging on in Europe.

The Ponevezh Yeshiva sits on top of a hill, and from the outside, it is awe-inspiring, especially given that it is in Bnei Brak, where the depressive Bauhaus style reigns supreme.

According to published reports, there are more than two thousand students in the yeshiva, though the main study hall seems to have fewer than one thousand seats.

But what a study hall! Take a look, my dear, at the gold-plated Holy Ark, awesome in design and a marvel of sacred art. You can't find a Holy Ark like this in the Vatican.

The hall is packed with students, but there's an empty spot on a bench in the middle of the study hall, on its right side, and I take it.

I look at the students around me.

Unlike the yeshivas in Jerusalem, no one here talks to me. I watch the young men, dressed in white dress shirts and dark pants, and listen to them studying in *ḥavruses*. I enjoy listening to them analyze and argue Talmudic texts and complex religious legal codes, passionately debating one another about issues that have no real consequence to the rest of humanity but mean the world for them. I remember those days when I studied in a yeshiva, and we spent hours every day on hair-splitting arguments, passionately debating delicate issues such as: When sitting on a chair, what does it mean? Does it mean that you are sitting on the chair, or does it mean that the chair is seated underneath you?

Yeah, those were the days.

If the Gerer Rebbe Yaakov Aryeh Alter sat here and listened to these scholarly guys, he would probably get such a big headache that he would end up on the Mount of Olives before sunset.

As far as the guys here are concerned, they are busy debating between themselves, and they couldn't care less who is sitting where. Here I sit, but for them, I don't exist.

They ignore me.

Five minutes pass, ten, fifteen, and nothing.

It's time, I say to myself, that I make a move.

This is Ponevezh, right? I ask one student.

"Yes. And who are you?"

A Jew.

"Where from?"

From the world.

"From where in the world?"

Here and there.

"Where is here and there?"

There and here.

"Interesting."

Is Rabbi Shmuel Markovitz in today?

Rabbi Markovitz is a relative of mine, but I haven't seen him since childhood. I wonder how he looks these days.

"No."

His *ḥavruse* interjects: "He's actually in."

Where?

Pointing to the other side of the study hall, he says, "There."

Where there?

"There, the one with the jacket."

I don't see. Where?

"The one scratching his head."

Oh, yes, now I see. Wow. That man is old; I don't remember him like this. Why is he scratching his head? Is he lost?

How is he, do you like him? I ask.

"He is not our rabbi."

Whose rabbi is he?

"Of the other half."

What other half?

"The other half of the yeshiva, which in truth is another yeshiva."

What are you talking about?

"Two yeshivas are using this study hall."

Who are they, the ones with Markovitz?

"The Terrorists."

Interesting. And who are you?

"The Haters."

Nice names.

"Excellent!"

There are many videos on the internet, they tell me, showing the Terrorists violently attacking the Haters in this very study hall, throwing pieces of furniture on them, and often the police enter the yeshiva grounds to restore order.

What's the story of the study hall?

"This study hall is divided in the middle. No physical partition, but a partition, an invisible fence. Half of the hall is ours, and the other half is theirs. The dispute between the two sides is presently in court, and until the court decides to which of the two sides this study hall belongs, neither of us crosses the invisible fence from one side to the other."

This is a sad story.

Following the passing of Rabbi Yosef Shlomo Kahaneman, two of his heirs engaged in a bitter fight: his son, Rabbi Eliezer Kahaneman, and his brother-in-law, Rabbi Shmuel Markovitz. It's a fight about money, many millions, honor, prestige, and power. And as matters stand now, each of the camps has about one-half of the student body, though Rabbi Eliezer Kahaneman has slightly more students.

Do families of the Haters and the Terrorists marry one another?

"No!"

When was the last time furniture was flying here above your heads?

Another student intervenes. "You mean all those clips on the internet?"

Yes.

"That's made up."

What do you mean?

"What was shown in those clips is not true. Didn't happen. Not here. Don't believe anything you see on the internet."

As we chat, more and more students join the conversation, and it occurs to me that such a scenario couldn't have happened in my time. In my time, a rabbi or three would immediately ask me to leave, and no student would even dream of talking to me, a stranger who might, God forbid, talk about Beautiful Girls. These students, however, are much more open than the ones of my time, and the rabbis, it seems, don't order them around as much as they did us.

I share with the students, a crowd that keeps growing, an anecdote from my life in the last few hours: last night, I went to the Ḥazon Ish, Lederman Synagogue, and hundreds of men were praying for matches.

A student comments: "They were crying, right?"

Yes, they were. And I have a question: Who started this kind of prayer?

"What do you mean?"

I grew up in this city, on Rashbam Street, and we never had that.

A student, who comes from a distinguished rabbinical family, but doesn't want his name mentioned, says: "All those organizations, like Rina shel Torah, are corrupt money grabbers, and they organize events to raise money for themselves."

If I'm not mistaken, Rina shel Torah is under the leadership of Rabbi Ḥaim Kanievsky. Are you telling me that he's all about money?

"In defense of Rabbi Ḥaim, and for the sake of his honor, let me tell you: he's an old man, he's senile, and he doesn't know what he's doing or saying. Everything you hear in his name or read that he had signed is not him but his grandson, Yanki. Yanki does deals with many organizations and individuals, and it's all about money. He is using his grandfather to enrich his pockets."

Hearing this, the student who told me not to believe anything on the internet now says to his friend: "No, it's not Yanki, it's Rabbi Ḥaim. He's not senile, Heaven forbid. There are many video clips on the internet where you can see the miracles that Rabbi Ḥaim performs!"

What do you think of the Pray for a Mate event I saw yesterday?

"What do you expect a thirty-year-old man who is not yet married to do?"

If he's thirty and still not married, let him marry a young Sephardi girl, not spend his time crying in Lederman!

They laugh.

One of them then says: "This is not nice to say!"

I say what you guys think. Don't I? Let me ask you something: How many Sephardim study in this huge yeshiva, two?

"No way! In this yeshiva, at least 30 percent of the students are Sephardim!"

You must be kidding me, aren't you? Where are they? I can't spot more than a couple of Sephardim in this hall, if that.

Another student, responding to what his friend has just said, says to him: "What thirty? Where's thirty? What, every third student is a Sephardi? What's happening to you?"

At this point, there are more students around me than around any rabbi, and I feel like a Rebbe. It's an excellent feeling, let me tell you.

I ask them: Do you, dear students, pray at graves?

The guy who comes from a famous rabbinical family jumps fast to answer: "We, the Litvaks, have become worse than the Ḥasidim. They learned from us how to study Talmud, and we learned from them how to pray at graves. It's a shame! We are the laughingstock of the Ḥaredi world!"

The others hear this and say nothing. The man has spoken.

It's 1:25 in the afternoon, and the afternoon prayer will start in five minutes. At this point, all of them put on their jackets and hats in honor of The Name, Who, obviously, likes men in jackets.

I look at the praying students and notice an interesting fact: the less attractive the student, the more earnestly he prays. And these students, may I say, touch me the most. They pray so intently, begging The Name to help them, most likely asking Him for a beautiful match. But the question is: Why would a beautiful girl marry them? Yes, I know: they are looking for God to make a miracle and match them with beautiful girls, but this is not going to happen, sorry. Last night, after all, the Ḥaredi women of Bnei Brak asked God to give them the handsome men. And God, as we all know, fulfills requests of lonely people at eleven p.m. on the last day of Ḥanukah. The unattractive guys here, so sorry, missed the train. Perhaps that's why they are praying so intensely, begging God to throw them a few bones.

The Terrorists, I guess, don't pray that hard. If they don't get what they want, they have more than just a few pieces of furniture to throw around. And part of me, to be honest, wants to cross to the other side and see the Terrorists up close, but I think that I should show a little loyalty to the loveable Haters who have welcomed me so nicely.

And soon, the prayer ends, and I get ready to leave the yeshiva, a yeshiva I've never been to before, as tons of students accompany me on my way out.

Wow! So many students, all so eager to touch the world outside of their world, and so curious.

What can I say? I fall in love with these guys. Yes, they are Litvaks, but sweet Litvaks! So open, so curious, and what a spark in their eyes. Lovely.

To a slightly lesser degree, I experienced this curiosity and openness in the other Litvishe yeshivas I went to. In some of them, I could tell, by looking at the rabbis' faces, how the rabbis disapproved of the encounter between their students and a stranger, me, but they didn't say a word. There is a dissonance, I feel, between the younger generation of the Ḥaredi world, the students who want to engage with the outside world, and the rabbis, who wish to adhere to the practice of seclusion of the past. It's interesting to see how the younger of the Ḥaredi world are trying to open more and more, to throw at least some of the shackles of prohibitions away, while the world outside of them, the world of supposedly Free Thinkers, piles up more and more rules on its members and ever more prohibitions on its followers.

I leave Ponevezh without saying hello or goodbye to Rabbi Markovitz. Yes, we are family, but I never liked that part of my family too much. I thought that his father, also a rabbi, was a fake, and I guess that the apple didn't fall far from the tree. Rabbi Markovitz is not messing up things only in this yeshiva, by the way, but he's also one of the leaders of a strange group of people, called Peleg, short for the Jerusalem Peleg, known for its love of violence.

Last week, so I was told, his followers went to Jerusalem, Bar Ilan Street, to demonstrate against the infrastructure works undertaken to build train tracks in the area. When asked what's so wrong with having a train or why they bother with a train in a place they don't live in, his followers don't answer; they just throw stones at the police and engage in fistfights with people who ask them to please leave the area. Why is our Holy Rabbi getting involved with train tracks in Jerusalem? I'm not sure, but perhaps Rabbi Markovitz has a God complex, and he craves, for his mental survival, blood sacrifices from his followers. I admit it is a valid reason, and I'm not sure why he's busy scratching his head.

As for Yanki: I try to meet him, to hear his side, but he doesn't want to meet me. It's his right.

I walk on Ra'avad Street, passing the home of the late Rabbi Moshe Bergman, where my father often took me when he visited him. As I approach Varsha (Warsaw) Garden around the corner, I stop for a moment next to a store that once used to be a shoe repair shop where a Yemenite couple toiled hard to earn a living.

They were an older couple, those Yemenites. One day, I remember, they came to our home, shouting at each other, asking my father to help them. They didn't get along anymore, they said, and wanted my father to advise them if there was a possibility to restore the flame of love between them. I hid in an adjacent room and listened to what followed. Yes, my father told them, there's a way to restore the love between them, provided they kept his instructions. What were the instructions? "Every morning," my father said to them, "you must go together to the grocery store and buy the following: cottage cheese, three slices of yellow cheese, four slices of feta cheese, and one small container of cheese spread. You put the cheeses in a bag, and when you are back home, do the following: slice the yellow and feta cheeses into eight equal pieces and put them on a plate, add three spoons of the cottage cheese and two spoons of the cheese spread, and mix them all for five minutes. Leave on for four minutes, sit down at the table, and eat the cheese mix together for ten minutes. Do this every day for six days, Sunday to Friday."

After the couple left, I asked my father: Are you out of your mind? What's this cheese mix tale? "Have patience," my father replied.

A week later, a big box with all kinds of gifts arrived at our home, and a small piece of paper was inside the box. "Thank you, holy and genius rabbi, for making us love each other again. We are so happy!"

There you go. No graves, no *kvittels*, and no blessings. Just cheeses.

Up the road on Rabbi Akiva Street, there used to be a kiosk where one could buy all kinds of secular Israeli newspapers, but no more. I ask people where I can find a non-religious newspaper or book in Bnei Brak, but nobody knows. There are bookstores in this city where you can buy holy books, but if you want to hold in your hands a copy of, let's just say, *Crime and Punishment*, you'd better take a cab or a bus to another city.

There's a bus stop next to the kiosk, if you're looking for one. In the old days, bus number 54 used to have a stop there, but 54 is no more. Why, we asked back then, was the bus line called 54? Answer: every fifty minutes, four buses come together. You've got to be a Litvak to come up with this question and answer, I know, but truth be told, that was a fact as well.

It's the rush hour now, and I take the 53 bus, going further on Rabbi Akiva Street, the busiest street in Bnei Brak. A few Ḥaredi Sephardim, young men who are dressed like Litvaks, board the bus with me, but they don't pay for the ride. It's not the first time I see young Ḥaredi Sephardim doing this. Why are they doing this? Because. In Germany, fare dodgers are known as *Schwarzfahrer*, but don't say this word to these young Sephardim, because the word's literal meaning is "black rider," and they might be highly offended.

In any case, the bus is moving very slowly, because a garbage truck is making its rounds in front of it. Why is a garbage truck anywhere in sight here, on this street, at the height of rush hour? Don't ask me. A stupid thing like this, let me tell you, I did not encounter even once during my months-long stay in Jerusalem.

I get off the bus and walk on foot; it's faster. And what do I see? Almost everywhere I walk, I see trash, be it on the streets or in the fronts of many houses, that no garbage truck will collect because it's all over. I'm ashamed for the people living in this city. Do the inhabitants here have no sense of aesthetics?

Moments later, I reach a building known as Koilel Radzyn. There are three people inside, another testimony to the sad fate of the Ḥasidic dynasty of Radzyn, the horrific fate of my family.

I keep on walking, ever looking at the people around me, and they look as if all of them were made in the same Assembly Line in Heaven, where humans are supposedly manufactured.

Bnei Brak, it dawns on me, is an insular city, a place which no tourists visit. No outsiders come to stroll on the streets of this city whose buildings are ugly, in a location on the map where everybody and everything looks more or less the same. Unlike Jerusalem, there's no Jaffa Street in Bnei Brak where immodest women could tempt the righteous. Instead of tempting women, what my eyes see is dirt, trash, and garbage. Lucky Bnei Brak residents, they have a yeshiva of Haters and Terrorists – God only knows how they came up with such names – that supplies them with a bit of excitement. Bnei Brak, I get the impression, is a melancholic city. In Jerusalem, I saw people laughing often, but hardly here. No wonder Messiah ben David will not start resurrecting the dead in Bnei Brak. If he starts here, people might not notice that the dead have resurrected.

Should I ask them about the essence of their faith, who and what is God, and have them explain to me the idea of the white donkey, or am I going to make them even more melancholic by asking such questions? I don't know. The only thing I know is this: I'd like something sweet to eat.

If the Wind Blows on Your Hair, You Will Be Thrown Out of School

Why are the streets of Bnei Brak so dirty? Because Bnei Brak is a liberal city

When I was a kid, my mother used to take me to a bakery on Rabbi Akiva Street, Katz Bakery, where we would have a slice or three of apple strudel together. It was so good that I still remember it, and I'd like to have a slice now, right now!

It's early afternoon of the next day, and I go looking for the Katz Bakery. Will it still be there? So much has changed on this street – many shops closed and many new shops opened – that it would be a miracle if Katz is still around.

But yes, Katz is still around!

I go in and ask: Do you still have apple strudels?

Yes, the man behind the counter says, we still have. Would you like me to serve you a good, warm apple strudel, the same apple strudel we have been serving since 1961?

Please!

Wow! It tastes the same, and I feel like a little kid once more. I imagine my mother sitting next to me, enjoying her son eating the delicacies she ate when she was his age.

Having finished my apple strudel, I walk down Rabbi Akiva Street until I reach the famous Itzkovitch Shtiebelaḥ (*shtiebels*) on the corner of Rabbi Akiva and Herzl Streets.

There are more than ten *shtiebels* in Itzkovitch's, and according to Israeli media, seventeen thousand people pray in Itzkovitch's daily, which arguably makes it the most active synagogue anywhere in the world. If you look at it from the outside, the building is an eyesore, but it looks much better inside. The nicest thing about Itzkovitch is that here everybody can feel home: Ḥaredi and non-Ḥaredi, Ḥasid, Litvak, Sephardi, and a bunch of schnorrers from every conceivable background.

But oops, I got it wrong: Itzkovitch is nowhere near any Herzl.

Yes, once upon a time, the street was called Herzl, named after the founder of modern Zionism, Theodore Herzl, but now it's Rabbi Sḥaḥ Street, named after the late head of the Ponevezh Yeshiva. Who cares about the State of Israel, a little tiny country, when there's something much more significant to celebrate, the Ponevezh Yeshiva! In one more generation, perhaps, the street will be called The Terrorists and Haters Street.

Outside on the rainy street, whatever its name, I see a little kid, somewhere between four and five years of age, walking alone. He carries an umbrella, which is about as tall as he is, and he navigates his way on the wet street between cars and people, not a simple undertaking on the busy street, especially on a rainy day. Would I see something like this in New York, a kid of four or five walking all alone? I don't remember seeing anything like this anywhere in New York. Like many Ḥaredi kids I have seen, this kid is exceptionally independent, and I guess he'll do well in life. When he grows up, he might not know why God and the Messiah have no names, but I don't think that it will bother him much.

A few steps ahead of me, I see two signs at an entrance to a building. One sign says that the ground floor is a grocery, and the other sign says that it's a synagogue. Which of these two signs is correct? I ask a five-year-old girl.

"Both," she says.

Good!

Three blocks up the road, I read this big poster: "Why is open hair forbidden for female students, but is allowed for their female teachers? The teacher's response: Next time you raise this issue, you will have to find yourself a different school."

What's "open hair"? I have no idea. The only thing I know is that if you dare to raise this issue, you'll be thrown out of your school.

A rabbi passes near me, a nice-looking Litvak, a big black hat on his head, and a new-looking frock over his body, and I ask him if he has a couple of minutes to help a wandering Jew.

"What would you like to know?"

What's "open hair"?

What?

I point to the threatening poster.

"Ah, this is about hair that's 'flowing,' as opposed to braids."

Let me understand: If you let the wind blow on your hair, you'll be thrown out of school? What's the problem with flowing hair?

"None that I know. Whoever put this here is an idiot. Not everything you see on the streets of Bnei Brak has to do with Ḥaredi Jews. Many times, what you see is the work of disturbed people."

He happens to have a few sheets of ready-glue papers with him, and he covers the poster with them. "They are idiots, idiots," he mumbles, visibly angry.

Let me ask you something else: Why is Bnei Brak so dirty?

"You don't live here?"

No. I live abroad.

"Where?"

Here and there.

"And it's cleaner where you are?"

I would say so.

"Just a minute: Are you Tuvia? You used to live on Rashbam Street when you were a kid, right?"

Yes, that's true. But I don't remember you.

"That's okay."

So why are the streets so dirty here?

"Because of the little kids. They buy something, eat it, and throw the wrappers out. If they did that in Tel Aviv, people would yell at them to pick up the garbage; in Bnei Brak, nobody yells at them. We, in Bnei Brak, are more democratic and more liberal than the liberals of Tel Aviv!"

Are you?

"As long as the issue is not faith."

And why are the entrances to buildings so dirty, with or without wrappers?

"Ask Rubinstein."

Who's Rubinstein?

"The mayor. Who else?"

It is at this very moment that I feel a strong desire to eat the excellent meat patty I used to buy as a kid every Thursday afternoon from Teitelbaum's Deli, and I rush to the deli.

But there's no deli anymore. "Teitelbaum passed away years ago," a man standing next to the old deli tells me. "But if you want something good, go to Kurnik, two blocks down the road, after the traffic light. It's good."

I go to Kurnik, and there I find two Ger Ḥasidim, one who follows the Gerer Rebbe, Yaakov Aryeh, and one who follows Rabbi Shaul. "There's no two Ger," the Rebbe's follower tells me as he hands me a potato kugel. "The other ones, those others, let's not talk about them. They don't exist!"

What can I say? I didn't think that I would ever say it, but this potato kugel, here in Bnei Brak, is my best yet, the best of the best of the potato kugels. It's in no way an endorsement of Old Ger, just a report about a kugel, a kugel sold by a Gerer in Bnei Brak, of all places.

Will the Ger story follow me to Bnei Brak?
We shall see.

Did My Father Rise from the Dead?

An old Jew rents a room next to the grave of his late wife

During the week, my father and I prayed at Lederman, but on the Sabbath, we went to Volozhin.

I walk over to the Volozhin Synagogue, named after the original nineteenth-century Volozhin Yeshiva, known as the "mother of all yeshivas." This synagogue was unique because its rabbi, always meticulously dressed, with a long, snow-white beard, lived on the premises, something rarely seen at the time. That rabbi is no longer alive, nor is my father, but when I enter the hall, which looks like it did in the old days, it hits me, and very deeply. I see my father in my mind, with his long peppery beard and sidelocks, and he invites me to sit with him. This encounter with my past is very vivid, as if it's real, as if it is taking place right at this very moment. I hear my father's voice, I see his eyes, and I see him pointing with his right index finger at the empty seat next to him. He looks at me now, with his penetrating eyes. Oh, God, it's frightening and magical at the same time. Has he been resurrected?

I run out, and the first Litvak I find, I stop and ask: Tell me, dear, do you believe in the resurrection, that story with the donkey?

"Yes, of course," he says.

Are the dead who come back to life the same age they were when they died?

"The resurrection does not necessarily mean that the bodies of the dead will rise from their graves."

What, then, does it mean?

"Their spirit will rise."

Will we not see them again?

"No."

What? That's it?

Well, "Yes," he says, and then adds, "Perhaps," and then asks me not to mention his name, not even his first name. As if I even knew his name.

I think, though I don't tell him, that he is wrong. I have just witnessed the resurrection of my father; how can he say that the dead don't resurrect?

I don't ask him this question. Instead, I ask: What is God? Who is God?

"The Creator."

My question is not what He did. My question is, Who is He?

"Who is He? I don't know, but I know that He is."

At this juncture, and for whatever reason, the man doesn't feel comfortable anymore, and he walks away.

I walk, just walk.

I pass by the apartment building I grew up in and try to enter the apartment, my childhood home, but the current owner refuses to let me in. "No way," he says.

An old man, walking by, stops near me. "You are Tuvia, aren't you?"

Yes, I am.

"You are the son of the genius Rabbi Akiva, my teacher in the yeshiva when I was a young man. Oh, God, what a miracle to see you. I loved your father. What a man!"

Oh, Lord.

The old man tells me that he rents a room in a nursing home in Kiryat Vizhnitz, even though it's prohibitively expensive, NIS

12,000 a month, but he does it because his wife is buried not far, and he wants to live next to her.

That's love.

Did you ever imagine that Ḥaredim could love like this?

If You Want to Get Married, Wear a Tallit That Was in a Grave

The exciting Bnei Brak show: an old lady feeding a street cat

I walk the streets of Kiryat Vizhnitz, where the Aristocrat Hotel is, and I see an old lady carrying a plastic bag with old bread and leftover food. She stops next to a bench, sits down, and throws little pieces of food for a passing street cat. The cat starts eating the kosher food, and a bunch of kids on the other side of the street rush over to look at the eating cat. I don't remember seeing Mea Shearim kids getting excited by a cat eating anything, but this is Bnei Brak, a city of reportedly over 200,000 residents, yet insular and secluded from the rest of the world to the point that a street cat excites its little ones.

After feeding the cats, the old lady takes out her leftover bread and *ḥallah*s and throws them on the ground, and in seconds, about fifty doves fly in and have a feast with the bread and *ḥallah*s. For the doves, the thought comes to me, this woman is a Rebbe, and they flock to eat her *shirayim*.

Nice.

And then I meet a middle-aged man, a Litvak who used to have a program on a Ḥaredi radio station that broadcasts mainly to Sephardim.

What kind of program was it?

"Spiritual advice."

What kind of advice did people seek the most?

"How to find a mate."

And what was your advice for the lonely souls?

"I advised them to go to Amuka."

You did what?

"I started the trend of going to Amuka; very few people went there before I made it trendy."

Why did you do that?

"Seventy percent of the listeners, mostly Sephardim, asked me for advice about matches. What could I tell them? I told them to go to Amuka. I'm also in the tallit business, and one day, I took several people to Amuka, had each wear a tallit, and prayed special prayers. Then I collected the tallits and sold them as Amuka Tallits, tallits of Special Merits that could help those who buy them find their mates."

There you go. *Na, naḥ, naḥma, Naḥman me'Uman*, Amuka Tallits, and Bat Ayin: foolish acts that became essential articles of faith.

After the Amuka salesman departs, I get a message from Reb Moishe, the Lelever Ḥasid who invited me for a Sabbath meal at his home in Jerusalem quite some time ago. He had just read in one of the Sabbath bulletins, he writes to me, a two-page article about the father of my grandmother, who happened to be the grandson of Rabbi Akiva Eiger, one of the most renowned leaders in the history of European Jewry. It's incredible: these Ḥaredim know about my family more than I do. I am, of course, elated to learn where I come from, and maybe one day, you never know, I'll also be known as the Prince of Torah. With such a pedigree, what other title could I be known by? Me, Prince. I love it.

The Power of the Pinky of the Ḥasidic Lady

The luckiest of men get a bite of Holy Gefilte

As Friday evening comes, I join other guests of the Aristocrat Hotel for the Sabbath meal. Look at them, look at the Ḥaredi girls and their daughters, and how they are dressed! Glitzy velvet dresses, with gold linings and pinkish flowers, like European princesses of long ago, and they all have perfect figures. How do they do it? You can't find actresses in French festivals dressed like this! They look amazingly gorgeous, these Tempting Ḥaredi ladies, and I wonder if their rabbis are not going crazy just knowing that these gals exist.

The food, by the way, is delicious. Top Ḥasidic food, and plenty of it, to fit every self-loving aristocrat. When I was a kid, kosher food was quite bad, but the kosher food industry has improved tremendously since those days, and I love every bite of it.

Yes.

With my belly satisfied, and after singing love songs to the Sabbath, I go to the *tish* of the Rebbe of Vizhnitz, joining thousands of Vizhnitz Ḥasidim who go there as well. On the road leading to the shul, which like all the streets of Bnei Brak is closed for traffic on the Sabbath, the community leaders put partitions in the middle of the road: one side of the road is for men, the other side for women. When men and women walk on the street of this holy community, men mustn't encounter, Lord save us, a woman's face or pinky.

I don't know if I should tell you this, and I'll certainly never admit it in public, but I take my time to look at the pinkies of the ultra-righteous Vizhnitz ladies. Oh, my Lord, Creator of Heaven and Earth, these pinkies are the most luscious, loveable, sexy, and romantic pinkies the world over! If the Messiah has a pinky just half as potent as these Ḥasidic ladies, he will be able to raise one million dead Jews per second. I swear.

I move on to the *tish*, joining the holy Vizhnitz Ḥasidim.

They sing, while the luckiest of them also get crumbs of *shirayim*. I'm so jealous. In between songs, the Rebbe gives a speech, but nobody can hear a word he's saying aside from the select few right next to him. He talks, talks, talks, and then more, and nobody minds not hearing their Rebbe. It reminds me of the Slonimer Rebbe on the eve of Yom Kippur. One of the Ḥasidim offers me a big bottle of cold soda to drink while the Rebbe is mumbling, and when I thank him in Yiddish, he falls in love.

Such a Yiddish, he says, I must be a holy man.

His grandpa and my grandpa, I guess, meet.

This Ḥasid is a lucky man, as now he has two holy men protecting him, the Rebbe and yours truly.

Oh, God, I missed my calling. I should have been a Rebbe.

The Vizhnitz songs sung at this *tish* are sacred Jewish melodies, uniting the Jewish soul to its origin in Heaven, a Ḥasid explains to me, and I wonder: Who composed them? Was it Moses the Lawgiver, King David, the Patriarch Abraham? There's no Ḥasidic Judaism without Ḥasidic music, as every child knows, but who originated it?

Ḥaim Banet, on whose music I grew up, is arguably the most prolific composer of Ḥasidic music for the past few decades, and he might have the answer. Born in Romania, he lives in Haifa and has his studio in Bnei Brak. The melodies he composes are in the style of the Vizhnitz melodies of old, and he is indeed a Vizhnitz

Ḥasid (Seret-Vizhnitz, to be exact). I arrange to meet him in the next few days via his son, Ruvi, the manager of Motty Steinmetz, and I hope he will enlighten me.

Small world. Motty first put the idea in my brain to come to Vizhnitz to experience this Ḥasidic court and its music. And I'm here, trying to decipher the biggest of Jewish music secrets.

God Is a Word. Period.

Beautifully clad Ḥaredi women kill righteous Ḥaredi men

On this Sabbath, a bar mitzvah is being celebrated at the hotel by one of the most esteemed Bnei Brak families, the Povarsky family, whose late grandfather was the head of the Ponevezh Yeshiva for over fifty years. Dozens of relatives are staying in the hotel, and the celebration goes nonstop day and night. One of the relatives, a nine-year-old kid, entertains the crowd spiritually by singing various Jewish texts, in which he begs The Name to accept the prayers of His Suffering Children, the Jews. His father, a lawyer in real life, sits behind him and encourages him every step of the way, softly singing with him in complete harmony.

The kid has a fantastic voice and a very warm presence, qualities that enable him to create for us in the audience an image of a kid speaking with The Name on our behalf, serving as our mouthpiece before The Name. The words sung are undoubtedly too heavy for a kid of his age, but the people don't think about that. What matters to them is that the words are uttered, even if this kid has no idea what he's saying. What matters is that the words, in the proper Litvishe accent, are comforting them. The words have a life of their own, living by themselves, and it doesn't matter if the one delivering the words understands them or not. These people's connection to God is made via the use of words.

The Name, it now strikes me, exists in words, words of the prayer, and the more words the believers utter, the closer and stronger they are to The Name. They know The Name exists because they utter words that say that He exists. The Name, hear me out here, is a Word. Can anyone doubt it? Can anyone doubt the existence of The Name, the presence of the Word? His name, if you wish, is Word. That's why, if you wonder, He has no name. He *is* the name. A Word. And His Torah, words, is Him.

Wow! Am I not brilliant?

I keep thinking about this for some time, proud of my finding, and then I meet Pini, a religious but not Ḥaredi cabbie working in the area, who brings me back to earth, showing me that nothing is as simple as it looks.

We meet on the street, outside the hotel. "There used to be a time," he tells me, "that when two Ḥaredim sat in my car, they constantly talked about the Talmud and *halaḥah*, but no more. Today, every time two or three of them get in my car, they talk about money, money, and money. That's the only thing they have on their minds. They are manipulators, thieves, liars. They are a mafia. The Talmud says that just before the arrival of the Messiah, the face of the people will look like the face of dogs, which is how the Ḥaredim look today. All they want is to eat. So, maybe there's a good thing about it because now we can expect the Messiah to come very soon."

Why do you talk so badly about them?

"They are violent people, these Ḥaredim. What, do you think that I don't know what's going on in this community? A few years ago, before the late Rebbe of Vizhnitz died, two of his sons planned to take over. Some Ḥasidim went with one son, and the others with the other son. You had to see what was going on, on these streets! They were beating one another up ruthlessly, and there was blood on the street. In the end, the two brothers became Rebbes, each of them with his set of followers. But it wasn't pretty!"

Speaking of pretty: in a neighborhood not far from here, I'm told, a group of Ḥaredim are gathering to listen to a speech by an old local rabbi. What does he say? He says that a few people in the neighborhood have passed away recently. Why? Because of the fashionable clothes that Ḥaredi women wear, clothes that make them look pretty, clothes that cause men to look at them. Such clothes, says he, are forbidden by the *halaḥah*, and they cause men to lose their lives.

There goes my theory, my big Word theory. It is as good, sad to say, as my old theory that The Name's real name is Pinky. Me and my dreams. In real life, no big ideas about Word and Pinky exist, just an old rabbi who's afraid of pretty ladies and two jealous brothers out to ruin one another.

What's the real story about these two Rebbes?

I get curious, and when I get back to the hotel, I chat with a few Ḥasidim about the two Rebbes that Pini mentioned to me, and they tell me the story of the two cuties. The Vizhnitzer Rebbe, the one to whose *tish* I went, is Rabbi Israel (Yisroel) Hager, and he is the main Vizhnitzer Rebbe. Per his late father's wishes, he leads the Vizhnitz dynasty, centered in Kiryat Vishnitz, exactly where I am. All in all, he leads about five thousand families, making his court one of the largest Ḥasidic courts in Israel after Ger and Belz.

His brother, Menaḥem Mendel Hager, did not accept his brother's leadership and founded his own court, Vizhnitz Center, in Bnei Brak but outside of Kiryat Vizhnitz, where he leads about seven hundred families, a much smaller Ḥasidic court. This Rebbe, Menaḥem Mendel, calls himself Der Heilige Rebbe, meaning the Holy Rebbe, and his followers are called die Schwänze, meaning the Tails, like a tail of a monkey or cat. In other words, he's the holiest of holies, The Lord, and his followers are little tails. Strangely, his Ḥasidim love it and give him every penny they've got. This past Ḥanukah, one of the Ḥasidim tells me, Der Heilige Rebbe announced his plan to build a new Ḥasidic Center and demanded that each of his Ḥasidim donate at least NIS 120,000 for it.

In a schnorring speech before the kids of his community, he told them: "I cannot ask you for money, but you have to understand that from now on, your parents will have less money to spend on you. If you are used to having two chicken dishes every week, from now on it will be only one dish of chicken per week. If you are used to getting one pair of shoes once a year, from now on it will be one pair of shoes every two years."

Is this true? Did he say it? I don't know, and I'll try to go to Der Heilige's shul and see what's going on over there.

But not now. Now I have to do something else, because I just got an interesting message. It comes from the unnamed person I met in Hatzor, stating that the ugly split between the two sections of Ger will show its ugly face tomorrow outside the borders of the Ḥaredi world. To be precise, in an Israeli court in Tel Aviv.

I shall be there.

A Ḥasid with a Beard Declares War on God

When Ḥasidim try to blow up the head of a fellow Ḥasid

On behalf of Akiva Greentzeig, Attorney Shlomo Elbaum is suing Shlomo Tsvi Alter, the son of the Gerer Rebbe Yaakov Aryeh Alter, plus seventeen leaders of the Old Ger, on charges of defamation before Her Honor, Senior Judge Yael Pradelsky, in the Magistrate Court, Tel Aviv.

It is a rare sight in Israel's official court system to see a group of Ḥasidic leaders, not to mention a son of the biggest Rebbe, brought to court as defendants, as criminals, a sight that the powerful Ger establishment, in control of about 100,000 followers, doesn't like to see and is determined to fight tooth and nail.

The hearing takes place in Hall C, Room 306, and the proceedings for today are mainly technical. Due to another wave of the coronavirus at present in Israel, all present must wear a mask. As for Ḥaredi garb: I'm the only one in the courtroom who's not wearing Ḥaredi garb, and I wonder why no news organization has found it proper to have reporters attend this session. Be that what it may, the Court adjourns in less than half an hour, not before deciding to reconvene in about eight months.

What's the story here? I ask Shlomo Elbaum, a man with a long beard and a long black coat, with whom I chat on our way out of the court. It's about a false accusation leveled against his client. What was the accusation? "That he threatened Ger Ḥasidim with tear gas."

What?

"Later today, there will be a demonstration in front of my house. Fifteen thousand demonstrators are expected to attend," he shares with me.

I will make it my business to be there, I say to him.

What is this all about?

As it turns out, the Old Ger establishment has put out a video claiming to show Akiva Greentzeig, reportedly a supporter of Rabbi Shaul Alter's group, using tear gas against innocent Ḥasidim waiting to enter the Rebbe's room. On the other hand, photos released of Akiva after his supposed attack show him bleeding badly in his face, as if somebody had tried to blow up his head, and paramedics who were on the scene immediately afterward said that there was no evidence of tear gas being used, at least not in quantities that would be detectable.

If one believes the paramedics, who are not party to the Ger dispute, the Ger official establishment is made of outright liars. Granted, no one can accuse them of anything before the Court issues its verdict, but looking at the evidence currently available puts their reliability in question.

Later in the day, during the evening hours, twenty thousand men, according to the Ḥaredi media, have shown up on Ḥazon Ish Street to demonstrate against Attorney Elbaum's home nearby and shame him into withdrawing the lawsuit.

I join the crowd and walk leisurely among the Ḥasidim.

I don't know how to estimate crowds, but since the Ḥaredi world often exaggerates, including in its counting of angels and seeds, the initial figure of fifteen thousand is probably closer to the truth.

Whatever the exact number, everywhere I walk along the central part of Ḥazon Ish Street, I see Ger Ḥasidim, males only, wearing their signature *hoisensocken* (where the bottom of the trousers is under their black socks), block after block after block. There is also a strong police presence, including at the entrance to the attorney's home, to make sure that nobody gets any wrong ideas on how to eliminate the man.

There's no Ger music playing at this gathering, but there are speeches aplenty.

Speaker after speaker, all rabbis, threaten the attorney with the harshest consequences if he doesn't withdraw the lawsuit, decreeing that his soul will never enter Paradise and reminding him of the punishments awaiting those who hurt God's Messiah.

Yes, Yaakov Aryeh is herein called God's Messiah. One day he's God, the next day he's God's Messiah.

Good.

The lead speaker, Rabbi Flakser, urges the thousands of demonstrators to repeat after him three times the biblical words (from Exodus) of "We will do, and we will hear," which in this case means a promise to obey whatever the Rebbe commands, no matter what the command is. Rabbi Flakser then says, three times, "We will do, and we will hear," but for the life of me, I can't spot one Ḥasid uttering these words, much less repeating them three times.

Why aren't you repeating the words you have been told to repeat? I ask a few Ḥasidim, but they just laugh.

It seems that they are here because they were ordered to be here, but their hearts are not in the same place as their feet. It's very interesting to watch. I have seen Ḥasidim who didn't believe in God, but I have never seen Ḥasidim who didn't believe in a Rebbe until now.

Wow!

Checking the Ḥaredi news sites, I read that earlier today, the Rebbe of Vizhnitz was taken to the hospital unexpectedly, suffering from an undisclosed disease, and they urge people to pray for him. I saw the Rebbe just a couple of days ago, and he seemed healthier than I ever was. What is the mysterious disease he's suffering from?

I'll try to find out.

As of now, I'm in a demonstration and, apart from the "We will do, and we will hear" fiasco, the rest of the operation resembles an army operation. The Ḥasidim show up on time, stay in place on order, and disperse on order ninety minutes later. When the operation is over, the Ḥasidim are ordered on loudspeakers not to engage in any violence while dispersing, and to walk to the buses waiting to take them back to where they came from. They obey. The Ḥasidim were called to shame a man, a Ḥasidic attorney, and they did it. Now it's time to go, and later we shall see if the attorney is willing to give up Paradise.

I ask myself: How does a man facing so many thousands of demonstrators feel?

On the next day, I go to visit the man, whose office is on the eighth floor of an office building in Bnei Brak.

When I ring the bell, Mr. Attorney Shlomo comes to open the door. No secretary do I see, and no fellow attorneys working alongside him. Is this a one-man show against the most powerful Rebbe of the land?

Shlomo greets me with a disposable plastic cup filled with plain water, the kind of water Dushinsky Ḥasidim make Tashliḥ on, and we sit down to chat in a lackluster conference room.

First off, I ask him for a copy of the criminal complaint as filed with the court, and he hands me a copy. The official paper, I read, lists the charge as "public defamation with intent to harm."

The complaint lists twenty-four witnesses, all women, plus Akiva Greentzeig. Why no man? This is a bit bizarre, but here goes: Ger, unlike most Ḥasidic courts, does not believe in writing down the most important parts of its various rules, and it also does not believe in keeping records of sensitive gatherings or presentations. The Takunnes, for example, are not to be found in any official document of Ger, even though they are the very core of Ger's being and behavior. Similarly, various orders by the High Command of Ger are not published and not recorded. They are presented in shuls, *shtiebels*, closed-room meetings, or yeshivas, but there is no paper trail. Same rules apply, of course, for Special Presentations.

What are Special Presentations? This is interesting. An example of a Special Presentation is this: a couple of Ḥasidim carry a computer or video player and go from place to place, where they show a video presentation or play an audio presentation. When this is done, they move on with their equipment. It's crucial to keep important matters secret, mind you.

But on one occasion, in one city in Israel, in Arad, Shlomo was told ahead of time that a presentation would take place for the local Ger women, and he made sure that somebody recorded the whole spiel with a hidden camera – hence the female witnesses.

What was this presentation about?

The complaint states that the Ger establishment forced Ḥasidic groups and members to watch an official video presentation. In it, Akiva is seen in the Ger Palace, in the Rebbe's waiting room, the place where Ḥasidim wait in front of the Rebbe's room for their turn to meet the Rebbe, normally with a *kvittel*. According to the complaint, Akiva is seen in the presentation spraying tear gas for no reason, and it insinuates that his real target was not the Ḥasidim, but the "Holy of Holies," the Rebbe. Akiva and those who follow Rabbi Shaul, in case you are curious to know, are referred to as "Satan."

The facts on the ground, the complaint charges, were totally different: Akiva was brutally attacked by the Ḥasidim for no reason, and the CCTV cameras on site would prove it. However, requests to examine the CCTV recordings were flatly denied per the complaint.

I tell Shlomo that I passed by his home last night during the demonstration, and a small child pointed to his apartment and told me, "He lives there, on the top floor."

"Why didn't you come up?" he asks.

The police were in front of the staircase, blocking people from entering the building.

"You should have called me! My family had a big party in our home; you should have come!"

His children, he tells me, loved it; for them, it was a memorable experience, something that might not repeat itself soon.

How did it feel, seeing thousands of people demonstrating against you?

"Of the fifteen thousand demonstrators last night, I can tell you that many thousands of them are on my side. Thousands of people have contacted me saying, 'Continue! What you do is the only thing that can save us.' Just before you came in, a Ger Ḥasid stopped by and begged me not to give up. 'Go all the way,' he said. I get many emails from Ger Ḥasidim, and when I read them, I cry."

I noticed that when Rabbi Flakser asked the people to repeat after him three times, "We will do, and we will hear," they didn't.

"Do you know why they didn't? I'll tell you. 'Words that come from the heart enter the heart,' but his words did not come from the heart. His words, asking people to recite that line, did not come from his heart. I know Rabbi Flakser, and I know that he thinks exactly as I do."

This picture that he paints, of total joy in the middle of mayhem, does not cover the whole canvas. Demonstrations are one thing, but being boycotted is another. "I married off my daughter about a month ago. My brother didn't come to the wedding. Three of my brothers-in-law didn't come. The groom's father has ten siblings, and they didn't come to the wedding. It looked like a wedding after the Holocaust: no relatives," he shares with me.

The story with Akiva took place in the same shul where I joined the Ḥasidim for the Yom Kippur prayer and was witnessed in part by his sister, he tells me. Akiva, who was waiting to enter the Rebbe's office, was pushed and beaten by some Ḥasidim. Aided by a guard, they pushed him outside, and the beating continued.

"My sister, who's a widow, was in the vicinity with her children, and she saw it – she saw how Akiva was beaten up. She saw the guard beating Akiva in the head so hard, my sister told me, that she and her daughters couldn't believe that he survived the attack alive. The guard was beating Akiva in the face, very hard, boom, boom, and the Ḥasidim were standing around, she told me, cheering him on. They clapped and said: 'Beautiful, beautiful.

Finish him off!' For the next three hours, my sister and her children cried uncontrollably; they couldn't stop."

The root of all this evil, Shlomo explains to me, is the Takunnes. The Takunnes are so hard to keep that to make sure that people abide by them, the Ger leaders had to make the Ḥasidim feel that they were the closest people to God.

The question is, as you might imagine, who is God?

"Before I got married," so says Shlomo, "I was told, 'The Sages say: There are three partners in the creation of man – his father, his mother, and the Holy One Blessed Be He. But we, the Ger Ḥasidim, say: There are four partners in the creation of man – his father, his mother, the Rebbe, and the Holy One Blessed Be He.'"

What does this mean? I'm not sure, but Shlomo explains it all to me in numbers: "In Ger, 90 percent of Judaism is about the Rebbe."

Would you say that in Ger, the Rebbe is God?

"Yes. The Rebbe is the Creator."

This I already know; I have seen the clip. "A word of the Torah: the Rebbe, that's God."

If I remember correctly, Mormons believe that God was once a man. Ger Ḥasidim believe, if I get this right, that a man is God. These two are brothers in faith and should pray together in the same house. Imagine Mormons in Utah wearing *shtreimels*!

Yeah, yeah: I can joke about this, but Shlomo can't.

What gives you the strength to go on? I ask Mr. Attorney.

"When I was a child, I read a book about the rebels in France, how they fought the Vichy government, and I said: 'I should have been there!' Until my last drop of blood, I will fight for people's right to pray where they want to pray, to celebrate the Jewish holidays where they want to celebrate them. This is a war!"

He tells me that last night's demonstration is not the first time the Ger establishment has sent people to demonstrate against him. One day, when he was in Tiberias, several Ḥasidim from Hatzor were sent to demonstrate against him and blow shofars in front of the house that they thought he was staying in. He didn't even see them, Shlomo tells me, because at that exact time he was by the sea, swimming. Two days later, the leader of the demonstrators got sick with the coronavirus, and members of his family asked Shlomo to forgive him. He told them that, of course, he forgives him.

Did he survive the virus?

"No, he passed away."

No, Shlomo doesn't think that the man died because of him, and neither do I. Had Shlomo been a woman, dressed fashionably, that could have explained the leader's death, as the old Bnei Brak rabbi would surely agree.

I leave Shlomo's office searching for a fashionably dressed Ḥasidic lady, but instead of finding Ms. Bnei Brak, I meet an ex-Ḥasid, a man of no *shtreimel* and no golden caftan.

What Is God? A Battery

Swallow this pill, and you will never spill your seed again

The ex-Ḥasid's father is one of the old Ger's top leaders, he tells me, and he asks that I not mention his name.

No problem.

Outwardly, this man seems to have made a smooth transition from the Ḥasidic to the average Joe. He wears a blue shirt, grayish pants, carries a smartphone, and speaks modern Hebrew. But when he tells his dark story, you know this is no Mr. Joe. He was married to a Ger woman for over five years, he tells me, but slept with her only once because, he says, he was not attracted to her. His guide, the Ger guide assigned to married couples to guide them on sexual matters, suggested that "I get a certain kind of a liquid to inject into my penis, but I said to him that this was not the problem. 'I masturbate every day,' I told him."

The guide was shocked. How could a Ḥasid, God help us, spill his seed so brazenly, each and every day? Not only was he shocked, but he was also afraid that the sky would fall if this Jew kept wasting his semen. What did he do? He sent the masturbating Jew to a special doctor. The special doctor, working together with the Ger establishment, gave the masturbator a prescription for special pills. But before going to the pharmacy with the prescription, the masturbator checked what those pills were for. And he found out. "The pills were designed to make me extra weak, physically and mentally, so that I would not be able to masturbate and spill my seed."

He never went to the pharmacy.

"But other guys do, many. That's how Ger controls its Ḥasidim. If you stray, they will fix you with a pill and damage you for life."

Before we depart, he shows me a few photos of his father standing by the Gerer Rebbe. "Many times, when you see a photo of the Rebbe, you will see my father standing next to him."

Speaking of Rebbes: surprise, surprise, the Rebbe of Vizhnitz is out of the hospital, and he feels well, thank you for asking.

What's the story? How did he recover so soon from his mysterious illness?

I contact some people, those in the know, and they explain it all to me. The Vizhnitzer Rebbe, they tell me, was not sick; he just had a little problem that he was trying to solve. What's the problem? He was under pressure from Old Ger leaders to join the demonstration against Shlomo, but he didn't want to do it. And he didn't want to tell them that he didn't want to do it. So, he checked himself into a hospital under the pretext of a mysterious illness. As often happens with mysterious diseases of this kind, the mysterious illness left as mysteriously as it came, once the demonstration was in the past.

If true, that's how one Rebbe deals with another Rebbe. You can call it Rebbe Diplomacy, and it's funny, but the essence of what transpires these days in the world of Rebbes and rabbis is not a laughing matter.

The Ger story, to say it succinctly, is not confined to the Ger Court; it is a story about what happens when a Rebbe thinks he's God. Akiva miraculously survived, but the next one might not.

Another God Rebbe in the news these days, in case you didn't have enough Godly inspirations so far, is Rabbi Eliezer Berland. Protected by his followers who won't testify against him, despite his supposed pleas for them to do so, as Ḥaya told me, the Israeli prosecution could not build a criminal case against this old God, and he is being released from prison. Ḥaya must be jumping for joy. God is back! God is back! God is back!

But who's God?

It is in the lobby of the hotel, later on, that I pose this question to a Litvishe couple: Who is God?

"Everything," the woman answers.

What do you mean by "everything"?

"Everything."

What does it mean?

"The very being."

What's that?

"The power behind everything," the man contributes.

What power?

"Like a battery."

Is God a battery?

"A never-ending battery."

Like the newest iPhone battery?

"You have to talk to Rabbi Zamir; he knows how to answer this kind of question," the woman interjects.

I love conversations like that.

An Invite for a Sabbath Meal Is Withdrawn

"What's your name and the name of your mother?"

In front of my hotel, a white car, with two nicely clad Ḥasidim in it, stops in the middle of the street just as I start crossing it. "What are you doing here?" the driver asks.

Breathing, I say.

"Where do you plan to go?" he asks.

Rabbi Akiva Street, I say.

Where on Rabbi Akiva Street?

Anywhere. Maybe in the middle.

"Would you like a ride?"

Yes.

"Get in."

I get into the car, sit in the back seat, and the man asks: "Do you have a place to eat on the Sabbath?"

Not yet.

"Would you like to come to us for the Sabbath meals? You can come to me for the evening meal and go to my friend here for the morning meal. Would you like that?"

Yes!

"Tell me: On the Sabbath, what do you wear? What clothes do you wear on Sabbath?"

White shirt, black trousers, suspenders, black shoes, and a black yarmulke.

"Just that?"

Yes.

"I see."

Any problem with that?

"No, that's fine."

Where do you live?

"In Kiryat Vizhnitz."

I'm looking forward to being with you on the Sabbath!

He scratches his chin, entirely covered by his long beard, scratches more, and more, and more, and more, and finally says: "I have to ask my wife first."

Ask her what?

"She might want to go somewhere else on Sabbath."

I see. Then we won't meet on the Sabbath?

"We'll see."

He arrives at Rabbi Akiva Street.

Thanks for the ride!

"Before you go, what's your name and the name of your mother?"

Do you want a *kvittel* from me?

"Close enough."

The other passenger says, "He is very good at these things! He can tell everything by the name. Just like a Rebbe!"

Tuvia Yeshayahu, son of Dvora Leah, I say.

The driver, the holier of the two, repeats my name, opens the Book of Psalms, and mumbles a verse or two. He closes the holy book and tells me my future. "You will have a lot of success and good health," he prophesizes.

Thank you, I say, and get out of the car.

He drives off. Who is he? I don't know.

Interestingly, he asked me what I wear on the Sabbath, which probably determined his going back on his initial invite. This is Bnei Brak, not Jerusalem; this is Kiryat Vizhnitz, not Mea Shearim, and here people worry, it seems, that their neighbors would spread all kinds of rumors when they see a man without a hat and coat coming over for Sabbath meals. In general, the hospitality I experienced in Mea Shearim, where I was invited to people's homes many times, doesn't exist here.

This is Bnei Brak; this is not Jerusalem.

A Bored Litvak Is Looking for Something Exciting to Do

Do angels interfere with cellular connections?

Taking public transportation has enormous benefits, especially if you happen to live in Bnei Brak, insular city that it is, where nobody invites you anywhere.

And this is precisely what I'm doing right now.

I am on a public bus in Bnei Brak, and behind me sits a Litvak, and he's on the phone, a kosher phone, talking about important issues he's involved with: the future of a yeshiva student whose life he wants to manage.

What's the story?

There's this yeshiva student who studies in a particular yeshiva, but he doesn't like it. Just so. Not that he has become an infidel, The Name forbid, or that he wants to study in a university instead of a yeshiva, which is another major sin. All this guy wants is to study in another yeshiva, in another of a hundred yeshivas, all super kosher. But moving from one yeshiva to the other, as I learn while eavesdropping, is not a simple transaction, because it needs the approval of the rabbis. Many a rabbi. First, the rabbi of the yeshiva, who would agree to let the student leave. Then the rabbi of the other yeshiva, who would agree to accept this young man into his yeshiva. Then the permission of the student's father will be required for such a transfer. And then one more rabbi, the father-in-law of the man who is talking on the phone.

Now, what this Litvak is trying to do is to arrange a meeting with the yeshiva student to find out why, exactly, he wants to move out of his current yeshiva. Once he has spoken with him and gotten all the details, he will connect with all the rabbis again to get their approval. Will they approve?

At this point, the Litvak gets off the bus, and I have no idea how this story will end.

This Litvak is a *koilelnik*, or *avreḥ*, a married man who studies in a yeshiva, and he seems to enjoy his involvement in this story. He has no job, so he has plenty of time on his hands.

Avreḥim, who stay in yeshiva after marriage (some for just a few years and others for life), are exempted from army service, a mandatory service in Israel for all healthy Jews. This exemption is a sore point for many Israelis, who view it as unjustified, but the *avreḥim* couldn't care less. And that guy is one such *avreḥ*, a man with not much excitement in his life. He gets up in the morning, prays and eats, then studies for hours, or pretends to study, goes back home, eats, and sleeps. Day in, day out. A man like him cherishes some action in life, any action. And dealing with the issue of a non-married yeshiva student wishing to move to another yeshiva is a godsend. He'll squeeze every drop out of it and get ever more rabbis involved, which will keep him busy for at least a week or a month, whichever comes first.

Fifteen minutes or so after the Litvak has gotten off the bus, and once the bus reaches central Tel Aviv, I get off as well.

Walking on the streets of Tel Aviv, a secular city, after spending a considerable amount of time in Ḥaredi Bnei Brak, I notice a few things that I usually neglect to see. For the most part, Tel Aviv residents don't know each other; there are very few children walking around, but there are dogs; streets are cleaner; there are tons of restaurants, and my smartphone has excellent reception. Yes, in Kiryat Vizhnitz, the reception is usually bad, and I just got used to it, but all of a sudden, here in Tel Aviv, even my GPS is working properly. Wow. Why is the reception so good in Tel Aviv and so bad in Kiryat Vizhnitz? I have no idea. Maybe, who knows, in Kiryat Vizhnitz, many white angels are flying around, since there are so many righteous Ḥaredim there, and the angels interfere with the reception. Some angels, as you know, set birds on fire; others might interfere with cellular reception.

I sit down at a restaurant, where they serve anything but gefilte fish and kugels, and there's music in the background, music about love and longing, a longing for the flesh, not The Name. How absurd.

I look at the people around me, and no one is dressed modestly. No Golden Boys, no beautiful ladies.

Well, this is too bizarre, and I return to Kiryat Vizhnitz, joining the Aristocrats yet again.

It's late in the evening, and I get an urgent message.

What's Better, Cutting Off the Attorney's Sidelocks or His Beard?

Ḥaredi journalists afraid to report the news

"Attorney Shlomo Elbaum was attacked just now; they cut off one of his sidelocks," the message reads.

Who did it, if this is true? Old Ger Ḥasidim. Who else?

I check the Ḥaredi media, but there's no mention of the story. I contact a few Ḥaredi journalists, and the first to answer, one of the most prominent Ḥaredi journalists, replies: "Elbaum has short sidelocks. If anything, they would have cut his beard."

Do you know anything about the story?

"Let me check."

A few minutes later: "I see the story all over in 'Groups,' but not in the normal media."

More time passes, and I get another message: "He was attacked. No info as to how serious it is. Will update."

About an hour later, I get this message: "He was attacked outside his home and was beaten up by attackers. Police on the ground, investigating."

Still, nothing appears in any Israeli media.

Why is the Ḥaredi media not writing anything about it? I ask the journalist.

"Ḥaredi media? Tuvia, what Ḥaredi media? There's no Ḥaredi journalism. We are just making things up as we go. What Ḥaredi journalism? Nobody wants to write this."

Around midnight, I approach Shlomo Elbaum via WhatsApp: Are you okay? I heard some rumors that you have been attacked, and I hope they are not true.

"They are true," he writes back at 12:42 a.m.

Speedy recovery. How do you feel? Are you at home or in a hospital? How many people attacked you?

"In the hospital. Together with my son. Two people attacked us."

I assume I know your answers, but let me still ask: Will this attack cause you to stop? Are you worried about your safety and the safety of your family? What will this attack do to you?

"With all my power," he answers. In other words: I will go on even harder.

Keep safe. G'night.

"Thank you very much," he answers, and now it's 1:35 a.m.

I contact another top Ḥaredi journalist. Does the story appear anywhere in the Ḥaredi media? I ask, since I still can't find anything about it anywhere in the Ḥaredi press.

"You think anyone in the Ḥaredi media will dare to write against Ger? This is a lesson for you what Ḥaredi journalism is all about," comes the reply.

In other words: no one in the Ḥaredi media will publish anything negative against a powerful Ḥasidic court.

Are you not going to write about it?

"No."

Why not?

No answer.

"If the general media write about it, we will write about it too. Not before they write," a top Ḥaredi editor tells me.

At about nine a.m., I contact non-Ḥaredi journalists and am told that unless the Ḥaredi media write about it, they won't either.

Why? "One hand washes the other. That's the face of Israeli journalism. It's a shame, but that's what it is."

Another reply I get: "Wake up, Tuvia. The media in Israel is very weak, no heroes here. Ger can sue. They have all the money in the world."

Sad.

The truth is that Ger will not sue. "Ger" doesn't legally exist. The Catholic church, for example, cannot sue anyone reporting that a "Catholic" attacked an attorney. But Ḥaredi journalists are afraid, so they tell me, after I push a bit harder, that the Gerer Rebbe would issue a command to his followers not to read any Ḥaredi media that reports on an issue such as this, which translates into a loss of cash.

I leave the hotel and go on walking in Kiryat Vizhnitz; perhaps the Vizhnitz Ḥasidim can enlighten me. What do you think about what happened with Shlomo Elbaum? I ask the first Vizhnitz Ḥasid I meet. His answer? "I heard – I don't know if it's true – that they cut one of his sidelocks. He's lucky. Next time, they will cut off his *bris*, making him a woman, and that will be the end of the story."

Are Ger Ḥasidim capable of doing such a thing?

"They are gangsters. Ger is a mafia. The Rebbe has millions upon millions. Why is he behaving like this? Because. Mafia. Just in our area, he owns properties worth fifty million shekels. Why is he so afraid of Rabbi Shaul? He is a sick man."

Another Ḥasid tells me: "We, the Ḥasidim, are good people, but our leaders are corrupt. My wife drives a car, and because of that, I can't send my children to normal Ḥaredi schools; they won't accept them. Unless, and you might have heard this before, I pushed some fat envelopes under the table. All cash. But I refuse to do it. Corrupt. The leaders of the Ḥaredi world are corrupt."

Let me ask you a question. I was in Tel Aviv before, and my cellphone reception was excellent, but in Kiryat Vizhnitz, it's bad. Do you know why?

"Guess! Ḥaredi activists put internet blockers in Kiryat Vizhnitz and some other locations in Bnei Brak because they don't want people to use smartphones. Who gave them the right to do it? Their Rebbes and rabbis. It's illegal, but nobody stops them. Corrupt!"

It is at the entrance to the hotel that I meet Yoni, or at least this is what he says his name is. He is a Ger Ḥasid, a devout follower of the Rebbe, Yaakov Aryeh Alter. I ask him if he has any idea why the Ḥaredi media didn't even mention the attack on Shlomo Elbaum. "Do you really want to know?" he asks.

Yes, I do.

"They didn't poison you?"

Who?

"The followers of Rabbi Shaul."

Why would you think such a thing?

"I saw the photo of the court proceedings, and you were there."

He refers to a photo published in many a Ḥaredi media of the court proceedings in Tel Aviv, where I sat in the middle, between the two sides, next to Akiva.

This doesn't mean that I'm on anyone's side. If I were on their side, I guess I wouldn't be talking to you. Would I? I say to him.

"Good. I'll tell you why they didn't mention the attack."

I listen.

"It didn't happen. It's all a lie."

Can you prove it?

"I will send you a notice before legal action on charges of defamation, sent by a lawyer to the person who made up the whole story, Yossi Shtark."

Please do.

He sends me a copy of the warning, written by Attorney Israel Hecht, notifying Yossi, who tweeted that Elbaum was attacked. Yossi did not mention any name, but someone else mentioned two people by name, referring to this tweet. Why would Yossi be liable for any defamation, even if the attack did not happen, when he didn't mention any name? I ask Yoni.

Yoni doesn't know. What he does know is this: "We have proof that the story about Akiva Greentzeig, the subject of the defamation lawsuit in Elbaum's criminal complaint, is fake!"

Can you send it to me?

He calls up a friend of his and asks him to send him the "three-step photo of Akiva's supposed injury," which will prove, he says, that that attack was also made up.

About an hour later, I get the material. What is it? It's a color copy of three photos, supposedly taken in sequence, claiming to prove that Akiva was not attacked. The first photo in the three-photo sequence shows Akiva holding a little tissue with a droplet of blood. Photo 2, in which blood covers his nose, is said to result from Akiva's rubbing the tissue on his nose to make it look like he was bleeding. The third photo, where the blood is more visible, is supposed to show a further rubbing of the tissue. In short: no one was attacked, and it's all made up.

Not so fast.

Enlarging the third photo, I notice that the area around Akiva's eyes shows that he was beaten up badly, and the blood seen there is not on the skin but underneath it. It's not just red, but also black and blue. The fact that the man didn't go blind is a miracle.

Photo 3, I write to Yoni, shows internal bleeding under Akiva's eyes. Do you know what this is about?

"According to him [Akiva], this happened after he was beaten up in the nose."

In other words, somebody beat him up real bad. Correct?

"I don't know."

End of conversation.

If this is the line of defense the Old Ger will be using in court, I don't see how any judge will accept their claims. But I'm not a judge, and this is not up to me to decide.

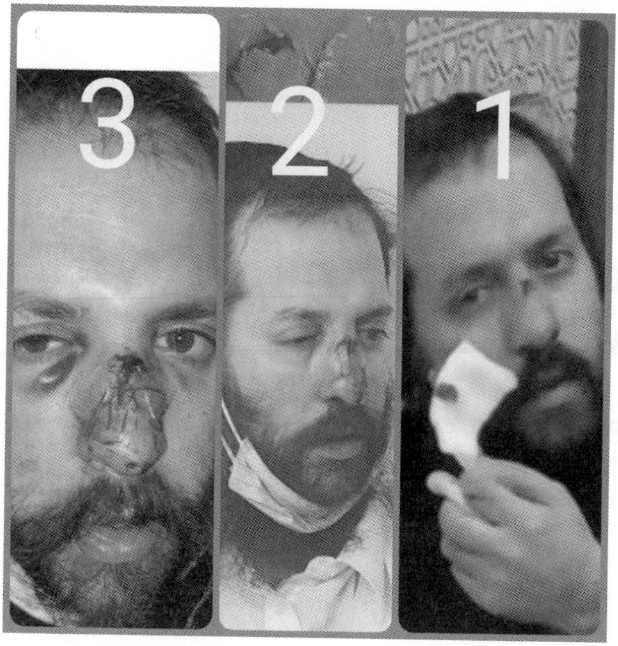

I'm not done, not yet. I shoot a message to Shlomo Elbaum: How come the Ḥaredi media didn't cover the story?

"Good question," he answers.

Hand in Hand, God and I Go for a Walk with a Quail in Kiryat Vizhnitz

A Gypsy with a shtreimel

Luckily, the little children of Kiryat Vizhnitz don't have to bother with the Ger story.

I see them in Vizhnitz Garden, a two city-block-long neighborhood "garden," with benches on both sides and playgrounds for children in the middle, as they congregate around a quail, a beautiful quail, and take turns caressing it and attempting to feed it a little piece of a green apple. They are extremely excited about this bird.

What bird is this? I ask them.

"*Slav*," they say.

Is this bird a Ger Ḥasid? I ask them.

"No!"

Then what kind of Ḥasid is it?

"Vizhnitz!"

What makes it a Vizhnitz Ḥasid?

"This is the same bird that's mentioned in the Bible."

In what context?

"After the Jews left Egypt, when they were in the desert on their way to the Holy Land, they complained to The Name that they didn't have food, and The Name sent them many *slav*s!"

Sweet kids.

Everything in the Ḥaredi world, from the moment of birth to the moment of burial, is connected to the faith. And for these kids, this quail, this *slav*, is not just a quail, but a biblical bird that survived thousands of years, from the Jews' days in the desert, until this very moment. From Egypt and the desert to Kiryat Vizhnitz, Bnei Brak. This quail saw it all. It saw the Jews leaving Egypt wearing beautiful *shtreimel*s thousands of years ago, and it popped in for a visit in Kiryat Vizhnitz today. Who needs cell phone connections when a little bird connects thousands of years in just one little appearance! This *slav* is proof, oh, yes, of the truthfulness of the Bible. It's a Vizhnitz bird, my friend, not a Ger bird!

When I started this journey, I said: If I'm lucky, I'll get to meet Him face to face while walking the land. I think, believe it or not, that I've finally succeeded. He is standing behind this *slav*, looking at me. I offer Him my hand, and together we walk the Garden of Vizhnitz, hand in hand, as the *slav* follows us.

Can you see? Open your eyes wide, and you will.

I keep looking at the kids, how they connect with the Bible via the *slav*, and I see myself in them. We are connected by a *slav*, and by our grandparents.

It is time for me now, I think, to meet Ḥaim Banet, the man who will take me with him to an era earlier than any *slav*, to the time of the Patriarch Abraham, when Jewish music first started.

Ruvi, Ḥaim's son and one of the nicest men I've met in Bnei Brak, comes to my hotel to pick me up. Aristocrats like me need personal service; don't you know?

The studio, first used decades ago, shows its age. It's in the basement level of a multi-story building, and the way to the studio from the elevators is adorned with exposed cement, making me feel as if I have just entered an army bunker in Afghanistan.

After a walk through the world of cement, we finally reach the studio, a studio that disguises the greatness of the man operating in it and at the same time reveals the passage of time. Ḥaim and his wife greet me, and both immediately capture my heart. They have a warmth that shines on every inch of the hard floor, and I am greeted with a sugar-free cheesecake, yogurt, and multiple other goodies, including cottage cheese. I love it!

What's the origin of Ḥasidic music? I ask Ḥaim, the most legendary composer of his time, whose songs I've been singing for years, the man who has touched the very core of my heart with his moving, grateful melodies.

I expect him to tell me stories about white angels, nine wings each at least, holy Rebbes from his motherland, and ancient shuls long ago burned either by the Nazis or by some other anti-Semitic fascists. But no. The origin of Ḥasidic music, he tells me, depends on the Ḥasidic court in question. Was the Ḥasidic court founded in Poland, Russia, Ukraine, Belarus, Hungary?

The origin of Ḥasidic music, of Ḥaredi music, including music composed during our time, is in the lands from which the different Jewish groups come, he tells me. "In Chabad music, the origin is in Russian folk songs," he says. He sings for me some Chabad songs, and he says, "You can feel the Russian style in them." The melodies of the Ger Ḥasidic court, he teaches me, have their origin in Polish *marsz* music.

I ask Ḥaim, a Vizhnitzer Ḥasid, to tell me about the roots of his music, and of his Ḥasidic court's music. "Many of the Gypsy songs have found their way into our music," he answers. The origin of Vizhnitz music, I discover today, has nothing to do with any white angels or the Patriarch Abraham.

Oops.

Ḥaim sings for me a Vizhnitz song whose words are in Hebrew, but its tune, he tells me, is Gypsy. It's a song I grew up on, and I always thought its tune was the most "Jewish" one could ever imagine, but no. The music I always connected with Yiddish, with Psalms, with Jewishness, with Ḥaredim, with a *shtreimel* and a caftan, it now turns out, is Gypsy. He sings a few more Ḥasidic tunes and tells me that their origin is in the Hungarian Gypsy *csárdás* music.

Csárda, by the way, means tavern in Hungarian.

Yes, my pure, sacred, and holy Ḥasidic music comes from a Hungarian pub. That's sacred, that's holy, pure vodka.

Yes, the roots of my Jewish soul go all the way to Gypsy land. We are, you would never guess, Gypsies with *shtreimel*s.

"I want to tell you a story," Ḥaim says to me.

Go ahead!

"This is a story I remember from my childhood. During a *tish* at the old Rebbe, the grandfather of the present Rebbe of Seret-Vizhnitz, the Ḥasidim were singing a certain song and, suddenly, in the middle of the song, the Rebbe asked that they immediately stop singing that song. We didn't understand why he wanted us to stop singing; it was bizarre. But we didn't say anything; we just stopped singing.

"After the *tish*, when the Rebbe went home with his gabbai, the gabbai asked the Rebbe why he had so suddenly asked us to stop singing. The Rebbe answered: 'That song is a Gypsy song, and when we were singing it, I saw a Hungarian Jew who just came in, as we were singing, and I know that that Jew knew the original song, with its original lyrics, and I didn't want him to recall the lyrics of the song, and that's why I asked to stop singing it.' A week later, I was at my parents' home, and I sang that tune, and when my mother heard it, she came to me and said: 'Ḥaim, what song are you singing? Do you know what the words of this song are?'"

What were the words? Were they some Nazi, Fascist lyrics?

"No, God forbid."

So, what were the original lyrics?

"It was a love song."

Oy vey, vey, vey. The Rebbe and Mama were afraid that a Jew would recall the original words of the song, of a Gypsy in love with a Romanian or Hungarian girl, words that could tempt the most righteous of men, The Name save us, and make him spill something that we shouldn't even mention, may Heaven protect us.

Oy vey, vey, vey.

Yeah. No white angels, no holy Rebbes, no Moses, no Abraham, and no donkey. Just Gypsies. Can you believe it?

Back in my hotel room, I do a little research and find out that, yes, Ḥaim is right. It's Gypsy.

But don't worry. We Jews have Heilige Rebbes.

Yes!

Der Heilige and die Schwänze

Have you got one million for me?

Der Heilige Rebbe, how lucky I am, is not far from my hotel, and on Saturday night he is making a Sabbath Third Meal *tish* late into the night, long after the Sabbath is over, a local tells me. Why would anyone have a Sabbath meal after the Sabbath? This he doesn't know.

I go there.

Are you the Schwänze? I ask a group of Ḥasidim when I arrive at a big yard outside of their shul, where many of them congregate.

They laugh and smilingly answer, "Yes, we are. Welcome!"

Why is your Rebbe having a Sabbath meal after the Sabbath?

"The Sabbath doesn't end before the Rebbe has the Third Meal of the Sabbath," answers one of them, a Ḥasid by the name of Reb Yitzḥok.

What do you mean?

"The Rebbe extends the Sabbath."

Why would he even try to do that?

"The Sages say that all punishments in Hell pause on the Sabbath, and that's why the Rebbe extends the Sabbath, so that those Jews who have been sent to Hell will have a longer period of break from Hell. The Rebbe loves Jews, all Jews."

Yes, that woman and her daughter, from the story in *Shoimer Emunim*, are resting now.

And how is it to be a Schwänze, a tail? I ask Reb Yitzḥok.

"Oh, that's the greatest pleasure in life!"

All others present agree, with a big smile on their faces.

How so?

"Come to the *tish*, and you'll see!"

Sounds fair, and we enter the main hall of the shul.

At the center of the hall, and just like at the Third Meal of the Belzer, there is a gigantic table, which is surrounded by bleachers around three of the hall's walls, with a big table by the fourth wall for the Rebbe.

Before I can say Jack Robinson, hundreds of Ḥasidim fill up every possible inch on the bleachers, and Reb Yitzḥok finds me a place to sit in the middle of the hall.

The *tish* is scheduled to start at eight p.m., and just a few minutes after eight, the Rebbe enters.

First, he washes his hands and then dries them with a towel. I like this. Normal Rebbes do a big spiel before they start anything; they pray, *shokel*, mumble, pray more, and more, and usually, nobody can hear them, and then they pray more, more and more, and the whole thing schleps forever. This guy, on the other hand, immediately goes to business.

Well, almost. As I can now see, this guy is schlepping the hand-washing ceremony.

Washing one's hands should take about five seconds, but it takes him a few minutes. As the hundreds of Ḥasidim watch, Der Heilige dries one finger at a time, over and over each finger, all ten of them, and then again, one finger at a time, over and over each finger, all ten of them, and then again, again, and again. But then the *ḥallah*s come – looonggg *ḥallah*s, Vizhnitz *ḥallah*s, which are the best *ḥallah*s in the world (trust me on this!) – and a Ḥasid comes to give Der Heilige a knife, a long knife, and Der Heilige cuts one of the *ḥallah*s.

When the Ḥasid moves away, he walks backward. You never, my dear, show your behind to Der Heilige!

Another Ḥasid comes with a knife longer than the one owned by the Angel of Death, and he cuts little pieces of the *ḥallah*s, pieces that are to be distributed amongst the lucky Ḥasidim who will have the chance to put a piece of Der Heilige's *ḥallah*s in their mouths.

I get a piece. Oh, boy, oh, girl, so delicious! These Schwänze get to eat the best *ḥallah*s on earth!

Once *ḥallah* is in the bellies, Der Heilige greets some of the Ḥasidim by name. Surprisingly, he looks at me, sitting quite far from him, and asks his gabbai, "What's his name?" The gabbai gives him my name, and Der Heilige greets me in front of all the Ḥasidim: "To life, Tuvia Tenenbom!"

How does the gabbai know my name, I ask Reb Yitzḥok.

"I told him," he answers. When did he have time to do this? Beats me. Everything works here, it seems, like in the Israeli Secret Service. Fast, smooth, secretly, and nobody knows how they did it.

In any case, the gefilte fish now comes. Slowly Der Heilige eats his gefilte, and he seems to enjoy every bite. He eats more, more, and more, and the Ḥasidim watch, watch, watch, and watch, each eager to get a piece of the gefilte on their tongues. I have never seen a Rebbe enjoying his gefilte in a *tish* like this Heilige!

It is at this point that Der Heilige tells his gabbai to deliver a portion of gefilte fish to me. "You don't know how lucky you are," a Ḥasid tells me. "Der Heilige likes you. You must be a remarkable man!"

Yes, I am.

It is with these *shirayim* that I put in my mouth that my body unites with the holiest of this world and all other worlds, up to the Seventh Heaven, where the souls are.

Up to this point, this *tish* is more or less similar to other *tish*es that I've been to before, but then the unbelievable happens. All the lights go off – not a single light stays on – and we are in pitch darkness, like the darkness in Egypt. And Der Heilige, the Rebbe, sings: "Oy vey, vey, vey, vey," and the Schwänze answer: "Oy vey, vey, vey, vey." The Heilige sings loud; he has more energy than his brother, thousands of times more, and his Schwänze answer him in kind. At times he sings verses from Psalms, such as: "Even when I walk through the valley of the shadow of death, I will fear no evil: for You are with me," and the Tails answer: "Even when I walk through the valley of the shadow of death, I will fear no evil: for You are with me."

This goes on for over thirty minutes, and it is so theatrical, powerful, and fascinating that you feel it in the deepest, most intimate parts of your being. Amazing! Amazing! Amazing!

Candles are brought in and put in the back of the hall, giving us a bit of light, and the crowd is seen as shadows, which is also powerful.

A few minutes later, the house lights come up again, and I feel as if I have woken up from a bewitching dream.

Is this what being a Schwänze means?

I walk out, and Reb Yitzḥok comes out with me. I ask him: Is it true that Der Heilige asked each of the Schwänze to come up with NIS 120,000?

"Yes, it is."

Did you come up with the money?

"So far, I came up with close to a million."

Are you a rich man?

"No. Der Heilige didn't ask us to give him our money, only to raise the money, and I raised it, much more than he asked."

Is it true that Der Heilige said to the kids that they would have to give up on their chicken dishes?

"Don't worry. Our kids eat very well! No kid is eating less than they did before. We just have to raise the money; we get the money from rich people, not our kids. Whatever you heard is not true."

How does it feel to be a Schwanz?

"Look, our Rebbe, Der Heilige, personally knows each of us by name, and he loves us. How many Rebbes know their Ḥasidim so intimately? Whatever one calls us, Schwänze or any other name, we feel lucky to have Der Heilige."

Are you the tail of the Rebbe?

"For us, being a Schwanz means to worship The Name, nothing else."

I would like to see Der Heilige face to face. Can you arrange this for me?

"Give me your cell number, and I'll call you tomorrow."

I give him my number, and the next morning, I get a call from him.

"Can we come to you?" he asks.

Yes, of course.

He'll come, he says, with another Ḥasid.

In minutes, they show up at my hotel, and we meet in my suite.

The other Ḥasid brought something for me, he tells me when we sit down to chat.

What is it?

It's a schnorring letter. In it, I read that the late Vizhnitzer Rebbe, the father of the Heilige, promises every donor to Vizhnitz that he will pray for him from his place in Heaven and approach God, right next to the Holy Seat, on the donor's behalf. In addition, Der Heilige blesses the donor with good life, health, and happiness, if he donates to the new Vizhnitz Center, the name of his Ḥasidic court.

The new Vizhnitz Center building will cost, they tell me, NIS 250 million, and it would be nice if I could donate a million or two, they say to me.

Me?

Yes, why not?

These two Ḥasidim think that I'm a millionaire. I love it!

Yes, they are naïve, thinking that this millionaire will part from one million or two this very morning, but there's something sweet to this. Der Heilige, they tell me, asked them about me earlier in the morning. "He is interested in you," Reb Yitzḥok's companion, Reb Meir, tells me.

And now I hear an interesting detail. The father of the current Vizhnitz Rebbes left NIS 270 million for the younger son, Der Heilige, but the older son, the man in whose *tish* I was on Friday night of my first week in Bnei Brak, wouldn't give him the money. "Der Heilige said, 'I'm not going to fight this; The Name will provide,'" they tell me.

Is this true? I don't know, but the people sitting with me are sure it is.

These two are dreamy boys, and their naivete touches me because it's so pure and it's filled with so much hope and faith. Perhaps they were even sent by Der Heilige himself, but I love their devotion no matter what. And their simple belief that I would give them a million or two, just because they noticed that I liked their Rebbe's *tish*, is fascinating.

If I give the million or millions, they tell me, Der Heilige would love to see me and talk with me in person. He would even come to meet me in this hotel. Yes.

I tell them that, sorry, but a donation to see a Rebbe is against journalistic ethics. "Oh," says Reb Meir, "it doesn't have to come from your publisher. It can come from your own pockets! You have this kind of money, we think."

That's nice to hear.

Had it come from the publisher, I tell them, there would be no ethics problem, because publishers can do whatever they want. The ethics issue, I the millionaire, explain to them, is a problem only if I give it. But you know what? I tell them, perhaps I could connect you with millionaires.

They love it. If I do that, Der Heilige would be pleased as well, they tell me, and perhaps Der Heilige, the million-donor, and myself would meet all together.

How about, I try my luck, I first meet Der Heilige, and then I will see if I can get the donor as well? After all, the mysterious donor would want to get a detailed report from me.

Well, they say, they will talk to the gabbai, and perhaps they could arrange a meeting between Der Heilige and myself in the next few days.

Settled.

Shlomo Elbaum, one of the most colorful of Bnei Brak people, a man fighting a system much stronger than him, keeps at it. His date in court with the leadership is still a few months ahead, but he's not sitting on his laurels. He sends various warnings to different Old Ger officials and lieutenants, and sometimes I don't know if I should laugh or cry when I read some of the stories he mentions in those warnings.

Here are three examples of what the Rebbe's Ḥasidim believe, according to him: 1. The Rebbe, Yaakov Aryeh Alter, said on the day of the wedding of one of his grandchildren that he stopped the rain for that day, but it was very difficult for him. He asked that henceforth the weddings of his other grandchildren take place only during the summer when it doesn't rain in Israel. 2. The shape of the Rebbe's image is engraved under God's Holy Seat in Heaven. 3. There are times when the Rebbe signals incomprehensible movements with his hands, but he does this for a reason. These movements are directed at souls floating in the air near the Rebbe, and he signals to them that they cannot hide from him.

Yeah.

That's Bnei Brak, a Ḥaredi city of over 200,000 people, a city I thought I wouldn't like, but I do.

Is all fine and dandy in the Ḥaredi world of this city?

Not exactly, at least not for everybody.

Ḥaredim in Appearance, Atheists at Heart: These Are the Anusim

Am I a Ḥaredi or an infidel?

Toward the end of my stay in Bnei Brak, as the rumors spread around that there is a Jew guest in town, yours truly, who writes about the Ḥaredi world, more and more people flock to see me, to tell me their personal stories. The ones I find to be the most interesting are the Anusim, the Coerced, people who lost faith but wouldn't leave the community.

The term Anusim, first used in the eleventh century in Germany, and most prevalent a few centuries later for Jews in Spain, during the Spanish Inquisition, refers to Jews who were forced to convert to Christianity but continued to practice Judaism in secret. This term, what a paradox, is now used in Israel for Jews born in the Ḥaredi world who are still part of it but don't believe in God anymore. They still practice the religion, not out of faith but out of fear. Some of them are single; others are married with children. Some share their new status as unbelievers with their spouses; others don't. The common denominator to all: they believe in God no more, but they don't have the guts, the stamina, the financial means, or whatever, to leave the Ḥaredi world. They live in fear, a constant fear of being discovered, and they unite if they can with fellow unbelievers in secretive Groups on the internet.

This evening, I have three of them in my hotel suite: two of them are Ger Ḥasidim, a man and a woman; one is a Litvak, a woman. The Ger Ḥasid, dressed like any Ger Ḥasid, tells me right from the top, "I don't believe in God, but I'll never leave Ger."

Why?

"If I leave, my family will not talk to me ever again, my father-in-law will renounce his daughter, my wife; and my children will be taken away from me. Plus, I'll lose my job."

This man has been married for over twenty years, has children, and never called his wife by name, or she him.

What's your wife's name?

He stares at me.

What's her name?

He stares at me.

What's your wife's name?

He stares at me.

I look at him, and he gets scared.

What's your wife's name?

His lips tremble.

What's her name? You can tell me.

He has a scary look in his eyes; his lips are shaking.

It's okay; you can tell me her name. What is your wife's name?

He whispers her name, and I can hardly hear him, even though he is sitting right next to me.

"Please," he tells me, "don't mention my name to anyone, and not my wife's name. Please!"

No problem. What made you lose your faith?

"It started when I felt that in Judaism, we think of ourselves as Chosen People, the best of people, and I don't think it's true."

And that's why you lost your faith, because you don't think you're special?

"Yes, that's how it started."

The woman who sits next to him, also of Ger, tells me what made her stop believing. "My Ger marriage guide told me before

I got married that when I have intimate relations with my husband, I should imagine the Rebbe. I did it; I had so many orgasms with him, imagining him every time I slept with my husband! But after a while, I realized how weird this is, to imagine an old man when I sleep with my husband, and it turned into horror." Her husband, she tells me, left the faith as well, and they practice atheism together.

And then there is this Litvak, an attractive lady who shares with us that she doesn't believe in any God but keeps all the laws of Judaism. "This is my agreement with my husband: I don't believe, but I behave as if I did believe. I keep a kosher home, and on the Sabbath, I clean the dishes with cold water because hot water is not allowed to be used on the Sabbath. This Sabbath, I used warm water. If my husband caught me, he might have left the house."

Does he know you are here?

"No."

What will you tell him if he asks you where you have been?

"I don't know. I haven't thought about it yet."

What's the future?

"No future for me. I'm done."

You are a beautiful lady, in the prime of your life, and you are giving up on everything?

"What are you talking about? I'm an old woman!"

How old are you?

"Forty."

That's old? I'm sorry, I don't get you.

"Yes, I'm old. What do you think, do you think that I can leave my husband and children and start life again? I have no money of my own; I didn't go to university, I have no profession, what am I going to do? There's nothing I can do."

Do you love your husband?

"Yes, I do."

Even if you know that he might leave you if he catches you cleaning dishes on the Sabbath with warm water?

"I won't do it again."

You make no sense to me.

"I know, but that's my life."

All three know each other from Groups, and this is the first time these three have seen each other in person.

Why did they come to see me this evening? I don't know. Perhaps they feel that they share something with me. Do they? We all left the Ḥaredi world, but as much as I try, I find no common denominator between them and me. They divorced themselves from their former world, even if their bodies are still in it. I did the opposite thing: my body left the Ḥaredi world, but my soul is still in it. I never thought so. Only now, when I look at these Anusim, I realize for the first time what it means to leave a community, what it means to divorce yourself from a community, but that's not what I did. They did, I did not. The Ḥaredi Jew deep in me, I realize as I look at them, never left. The Jew in me is solid. It's funny, yes, but I feel more connected to the Schwänze than to these Anusim.

How many Anusim are there? Nobody knows. Some people estimate that most Anusim are in Ger, but I don't have any source for it, and I doubt anyone has.

As the Anusim get up to leave, I crave to share some words of wisdom with them, but I have none. Be strong, I say, the only two words that come to my lips. One day perhaps, when they get older, much older, and have nothing to lose, they will find the strength to move, maybe to Jaffa Street in Jerusalem, maybe to Unter den Linden in Berlin. There they will sit in a café and sip a cup of herbal tea with lemon. They will no longer be told that they are the Chosen, they will make love with no Rebbes, and they will be able to use hot water on the Sabbath, finally.

As for me, I'm about to leave Bnei Brak, but before I do, I take one more walk on its streets. And who comes my way? Reb Yitzḥok, the Tail of the Holy. "Sorry," says he, "that we couldn't arrange a meeting between you and Der Heilige because Der Heilige was very busy. But we'll try to get it done. How do you like Bnei Brak?"

Pointing at a bunch of kids passing by us, I say to him: I love walking on the street and seeing so many little children everywhere I look.

"Yes, it's nice to look at them. And at the girls."

I can't believe he said that, but it's refreshing to hear such a comment coming from a Tail.

I keep on walking, and soon enough, I get a call from Reb Meir, the other Tail. Der Heilige, he tells me, plans to go to the Red Sea to celebrate the Splitting of the Sea, recalling the journey the ancient Jews made from slavery in Egypt to freedom in the Holy Land of Israel. Would I like to join Der Heilige and his Schwänze? I thank Reb Meir for thinking of me but tell him that I can't make it this time. I'm sure Der Heilige will do outstandingly well also without me, and I can already imagine how he'll use the Red Sea as a staging area for his theatrical genius. Maybe on Passover, when the Jews celebrate their freedom from their Egyptian enslavers, Der Heilige will return to the Red Sea, and if he does, I will do my best to join him then.

I pack my suitcases, get into a cab, and drive out of Bnei Brak.

When I started the journey, I was filled with memories of the sweet boy I once was and thought he had died long ago, forever gone.

Today, I know a little better. That boy has never gone, and he doesn't plan to go anytime soon.

The Ḥaredim are my family, whether I want it or not, whether they want it or not. The umbilical cords of our grandmothers attach us, and we can't separate.

But there's more to it.

For me, being a Jew means leading a life of endless questioning, including the question: Does God exist? To them, being a Jew means never questioning anything about God, never getting too close to Him, and never knowing much about Him. Aren't we one and the same? We both, hear me out, don't know. Yes. We are of the same cloth from birth until death, and we have the same past and the same future. After all these months of living with the Ḥaredim, I realize that it's not just my grandparents talking with their grandparents, but me talking with them and them with me. We share the same God, the same Jewish God, if we believe in Him and if we don't. If He exists or if we invented Him, He is our God, our Lord, and we are the Children of the Lord.

Some time ago, I interviewed Yair Lapid (Israel's fourteenth prime minister), whom the Ḥaredim hate passionately. "My father," he said to me, "was the most famous atheist in Israel. I said about him, and it's very true, that the God he didn't believe in was a Jew!"

Yes, he's right.

Where am I going from here? It doesn't matter. Let the car drive. Wherever it reaches, wherever I end up, I will carry Jerusalem with me, and I will carry Bnei Brak with me. Forever united.

And as I sit in Prenzlauer Berg, sipping my hot Italian coffee, a car drives in Jerusalem announcing the funeral procession of the most righteous of all, my childhood neighbor Rabbi Ḥaim Kanievsky. Hundreds of thousands of people, according to local media, participate in the procession – but not I. I am in Berlin, in a café, and I light up a clove cigarette. I stare at the smoke rings and see Adam and Eve, with the nicest *shtreimel* and *tiḥel*, passing by with three of their children, Zisale, Rachel, and Feigele. No Patricia. And up there, in the Garden of Eden, look up to the sky, and you will see. Who is that? Do you recognize Him? Yes, that's The Name, and He's busy, very busy. He has just welcomed Reb Ḥaim to the Heavenly Court and is now preparing the best omelet for Zisale, the most delicious of potato kugels for Feigele, a mouth-watering gefilte fish, prepared by Teraḥ, father of Abraham, the owner of the white donkey, for Rachel, and He pours the best ever chicken soup, prepared by the whitest of angels, for Adam and Eve, and together they all sing: "Ta, ta, ta, pa, pa, pa, ma, ma, ma, da, da, da, ya, ya, ya," as around them the beauties of Mea Shearim and Bnei Brak dance wildly, joining in song, and the Lord pours Himself the heavenly brandy, 77726, loudly uttering the best ever blessing: "To life!"

I look up to Heaven, ever higher, and intense longing overtakes me for the place I left behind. What shall I do?

The Light Train Carries Your Bulls to the Holy Temple

Murderers, get out!

The days pass, and after I travel here and there, I find myself in the Holy Land again, resuming my old activities, hard-to-get-rid-of habits: a *tish* here and there, watching the ladies there and here, and lovely strolls on the Godly streets.

Not a boring day, my dear.

One day, for example, a man and his wife, both members of Rabbi Shaul Alter's camp, confront their previous Rebbe, Yaakov Aryeh Alter, in a public place. Using a loudspeaker, they let out their frustrations and pain and shout at the Rebbe. Their daughters, it seems, have been brainwashed by the Rebbe's followers to run away from home. For good.

What a sad story.

No, it's not sad because the girls ran away from home, it soon becomes clear, but because the parents dared to show their frustrations in front of God, Yaakov Aryeh.

Such an attitude cannot pass without consequence, the Ger establishment decides, promptly issuing several directives, calling the Ḥasidim to act.

And act they do.

Across this small country of Israel, hundreds of Ḥasidim start chasing followers of Rabbi Shaul. They chase them on the streets, and they chase them inside shuls.

"Chase" is a nice word. They do much more than chase. They beat them so severely that some of the injured require immediate medical care, even a hospital.

Thusly shall be done, forever remember, to anyone who stops following God. A Ger Nadlan Ḥasid, who happens to be home chatting with his wife, Mrs. Psss, must leave the house immediately and run after Rabbi Shaul's people to beat them up. No mercy.

How charming.

Video clips of this Special Action appear all over the Jewish net, but according to *Haaretz*, no one is arrested.

The power of Ger.

The Ger Ḥasidim are not the only people busy here, mind you. The Jerusalem Peleg and other folks who have nothing better to do keep demonstrating on Bar Ilan Street against the light rail. They don't want the light rail, come Hell or high water. But the Jerusalem Municipality, heavily invested in the project, is fighting back. The good officials have just issued a pamphlet, a brochure, geared to convince every good Jew how important the future light rail train is for the Jews. How so? Well, for the sacrifices in the Third Temple.

Yes.

In the colored brochure, supposedly written sometime in the future, one can read the story of Yudi and his father, who have joined many other Jews on a unique train ride. They were accompanied by bulls, you will happily find out, for the animal sacrifice at the Temple.

> Yudi and his father joined the crowds that packed the roads. They were directed by the many ushers who welcomed the arrivals and showed them to the stations. "Did you arrive here on the light rail train that came

> from the Great Sacrifice Market by Kanfei Nesharim Street, or rather on the blue line?" an usher asked, glancing at the page in his hand. "Peace be upon you. Welcome! You've cleansed yourselves, I believe, haven't you? Advance to the terminal through the gate at the right; the next train will leave in one minute and thirty seconds. Please place all bulls in the front car, the Sacrifices Car, only!"

And so it goes on and on and on. "Let us resume our study of tractate *Bikkurim*," Yudi's father tells him. "Soon, Moses the Lawgiver is going to deliver a class!"

Yes. Moses the Lawgiver is about to give a class on tractate *Bikkurim*, right here by the train tracks, and Yudi better be prepared!

For those who are hard of understanding, illustrations are included.

Time passes, and since the Messiah has not arrived yet, the Magistrate Court date for the Ger leaders and Attorney Shlomo Elbaum does arrive.

How is it going?

Nobody knows, it seems.

In the Ḥaredi media, mum's the word. The general media too. I can't find a trace of information about it anywhere. This court case is the same one that brought about fifteen thousand people to the streets of Bnei Brak just a few months ago to vilify Shlomo Elbaum. Yet the media is quiet.

But the legal process does take place.

Senior Judge Yael Pradelsky, not a Ger Ḥasid, said last year that she would be here on this day, and she is.

Nu, you probably ask, what's cooking?

Well, well.

After hours of back and forth, long story, the sides agree as follows.

Attorney Shlomo Elbaum agrees to withdraw the criminal complaint, saying, "In light of the fact that the [Special] Presentation is no longer displayed, we will agree to the cancellation of the [Criminal] Complaint under section 94 (b) of the Criminal Procedure Law, subject to the condition that the Presentation will not be displayed in the future."

The defendants, leaders of the Ger establishment, accept this condition. Kind of. They "do not know the Presentation," they say via their attorney. "They have not seen the Presentation, are not responsible for the Presentation, and in any case, have no future intention to do anything with a Presentation they are unfamiliar with, and they can commit to that."

In other words, they promise not to give what they say they don't have. Brilliant!

The days and weeks pass by, and nothing out of the ordinary is taking shape, except for two special events: one is taking place high up in the heavens, where a great commotion, whose echoes are heard down below, is underway. At the conclusion of a lengthy trial in the Heavenly Court, Queen Elizabeth of Britain enters Paradise. Yeah. That's something, you must admit. The second, down on earth, is in Mea Shearim: a stormy demonstration right under my nose.

Today is Thursday, and in the early evening, a demonstration starts at the intersection of Tsfanya and Yeḥezkel Streets, exactly where your faithful servant resides. A group of young people push a "frog" from Tsfanya Street toward the intersection and set its contents on fire, much to the disappointment of the Jerusalem Municipality, if it really thought that frogs could not be pushed. Soon enough, hundreds of ultra-Orthodox men show up, this time mostly Ashkenazi Jews, some of whom are particularly violent and loud. A young man is standing next to me, cursing the police officers who came in to disperse the demonstration. "Nazis!" he screams.

Which sect are you from? I ask him.

"Breslev," he answers, the people famous for Wasted Semen remedies.

What exactly is the demonstration about? Most people I ask have no clue. Some are here, I guess, because they have to release internal bodily and mental pressures by screaming as loud as they can, and others are here because they enjoy the free street theater. So be it. In the meantime, Egged buses get stuck on the street without being able to move, and a few bored guys push a frog downhill on Yeḥezkel Street. The frog rolls down fast, at high speed, smashing the body of a Ḥasidic woman, Mirel, a mother of eleven children. Severely wounded, she is taken to the hospital, where she is fighting for her life.

The guys who pushed the frog down the street "saw a woman being crushed and fled the scene," I read on the Ḥaredi website Kikar Hashabat. How did we get to this low point where ultra-Orthodox men behave like the worst of humans? I don't know. Most of the people here, I'm sure, are anything but violent, but I believe that the time has come for the ultra-Orthodox to get rid of the criminals among them.

Will it happen?

Three days later, many Ḥaredim gather once again to protest.

They haven't had enough yet.

I look away, staring at the distance, when the image of the sweet boy I once was appears in front of me, tears flowing from his eyes.

"There are violent people here, and they threaten everyone," one of the residents tells me.

Why don't the other residents stop them?

"In this society, you don't initiate things."

Why?

"If you get involved with what happens on the street, people will disrespect you."

Come next evening, I go to see how the protests start, from the beginning, long before they turn violent.

What do I see?

A small group of people come to the intersection and start screaming: "Cursed Zionists," the battle cry of the demonstration leaders. Hearing this call, all available idiots, primarily young men, show up and look for Egged buses to block.

Minutes later, yeshiva boys from abroad, who study in the Mir Yeshiva, creatures who love free shows, appear.

The circle of the audience grows.

Curtain up; the show is about to start.

Ordinary Ḥaredi men, who happen to pass by, mutter, "Idiots! What blasphemy!" but their voice is heard only by angels, white and black. They don't do much more than mutter; they don't want anyone rolling a frog or two at them.

But what a miracle! Tonight, I'm not the only one who came to see how a demonstration starts from the very beginning; the police are here as well. And since the protest has not yet matured enough, they succeed in nipping it in the bud.

Within minutes, the demonstrators and the non-paying audience disappear.

And there was evening, and there was morning, as the Bible says, and another day has dawned. And when the evening comes, a new demonstration is born.

What's going on here? For months, God knows, there were no demonstrations, and now there isn't a single evening without one.

Bizarre.

I'm going to the intersection.

What do I see? It turns out that a group of ultra-Orthodox rioters have pushed a garbage container into the intersection, intending to set it on fire, which they are trying to execute right now. Only there's a sudden twist in the plot: another group of ultra-Orthodox men appears, and they forcibly push the rioters away. "You're screwed up in the head; you are murderers!" shouts one of them at the rioters, and he and his friends push the container to the sidewalk.

Not one police officer can be seen in the area.

I walk to the next intersection, not far from where Mirel was severely wounded, where another rough story seems to unfold. "Five men between the ages of twenty and forty dressed in ultra-Orthodox clothing pushed the frog into the intersection, set it on fire and ran away," an ultra-Orthodox man standing next to a burning frog tells me. "I hope no idiot is planning to roll this frog down the road and injure another person."

It won't happen, not this evening. A few ultra-Orthodox men appear, and they push the burning frog toward the sidewalk and the rioters as well.

Bus traffic resumes.

I guess I was wrong. People here *are* trying to get rid of the criminals among them.

And it pays off. The rioters, pushed to the sidewalk, disappear as if swallowed by the earth. Only some spectators remain in place, all ultra-Orthodox men, and they go away in less than half an hour. Not one police officer, by the way, can be seen anywhere around.

On Friday, big announcements are pasted on the walls of the neighborhood. They read, in part:

> Murderers, get out of our quarters!
>
> For a long time now we, residents of Jerusalem's neighborhoods, have suffered at the hands of thugs, destroyers of the city, who engage in acts of violence, vandalism, burning trash cans and cars, and much more.... Get out!

In my youth, no one dreamt of making public such a call.

A man with a *shtreimel* on his head and a golden caftan on his body passes by and says: "They are right. It's a horror what's happening here!"

Two young Litvaks from the prestigious Brisk Yeshiva pass by next, and they read the announcement with great interest.

On which side are you, I ask them, those who set frogs on fire or those who fight them?

"Both sides are right," they answer.

I stare at them, Litvaks who don't eat kugels on the Sabbath, and I give up on them for good.

רוצחים
צאו ממחנינו!
הגיעו הדברים לידי כך שכמעט וגדעו רגלו של ילד ועתה הביאו לשפיכות דמים של ממש כאשר
אמא ל 11 ילדים כ"י,
נתונה בשל מעשיהם
בשערי מוות רח"ל
וזאת למודעי
ובערת הרע מקרבך!
קרעו שערי שמים לתפילה להצלת
מרת מירל בת רחל לאה לרפו"ש
ועד התושבים להצלת ירושלים תובב"א

These are the ultra-Orthodox, my dear: groups of people who disagree with one another on almost every issue. They are creatures who create an infinite number of angels, white and black, and they spend their lives traveling from one cemetery to the other, from Zfat to Uman, and every tomb in between. They are the same people who speak in the name of God, The Name, a God whose name they don't know, but they are forever proud to be Jews.

This is the one thing, let me tell you, that the various peoples here share: pride in being Jewish. They, the Chosen People, see themselves as the Chosen Jews: better and wiser than all gentiles and all other Jews.

Personally, I enjoy being surrounded by people who think that they are the best, most beautiful, sexiest, kindest, wisest, most loveable people in the world. It's a beautiful way to live, thinking that you are the best, the Chosen of the Chosen.

Life is not perfect, though, and there's a little problem with the picture that I've just painted: dancing above the heads of these wise and good people are the Super Chosen, to whom the "people" must bow. Who are the Super Chosen? The rabbis, a class of beings who believe themselves to be so holy and so pure that they can tell God what to do, not the other way around. Relying on an old saying, "The righteous decrees, and the Holy One Blessed Be He fulfills," they shamelessly crown themselves "righteous." They are the elite, the crème de la crème, and all others are "commoners," born to serve them, their children, and their families.

As a result, the ultra-Orthodox rabbis are often enough admired, feared, loved, and respected more than God. God is more like an afterthought, while the rabbis are supreme, the first in line of holiness.

Perhaps, just a thought: let the Ḥaredi people start uttering the name of God, not calling Him The Name, and maybe nobody would ever again confuse God and the rabbis.

Not a bad idea, right?

In any case, the biblical Moses, the one who, according to the Bible, gave the Jewish people their religion and about whom the Torah says that there was no man closer to God than him, is the same one about whom the Torah testifies, "Moses was a very humble man, more humble than anyone else on the face of the earth." Does this, the quality of being humble, mean anything to the Ḥaredi rabbis?

I have long searched for humble leaders in the ultra-Orthodox world and found but a few, such as the Rebbe of Toldos Aharon or the Rebbe of Karlin. I met many ultra-Orthodox leaders, many more than mentioned on these pages, and they were anything but humble. On the other hand, slaves – of the rabbis, not of The Name – I found aplenty. The Holy and the Tails, whom I'm sure you remember, are not just one separate, unique community, but a mirror image of the others. There are the rabbis, and there are the tails. And the twain shall never meet. Period.

Rabbis come with families. Yes, families. What this means is simple: since rabbis are so pure, their offspring are also pure, and *their* offspring as well. Hence the importance of pedigree. If you have the right pedigree, if you come from a rabbinical family, your life will be full of honey. Otherwise, may God help you. Oy to you, my dear, if you are Sephardi, oy to you if you are a convert, and oy to you if you are a severely wounded secular Jew lying down on the street in urgent need of medical care on the Sabbath. Oy, oy, oy.

Yet despite the above, the bitter hatred of the ultra-Orthodox by those who are not ultra-Orthodox is not only misplaced but reeks of outright anti-Semitism and pure racism, even if the haters are themselves Jewish. The assertion that the ultra-Orthodox are violent, sex offenders, thieves and robbers, primitives and cheaters, and other similar titles, is a gross and despicable lie that has no place in the civilized world. The ultra-Orthodox community, as I have found during my extended stay with them, is one of the most generous and humane I have encountered in my lifetime. Of course, this does not mean that there are no violent people among them, but what society doesn't have violent individuals in it? Does the Palestinian society, that darling of the Israeli left, lack violent people? There are also thieves and fraudsters among the ultra-Orthodox, yes, but what other society is clear of liars and cheats – the Vatican?

In one field, as you already know, the Ḥaredim differ hugely from any other: their sense of humor. They are the funniest people on earth.

Well, the Ḥasidim of them.

In case you are curious to know: to date, not a single Ḥaredi yelled at me, "Infidel, get out!"

The only ones who have been asked to leave this place are the "murderers."

Still, and sorrowfully, I'm not going to stick around here for long.

I feel more at home here than I ever felt in New York or Berlin, and this I will never deny. Here is the only place in the world where no one hates me because I am a Jew. Not only that, but they even love that I'm Jewish, which for me is a fantastic experience. But I am not willing to disrespect Judaism so much by allowing myself to surrender to the God-replacement rabbis and enslave myself to them.

No.

It won't be easy for me to leave, that's certain. I love the people here, and I will miss them, especially when I wander again among the ugly non-binary Progressives of America, Germany, and the rest of the crumbling Western democracies of our time.

I can tolerate the *meshigene mentschen* (crazy people) of the West because they are not my *meshigene mentschen*. It's always harder, don't you know, when the idiots are part of your family, not somebody else's.

For the next few months, I find myself in and out of Mea Shearim, and when the next Simchat Torah, Simḥas Toireh, comes around, I'm of course excited to celebrate the happiest holiday on the Jewish calendar with my favorite *meshigene mentschen.*

Only this Simḥas Toireh, sadly, turns out to be anything but happy.

Early in the morning, as the people of Mea Shearim get ready to dance the day away, loud sirens are heard, followed by sounds of explosions coming from high up in the sky.

We all go out to the street, looking up and down, trying to figure out what's happening.

Not one of my neighbors knows.

Truth be told, how could they? On the Sabbath and Jewish holidays, they don't use phones or any other electronic devices.

So they approach me. Do you, they ask, know what's going on? They assume that since I'm not religious like them, I might know more.

Well, not really.

I return to my room, turn on the iPhone, and connect with Michal, a journalist from Tel Aviv.

She sends me a video. In it, I see a pickup truck, inside of which lies an almost fully naked woman, probably dead. People sit on her body, and one of them grabs her hair in sadistic pleasure. They have fun. The truck drives through the streets of Gaza, and people all around shout "Allahu Akbar," God is the Greatest, each of them happier than any Hasidic Jew with his gefilte fish.

What's this?

"A kidnapped Israeli girl," Michal writes.

And then I see more videos, some on the Hamas Telegram channel and others on Al-Jazeera TV in Arabic. Shot by Hamas, who are obviously proud to advertise their brutality, the videos show dead Jews, their bodies mutilated, and crowds of young Gazans fighting one another to mutilate the bodies ever more.

What is this?

It takes me some time to figure this out, but slowly, the picture becomes clear, or at least clearer. Thousands of Hamas men, it turns out, stormed into Israel earlier this morning, kidnapped hundreds of Jews, some of whom they slaughtered on the way, and are now having fun mutilating their bodies in public.

And it doesn't end there. Houses, I see, are set on fire, the border fortification between Israel and Gaza has crumbled, babies and their mothers have been brutally kidnapped, bombs are flying all over, and countless Israelis lie dead on the streets.

Is Israel itself about to crumble?

I leave my room and share what I saw with the people. They are shocked, and they are horrified.

"They do to us what the Nazis did to our grandparents," they tell me.

"We are all Jews," they say about the slaughtered Israelis in the south of the country, almost all of whom are secular.

By evening, when the holiday is over, my neighbors drive by with loudspeakers. "Father in Heaven, have mercy on us, on our children and our babies," they pray, calling on the residents to beg God to protect His Children, whether religious or not.

I feel protected by them, part of them – a proud member of the tribe.

It takes some time, some precious time, but finally the Israeli army takes control of the border, and its forces push their way into Gaza.

Some weeks later, as the war still rages in Gaza but Israel seems to have gained the upper hand, I pack my belongings and get ready to go.

Where am I going from here?

I shall see.

Be well, my handsome and beautiful brothers and sisters. And though I leave you, I will forever carry you in my heart.

Oh, yes, it has come to my attention that some of you are in the process of raising the necessary funds to buy me, the Rebbe of Lodz, a *shtreimel*. Please note: my size is 62.

Thanks and Acknowledgments

Many thanks and deep appreciation to the ultra-Orthodox people who opened their hearts to me, led me into the depths of their souls, invited me to their homes, and graciously honored me with their presence at my abode.

My thanks to the Grand Rabbis who let me interview them and showered me with their blessings and prayers; to their followers who prepared a place of honor for me at the various *tish*es and shared with me the last pieces of the "holy foods."

I thank the yeshiva students that I came to interview but ended up interviewing me, teaching me the secrets of their crafts.

Thanks also to the Sephardi ultra-Orthodox who lovingly treated me to their spicy pickles, known to cure all diseases.

I am in debt of gratitude to the demonstrators who, while preparing to set garbage containers on fire, happily discussed with me all the intricacies of Jewish Law on the use of iPhones, cheeringly explained to me the secrets of mating in dark rooms, and gladly taught me everything I needed to know about the World to Come.

Thanks to the Israeli police officers who gave me free access to every burning container in This World.

To Florian Krauss, the best videographer in both This World and the World to Come, my deep gratitude for the countless days of recording anything that moved with his various devices.

May the blessing of Heaven above fall on the head of my German editor, Winfried Hörning, of Suhrkamp in Berlin, for coming up with the idea of writing this book.

To the owner of Tzefania Hotel, Itzik Giladi, my thanks for the fantastic omelets every morning, free of charge; to his son, Asaf, for taking care of everything; and to Yossi Sheetrit, who greeted me every day with lovely songs and amazingly imaginary tales.

And to my gentle and devoted mother-in-law, Isa, who always embraces me with love and care as if I were her only son – my deepest thanks.

About the Author

TUVIA TENENBOM is a bestselling author, journalist, playwright, and director whose books and dramas have been translated into many languages. He holds advanced degrees in fine arts and science and is the founder of the Jewish Theater of New York. Tuvia's articles and essays have appeared in leading Western media, including *Die Zeit* and *Der Spiegel* of Germany, *Corriere della Sera* of Italy, the *Jerusalem Post*, *Yedioth Ahronoth*, and *Israel Hayom* of Israel, and the *Forward* and *National Review* of America. His plays include *Father of the Angels*, *Like Two Eagles*, *One Hundred Gates*, *The Last Virgin*, *The Diary of Adolf Eichmann*, *The Beggar of Borough Park*, and *Last Jew in Europe*. His previous books include *Catch the Jew!*, *The Lies They Tell*, *I Sleep in Hitler's Room*, *Hello Refugees!*, *The Taming of the Jew*, and *From New York to Brno*.